"Those Who Labor for My Happiness"

JEFFERSONIAN AMERICA

Jan Ellen Lewis, Peter S. Onuf,
and Andrew O'Shaughnessy
Editors

"Those Who Labor for My Happiness"

Slavery at Thomas Jefferson's Monticello

LUCIA STANTON

University of Virginia Press

CHARLOTTESVILLE AND LONDON

in association with

MONTICELLO
Thomas Jefferson Foundation

MONTICELLO

This book was made possible by support from
the Martin S. and Luella Davis Publications Endowment.

University of Virginia Press
© 2012 by the Rector and Visitors of the University of Virginia
All rights reserved
Printed in the United States of America on acid-free paper

First published 2012

3 5 7 9 8 6 4

Library of Congress Cataloging-in-Publication Data

Stanton, Lucia C.
    "Those who labor for my happiness" : slavery at Thomas Jefferson's Monticello / Lucia
Stanton.
        p.   cm. — (Jeffersonian America)
    Includes bibliographical references and index.
    ISBN 978-0-8139-3223-1 (pbk. : alk. paper) — ISBN 978-0-8139-3222-4 (e-book)
    1. Jefferson, Thomas, 1743–1826—Relations with slaves.   2. Plantation life—Virginia—
Albemarle County—History.   3. Slaves—Virginia—Albemarle County—Biography.
4. Monticello (Va.)—History.   5. Hemings, Sally—Family.   6. Jefferson, Thomas,—
1743–1826—Family.   7. African American families—Virginia—Albemarle County—History.
I. Title.   II. Title: Slavery at Thomas Jefferson's Monticello.
    E332.2.S74 2012
    973.4'6092—dc23

                                                                                            2011035898

Contents

"We Will Prove Ourselves Men": Hemings Descendants in the

Fulfilling the Declaration: Descendants of Monticello's African

Introduction

PETER S. ONUF AND
ANNETTE GORDON-REED

MONTICELLO occupies an iconic place in the American imagination as a site of breathtaking natural and physical beauty and as the home of Thomas Jefferson, the man who wrote the American charter of freedom, the Declaration of Independence, and who has been called reverently—and sometimes irreverently—"the Apostle of Liberty." Over the years, millions of visitors have walked the paths that Jefferson walked on his mountaintop home in Albemarle County, Virginia, imagining the ways in which the place both reveals his character and helped to shape what we know of it. Scholarly attention has been paid to the place almost from the time of Jefferson's death in 1826. It has only been in recent years, however—since the early 1990s—that Monticello's other important residents have come into clear and considered focus: the hundreds of enslaved men, women, and children whom Jefferson owned over the course of his very long life. Monticello was not just the place from which Jefferson dreamed and projected his hopes for the future of a new nation: it was a slave plantation where human beings had the legal status of property in seeming violation of all of Jefferson's stated ideals. Nowhere is America's foundational contradiction on more vivid display.

No one has done more to focus our attention on slavery at Monticello, the lives of the individuals enslaved there, and Jefferson's relationship to them than the author of this collection of essays, Lucia ("Cinder") Stanton. During over thirty years working as a historian at the Thomas Jefferson Foundation, which runs Monticello, Stanton has acquired unparalleled knowledge of Jefferson's personal life and the lives of his slaves. Over a twenty-year period, she, along with James A. Bear, edited Jefferson's voluminous *Memorandum Books*, two volumes of his meticulously kept daily records of expenditures from the days of his twenties into his eighties.[1] The records contained in the *Memorandum*

Books not only reveal Jefferson's life through his financial transactions but also shed light on the lives of the enslaved blacks who were the objects of his actions, whether repaying his wife's enslaved half brother Robert Hemings money he borrowed or recording the sale, purchase, or hiring of enslaved workers.

Stanton's deep knowledge of all aspects of life at Monticello gained while working on the *Memorandum Books*, along with her great insight and humanity, make her uniquely qualified to explain Monticello to the world. Her work invariably gives readers a clear window through which to see the world that enslaved people inhabited with the third president over the course of more than five decades. But the perspective presented has been no more static than the institution of slavery itself or slavery at Monticello in particular. The evolution of views about Monticello and slavery—the Foundation's realization that it should be presented as the slave plantation it was—tracks Stanton's own development as a historian. She helped drive a process that, in turn, helped transform her own understanding of the subject matter that has been her life's work. The following essays show the progress of the modern evolution of Monticello, and of Stanton, who has become the leading interpreter of Jefferson's life as planter and master and the lives of those whom he enslaved as well as their descendants.

The Monticello that Stanton first knew (she came in 1968, stayed one year, then returned in 1975 for two and a half years, and settled permanently in 1979) was a place where enslaved people were still referred to as "servants,"[2] a term that Jefferson himself used to dull the impact of the reality of life on the mountain. Jefferson the Apostle of Liberty, the architect, the horticulturalist, the wine enthusiast, and the lover of gadgets were, by far, the Foundation's most favored representations of the Master of Monticello. By the late 1980s it had become more than apparent that the Foundation was well behind the curve of modern scholarly treatments of slavery. From at least since the publication in 1956 of Kenneth M. Stampp's monumental *The Peculiar Institution*, the mainstream historiography of slavery had moved away from the master-centered focus and embraced the idea, long present in the scholarship of black historians, that the lives of enslaved people actually mattered to the study of slavery. What followed was the flowering of a body of scholarship that reworked the narrative of American history in ways that are still unfolding to this day. Recognizing that it had come late to these developments, understanding its unique capacity to educate the public about the history of slavery in America, and desiring to attract a more representative and diverse range of visitors, the Foundation decided to shift gears, to focus on reinterpreting Monticello as a working plantation and highlighting the role of slaves—as they would now be known—in making it, and Jefferson's life, work.

Stanton was at the very core of this reformation. An assiduous researcher, she not only undertook the arduous and exhaustive task of annotating the *Memorandum Books,* she became the "go-to" person for all aspects of Jefferson's life, researching and answering questions from all over the world about issues, great and small, at the plantation. It was only natural, then, that Stanton was called on to provide documentation and evidence for the Foundation's new interpretative thrust. Coincidentally, the University of Virginia began to mobilize for the 250th anniversary of Jefferson's birth (on April 13, 1743), and Stanton was invited to draft a paper on Jefferson as a slaveholder. That paper, now the essay that begins this volume, was first published in *Jeffersonian Legacies,* the book that grew out of the conference of the same name.[3] " 'Those Who Labor for My Happiness': Thomas Jefferson and His Slaves," now recognized as a classic in the field, launched Stanton's career as a historian—a career for which she had not trained professionally and with a focus that was accidental and unintended. Stanton was able to seize the moment, however, because of her unparalleled mastery of the Jefferson archive. Before Stanton, historians wrote about what Jefferson wrote or said about slavery, not about how he actually lived his life as a slaveholder. To know this thoroughly, one has to know (and care to know) about the lives of the individuals who shared Jefferson's life, a task that Jefferson's biographers had not wished to perform. The materials to learn about the enslaved at Monticello—the abundant records of life on the plantation—were simply not touched, much less subjected to deep analysis. Armed with her keen intelligence, skills as a writer, and extraordinary empathy for her subjects, Stanton filled a scholarly void and forever changed the way historians think about Jefferson and slavery. That contentious topic, already in the forefront of public concern before revelations of his relationship with his slave Sally Hemings, has dominated Jefferson studies and the Jefferson image over the last generation. All serious work on the subject now begins with Stanton.

This book is divided into three parts, sections that mirror the trajectory of Stanton's engagement with Monticello, from her first near-exclusive focus on Jefferson, to her later treatments of the lives of individuals in Monticello's enslaved community, and finally, to her consideration of the descendants of those enslaved on the mountain. The first group of essays, in part I, titled "Jefferson and Slavery," examines the "character" and psychology of Jefferson, now situated on his plantation and in interaction with his human property. Though we consider the subtle and eloquent analyses in " 'Those Who Labor for My Happiness' " and "Perfecting Slavery" to be devastating in their implications, the portraits that emerge do not demonize the master of Monticello, and some of Jefferson's most ardent defenders acknowledge their verisimilitude. " 'A Well-Ordered Household'; Domestic Servants in Jefferson's White House" presents

Jefferson removed from the context of plantation slavery and set down in the ambiguous household he assembled while president, mixing enslaved workers with free, white with black. We see how he attempted to deal with the reality of his status as a slaveholder while maintaining his image as the enlightened opponent of slavery under the intense scrutiny that attended his life as a public official. "Jefferson's People: Slavery at Monticello" reconsiders the themes first set forth in "'Those Who Labor'" in the broader context of his life as a planter and with a focus on changes over time. "Looking for Liberty: Thomas Jefferson and the British Lions" presents Jefferson as a slaveholder through the eyes of British critics, with judgments that ranged from the extremely positive to extremely negative. From the time he stepped onto the world stage, Jefferson the slaveholder was subject of curiosity and comment.

The essays in the next section, part II, titled "Families in Slavery," expand on material only tantalizingly hinted at in her writings about Jefferson's attitude about slaves and slavery as Stanton shifts her focus to hone in on the enslaved community of Monticello, recovering slaves' individuality, agency, and experiences with one another and with Jefferson. The lead essay says it all: "The Other End of the Telescope: Jefferson through the Eyes of His Slaves." This essay, as well as the next essay, "Free Some Day: The African American Families of Monticello," uses narratives of former slaves at Monticello, including that of Madison Hemings, whom historians now believe was Jefferson's son by his slave Sally Hemings, to repopulate Monticello, moving out from the celebrated house to look back at Jefferson from through the eyes of those who lived under his dominion. "Free Some Day" presents the history and genealogies of several Monticello slave families, restoring their true names and demonstrating the ties that bound them together during slavery and freedom.

"The Other End of the Telescope" was Stanton's first extended treatment of Thomas Jefferson and Sally Hemings and makes clear that slavery at Monticello was not just a system in which people worked for no pay and were subject to the control and caprice of those who claimed to own them. It was a place of blended families and interracial unions. If Stanton gives us a new view of Jefferson, her accomplishment in reconstructing the lives of his slaves is even more remarkable—for these were people who had disappeared from the view of scholars and the general public. It is stunning to think that material this rich and instructive, and so accessible, had gone unexamined for so long. These essays should be seen as acts of restoration, for Stanton depicts the enslaved people at Monticello as acting as fully as they could within the boundaries of Virginia's slave society to shape their plantation world and to make lives for themselves once they left the mountain.

Finally, in part III, "Families in Freedom," Stanton reaches beyond the inhabitants of Monticello during the era of Jefferson to take up the story of the descendants of Monticello's enslaved community. One of the results of interracial unions was the emergence of a cadre of free blacks who began life as slaves but gained their freedom decades before the end of the Civil War, a group explored in "Monticello to Main Street: The Hemings Family and Charlottesville." Stanton broadened her research on Monticello slaves and their descendants in the Getting Word project, the Foundation's ambitious effort to craft a new vision for Monticello. With the aid of Dianne Swann-Wright, Stanton found and interviewed dozens of individuals descended from members of Monticello's slave community to determine what, if any, memories of slavery survived. The results of the partnership can be seen in "Bonds of Memory: Identity and the Hemings Family," a remarkable work that blends history with contemporary observations about race and family. Of the many things learned while working on Getting Word, one of the most poignant and ironic facts was the extent to which those descended from slaves at Monticello worked to make the words of Jefferson's Declaration of Independence, "All men are created equal," come to life. Stanton explores their efforts in two new essays that close out the volume, "'We Will Prove Ourselves Men': Hemings Descendants in the Civil War" and "Fulfilling the Declaration: Descendants of Monticello's African-American Families."

Stanton's scholarship has been enormously influential among scholars; it has also shaped the ways in which a much broader, more general public has begun to understand Monticello's slaveholding master when they visit his home. In complementary combination the various strands of Stanton's research and writing have made Monticello much more than a shrine to Thomas Jefferson. The plurality of perspectives that she has brought into view—most notably those of enslaved workers, their families, and descendants—makes it possible for us to see life on the mountaintop in all its dimensions. By re-peopling Monticello and recapturing its business—and busy-ness—the Jefferson Foundation has built on Stanton's work to interpret it back to life. The Foundation's ostensible goal, to reconstruct Monticello, its furnishings, and its surroundings at the moment he left public life in 1809, invites visitors to remember what came before in the career of a great, often controversial statesman and to look forward, with Jefferson, to a long, eventful, and productive retirement. But Jefferson's was only one of many lives enacted in this seemingly peaceful and idyllic scene, and his life only makes sense in the human context of this larger community. Opening the way to recognizing those other lives, Stanton's work invites us to look deeper, into the shared experiences of Monticello families, white and black, free and enslaved.

Jefferson's performances on the stage he set for himself at Monticello depended on the performances of many others. As much as they could, these actors interpreted the lines Jefferson wrote them in their own way; sometimes they followed scripts that the director himself only dimly discerned. No one better grasped Jefferson's performances as a master than those who "labored" for *his* "happiness" while attempting to secure some measure of happiness for themselves. By helping to imagine, with his slaves, what the great man looked like, Stanton's revisionist work does not simply or necessarily diminish him. Quite to the contrary, this new perspective brings Jefferson back to life: he is both more recognizably (and comfortingly) "human" and recognizable to us in his day-to-day transactions with his slaves, but he is also, as a master, as the owner of these equally recognizable people, an alien and alienating figure, the very embodiment of the despotism that the patriots of 1776 had sought to demolish.

As we look more deeply into life as it was actually lived at Monticello in, before, and after 1809, we become more acutely, self-consciously aware that we are looking back and that the past is indeed "a foreign country."[4] But just as the past is the complex, joint production of many actors, so too there are many ways to look at that past—or those pasts. The family stories that Stanton and her colleagues have collected from descendants of Jefferson's slaves enable all of us to see and "remember" life at Monticello in new, more inclusive, and ultimately more generous ways. This is hardly to say that the experience of slaves was as "happy" as Jefferson liked to think or that the peculiar institution did not exploit, maim, and destroy many lives. Yet it is also true that the plantation was home for Monticello slaves and the families they made there and that their free descendants have looked back with pride to the new lives their ancestors first dreamed about and then made for themselves. They continue to do so, as may all visitors to Monticello, in the knowledge that Jefferson's slaves have at last fulfilled his and our most cherished vision of freedom, equality, and independence.

Great men and women cannot make history all by themselves. But a few gifted and fortunate historians can make history seem different and therefore enable us to see ourselves differently. Cinder Stanton has played this role at Monticello. Her career—like most careers—was shaped by accident and contingency; but in her generous empathy, in her determination to do justice to her subjects, in her insistence on telling the story—or, more accurately, the many stories—of Jefferson and his slaves, she has made Monticello a much different place than it had been before, a place that was truer to the experiences of those who once lived there and "labored" for their master's "happiness."

Author's Note

Two of the essays in this volume are published for the first time. The other nine were published over the course of eighteen years, from 1993 to 2010. I have made no attempt to improve or update my conclusions with insights gained since their original publication. For instance, the long note on the Hemings-Jefferson controversy in the first essay remains as it was in 1993. Changes have been made, however, to expedite access to previously unpublished manuscripts, by citing them to works published in the meantime. Also, enslaved individuals who had been known only by their first names have been given their full names, by incorporating surnames learned in subsequent research. A handful of factual errors and misstatements have been corrected.

My debt to the many people who have provided essential advice and support has been expressed throughout this volume. Here I would like to reiterate my deep gratitude to a few whose wisdom and friendship have enlightened and sustained me over the long haul: James A. Bear, Jr., gave me my first real job and introduced me to Monticello and its residents. His humane curiosity about people famous and forgotten, black and white, inspired my efforts to understand those who lived in the past and the daily choices they had to make. I am forever thankful to Jim and Mary Caperton for their invigorating conversation and inexhaustible hospitality. Peter Onuf challenged me to publish in this field for the first time (the essay that provides the title of this volume) and has been egging me on ever since. I have benefitted from his uncanny ability to detect and articulate one's embryonic ideas and have delighted in and relied on his and Kristin's friendship. Dianne Swann-Wright and Beverly Gray, my partners since 1993 in the Getting Word oral history project, introduced me to an aspect of the American experience from which I had been insulated for far too long. It has been a life-changing and life-enhancing collaboration, whether talking around kitchen tables or exploring the back roads of Ohio. Annette Gordon-Reed appeared out of the blue in 1995, fully in command of a part of Monticello's history that I had been thinking about in a relative vacuum. Our discussions since then have sharpened and enriched my understanding of key issues of American history.

I would also like to thank Bob Vernon, Gayle Schulman, and other more recent associates in the local history group now known as Central Virginia History Researchers, who have been unfailingly generous in sharing their broad knowledge of public records and the African American experience in Virginia.

And, finally, I am deeply grateful to the Thomas Jefferson Foundation and Daniel P. Jordan and Leslie Greene Bowman, its leaders since Jim Bear's retirement, and to Douglas Wilson, James Horn, and Andrew O'Shaughnessy, directors of the Robert H. Smith International Center for Jefferson Studies, for providing a stimulating and supportive environment for my adventures in scholarship over the years.

Part I

JEFFERSON AND SLAVERY

"Those Who Labor for My Happiness"

Thomas Jefferson and His Slaves

> To give liberty to, or rather, to abandon persons whose habits
> have been formed in slavery is like abandoning children.
>
> —*Thomas Jefferson to Edward Bancroft, January 26, 1789*

ON January 15, 1827, Monticello blacksmith Joseph Fossett may have left his anvil to watch the bidding begin. His wife Edith and their eight children were among the "130 valuable negroes" offered in the executor's sale of the estate of Thomas Jefferson. "The negroes are believed to be the most valuable for their number ever offered at one time in the State of Virginia," declared the advertisement placed by Thomas Jefferson Randolph, Jefferson's grandson and executor. Despite bitterly cold weather, a large crowd assembled for the five-day sale, and bidding was brisk. Surprising sums were paid for faded prints and old-fashioned tables, while the slaves brought prices averaging 70 percent more than their appraised values.[1]

By the terms of Jefferson's will, Fossett would become a free man in July. Now, his wife, two infant sons, and two teenaged daughters were sold to three different bidders for a total of $1,350. "Thank heaven the whole of this dreadful business is over," wrote Jefferson's granddaughter on January 25, "and has been attended with as few distressing occurrences as the case would admit." Her brother remembered that week over forty years later as "a sad scene" and likened it to "a captured village in ancient times when all were sold as slaves."[2]

The monumental debt kept in check by Jefferson's presence overwhelmed all the residents of Monticello, both black and white. In the three years after his death the black families were dispersed by sale, and the white family left the

This essay was originally published in *Jeffersonian Legacies*, ed. Peter S. Onuf (Charlottesville, 1993), 147–180. In 1997 it was republished in book form, with illustrations, under the title *Slavery at Monticello*, by the Thomas Jefferson Memorial Foundation, Inc.

mountaintop and put the house on the market. The plantation "family" that Jefferson had nurtured and controlled for sixty years was no more. In the end, he had abandoned his "children."

"My Family"

In 1776 Jefferson made a census of the "Number of souls in my family."[3] His Albemarle County "family" numbered 117, including, besides his wife and daughter, 16 free men (his overseers and hired workmen), their wives and children, and 83 slaves. Throughout his life Jefferson used the word "family" for both a group of people connected by blood and—according to more ancient usage—all those under a head of household or, in his case, plantation owner. In 1801 he vaccinated "70 or 80 of my own family" against smallpox; in 1819 he spoke of the voracious appetite for pork of "our enormously large family." At times this usage required the addition of qualifying adjectives. Jefferson wrote that his son-in-law's "white family" had recovered from a prevailing illness in 1806, and in 1815, he noted the surprising number of sick "in our family, both in doors and out"— making a neat spatial distinction between the Jefferson-Randolph family inside the Monticello house and the black men, women, and children living in cabins on the mountaintop and adjacent farms.[4]

Joseph Fossett joined this family in November 1780, born to Mary Hemings (b. 1753) and an unknown father. She was the oldest child of Elizabeth (Betty) Hemings (ca. 1735–1807), who, with her ten children, became Jefferson's property on January 14, 1774, on the division of the estate of his father-in-law John Wayles.[5] On that date Jefferson acquired 135 slaves who, added to the 52 slaves derived from his inheritance from his father, made him the second largest slaveholder in Albemarle County. Thereafter, the number of slaves he owned fluctuated above and below the figure of two hundred—with increases through births offset by periodic sales that were part of an attempt to pay off the almost £4,000 debt that accompanied the Wayles inheritance. Between 1784 and 1794 Jefferson disposed of 161 people by sale or gift.[6]

Unlike his father-in-law, Jefferson never engaged in the commercial buying and selling of humans. His infrequent purchases were usually made to fulfill needs of the moment, and selling was primarily a reluctant reaction to financial demands. As Jefferson wrote in 1820, he had "scruples about selling negroes but for delinquency, or on their own request."[7] Several known transactions were intended to unite families. The purchase of Ursula in 1773 involved buying her husband George Granger from a second owner. In 1805, Jefferson "reluctantly" sold Brown Colbert, a twenty-year-old nailer, to unite him with his wife, the slave of a brick mason about to leave Monticello. On this occasion Jefferson declared himself "always willing to indulge connections seriously formed by those people, where it can be done reasonably."[8]

In 1807 Jefferson bought the wife of his blacksmith Moses Hern when her owner emigrated to Kentucky. "Nobody feels more strongly than I do," he wrote at the time, "the desire to make all practicable sacrifices to keep man and wife together who have imprudently married out of their respective families." This final phrase, a telling indication of the dual nature of Jefferson's recognition of the importance of the black family, reveals his hope that his slaves would seek spouses only within their master's domain. "There is nothing I desire so much as that all the young people in the estate should intermarry with one another and stay at home," Jefferson wrote his Poplar Forest overseer. "They are worth a great deal more in that case than when they have husbands and wives abroad." His methods for discouraging romance beyond the plantation boundaries are not known, but he did use rewards to encourage "prudent" courtship. To the slave women, for instance, he promised an extra pot and crocus bed "when they take husbands at home."[9]

[margin note:] wanted everyone "at home"

Jefferson realized the potency of family bonds for the African American members of his extended household. In 1814, there is even a note of envy in his comparison of the lot of English laborers and American slaves. Slaves "have the comfort too of numerous families, in the midst of whom they live without want, or fear of it." This "comfort" was not always possible for whites. Jefferson all his life sought to draw to the neighborhood of Monticello both kin and kindred spirits, but with only limited success. The mobility of white Virginians separated parent from child and sibling from sibling. His sister emigrated with her husband to Kentucky, and his younger daughter's husband could not be persuaded to leave his Tidewater plantation. Jefferson's fatherly tenacity kept his elder daughter Martha always at or near Monticello, at considerable jeopardy to her marriage.

His rosy picture of the "comfort of numerous families" was drawn at a time when Virginian society was progressively destabilized by westward migration. He must, therefore, have witnessed how frequently the ties within extended slave families were severed, and he would have heard constant expression of the "dread of separation" that Frederick Douglass called the "most painful to the majority of slaves."[10]

Jefferson's awareness of the slave's attachment to a particular spot on earth and the extended network of relations that lived on it played a significant part in his actions as a slaveholder. He could foster family ties through benevolent intercession, he could exploit them to control behavior, or he could ignore them in the interests of efficient management. These ties could even inhibit his actions toward improving the lot of his slaves through emancipation or removal to cotton

[margin note:] How TJ used family bonds

country, where conditions were considered more favorable to their well-being. Even freedom was not, in Jefferson's mind, sufficient justification for uprooting whole families. In 1814, he wrote that "the laws do not permit us to turn them loose," evidently referring to the 1806 act declaring that freed slaves must leave the state within a year. When his son-in-law Thomas Mann Randolph launched a scheme in 1802 to take his slaves to "a mild climate and gentle labor" in Georgia, Jefferson did consider sending "such of my negroes as could be persuaded to it." But in 1822, Martha Randolph knew her father "would never listen . . . for a moment" to the family's latest plan to try their fortunes further south—"although moving [his slaves] in a body would occasion little or no distress to them."[11]

Slaves were both humans and property, and as the protector of a large household and the manager of a working plantation, Jefferson always had to play two roles. He was gratified when "moral as well as interested considerations" were in accord, as when prescribing lighter labors for women with infant children in 1819: "I consider the labor of a breeding woman as no object, and that a child raised every 2. years is of more profit than the crop of the best laboring man. In this, as in all other cases, providence has made our interest and our duties coincide perfectly." But he must have had daily reminders of the frequent contradiction between "interest" and "duty."[12]

In his role as plantation manager, Jefferson's efforts to maximize the utility of each man, woman, and child led to regular interference in the family lives of his slaves. The demands of productivity limited his respect for the integrity of the black family. Like many other enlightened Virginians, Jefferson always specified that slaves be sold in family units: husbands were not separated from wives, nor parents from young children. But once black boys or girls reached the age of ten or twelve and their working lives began, they lost their status as children and, with it, the guarantee of family stability. Teenagers were often separated from their families through sale or transfer to other plantations. Four boys from Poplar Forest, aged ten to twelve, were sent to Monticello to work in the nailery in the 1790s, and in 1813 two fourteen-year-old girls left Bedford County to learn weaving and spinning in the Albemarle County textile factory. The privileged household servants were particularly vulnerable to teenage separation, as their young masters or mistresses grew up and married. Betty Brown left her family to attend the newly married Martha Jefferson at age thirteen, and her niece, Betsy Hemings, was fourteen when she was given to Jefferson's daughter Maria on her marriage in 1797.[13]

Dinah was sold in 1792 with "her younger children" to accomplish the double objective of paying off a debt and uniting her with her husband. When Jefferson purchased the weaver Nance Hemings from his sister, he listened to a mother's

plea. Nance "wishes me to buy her children," he wrote, "but I would not purchase the boy; as to the youngest child, if she insists on it, and my sister desires
it, I would take it." Fifteen-year-old Billy was left in Louisa County, and twelve-
year-old Critta only came to Albemarle because she was bought by Jefferson's
son-in-law.[14]

Joe Fossett was also separated from his mother by sale. During Jefferson's five-
year absence in France, Mary Hemings was hired out to Thomas Bell, a respected
Charlottesville merchant. In 1792 she asked to be sold to Bell, the father of her
two youngest children, Robert Washington and Sally Jefferson. Jefferson asked
his superintendent to "dispose of Mary according to her desire, with such of her
younger children as she chose." Bob and Sally remained with their mother and
became Bells, and eleven-year-old Joe and nine-year-old Betsy were now on their
own at Monticello.[15]

Joe spent his days in and around the Monticello house, one of nine house servants. He and three of his cousins were the fetchers and carriers, the fire builders,
the table setters and waiters; they met guests at the east portico and ventured
forth on errands. They were the "boys" that Martha Jefferson Randolph finally
got "in tolerable order" during Jefferson's absence, after some accidents to the
household china.[16]

In the house Joe was surrounded by members of his own family, all Hemingses. The household staff included his uncles James and Peter, his aunts Sally
and Critta, his cousins Wormley, Burwell, and Brown, and his sister Betsy.[17] From
their arrival at Monticello as part of the Wayles estate in 1774, the children of
Betty Hemings had assumed the primary roles in the Monticello household.
Robert Hemings (1762–1819) replaced Jupiter as Jefferson's valet and traveling
attendant; Martin Hemings (b. 1755) became the butler; Betty Hemings and her
daughters were employed in cleaning, sewing, and in personal attendance on
Martha Jefferson and her children. In the period of Jefferson's retirement to
Monticello from 1794 to 1797, visitors who did not wander over to Mulberry Row
or down to the cellar dependencies would have seen only Hemingses.

Jefferson's grandson Thomas Jefferson Randolph recalled a slightly later period,
when the "entire household of servants with the exception of an under cook and
carriage driver consisted of one family connection and their wives. . . . It was a
source of bitter jealousy to the other slaves, who liked to account for it with other
reasons than the true one; viz. superior intelligence, capacity and fidelity to trusts."
Monticello overseer Edmund Bacon spoke of the women of the household: "They
were old family servants and great favorites. . . . I was instructed to take no control of them." And more than one visitor would have noted, as did the duc de La
Rochefoucauld-Liancourt in 1796, that the slaves visible at Monticello were

remarkably light skinned. "I have even seen," he wrote at a time when Sally Hemings's children were not yet on the scene, "and particularly at Mr. Jefferson's, slaves who have neither in their color nor features a single trace of their origin, but they are sons of slave mothers and consequently slaves."[18]

According to her grandson, Betty Hemings was the daughter of an African slave and an English sea captain, and at least seven of her children had white fathers. Isaac Granger (later Jefferson), former Monticello slave whose reminiscences were recorded in 1847, recalled that Betty's children Robert and James Hemings were "bright mulattoes" and Sally was "mighty near white."[19] Many of the third generation of Hemingses were even lighter. Without reviving the debate over the paternity of Sally Hemings's children, it is sufficient to note here that several and perhaps all of Betty Hemings's daughters formed relationships with white men.[20] In at least one case, that of Sally Hemings, the children had seven-eighths white ancestry and thus were not black by Virginia law, which declared that a person "who shall have one fourth part or more of negro blood, shall . . . be deemed a mulatto."

Jefferson looked up this statute in 1815 and, after demonstrating its effects in a series of algebraic formulas, stated that "our Canon considers 2. crosses with the pure white, and a 3d. with any degree of mixture, however small, as clearing the issue of the negro blood." "But observe," he continued, "that this does not reestablish freedom, which depends on the condition of the mother." If the issue of the third cross were emancipated, "he becomes a free *white* man, and a citizen of the US. to all intents and purposes."[21] Thus, future citizens of the United States were being held in bondage at Monticello.

Jefferson did free all of Sally Hemings's children. He allowed Harriet and Beverly to "run away," providing Harriet money and stage fare to the north, and gave Madison and Eston Hemings their freedom in his will. Overseer Edmund Bacon remembered Harriet's departure, when "people said he freed her because she was his own daughter" (Bacon's own candidate for paternity was deleted in the published version of his reminiscences), but the reasons given by Jefferson's granddaughter Ellen Randolph Coolidge accord with his racial formulas. In 1858 she stated that it was her grandfather's principle to "allow such of his slaves as were sufficiently white to pass for white men, to withdraw from the plantation; it was called running away, but they were never reclaimed."[22]

"It is almost impossible for slaves to give a correct account of their male parentage," wrote former slave Henry Bibb in 1849. The fathers of most of Betty Hemings's children and grandchildren cannot be positively identified. The only certainty is that some of them were white men, and those implicated by their contemporaries ranged from overseers and hired artisans to sprigs of the local aristocracy, family kinsmen, and even the master himself.[23] Jefferson, thus, who often stated his "aversion" to racial mixture, lived surrounded by its examples.[24]

Little is known about miscegenation at Monticello beyond the Hemings family. The presence of two mulattoes in the legacy of Peter Jefferson suggests that the crossing of racial lines was nothing new on the mountain.[25] Nevertheless, the Hemings family—as Thomas Jefferson Randolph's statement indicated—seems to have been a caste apart.

All the slaves freed by Jefferson in his lifetime or in his will were members of this family. Two, Robert and Martin, were allowed a measure of mobility no other slave had—they often hired themselves out to other masters during Jefferson's long absences in public service. Only Betty Hemings and her daughters were spared the grueling weeks of the wheat harvest, when every healthy slave was drafted to bring in the crop. None of her twelve children and only two of her more than twenty grandchildren found spouses "at home." One of the latter, Burwell Colbert, even married his own first cousin. Known husbands were drawn from the local community, both free black and white, and wives from the household staffs of neighboring plantations.[26] Only Joe Fossett and Wormley Hughes, who married a niece of Isaac (Granger) Jefferson, found wives at Monticello.

At the boundary between the black and white worlds at Monticello, the Hemings family has occupied the foreground of all accounts of the slave community there because we know more about them. Their domination of the documentary record derives from the positions they occupied in the household and Mulberry Row shops, under perpetual observation by their master and his family.

"To Labor for Another"[27]

In 1794 Joe Fossett's life took on a new dimension. He was one of "a dozen little boys from 10. to 16. years of age" whom Jefferson installed in a new nailery on Mulberry Row.[28] Retired to Monticello, Jefferson devoted most of his energies at this time to the reformation of his farms, impoverished by thirty years of the extractive rotation of corn and tobacco and the unsupervised management of stewards and overseers. Expecting the change from tobacco to wheat production and the inauguration of his complex crop rotation schemes to cause a temporary decrease in farm production, he had determined to find a new source of income. He chose the production of nails, because it required little capital outlay and was within the capacities of his own slave labor force.

In the first three years of the nailery's operation, Jefferson was a daily presence. His surviving accounts reveal that he must have risen at dawn to weigh out the

Mulberry Row today. (Thomas Jefferson Foundation, Inc.)

nail rod given to the nailers and returned toward dusk to weigh the nails they produced. An "Estimate on the actual work of the autumn of 1794" summarizes the results of his daily balancing of the scales. "Moses wastes 15 lb. in the [hundredweight]," he began, writing down the name of each nailer and the average amount of iron he wasted in the nail-making process. Fourteen-year-old Joe Fossett was one of the most efficient, wasting only 19 pounds of iron per hundredweight, while two ten-year-olds—Burwell and James—were predictably the least efficient, making only seventy-one pounds of nails from every hundred pounds of nail rod. Another ten-year-old, however, the future wagoner David Hern, was the third of nine in efficiency.[29]

Here was a new scene for Joe, Wormley, and Burwell, who now divided their time between the Monticello house and the Mulberry Row nailery, where a dozen teenagers stood at their anvils around four fires, pointing and heading nails with heavy hammers until they had completed their appointed tasks. Because of his household duties Joe's daily task was about two-thirds that of the full-time nailers—250 to 350 nails, depending on size. Two years later, when he left the house to pursue the ironworking trade full-time, his task was increased. One page of accounts shows Jefferson apparently calculating the average production of his nailers to set a new and higher daily task. In an analysis Jefferson made in April 1796, Joe Fossett was the third most profitable nailer, making 326

TJ managing output thresholds

pounds of nails in three months and earning for his master an average daily profit of about sixty cents.[30]

The Mulberry Row nailery served as more than a new source of income. It allowed Jefferson to observe the abilities and attitudes of his young male slaves and to select their future careers. By the same token, in the nailery these young men had a chance to influence their future by their own actions. Many of them evidently chose to please their master by their performance and eventually occupied the most important artisan and household positions on the mountain. Several became blacksmiths, carpenters, and coopers; one became the head gardener and another the Monticello butler; a few were unable to avert the usual fate of farm labor; and at least one, James Hubbard, the most "wasteful" in 1794, chose the route of resistance.

The nailery was also an important part of Jefferson's perpetual effort to make the most efficient use of his labor force. His constant attempts to eliminate every pocket of idleness from his operation went beyond the ordinary profit seeking of plantation managers. Neither youth, age, illness, nor weather was allowed to stop the plantation machine. There is even a note of pride in Jefferson's accounts of his successful efforts to provide for all his wants by harnessing the energies of children. In the summer of 1795 he wrote that "a nailery which I have established with my own negro boys now provides completely for the maintenance of my family." A few months earlier he had declared that "my new trade of nail-making is to me in this country what an additional title of nobility, or the ensigns of a new order are in Europe."[31]

Twenty years later Jefferson's favorite project was the textile factory, which "only employs a few women, children and invalids who could do little in the farm." Appropriate tasks were found for slaves past the age for farm labor. "The negroes too old to be hired," Jefferson wrote his steward in 1788, "could they not make a good profit by cultivating cotton?" Some older women served as nurses or cooks in the quarters, whereas others joined the older men on the vegetable gardening team, dubbed by Jefferson the "veteran aids" and "senile corps."[32]

The sick who were not bedridden were treated with gentle doses of alternative labor. When all hands were diverted to the digging of a canal in 1793, the "invalids" were to "work only when they shall be able. They will probably be equal to the hauling away the earth and forming it into a bank on the side next the river." Poplar Forest's former "head man" Nace was to be "entirely kept from labour until he recovers." Jefferson suggested, nevertheless, that he spend his days indoors, shelling corn or making shoes or baskets.[33]

So that neither climate nor circumstance could interrupt the hum of activity on his plantation, Jefferson gave his laborers a variety of skills. Barnaby and Shepherd, whose main trade was carpentry, were to join Phil when he "proceeds to the making shoes for the people . . . in order to perfect themselves in shoe-making." Carpenters and coopers were also charcoal burners. Nailers were dispatched to the woods with axes when there was an immediate need for clearing land. Poplar Forest blacksmiths, when there was no work, could fell wood for charcoal or work in the fields; Bess made butter "during the season" and worked in the spinning house when there was no dairy work.[34]

Male domestic servants, in particular, were trained in a trade they could pursue during Jefferson's long absences in public service. Jupiter was a stonecutter as well as manservant and groom. Burwell Colbert, butler at Monticello for many years, was a skilled glazier and painter. Israel Gillette, a waiter and postillion, worked as a carder in the textile shop when his services were not needed by the household, and as already mentioned, the young boys in the house filled their extra hours with nail making. Although overseer Edmund Bacon wrote that the female house servants had "very little to do" when Jefferson was absent in Washington, later references reveal that some were expected to master textile skills and complete a daily carding or spinning task.[35]

Joe Fossett's own training probably began in earnest in 1796. In his Farm Book, Jefferson had penned a script for the childhood of his slaves: "Children till 10. years to serve as nurses. From 10. to 16. the boys make nails, the girls spin. At 16. go into the ground or learn trades." In 1796 Fossett—now sixteen—was issued overalls instead of his usual house servants' clothing allowance, and for several years he divided his time between nail making—becoming a foreman of nailers—and learning the blacksmithing trade. He first worked under Isaac Jefferson's brother George Granger and in 1801 began his training under a remarkable new teacher, William Stewart. Jefferson had found "the best workman in America, but the most eccentric one" in Philadelphia and employed him for six years—"several years longer than he would otherwise have done," wrote Edmund Bacon, "in order that his own servants might learn his trade thoroughly." Drink was Stewart's downfall, and when he got into "his idle frolics," Joe Fossett had to carry forward the work of the blacksmith shop on his own. When Jefferson's patience ran out at the end of 1807, Stewart was dismissed and Fossett became the head blacksmith, running the shop until Jefferson's death. Bacon described Fossett as "a very fine workman; could do anything it was necessary to do with steel or iron."[36]

The workmen hired to build and rebuild the Monticello house also imparted their considerable skills to their African American assistants. Jefferson had friends in Europe and Philadelphia on the lookout for the best masons and woodworkers. Moses Hern was to be the "disciple" of a stonemason expected from Scotland. John Hemings worked first with David Watson, who had deserted from the British army in the Revolution, and then with a newly arrived Irishman, James

Dinsmore. Together Hemings and Dinsmore crafted Monticello's beautiful interior woodwork, to which, in Jefferson's opinion, "there is nothing superior in the US." Hemings alone was responsible for the interior joinery work at Poplar Forest, and he reigned in the Monticello woodworking shop for all the years of Jefferson's retirement.[37]

"To be independent for the comforts of life," wrote Jefferson in 1816, "we must fabricate them ourselves."[38] To enable his own slave laborers to produce both the necessities and some of the comforts of life, he imported to Monticello at various times a Scottish gardener, an English brewer, a German painter, and a French chef. He hired white masons, smiths, carriage builders, charcoal burners, and weavers for the time required to pass their skills to men and women who practiced their craft and in turn passed it on to others.

As an observant Madison Hemings remembered in 1873, Jefferson in the years of his retirement had "but little taste or care for agricultural pursuits. . . . It was his mechanics he seemed mostly to direct, and in their operations he took great interest." Jefferson was certainly most comfortable in the management of his artisans, with whom his methods of personal control and rational incentives to industry were so successful. His daily supervising presence in the nailery in its first three years made it both profitable and relatively tranquil. A sense of pride and esprit de corps was instilled through rewards and special rations. Isaac Jefferson remembered that Jefferson "gave the boys in the nail factory a pound of meat a week, a dozen herrings, a quart of molasses, and peck of meal. Give them that wukked the best a suit of red or blue; encouraged them mightily." The special clothing prize would have had particular appeal in a community that received the equivalent of uniforms twice a year, and the Farm Book confirms a larger meat ration.[39]

Financial incentives were reserved for adult laborers. The blacksmith George Granger, manager of the nailery, received a percentage of its profits. The Monticello coopers were allowed to sell for their own benefit every thirty-third flour barrel they made. Jefferson gave his slave charcoal burners a premium for efficiency, not just productivity. He paid them according to the average number of bushels of charcoal they could extract per cord of wood.[40] John Hemings, the joiner, and Burwell Colbert, butler and painter, were given an annual "gratuity" or "donation" of fifteen or twenty dollars—equivalent to one month's wages of a free workman.[41]

Joe Fossett and other artisans at Monticello carried on their work with a notable freedom from supervision. In 1798 Thomas Mann Randolph wrote an absent Jefferson about the slave manager of the nailery: "George I am sure could not stoop to my authority & I hope and believe he pushes your interests as well as I could." Jefferson was willing to give his tradesmen a remarkable measure of independence. On his departure from Monticello at the end of 1797, he left written instructions with his carpenters, merely asking his son-in-law to keep them "to their metal" by occasional questioning "as to their progress." A few years later he directed that Wormley Hughes and Joe Fossett work on their own, with auger and gunpowder, blasting rock in the canal. Overseer Gabriel Lilly, however, could not bring himself to let them do this dangerous work out of his sight. Randolph, too, had doubts about Jefferson's wisdom in leaving his artisans "under no command." He was convinced they would become "idle and dissipated" but admitted Jefferson's confidence was "less abused than I expected" and "it confirms them in honesty."[42]

punished
by shame
vs whipping

The power of Jefferson's personal control is apparent in an incident related by Edmund Bacon. About 1807 one of the nailers was discovered in the theft of several hundred pounds of nails. Brought before Jefferson, "he was mortified and distressed beyond measure. He had been brought up in the shop, and we all had confidence in him. Now his character was gone." Jefferson considered his shame sufficient punishment and, despite the expectations of the nailery manager, ordered no whipping. According to Bacon, the chastened offender found religion through this experience and was baptised soon afterward.[43]

After Jefferson's return to public life, nailery profits shrank as cheaper British nails came on the market and the cooped-up crowd of teenagers became unruly. William Stewart, the blacksmith from the North, was entirely unequal to their management. In Jefferson's opinion, "They require a rigour of discipline to make them do reasonable work, to which he cannot bring himself." Overseer Gabriel Lilly was ordered not to resort to the whip except in extreme cases. Jefferson wrote that "it would destroy their value in my estimation to degrade them in their own eyes by the whip. this therefore must not be resorted to but in extremities. as they will be again under my government, I would chuse they should retain the stimulus of character."[44]

Character
vs
whipping

"I love industry and abhor severity," Jefferson wrote in 1805, and no reliable document portrays him in the act of applying physical correction.[45] Overseer Edmund Bacon recalled that Jefferson "was always very kind and indulgent to his servants. He would not allow them to be at all overworked, and he would hardly ever allow one of them to be whipped. . . . He could not bear to have a servant whipped, no odds how much he deserved it." His intercession in the affair of the nail thief was only one of a number of such incidents. In the case of Hercules, a runaway from Poplar Forest, Jefferson suggested to his overseer that as "it is his first folly in this way," further punishment was inappropriate; his imprisonment in Buckingham County jail had been sufficient. Another Poplar Forest slave, Phil Hubbard, was not to be punished for running away to Monticello: "Altho I had let them all know that their runnings away should be punished, yet Phill's character is not that of a runaway. I have known him from a boy and that he has not come off to sculk from his work."[46]

In Hercules's case, Jefferson advised the overseer to let him "recieve the pardon as from yourself alone, and not by my interference, for this is what I would have none of them to suppose." And he gave Thrimston Hern, whose transgression is not specified, "a proper reprimand for his conduct" and assured him that punishment for any further misbehavior would be left to the discretion of the stonecutter for whom he worked.[47] Despite Jefferson's wish to remain hidden behind the cloak of his overseers' authority, it is apparent that first-time offenders, especially, turned to him frequently in expectation of leniency.

Jefferson's views on physical punishment no doubt reduced whipping on his plantations to levels well below those of many of his neighbors. The whip was, however, by no means eliminated. From the 1780s Jefferson employed on the Monticello plantation over twenty overseers with diverse temperaments and management styles.[48] Some were cruel, even by the standards of the day. William Page, "peevish & too ready to strike," spent four years in Jefferson's employ. When he later became overseer at John Wayles Eppes's neighboring Pantops, Eppes was unable to hire slaves in the neighborhood because of "the terror of Pages name." The "tyrannical" William McGehee, overseer at the Tufton farm for two years, carried a gun "for fear of an attack from the negroes." One of Monticello's white house joiners deplored the cruelty of Gabriel Lilly, overseer there from 1801 to 1805. Lilly whipped Critta Hemings's seventeen-year-old son James three times in one day, when he was too ill to "raise his hand to his Head." Yet Jefferson considered it impossible to find "a man who fulfills my purposes better than" Lilly and would have kept him longer, had he not demanded a doubling of his salary.[49]

The whippings that Jefferson himself ordered were mainly for the benefit of their witnesses. He had the chronic runaway Jame Hubbard brought to Monticello in irons and "severely flogged in the presence of his old companions."[50] And when the excuses of youth, sentiment, or special circumstances had been exhausted, Jefferson invariably rid himself of disruptive elements by sale. Overseer Bacon remembered his orders: "If there was any servant that could not be got along without the chastising that was customary, to dispose of him."[51]

In 1803 an unforgettable example was made of an eighteen-year-old nailer. The usual turbulence of the nailery boiled over into violence in May, when Cary nearly killed Joe Fossett's cousin Brown Colbert with his hammer. Jefferson wrote home from Washington: "Should Brown recover so that the law shall inflict no punishment on Cary, it will be necessary for me to make an example of him in terrorem to others, in order to maintain the police so rigorously necessary among the nailboys." He was to be sold either to "negro purchasers from

[margin handwritten notes: "Whipping as disciplinary spectacle" and "sale preferred to whipping"]

Georgia" or "in any other quarter so distant as never more to be heard of among us." It would seem to Cary's companions "as if he were put out of the way by death." In the language of this letter, Jefferson became increasingly vehement in his determination to deliver a shock to the family sensibilities of the African Americans who would continue to share his mountaintop. He continued: "I should regard price but little in comparison with so distant an exile of him as to cut him off compleatly from ever again being heard of."[52]

By all accounts, Jefferson was remarkably successful in surrounding himself with artisans and house servants of the proper "character," who united industry with trust. Jupiter and other "trusty servants" traveled alone all over Virginia, carrying large sums of money. In 1811 Jefferson promised "a trusty negro of my own" a reward in exchange for information on the whereabouts of a runaway.[53] Whereas George Washington's letters abound with exasperation at the performance of his craftsmen, Jefferson's are surprisingly silent on this head. Since it is doubtful that his expectations were lower, this suggests both the talents of his tradesmen and the success of his management methods.

With his farm laborers, however, Jefferson was less successful. He was always wrestling with the overseer problem. As his son-in-law expressed it, an overseer "will either reject all restraint or use it as an excuse for making no profit." Jefferson stated the case in the usual two parts in 1792, when he was contemplating a novel solution: "My first wish is that the labourers may be well treated, the second that they may enable me to have that treatment continued by making as much as will admit it. The man who can effect both objects is rarely to be found." He sought that rarity—an overseer both humane and productive—in Maryland, where, because of the mixture of free and slave labor, "the farmers there understand the management of negroes on a rational and humane plan."[54] But the tenures of his Maryland overseers were short and, for unknown reasons, not happy.

In 1799 Jefferson wrote: "I am not fit to be a farmer with the kind of labour we have." And in the same period he indicted the labor system that harmonized so imperfectly with the systematic agricultural reforms he tried to introduce on his plantations: "My last revulsion from retirement has overshadowed me with despair when I contemplate the necessity of reformation in my farms. That work finds obstacles enough in the ignorance & unwillingness of the instruments employed, even in the presence of the master. But when he is obliged to be absent the half of every year no hope remains of that steady perseverance in a fixed plan which alone can ensure it's success."[55] After the overseer experiment of the 1790s, the men and women who labored in Monticello's fields had to take their chances with a long succession of local overseers.

In the summer of 1806 one of Jefferson's tradesmen stepped out of character. Joe Fossett startled him by running away from Monticello just five days after

Jefferson returned from Washington. He sent his head carpenter "in pursuit of a young mulatto man, called Joe, 26. years of age, who ran away from here the night of the 29th. inst[ant] without the least word of difference with any body, and indeed having never in his life recieved a blow from any one." His disbelief at this insubordination from one of his most privileged slaves was soon modified by a glimmer of understanding. "We know he has taken the road towards Washington," Jefferson continued. "He may possibly trump up some story to be taken care of at the President's house till he can make up his mind which way to go, or perhaps he may make himself known to Edy only, as he was formerly connected with her."[56]

Fossett's uncharacteristic action forced Jefferson to consider, for a moment, that his slave had a life of his own. Fossett had not been running away from Monticello. He ran *to* the President's House, where Edy had been in training under a French chef since 1802. Fossett's desperate journey was evidently precipitated by something he heard from two hired slaves who had accompanied Jefferson from Washington. The situation may have been similar to that of the wagoner David Hern and his wife Fanny, as remembered by Edmund Bacon. Fanny, too, was a trainee cook at the President's House, and she and her husband "got into a terrible quarrel. Davy was jealous of his wife, and, I reckon, with good reason." Bacon was summoned to take them to Alexandria to be sold. "They wept, and begged, and made good promises, and made such an ado, that they begged the old gentleman out of it. But it was a good lesson for them."[57]

The pressures of separation had nearly destroyed the relationship of Davy and Fanny Hern, who saw each other two or three times a year when he carted trees and plants or led horses to and from Washington. Joe and Edy Fossett, on the other hand, may have seen each other very little, if at all, between at least 1802 and Joe's sudden appearance in 1806. Any necessary repairs to their relationship were made quickly, for shortly after his arrival, Fossett was caught by Jefferson's Irish coachman leaving the President's House and put in jail. No record has survived of the reception the runaway met on his return to Monticello, where he waited three more years for Edy to return with the retiring president. There they renewed their connection and raised eight children.[58]

"In the Mountain with Old Master"[59]

The descendants of Joe Fossett and his relatives still tell stories about the starring roles played by their ancestors in the momentous events of the summer of 1781. The hero of one tale was the Monticello blacksmith who foiled the pursuing British dragoons by shoeing Jefferson's horse backwards. Other family members took part in the preservation of the family silver. In one version, the

[margin annotation: heroic family oral histories]

blacksmith's wife devised a scheme for hanging the valuables on iron hooks in the well. In another story a slave, in the act of secreting the silver, is trapped under the front portico by the arrival of Banastre Tarleton's troops. Joe Fossett, then actually only seven months old, is given the part of bringing this man food and water for two days, until the enemy leaves the mountain.[60]

These family traditions carried down through the generations the memory of skills and ingenuity that enabled slaves to participate in epic world events and made them indispensable to their master. They also reveal the slaves' consciousness of the larger stage on which their master moved. The dash southward along Carter's Mountain in 1781 may not have been Jefferson's finest hour, but the participants in the events of the first days of June knew the importance of preventing the governor's capture. Isaac Granger, taken to Philadelphia in the early 1790s to learn tinsmithing, actually saw his master in action as a public man in his many-windowed house on Market Street and, in memory, promoted him to president. As Martha Randolph remembered, the Monticello slaves believed her father to be "one of the greatest, and they knew him to be one of the best men and the kindest of masters."[61]

Jefferson would probably not have been able to reciprocate with tales of those living around him on the much smaller stage of Monticello. To protect himself from the realities of owning human beings, he needed the same psychological buffers as other well-intentioned slaveholders. The constant tension between self-interest and humanity seems to have induced in him a gradual closing of the imagination that distanced and dehumanized the black families of Monticello.

His records demonstrate this limited view. In the infrequent descriptive phrases of his correspondence, his slaves are singled out for characteristics—trustworthiness or unreliability, intelligence or stupidity, sobriety or drunkenness—that bear entirely on performance.[62] In the Farm Book they are given only first names, and diminutives at that. The husband and wife known as Joseph and Edith Fossett to their family members were just Joe and Edy to Jefferson. If Israel Gillette Jefferson's reminiscences had not been recorded by an eager journalist in 1873, we would never have known that the Ned and Jenny of Jefferson's records knew themselves as Edward and Jane Gillette. A negative picture emerges from correspondence with overseers and family members. There are discussions of misbehavior rather than comments on craftsmanship. Illness fills many pages, along with descriptions of the death throes of several slaves. Even Jupiter, Jefferson's lifelong companion as manservant and coachman, passed from the scene accompanied by words that demonstrated the inextricable connection between his humanity and his value as part of the labor force. Jefferson wrote that "I am sorry for him as well as sensible he leaves a void in my domestic administration which I cannot fill up."[63]

Jefferson lived long enough to become fully entangled in the net of slavery's realities. His unsuccessful early efforts to curb or end slavery were followed by years in which he uttered simultaneous protestations of the impracticability of emancipation and cries of alarm about the consequences of inaction. The man who in 1786 wrote of "a bondage, one hour of which is fraught with more misery" than ages of the tyranny that American revolutionaries had just thrown off, was not the man who in 1814 told Thomas Cooper that American slaves "are better fed . . . warmer clothed, and labor less than the journeymen or day-laborers of England," living "without want, or the fear of it." His insights into the kinds of behavior caused by enslavement were forgotten, and his suspicions of racial inferiority gained the upper hand, perhaps serving as a defense against stings of conscience. While Jefferson was shocked at the sight of French and German women driving the plows and hoeing the fields of Europe—it was "a barbarous perversion of the natural destination of the two sexes"—he never expressed misgivings about the long days of hard agricultural labor of the women he owned. His farms always were cultivated by "gangs of half men and half women." According to one visiting Englishman, Jefferson expressed the opinion in 1807 that the "Negro race were . . . made to carry burthens." He appears to have convinced himself that those who were, as he suspected in print in the *Notes on Virginia*, "inferior in the faculties of reason and imagination," and whose griefs were "transient," might find happiness in a bondage mitigated by a benevolent hand.[64]

Jefferson's own efforts turned to reforming slavery rather than ending it. In 1787 he wanted to put his slaves "ultimately on an easier footing," and five years later his experiment with Maryland overseers was inaugurated to place his slaves "on the comfortable footing of the laborers of other countries." While in Paris he briefly contemplated importing Germans to settle on fifty-acre farms, "intermingled" with his slaves, and "all on the footing of the Metayers [tenants who pay in kind] of Europe" (he prefaced this proposal with his opinion that freeing slaves was "like abandoning children"). But the overriding demands of debt made even his reform efforts contingent on the impossible. The ultimate "easier footing" could be realized only after the slaves "have paid the debts" due from the Wayles estate. In 1792, when the Maryland overseer plan was aired, the improved treatment of the slaves was made to depend on their own exertions; they must "make as much as will admit" the continuation of better conditions.[65]

Neither Jefferson nor his slaves ever succeeded in clearing away his massive debts, which only grew with the years. It is impossible to know, partly because his exact intentions were not expressed, just how much he was able to carry out his wish to ameliorate the condition of his own slaves, to contribute to their happiness as he perceived it. There is plentiful evidence, however, that the Monticello slaves were made more "comfortable" in bondage than most of their fellows, even in Virginia.

Edith Fossett returned to these conditions in the spring of 1809. She probably moved into the cook's room—a 10-by-14-foot space with brick floor in the stone-built south dependencies of the main house. Two other rooms there were occupied by slaves, but most lived in log cabins on Mulberry Row or elsewhere on the mountain slopes. A visitor from Washington in 1809, although struck by "a most unpleasant contrast" between the slave dwellings and the neoclassical "palace" standing together on the leveled summit of Monticello, declared that "they are much better than I have seen on any other plantation." Their superiority could not have been due to their size or materials—they varied from 12 to 14 feet wide and 14 to 20 feet long and had wooden chimneys and earth floors. Perhaps they were more carefully built and maintained. In 1809 Peter Hemings was to move to a cabin on Mulberry Row, fitted up "in an entirely comfortable and decent manner," and instructions to overseers regularly mention the winter "mending" of slave cabins.[66]

Despite the hours she spent each day in the main kitchen, Edy Fossett still received the normal weekly food rations—a peck of cornmeal and a pound of pork, but she was probably able to vary this monotonous fare for her family with kitchen leftovers and her own skills. Her clothing allowance was similar to that on other southern plantations—two outfits a year, cotton for summer and a mixture of cotton and wool for winter; a striped blanket was issued once every three years. From at least 1815, when raw cotton prices were high, the summer cloth for her children was woven from a mixture of cotton and hemp.[67]

During the years of Jefferson's final retirement to Monticello, Edy and Joe Fossett filled two of the most important positions on the mountain. Almost a century later, Peter Fossett remembered that his mother was "Mr. Jefferson's favorite cook" and his father "had charge of all mechanical work done on the estate." Edy took over the new kitchen and prepared meals for a mounting flood of guests. While visitors' accounts are disappointingly vague about the food, all agreed on the quality of the fare. "The dinner was always choice, and served in the French style," wrote Bostonian George Ticknor. Daniel Webster recorded in 1824 that "dinner is served in half Virginian, half French style, in good taste and abundance."[68]

Joe Fossett ran the Mulberry Row blacksmith shop, which served the neighborhood as well as the master of Monticello. He was allowed to keep a shilling in every dollar of income from plating saddle trees for local saddlers in his free time. Fossett's workday, like that of most other Monticello slaves, lasted from dawn to dusk. Jefferson's chart of the daily tasks of his textile workers indicates that their labors grew from nine hours in the darkest winter months to fourteen hours in the longest days of June and July. Jobs that were tasked could provide early release for fast workers but, when the tasks were set by Jefferson the maximizer, could also lead to even longer workdays. "Jerry says that you tell him that he is to bring a certain number of logs a day," wrote Edmund Bacon, "and that it takes him till after night to do it." Bacon drew this situation to Jefferson's attention for the sake of the mules, not the wagoner.[69]

It is apparent that for many of the Monticello slaves a second working day began after dark. Mothers had to attend to their households, preparing meals, repairing clothing, and caring for their children. Both men and women pursued activities to supplement the standard of living provided by their master. Every slave household at Monticello had a poultry yard, and most raised their own vegetables. A typical Sunday is revealed in the household account book kept by one of Jefferson's granddaughters. Slaves carried to the mountaintop their chickens and eggs, cabbages and watermelons, to stock the Monticello kitchen, and took home dimes and half-bits in exchange. Some probably obtained passes so they could take their products into Charlottesville for sale as well.[70]

The nearby river and surrounding forests also provided opportunities for additional food or money. Hunting and trapping expeditions yielded raccoons, possums, and squirrels to add to the pot and skins to be sold. Isaac Jefferson's brother Bagwell Granger, a farm laborer, makes several appearances in Jefferson's accounts, selling him skins for a bellows, fish, ducks, hops, timothy seed, watermelons, cucumbers, and cymlin squash. Jefferson's grandson regaled his children with tales of midnight forays as a boy after possum and honey, in the company of the black men. After the dogs treed their quarry or a bee tree was felled, they returned to sit around the fire in a slave cabin. At "a little table covered with the best," one of the wives provided "a pot of hot coffee, fried meat and eggs, and a dish of honey."[71]

The pleasures of the quarters received little comment in the correspondence of Jefferson and his family. Apparently without curfews, his slaves took advantage of the freedom of the night. Jefferson observed, in the *Notes on Virginia*, that "a black, after hard labour through the day, will be induced by the slightest amusements to sit up till midnight, or later, though knowing he must be out with the first dawn of the morning." He knew his gardener John as a "great nightwalker" and thus unsuitable as a guardian for the main house. Former slave Isaac Jefferson remembered that his master's brother Randolph would "come out among black people, play the fiddle and dance half the night."[72]

There are further suggestions of the solace of music. Three of Sally Hemings's sons were noted musicians. Her oldest, Beverly (b. 1798), played fiddle in the South Pavilion for the Saturday night dances of Jefferson's granddaughters and young men at school nearby. He may also have provided the single note of holiday spirit in the quiet Christmas of 1821. Mary Randolph wrote her sister: "I have not had a single application to write passes . . . and except catching the sound of a fiddle yesterday on my way to the smokehouse and getting a glimpse of the fiddler as he stood with half closed eyes and head thrown back with one foot keeping time to his own scraping in the midst of a circle of attentive and admiring auditors I have not seen or heard any thing like Christmas gambols."[73]

The most remarkable evidence of the vigorous music and storytelling tradition in the Monticello quarters survives because of an interested foreigner and one member of Jefferson's household. His daughter Martha, who at fourteen had written her father, "I wish with all my soul that the poor negroes were all freed," was primed by the tales and songs of her childhood nurse. Even late in life, she had not lost her sensitivity to both the conditions and culture of the slave community around her. She shared corn-shelling and rowing songs and tales of Mr. Fox and Mr. Rabbit with interested visitors to Monticello. In the year she died Martha Randolph worried about the fate of some of her slaves, hoping to protect them from the laxer morals of the vicinity of the University of Virginia: "I feel anxious that these poor uneducated creatures should be placed in situations as little exposed to temptation as possible."[74]

The younger members of Jefferson's household made some of the only recorded efforts to enlighten those "poor uneducated creatures." Madison Hemings recalled learning his ABCs from Jefferson's granddaughters, while Joe Fossett's son Peter learned his letters from Jefferson's grandson Meriwether Lewis Randolph. Ellen Randolph wrote in 1819 that she was "anxious to have it in my power to befriend, and educate as well as I can" one of the motherless daughters of Monticello butler Burwell Colbert. In the absence of explicit statements on the subject, Jefferson's own attitude toward the education of his slaves is harder to determine. His response to Quaker activist Robert Pleasants's 1796 plan for instructing black children suggests qualified support for educating slaves destined for freedom. The only emancipation plan Jefferson considered feasible called for education, at public expense, in "tillage, arts or sciences, according to their geniusses," followed by deportation. This plan required the permanent separation of children from their parents, a necessity that Jefferson agreed would produce "some scruples of humanity, but this would be straining at a gnat, and swallowing a camel."[75]

Closer to home, Jefferson's never-executed tenancy plan called merely for bringing up the children "in habits of property and foresight." The blacks' apparent absence of foresight weighed heavily in Jefferson's mind as a stumbling block to emancipation. It colored his discussion of racial characteristics in the *Notes on Virginia*, and he brought it forth in conversation with visiting foreigners. A bemused British diplomat listened in 1807 to Jefferson's favorite example of the lack of forethought demonstrated by his own slaves. At the approach of summer they cast off their blankets, "without a thought as to what may become of them, wherever they may happen to be at the time, and then not seldom lose them in the woods or the fields from mere carelessness." No slave in the Upper South took blankets lightly, so it is possible that Monticello's blanket-tossers may have counted on Jefferson's willingness to replace their loss. It is even more likely that some of these apparently thoughtless slaves had discovered a way to acquire extra blankets for warmth or sale. Jefferson himself had noted, in 1806, that a recent Monticello overseer had failed to distribute a single blanket during his five-year tenure. This experience may have caused the very opposite of what the master saw—an effort to prepare for an unpredictable future.[76]

Israel Gillette (later Jefferson), a twenty-four-year-old postilion, overheard Jefferson tell the Marquis de Lafayette that slaves should be taught to read but not to write, as that would "enable them to forge papers, when they could no longer be kept in subjugation." The statement Israel Jefferson recalled, almost fifty years after the event, is difficult to verify. A number of Jefferson's slaves could read *and* write. John Hemings's surviving letters report on his joinery work at Poplar Forest, his brother James left an inventory of the Monticello kitchen, and there is one letter from Hannah, a Poplar Forest household slave. Several others could at least read: Jefferson left written instructions in his absences for the carpenters David Hern and John, and George Granger the overseer. Albemarle County records reveal that Mary Hemings Bell and Joseph Fossett could sign their names and probably could read and write, although they may have learned after they were freed.[77] It is not known how these slaves learned their letters, nor is there any direct evidence that Jefferson took an active role in educating the African American children around him.[78] There is also no sign that he took up his own challenge in the *Notes on Virginia* or emulated the example of his mentor George Wythe, by testing the intellectual powers of blacks through the cultivation of their minds in improved conditions. One clue to this vacuum appears in a letter Jefferson wrote questioning the educational aims of the African Institution of London: "I wish they may begin their work at the right end. Our experience with the Indians has proved that letters are not the first, but the last step in the progression from barbarism to civilisation."[79]

Religious instruction of slaves would, of course, have been completely un-Jeffersonian. The life of the spirit was pursued beyond the control of the master and thus escaped his commentary. Again it is the negative events that inspired the scattered references that can only suggest the vitality of religious beliefs in the Monticello slave community. Jefferson's granddaughter Mary complained of having to watch a visitor's children one Sunday because "mammy is gone *'to meeting.'*" Her sister told of the death of Priscilla Hemings, longtime head nurse in the

Jefferson-Randolph household, whose last hours included "a prayer meeting at her house" and a Bible reading before bedtime by her husband, John. African traditional beliefs are also evident, mainly in discussions of the ill effects of the prescriptions of black doctors—almost universally labeled "poisons" in Jefferson's papers.[80]

There were two worlds at Monticello, where medicine and beliefs in one were perceived as poison and superstition in the other. Jefferson had no access to the hidden world of his slaves, but they were a constant presence in his, listening and watching. From the slave women in the house to Israel Gillette on the carriage horse, they attended to all words and actions that might play a part in shaping their future. Joe Fossett, in the blacksmith shop, the closest thing to a neighborhood gathering place, may have been a monitor for the mountain, listening for assessments of the state of Jefferson's finances, so critical to the stability of the Monticello slave community. One of Lafayette's companions talked to the slaves in 1824, when they told him they were "perfectly happy, that they were subject to no ill-treatment, that their tasks were very easy, and that they cultivated the lands of Monticello with the greater pleasure, because they were almost sure of not being torn away from them, to be transported elsewhere, so long as Mr. Jefferson lived."[81]

Independence

On July 4, 1827, one year after Jefferson's death, Joseph Fossett became a free man. Six months earlier Jefferson's granddaughter Mary had reported to a sister the results of the Monticello dispersal sale: "The negroes with one exception I believe, are all sold to persons living in the state, many of them in this neighbourhood or the adjoining counties, and most of them I believe also, are well and satisfactorily placed, as much to their own wishes as they could be in leaving our estate." No reference was made to the breaking up of families this satisfactory placement entailed. Joe Fossett had watched his wife and children sold to at least four different bidders. Edy and their two youngest children William and Daniel were bought by Jesse Scott; twelve-year-old Peter's new master was John R. Jones; fifteen-year-old Elizabeth Ann was sold to Charlottesville merchant John Winn; and University of Virginia professor Charles Bonnycastle bought seventeen-year-old Patsy. The fates of three other siblings are unknown.[82]

Jefferson had described Fossett at the time of his 1806 escapade as "strong and resolute," characteristics greatly needed in his first years of freedom. The fragmentary records suggest that he worked at his trade with a steadiness demanded by his need to reunite his scattered family and prepare for removal beyond the boundaries of slavery. Spared the requirement to leave the state within a year by an act of assembly requested in Jefferson's will, he continued to pursue his blacksmithing trade in Albemarle County. He may even have remained in the Mulberry Row blacksmith shop until 1831, when Monticello was sold to James T. Barclay and Fossett bought a lot in Charlottesville with a shop on it.[83]

At some time before September 15, 1837, Joe Fossett became the owner of his wife, five of their children (two born subsequent to the sale), and four grandchildren, for on that date he manumitted them all. It is apparent that the key to family unity was Joe Fossett's mother, Mary Hemings Bell. She and her children by merchant Thomas Bell had shared in Bell's estate in 1800, and her daughter Sally had married Jesse Scott in 1802. Thus, it was probably the combined resources of Scott and the Bells that provided the $505 for the purchase of Edy and the two youngest children—and probably also the money for the purchase of the third child, Elizabeth Ann.[84]

It is evident that, beginning in the 1780s, when Mary Hemings was leased and then sold to Thomas Bell, the Monticello slave community had a toehold in the more complex free community of Charlottesville. Thomas Bell's house on Main Street, occupied by his "widow," then her daughter and son-in-law Sally Jefferson Bell and Jesse Scott, and their children, was the residence of Hemingses for a century.[85] Jesse Scott, a free man of color said to be part-Indian, and his sons, the "famous fiddling Scotts," enlivened dances at the University of Virginia, at the Hot and White Sulphur Springs, and throughout the state for a

Rev. Peter Fossett (1815–1901). (From Wendell P. Dabney, *Cincinnati's Colored Citizens* [Cincinnati, 1926])

good part of the century. In 1888 Ora Langhorne paid a visit to the last surviving member of "the Scott minstrels, long famous throughout the South and well known to all visitors at the Virginia springs." Robert Scott reported that "the taste for music shown by his family had early attracted Mr. Jefferson's notice, as he dearly loved music himself, and he had taken much kindly interest in the family. . . . Mr. Jefferson had always been very kind to [Jesse Scott] and had encouraged him to have his children educated."[86]

Peter Fossett was not one of the children his father was able to purchase and free before the family left for Ohio about 1840. He remained a slave for over twenty years after Jefferson's death, making at least two attempts to run away. The learning he had gleaned from his years as "a sort of family pet" in the Monticello household was increased by enlisting the aid of his new master's sons. Then Peter Fossett passed his knowledge on to a fellow slave by the light of pine knots, stealing away to a deserted cabin long after everyone else was asleep. Finally, again by the combined efforts of members of an extended network of kin, he was able to purchase his freedom and join his family in Cincinnati.[87]

Peter Fossett's story demonstrates the extent to which identity is buried by the dehumanizing institution of slavery. In freedom his life is known and becomes an expression of much that cannot be known about the rest of the Monticello slave community. Flourishing unrecorded in the Monticello quarters were singular skills, a hunger for education, powerful bonds of family and community, and deep religious beliefs. Peter Fossett became "the most prominent of the early caterers" in Cincinnati, worked with Levi Coffin in the Underground Railroad, and has been called a "father" of the Ohio black Baptist church. His flock at First Baptist Church helped him satisfy a desire, at age eighty-five, to return to his birthplace. In 1900, the "last surviving slave of Thomas Jefferson," who had abandoned him in 1826, was welcomed to the entrance hall of Monticello.[88]

Looking for Liberty

Thomas Jefferson and the British Lions

I N November 1803 a twenty-four-year-old Irishman landed in Norfolk, Virginia. The town struck him as "really a most comical place," where nothing "but dogs and negroes" were to be seen in the streets. Thomas Moore had launched his voyage to the wilds of America from the salons of London, in which he had been welcomed as the translator of the *Odes of Anacreon* and a memorable entertainer at evening parties. He sang his own songs at the pianoforte in an "inexpressibly sweet" voice, making men weep and women faint. In his first exposure to American culture, "Anacreon" Moore was cheered to find one friendly drawing room, complete with harpsichord. This "looked like civilisation," but, as he declared to his mother, "music here is like whistling to a wilderness."[1]

Six months later Moore followed Virginia's "break-neck" roads to Washington, passing "the Potomac, the Rappahannock, the Occoquan . . . and many other rivers, with names as barbarous as the inhabitants." He wrote home that "every step I take not only *reconciles*, but *endears* to me, not only the excellencies but even the errors of Old England." After accepting the hospitality of expatriate Tories and Virginia Federalists, he arrived in the capital well educated in the errors of Jeffersonianism. Further instruction came from his Washington host, the British minister Anthony Merry, still tender from his own experiences in a nation ruled by republicans.[2]

Sir Anthony's feathers were first ruffled at his introduction to Thomas Jefferson. The representative of His Britannic Majesty, in full diplomatic regalia, had been met by the American president "in slippers down at the heels, and both

This essay was originally published in *Eighteenth-Century Studies* 26, no. 4 (Summer 1993): 649–668.

pantaloons, coat, and underclothes indicative of utter slovenliness and indiffer-
ence to appearances"—in Merry's mind a deliberate insult to his government. Soon
afterward, Jefferson's application of his philosophy of democratic "pellmell"
instead of diplomatic precedence at presidential dinners so offended the majes-
tic Mrs. Merry that all further invitations to dine were refused, and the incident
threatened to have international repercussions.[3]

The Merrys "have been treated with the most pointed incivility by the present democratic president," Thomas Moore reported to his mother, and he certainly arrived for his own audience at the President's House poorly primed for
admiration. He was received "in the same homely costume, comprising slippers
and Connemara stockings in which Mr. Merry had been received by him, much
to that formal Minister's horror." The six-foot-two-and-a-half-inch American
gazed down on the diminutive Irishman (Sir Walter Scott called Moore "a little—
a very little man") and passed on with hardly a word. The offended poet hastened
on to Philadelphia, where, cosseted by Joseph Dennie and his anti-Jeffersonian
friends, he "passed the only agreeable moments which my tour through the
States afforded me." There, clever articulations of Federalist discontent completed
the transformation of the Irish republican into merely a British chauvinist. Now
"cured of republicanism," as he had hinted in an earlier letter, Moore began to
compose his diatribes on the American experiment.[4]

In three verse epistles published in 1806, Moore described his rude awakening
from a "golden dream" of an "elysian Atlantis" in America. Its principles corrupted
by the "foul philosophy" of France, as well as "the demon gold," the young republic exhibited only a "false liberty." The crudeness of its society mocked the grandeur
of its landscape, and its "present demagogues" were distinguished by a "hostility
to all the graces of life." Like the long train of foreign visitors that followed him
over the next fifty years, Moore used the incompatible institution of slavery to
make his point. The citizens of the United States, "poor of heart and prodigal of
words," "shout for rights, with rapine in their soul!" "Bastard freedom" waved
"her fustian flag in mockery over slaves." And fresh in his mind was the perfect
human symbol of this hypocrisy.[5]

A member of Sir Anthony's staff later wrote that Moore's reception by Thomas
Jefferson had "so nettled the poet that we probably owe some angry verses to the
circumstance, in which he has not spared the ci-devant President." It was Epistle
VII, "To Thomas Hume," that repeated the report that Jefferson had fathered
children by a slave mistress and closed with a line that reverberated for the rest
of the century. Moore, according to one historian, "the first British traveler to
mention Jefferson in print," honed to its sharpest point the favorite weapon of
Federalist wits:

The weary statesman for repose hath fled
From halls of council to his negro's shed,
Where blest he woos some black Aspasia's grace,
And dreams of freedom in his slave's embrace!

In his usual manner, Moore embellished the poem with a footnote in which he used a favorite Federalist pejorative: "philosophical." The President's House, "a very noble structure," was "by no means suited to the philosophical humility of its present possessor, who inhabits but a corner of the mansion himself, and abandons the rest to a state of uncleanly desolation, which those who are not philosophers cannot look at without regret."[6]

Jefferson had already weathered four years of abuse on the miscegenation topic. James Thomson Callender first broadcast to the world the story of Sally Hemings in September 1802, in the columns of a Richmond newspaper. Federalist presses immediately began to mix satiric verses about "Black Sal" and her children into their usual assaults on the president's character and philosophy. The story added spice to their censure of the three-fifths clause of the Constitution, which gave southerners, through their slaves, a much resented additional representation in Congress. As Thomas Green Fessenden wrote in 1806: "Great men can never lack supporters, Who manufacture their own voters."[7]

While Jefferson's friends and even some enemies rose to his defense, he chose to make no public denial of the charges; he wished to be judged only by his actions and the "tenor of my life." It was his "rule of life" never to "harrass the public with fendings and provings of personal slander." The relentless newspaper attacks caused his faith in the freedom of expression to falter but not fail. In 1805 he wrote that the "fiery ordeal" of a chief magistrate required "all the devotion of patriotism which inspired a Decius. His sacrifice was life. With us character must be offered on the altar of public good." He began to view the years of abuse as an experiment, with himself as the subject. "I have thought necessary first to prove" that a free press can never be dangerous, he confided to a friend in 1808. His time on "the gridiron" of the public papers forged a conspicuous pride in a republican people, who could spot the truth in a hail of lies. When German scientist Alexander von Humboldt came to Washington expressly to meet the president in 1804, his host flourished before him a newspaper filled with virulent personal abuse. Jefferson admonished him to deposit the document in a European museum, as a demonstration of the wisdom of the people and "the reality of our liberty."[8]

So, in 1806, Jefferson's response to the first missile from the other side of the ocean is not surprising. Thomas Moore's poem was handed to him by two

Thomas Moore (1779–1852), by
unknown artist, ca. 1800–1805.
(© National Portrait Gallery, London)

indignant readers, his daughter Martha and his loyal former secretary William A. Burwell. They pointed out "the obnoxious passages" to the victim, who glanced through them and "broke into a hearty, clear laugh." The somewhat crestfallen pair left the room before they, too, "joined heartily in the merriment." Sensibilities were still raw in August 1807, when Anthony Merry's secretary of legation, Sir Augustus John Foster, visited Monticello. Moore's verses, "if unminded by the father succeeded at least in giving some pains to his daughter," Foster recalled. "She told me she had much regretted Mr. Moore's reception had not been more flattering to him, but that from his low stature and youthful appearance her father had taken him for a boy, and as he had always professed to be of the liberal party in England he felt rather surprized at this bitter censure of a person so devoted to the cause of liberty as was the President."[9]

Foster's last comment is a clue to the family outrage at this single shot in the midst of a barrage. Over fifty years later Jefferson's granddaughter Ellen Coolidge was still taking Moore to task for his own contradictions: "The truth is that Liberty idealized he adored, Liberty in its practical effects he abhorred. He wanted old European aristocratic society, with his fine-spun theories of equal laws and rights. To such a man the United States and its practical democracy, even as it was half a century ago, would give more disgust than satisfaction under any circumstances." She had heard the story of Moore's presentation from her grandfather himself: "When he called it so happened, a thing very likely to happen, that Mr. Jefferson did not hear his name, nor recognize a distinguished poet in a small, insignificant man, and he therefore received him only as he would have done any other strange gentleman, paid him no particular compliment and did not talk to him about himself."[10]

The mutual aversion of Moore and members of Jefferson's family was considerably modified by time and further publication. In 1816, Moore regretted his "crude and boyish tirades against the Americans." He acknowledged that his sentiments had changed since his visit and that, "as a lover of Liberty," he would blush if he allowed "the hasty prejudices of my youth to blind me now to the bright promise which America affords of a better and happier order of things than the World has perhaps ever yet witnessed." Two years later, confessing that he had "judged by the *abuse*, not the *use*" of democratic principles, he wished he could retract "every syllable injurious to the great cause of Liberty, which my hasty view of America and her society provoked me into uttering." He nevertheless reprinted every syllable practically unchanged in 1841, and his views of Jefferson himself remained ambiguous. He confided to his journal in 1818 a standard Tory accusation, that Jefferson "seemed to delight in vulgarizing democracy to its lowest pitch," and he always deplored the French influence on his politics. But in 1831 he carried the volumes of Jefferson's correspondence with him to read on his carriage journeys and six years later seemed to delight in discovering, when shown some original Jefferson letters, that they demonstrated "a frequency of my own trick of erasures and corrections."[11]

Jefferson, for his part, had purchased an American edition of the Anacreontic translations and was such an enemy of the British royal family that he read his way through to the end of Moore's *Twopenny Post Bag*. This instantly popular collection of satirical verses contained lines like the following, written as if by the Prince Regent, after an evening of gastronomic delights:

> Our next round of toasts was a fancy quite new.
> For we drank—and you'll own 'twas benevolent too—
> To those well-meaning husbands, cits, parsons, or peers,
> Whom we've, any time, honour'd by courting their dears.

From Monticello Jefferson hailed the author's "great wit and humor" and his "proper use" of kings and princes as "butts for the ridicule and contempt of mankind." When Moore's best known work, his *Irish Melodies*, reached a remote mountaintop in Virginia, it took it by storm. Surviving Monticello scrapbooks and souvenir albums are filled with his songs. The critical granddaughter Ellen copied the Melodies into manuscript music books and, as the mother of five in Boston in 1831, went to great lengths to gather the words of two "wild *Moore-ish*" songs to send her distant family. She admitted in 1857 that "ill as I thought of Moore the man, I greatly admired his poetry."[12]

No one at Monticello was immune to the attractions of these extraordinarily popular expressions of the age in which bees, flowers, harps, and tears mingle with gloom, glory, swords, and liberty. Moore polished Celtic myth with classical erudition and bathed Epicurean notions in parlor sentimentality. Ellen was the first to show the *Irish Melodies* to her grandfather, who exclaimed: "'Why . . . this is the little man who satirized me so!' He read along. He had always sympathized keenly with the Irish patriots. The delightful rhythm fell like music on a susceptible ear. He presently exclaimed: 'Why, he *is* a poet after all!'" Jefferson no doubt enjoyed glimpses of the same Gaelic heroes who had appeared in his favorite Ossianic poems, and three of the Melodies were said to be his "special favorites." "Oh! Blame Not the Bard," in which the bard excuses himself for not sacrificing all to Ireland's hopeless cause, ends with a metaphor of enslavement. "When He Who Adores Thee" and "Oh! Breathe Not His Name" meditate on reputation after death; the latter, also beloved by Lord Byron, was a lament for Irish patriot Robert Emmet, who from the dock had asked that no man write his epitaph until "other times and other men" could do justice to his memory:

> Oh! breathe not his name, let it sleep in the shade,
> Where cold and unhonour'd his relics are laid:
> Sad, silent, and dark, be the tears that we shed,
> As the night-dew that falls on the grass oe'r his head.[13]

If Thomas Moore had encountered Thomas Jefferson at Monticello, first impressions would soon have been dispelled. As Jefferson's initial coldness vanished in delightful conversation and the rural elegance of Monticello tempered the barbarities of American society, the Irish dandy would have sat down at the harpsichord and been transformed. One witness of his performances recalled the poet, his head "cast backward, and his eyes upward, with the true inspiration of an ancient bard. . . . He realized to me, in many respects, my conceptions of the poet of love and wine; the refined and elegant, though voluptuous Anacreon." Moore, charmed by his host, might never have sought to personalize the paradox that was a standard British theme since Samuel Johnson asked in 1775, "How is it that we hear the loudest yelps for liberty among the drivers of negroes?"[14]

Although no classically educated Celtic bard came to the Monticello parlor, a young woman did arrive who brought some of the same echoes of both Ossian and Epicurus. Frances Wright, born a Scot and raised in England, was twenty-three when she made her first visit to the United States in 1818. A work Jefferson greatly admired, Carlo Botta's history of the American Revolution, had revealed to her a country consecrated to freedom, "where man might first awake to the full knowledge and full exercise of his powers." Her reactions to the American experiment form a striking contrast to those of Thomas Moore, and her adulatory *Views of Society and Manners in America* (1821) was full of praise of Jefferson. This "distinguished philosopher" was one of the "purest patriots and wisest statesmen that ever steered the vessel of a state." Although her brief taste of slavery (she traveled only as far as Washington) caused her to exclaim that "to inhale the impure breath of its pestilence in the free winds of America is odious beyond all that the imagination can conceive," she had no need to find a personal illustration of the great American anomaly. She dismissed the "scurrilous abuse" of the Federalist press as part of "the machinations of disappointed politicians and ambitious incendiaries." Jefferson and Madison, "with a dignity becoming their character and station, passed unheeded every opprobrium cast upon them."[15]

In 1824, when Frances Wright returned to the United States under the protection of the Marquis de Lafayette, she followed her "venerable friend" to Monticello. The "Guest of the Nation" arrived in November at the head of a cavalcade of dignitaries and enthusiastic citizens; Wright and her sister Camilla joined the household a day or two later without fanfare. She and her host had briefly corresponded four years previously, and she had sent him two works written before she was twenty. He read her tragedy *Altorf* "with great pleasure," citing its hero as "a model of patriotism and virtue well worthy of the imitation of our republican citizens," and extravagantly praised *A Few Days in Athens*, her fictionalized treatise on the philosophy of Jefferson's "master," Epicurus. It had been a treat "of the highest order," he told Lafayette in 1823, "and like Ossian, if not ancient, it is equal to the best morsels of antiquity."[16]

It must have been an extraordinary week. The two revolutionary veterans, who had not seen each other for thirty-five years, captivated the company with a flood of memories. One witness recalled that "when in the freedom of conversation over their wine after dinner, they reverted to the stirring scenes of their early lives, its reminiscences and incidents, so animated did they become, with such eloquence did they speak, that, carried away by the enthusiasm of the moment, the rest of the company involuntarily left their seats at the table and grouped themselves around the two sages, that they might not lose one of the eloquent words which fell from their lips." Fanny Wright said the days at Monticello would be treasured in memory "as among the most interesting of our lives." She enjoyed "one of the finest prospects I ever remember to have seen" from a mountain "consecrated by the residence of the greatest of America's surviving veterans." She described her eighty-one-year-old host, "his tall well-moulded figure . . . erect as at the age of 20," as physically weakened by age and illness but retaining the "full power" of his mind. "The lamp is evidently on the wane," she reported from the mountaintop, "nor is it possible to consider the fading of a light so brilliant and pure without a sentiment of deep melancholy."[17]

Some members of the Monticello household, however, were not so charmed by Miss Wright as its master seems to have been. A visiting cousin recalled the

Frances Wright (1795 1852), by Henry Inman, 1824. (Collection of The New-York Historical Society)

arrival of the twenty-nine-year-old "bluestocking" years after she had been branded as the "Red Harlot of Infidelity," the female embodiment of social disorder. "Miss Wright was quiet enough at Monticello," wrote Jane Blair Cary Smith in the 1860s: "To ladies she never spoke, except to Mrs. Randolph as her hostess, and to the youngest girl of the party, whom she noticed favorably as a mere child. But the Frenchmen told many instances of her masculine proclivities—on occasions she wd. harrangue the men in the public room of a hotel and the like." Jane Cary listened to George Washington Lafayette's resentful comments on Wright's influence over his father, and even forty years later the page she devoted to her still bears the freshness of the upstairs gossip Wright must have inspired at the time: "In person she was masculine, measuring at least 5 feet 11 inches, and wearing her hair a la Ninon in close curls, her large blue eyes and blonde aspect were thoroughly English, and she always seemed to wear the wrong attire."[18]

It is apparent that the subject of slavery was prominent in the conversations of that week. The marquis, as European standard-bearer for the American republic, had tired of having "this wide Blot on American Philant[h]ropy" thrown in his face. His letters in the 1820s warn Jefferson with mounting urgency of the need for action to eradicate this "Great draw Back Upon My Enjoyments." While at Monticello, in a conversation overheard by a young slave postilion, he urged on Jefferson the need for a plan of education for the slaves. He may have entered the Monticello cabins to converse with their inhabitants, as he did at Montpelier some months later. Frances Wright is silent on her reaction to seeing the architect of her ideals in his role as a slaveholder. She must have noticed Jefferson's resemblance to the Virginians she had described in *Views of Society*. The humanity to their slaves, in which they took such pride, struck her as merely "gilding" the chains of bondage. Why did they not serve justice by breaking those chains? When she posed this question to Jefferson—as she must have—he told her he hoped for the adoption that winter of "some steps wch. he considers as preparatory to the abolition of slavery at least in this state." But she also learned from her visit to Virginia, and particularly from the Sage of Monticello, of a "deeply rooted" prejudice against the mixture of the two races. "Emancipation without expatriation," she concluded, "seems impossible."[19]

Wright may have imbibed some of Jefferson's faith in the power of example, for not long after her visit to Monticello she began to implement a practical experiment that she hoped would demonstrate to Americans the feasibility of eradicating slavery. Her great enterprise for the next five years was an effort to cleanse the United States of its "one great evil" and help it exhibit the "perfection of freedom." In some ways her plan resembled Jefferson's own scheme for gradual emancipation, but formed on a small scale as a model. Slave children were to be brought up in habits of industry and then removed to a colony of their own. But in the meantime she had found another hero with more radical principles, which "are to change the face of the world as surely as the sun shines in the heavens." After meeting British reformer Robert Owen and viewing his trial utopia, New Harmony, Wright founded her own experimental community in western Tennessee on Owen's ideals of cooperative labor; Nashoba's slaves would work like Harmonists to pay for their freedom. When she communicated her plan to Jefferson in July 1825, it elicited a benevolent blessing rather than a ringing endorsement. Stating that emancipation had always been one of his "greatest anxieties," he viewed her proposal as "well worthy" of trial: "It has succeeded with certain portions of our white brethren, under the care of a Rapp and an Owen; and why may it not succeed with the man of colour?" Some suggested, he continued, that "moral urgencies" were insufficient motivation for the slave, "but this is a problem which the present age alone is prepared to solve by experiment."[20]

By this time Jefferson, too, had met Robert Owen, whose brief visit to Monticello in the spring of 1825 included a full communication of plans for New Harmony and the precepts of Owen's "New System" for society. "Less a man than a walking principle," as one biographer described him, Owen probably repeated for the Monticello household the substance of two lectures he had just delivered before Congress. Announcing that he had come to assist Americans to attain "a much more perfect system of liberty and equality," he expounded the plans for New Harmony, where the guiding principles would be "union, co-operation, and common property." Jefferson had previously agreed with another communitarian that "communion of property" was effective in small societies like those of the Rappites and Shakers but rejected the viability of its application "to an extended society" like the United States and other countries. Although Owen later described the master of Monticello as "my friend and warm disciple," there seems to be no record of Jefferson's reaction to Owen's visit and the effect of hearing firsthand his radical innovations in the pursuit of happiness. One member of the household, at least, was deeply impressed. Nicholas Trist, recently married to Jefferson's granddaughter Virginia Randolph, was captivated by Owen's proposals for a better world. He became an ardent if clandestine disciple of Owen—later nearly joining the community at New Harmony—and a lifelong friend of his son, Robert Dale Owen.[21]

Jefferson in 1825, "with one foot in the grave, and the other uplifted to follow it," smiled on Wright's and Owen's projects from the sidelines while they stood on public platforms invoking his name and the ideals he had articulated. While Jefferson lay dying at Monticello on the fiftieth anniversary of the Declaration of Independence, July 4, 1826, Robert Owen preached his Declaration of Mental Independence at New Harmony. The words of 1776 had proclaimed a political liberty that only "prepared the way to secure to you MENTAL LIBERTY," Owen told the members of his community. He then denounced a "hydra" of evils, "private, or individual property—absurd and irrational systems of religion—and marriage." For the "mental revolution," this "threefold, horrid monster" must be destroyed.[22]

In the meantime, Frances Wright had met and drawn another Monticello pilgrim into the community at Nashoba. George Flower, also a friend of Lafayette, had left England for the United States in 1816, seeking "a healthy and pleasant spot" for the pursuit of agriculture and "the pleasures of domestic life." He visited Jefferson at both Poplar Forest and Monticello, where "the chief charm of the visit was in the evening conversations with Mr. Jefferson," who recounted the "inner history" of events Flower knew only from published accounts. Jefferson evidently sought to persuade the young Englishman to settle in Virginia, but "the brand of slavery was upon the land." Flower recalled the "dilapidated fences, decaying homesteads, [and] worn-out land" that gave "an uninviting aspect to a country perhaps more favored by nature than any other portion of the Union." He ultimately helped found the English settlement at Albion in the free state of Illinois, enlisting Jefferson's aid in the early stages. Calling the United States a "Canaan" for the oppressed of Europe, Jefferson replied with his belief that settlements like Flower's would "consecrate a sanctuary for those whom the misrule of Europe may compel to seek happiness in other climes." When, later in life,

Flower wrote the history of his settlement, he was certainly thinking of his brief association with Nashoba as well as Albion's early trials—which included a bitter struggle to prevent the introduction of slavery into Illinois. He reminded his readers that idealistic Europeans often read the Declaration of Independence and the Constitution without reflecting that "a perfect theory on paper might be very imperfectly rendered in practice."[23]

When Robert Dale Owen followed his father to America, "the Canaan of my hopes," he too became involved in Nashoba, which he called "a bold and decided experiment to *live* according to correct principles." This biracial community failed to fulfill the expectations of its founders. But in 1828, before she turned to other causes, Frances Wright lured an unlikely recruit from England to the forests of western Tennessee. Anthony Trollope's mother Frances, who shuddered at the "frightful" table manners and spitting habits of the Americans, was wholly unprepared for the primitive appointments and malarial atmosphere of Nashoba. She quickly changed her plans and settled with her family in Cincinnati. There she heard the second of Fanny Wright's public lectures (the first had been at New Harmony on July 4) and described the sensation caused by this unprecedented behavior, especially in a country "where women are guarded by a seven-fold shield of habitual insignificance." Trollope herself marveled at the spectacle: "I knew her extraordinary gift of eloquence, her almost unequalled command of words, and the wonderful power of her rich and thrilling voice . . . [but] all my expectations fell far short of the splendour, the brilliance, the overwhelming eloquence of this extraordinary orator."[24]

The effect was practically ruined by Wright's reverent use of a quotation that acted on Mrs. Trollope like a red flag to a bull: that "phrase of mischievous sophistry," that "false and futile axiom"—"All men are created free and equal." Like Thomas Moore, she found the sight of slavery especially intolerable in a country where every breeze bore those "mocking words." In her *Domestic Manners of the Americans* (1832) she waved thirty lines of Moore's anti-American verses before the public once again but reserved her greatest scorn for the author of the hypocritical expression that so nettled her. His life was a "glorious commentary" on his words, she began, and continued with an extravagant version of the Sally Hemings story. Trollope described Jefferson as a "heartless libertine" who fathered children by not one but "a numerous gang of female slaves" and who derived particular pleasure from being waited on at table by his enslaved offspring.[25]

Lafayette, who had kept Jefferson informed of the activities of the Wright sisters ("My Young philanthropic friends"), pleaded with Frances Wright to counter the effect of Trollope's blistering criticism of his adoptive land. By then, however, Wright would probably not have been an effective champion. Her determination to live the principles of both Jefferson's and Owen's Declarations of Independence carried her far beyond the orbit of most of American society, including one of the most articulate and intellectual members of Jefferson's family. His granddaughter Ellen Coolidge had been at Monticello that memorable week in 1824, but by 1829 she could not swallow Wright's views on marriage and religion. From Boston she wrote her sister Virginia Trist of Wright's arrival to give a course of lectures, "which I hope no body will go to hear," and repeated the rumor of Wright's liaison with Robert Dale Owen. She must have been unaware that Virginia and her husband were both disciples of Wright and Owen, at this time broadcasting their radical views in New York's *Free Enquirer*. Virginia would distribute Wright's printed lectures a few weeks later, and Nicholas Trist had recently written his two "Friends," regretting that his contributions to their publication must remain anonymous: "I can't be *one of you*, and therefore must remain one of the silent herd."[26]

When Wright returned to Boston in 1830, Ellen wrote her mother:

> There are fortunately no black Fanny Wrights to wrest from the poor negroes such hopes and comforts of religion as they are able to obtain—this "unsexed thing who dares to scorn her God" is again in Boston, where she divides public attention with a Rhinoceros the first ever brought to the United States—it is strange that upon her last visit her competitor and rival was a learned Dog who could play cards and tell the hour by a gentleman's watch. She can do no harm in New England where she is an object simply of curiosity, but I feel mortified, as a woman, and as having formerly been a personal acquaintance, that one who is alike a disgrace to her sex and to her associates, should belong to me by either of these ties however general the first or disavowed the second. I wish she would go to Hayti and marry president Boyer who is said to be an admirer of hers.[27]

If Frances Wright never took up Lafayette's challenge, an eloquent Englishwoman did balance the scales a few years later. Harriet Martineau, in her *Society in America* (1837), displayed neither the indignation of Moore and Trollope nor the overzealousness of Wright. This clear-sighted portrait, full of admiration for republican principles and those who articulated them, includes long and perceptive discussions of that "one tremendous anomaly." The "discrepancy between principles and practice" caused by the presence of slavery clouded her visit to the University of Virginia in 1835: "The evil influences of slavery have entered in to taint the work of the great champion of liberty." A snowstorm prevented her pilgrimage to Monticello, then owned by Uriah P. Levy, an ardent admirer of Jefferson's views of religious freedom.[28]

Martineau had, however, already met Jefferson's daughter. A few weeks before, Margaret Bayard Smith hosted a small dinner party in Washington for the thirty-two-year-old Englishwomen, a "lion" who had received more attention than any foreigner since Lafayette. She invited Martha Randolph and her daughter Ellen and was relieved when Mrs. Randolph, who usually "disregards her toilette," arrived "handsomely dressed." Mrs. Smith wanted Martineau "to see the daughter of Jefferson to advantage." Unfortunately, Martha Randolph was so disconcerted by Martineau's deafness and her ear trumpet that she hardly spoke a word. Samuel Harrison Smith's method was, in the warmth of conversation, to take the wrong end of the speaking tube or to wave the right end about in the air, "quite forgetful of its use." Mrs. Randolph, by contrast, "kept the cup pressed so tightly on her lips, that she could scarcely open them." As Jefferson's daughter told Mrs. Smith afterward, "the very touch of the Tube, put all her ideas to flight." One can only imagine that she was also mistrustful of yet another British commentator and felt the burden of guarding her father's reputation. Ellen Coolidge later wrote that her mother "shrank from the thought that any part of her idolized father's reputation should rest upon her words or recollections." She continued by recalling that her mother's "faith in his ultimate triumph over all misconception and all malice was founded on her faith in him." She believed it impossible "that such a man could fail, sooner or later, to have justice done to his real character and his true greatness."[29]

Two years before her encounter with Harriet Martineau, Martha Jefferson Randolph might have seen Thomas Moore's famous line used again in Thomas Hamilton's *Men and Manners in America*, which added to the Sally Hemings story its final twist—that Jefferson sold his own children on the auction block. Fortunately she did not live to see a more widely read repetition in 1843. Readers of the serialization of Charles Dickens's *Martin Chuzzlewit* learned of the "noble patriot, with many followers!—who dreamed of Freedom in a slave's embrace." Hamilton had written that Moore's "single line gives more insight to the character of the man, than whole volumes of panegyric. It will outlive his epitaph, write it who may."[30]

As is well known, Jefferson wrote his own epitaph, with its faint echoes of Thomas Moore—it was prefaced by two lines from Anacreon in the Greek original. And the day before his death he handed his daughter Martha a parting message in verse, evidently of his own composition. It is less "Moore-ish" in its phrasing than flavored by the poetry of Mrs. Hemans and Mrs. Barbauld, great favorites in the Monticello household and even quoted on occasion by Jefferson himself. This scrap of paper was a cherished relic in his family. Martha brought it forth to show only her most trusted friends, and her children transcribed copies for themselves. Some added to Jefferson's "death-bed Adieu" a further phrase or motto in the valedictory vein. And one penned on the same piece of paper an "Irish melody" of Thomas Moore, suggesting that this lament might have been heard at Monticello, or other homes of the dispersed family, after Jefferson's death:

> It is not the tear at this moment shed,
> When the cold turf has just been lain o'er him,
> That can tell how beloved was the soul that's fled,
> Or how deep in our hearts we deplore him.
> 'Tis the tear through many a long day wept,
> Through a life by his loss all shaded,
> 'Tis the sad remembrance fondly kept,
> When all other griefs are faded.[31]

Jefferson's efforts to reform the world continued from beyond the grave. Or so said Robert Owen, who discovered in his eighties a new practical device to usher in the millenium—spiritualism. The spirits of the Duke of Kent, Benjamin Franklin, and "my friend and warm disciple" Jefferson appeared frequently at his seances and "confirmed" the correctness of Owen's plans for the "new moral world." While Thomas Moore and Frances Wright did not commune with Jefferson's spirit after his death, they continued to wrestle with the issues of dream and reality raised by his country. Wright reported that on her first visit to America she "seemed to hear and see her declaration of independence every where." Her own enthusiasm threw "a claud-lorraine tint" over the landscape. She was then imperfectly acquainted with the "breadth of distance between American principles and American practice" and only gradually realized that the principles of the Declaration would be "practically exhibited" only with the wider diffusion of knowledge. In 1841, Thomas Moore, in a collected edition of his works, exposed his early criticism of American leaders and institutions to the world for a second time. Although he confessed that he was overly influenced by disgruntled Federalists, he justified republication by "the perfect sincerity and earnestness" of his impressions in the only period in his life when he lapsed from his "liberal creed of politics." Even the "Epistle to Thomas Hume" was only slightly amended. In his preface Moore recalled the object of his unforgettable couplet: "My single interview with this remarkable person was of very short duration; but to have seen and spoken to the man who drew up the Declaration of American Independence was an event not to be forgotten."[32]

"A Well-Ordered Household"

Domestic Servants in Jefferson's White House

ONE morning in early December 1802 a Federalist senator, just arrived from New Hampshire, was ushered into the President's House with some fellow legislators. After a few moments "a tall highboned man" entered the room, wearing "an old brown coat, red waistcoat, old corduroy small clothes, much soild—woolen hose—& slippers without heels." William Plumer later wrote a friend, "I thought this man was a servant; but Genl Varnum surprised me by announcing that it was the President."[1] Plumer made no mention of the actual servant who had admitted him, resplendent in a new suit of blue and red, trimmed with silver lace.[2]

The contrast between Thomas Jefferson's personal appearance and the elegance of his surroundings was cause for comment throughout his eight years in the Executive Mansion. Hostile Federalists and disdainful British diplomats grumbled about a president as careless of his clothing as of customary etiquette. Even friendly observers remarked on the contradictions in his behavior. "However he may neglect his person," wrote Mahlon Dickerson in 1802, Jefferson "takes good care of his table. No man in america keeps a better."[3]

Others echoed Dickerson's assessment of Jefferson's table, the central focus and emblem of the well-regulated household he had been shaping from the start. Back in early 1801, Jefferson had pondered the formation of two administrations, one public and one private. The day after his election in the House of Representatives on the thirty-sixth ballot, he started to issue official invitations to prospective cabinet members. Three days later, even before asking Meriwether Lewis to be his private secretary, Jefferson sent off letters in search of a cook and a steward—or rather a *chef de cuisine* and a maître d'hôtel.[4] He wrote

This essay was originally published in *White House History*, no. 17 (Winter 2006): 5–23.

to Philippe Létombe, the French envoy in Philadelphia: "Being now obliged to fix myself here, I find as great difficulty in composing my houshold, as I shall probably find in composing an administration for the government. You know the importance of a good maitre d'hotel, in a large house, and the impossibility of finding one among the natives of our country. I have imagined that such a person might be found perhaps among the French in Philadelphia."[5]

In a city with thousands of French residents, Létombe did find such a person. For the first six months of Jefferson's presidency, Joseph Rapin gave "the most perfect satisfaction" in the position of majordomo.[6] His replacement was Etienne Lemaire, a "portly well-mannered frenchman," previously in the service of wealthy Philadelphian William Bingham.[7] Lemaire was remembered by Jefferson's grandson as "a fine looking man[,] honest and highly accomplished in his line."[8] Margaret Bayard Smith recalled that Jefferson's "maitre-d'hôtel had served in some of the first families abroad, and understood his business to perfection."[9] It was Lemaire who choreographed the presidential entertainments, in the French style that was the height of fashion in the new republic.

Observers duly noted the French cast of both Jefferson's politics and his hospitality. John Quincy Adams's wife listed the "French Servants in Livery; a French Butler, a French Cuisine, and a buffet full of choice wine," most of it French.[10] The admiring Margaret Bayard Smith recalled that "republican simplicity was united to Epicurean delicacy; while the absence of splendour ornament and profusion was more than compensated by the neatness, order and elegant sufficiency that pervaded the whole establishment."[11] Jefferson expressed his keen sense of the proper limits of grandeur in an injunction to his steward: "While I wish to have every thing good in it's kind, and handsome in stile, I am a great enemy to waste and useless extravagance, and see them with real pain."[12]

When Jefferson was unsuccessful in persuading his former slave James Hemings to return to his service as chef, Létombe found another Frenchman to fill the second position in the household.[13] Honoré Julien, aged forty-two, had been in the country for almost ten years and had worked in George Washington's kitchen in the last four months of his presidency.[14] According to Mrs. Smith, his "excellence and superior skill" were acknowledged "by all who frequented [Jefferson's] table."[15] Congressman Samuel L. Mitchill wrote that Jefferson's cook "understands the art of preparing and serving up food, to a nicety."[16]

In the third position in the domestic hierarchy was the coachman and head of Jefferson's stables. Jefferson later described Joseph Dougherty, a native of Londonderry, Ireland, and a holdover from the staff of John and Abigail Adams, as "sober, honest, diligent, & uncommonly intelligent in business."[17] While Federalists deplored the new president's habitual mode of travel—"a single horse," with no servant in attendance—Dougherty was also chagrined, as he seldom got to mount the box of the elegant presidential chariot.[18] Over the years, however, his responsibilities expanded beyond the horse stalls and carriage bays. As Jefferson later wrote, Dougherty served "rather as a riding agent than as the head of my stable."[19]

It must have been these three servants, who served for the full eight years, that Margaret Bayard Smith had in mind when she wrote that Jefferson "secured the best services of the best domestics, not only by the highest wages, but more especially by his uniform justice, moderation and kindness and by the interest he took in their comfort and welfare. . . . During the whole time of his residence here, no changes, no dismissions took place in his well-ordered household."[20]

There was less stability, however, among the lower-ranking servants, although none is known to have been actually fired. The men who played a shifting variety of roles as footmen, waiters, and porters were, besides Lemaire, the most conspicuous representatives of the domestic staff. In a society where livery was rare, they wore splendid uniforms: blue broadcloth coats with "crimson" or "scarlet" collar and cuffs, plated buttons, and a decorative woven edging, in silver, called livery lace; red waistcoats; and velvet or corduroy pantaloons—not knee breeches.[21] Whereas George Washington's red and white livery derived from his family coat of arms, the blue-and-red color scheme used by Jefferson was by this time a generic standard for servants' uniforms in Britain and America.[22] This liveried corps included Irishmen, a German, possibly a Spaniard and a Frenchman, an American soldier, and an enslaved African American.[23] Besides their visible roles in greeting visitors, waiting at table, and attending to guests, these men shouldered the major burdens of fetching, carrying, and cleaning behind the scenes. Jefferson revealed their multiple duties when he sought "one who could act as porter, and at the same time take care of the Cabinet, setting room, and Oval room, leaving the Dining room and hall for John [Freeman]. He should be sober, diligent and goodhumored."[24]

Abraham Golden did double duty as footman and manservant for Meriwether Lewis and Lewis's successor as Jefferson's private secretary.[25] When Golden decided that a life at sea was preferable to one of service, John Pernier—variously described as a free mulatto, a Creole, and a Spaniard—filled his spot for another three years, leaving in 1807 with Lewis when he returned to the West as governor of Louisiana Territory.[26] Robert Dougherty, the coachman's brother, took the position for the remainder of Jefferson's term.

Despite having trusted enslaved domestics at Monticello, Jefferson brought only three slaves to the President's House, a succession of apprentice cooks. As he wrote in 1804, "At Washington I prefer white servants, who when they misbehave can be exchanged."[27] Yet one of his favorite Washington domestics was an enslaved man. Jefferson hired John Freeman, aged about twenty, from a

Maryland physician and purchased him in 1804, the contract specifying that he become free in 1815.[28] A document of 1827 reveals that Freeman was five feet seven inches tall, "straight and well made . . . very pleasing countenance."[29] Freeman's duties included waiting at table, care of the hall and dining room, and possibly some personal attendance on the president. Jefferson had no servant who could be described as a valet de chambre, wholly dedicated to the care of his clothes and person. In fact, as a grandson-in-law, Nicholas Trist, recalled, Jefferson usually did without a "body servant," as the term was then understood. Trist cited a Jeffersonian maxim, "Never allow another to do for you what you can do for yourself," and added, "It was incompatible with the sentiment of Manhood, as it existed in him, that one human being should be followed about by another as his shadow."[30]

This aversion to the presence of a servant was the source of anguish for Jefferson's family members until his death. In 1803, for instance, his daughter Maria Jefferson Eppes deplored "the unsafe and solitary manner" in which her father slept upstairs in the President's House.[31] John Freeman was nevertheless important to Jefferson, accompanying the president on all his journeys to Monticello. In 1803, Jefferson sent Freeman to Monticello as escort for his departing daughters. After their arrival, Maria Eppes wrote her father that the horses "will set off tomorrow with John, whom I hear you have miss'd very much in the dining room."[32] Another African American, a free man named John (Jack) Shorter, was a stable hand from the fall of 1801 to the spring of 1809.[33]

There were also women workers in the presidential household, although their duties are largely unclear. Joseph Dougherty's wife, Mary, was on the staff for almost the entire eight years. The wives of Honoré Julien and footman Christopher Süverman worked for shorter periods. Sally Houseman and Biddy Boyle were resident washerwomen, assisted by local women hired in busy periods. Most of the nonresident workers were free blacks. Lemaire's accounts repeatedly refer to the "nègres" and "négresses" he hired on a daily or weekly basis for special jobs like cleaning the privies, sweeping the chimneys, taking care of the infants of the trainee cooks, and tending the presidential flock of sheep.[34]

Into this household of multiple nationalities were introduced three young women who had never left Albemarle County, Virginia. Jefferson began preparing for his retirement in 1801, when he brought an enslaved fourteen-year-old from Monticello to learn the art of French cookery in Julien's kitchen. Ursula Granger arrived at the largest house in the first city she had ever seen, staying only a year. Edith (Edy) Fossett, aged fifteen, replaced her in the fall of 1802, remaining for six and a half years. Her sister-in-law Fanny Hern, aged eighteen, joined her in the fall of 1806 and returned to Monticello in the spring of 1809.[35]

Jefferson's list of servants in the White House, October 1807, from his Memorandum Books. (Courtesy of the Massachusetts Historical Society)

The cast of characters is completed by mentioning a series of scullions, Jack, Isaac, and Sandy, who were probably free blacks. In the first three years, there was also a more highly paid *garçon de cuisine* named Noel. For most of his presidency, Jefferson had a staff of eleven, managing with only ten for the last year and a half. Their wages, like all the costs of stocking and running the President's House, came out of his own pocket. With an annual salary of $25,000, he had the deepest pockets of his life. Still, it took close to 15 percent of his income to feed, clothe, and pay his servants.[36] Their wages never varied over the eight years. No one received, or evidently even expected, a raise. In 1802, relieved that a new footman had been found, Jefferson wrote about another candidate: "Some difficulty might have arisen from the proposition for 18. dollars a month, lest that should have furnished grounds to the other servants to whom I give but 14 D. including drink to expect a rise of their wages."[37] The "drink" figure was a customary gratuity of two dollars a month for everyone except Lemaire and Julien, who, as quasi-gentlemen in a kind of class of their own, were not tipped. "Drink money" was the only remuneration for the enslaved household workers.[38]

Despite his expressions of trust in Lemaire, Jefferson kept a close watch on the transactions of his factotum, through whose hands passed as much as $10,000 in cash each year.[39] Every weekend Lemaire compiled and handed in his accounts, which Jefferson analyzed and transcribed into his memorandum book on Mondays. This analysis involved ever more complicated computations, by which

Jefferson sought to gauge the costs of his entertaining. He kept a running record of the weekly average cost of each guest's dinner, and from 1802, he separately calculated weekly expenditures for meat, vegetables, butter, and eggs. He compared the costs of dinners when Congress was in session and when it was not, and it is no surprise that he also determined how expensively his servants were eating during his twice-yearly absences.[40]

The Family

Margaret Bayard Smith, the only Washington commentator to discuss the servants in the President's House at any length, wrote that "without an individual exception they all became personally attached to [Jefferson]. . . . In sickness he was peculiarly attentive to their wants and sufferings, sacrificing his own convenience to their ease and comfort."[41] She also reported that, when describing the harmony of his political administration, Jefferson said that "we were one family."[42] Everyone from scullion to steward was also "family," according to its then-customary meaning of an entire household. In his search for a maître d'hôtel, Jefferson had asked for someone who could "take charge of the family." Every summer Lemaire and Joseph Dougherty wrote to Monticello some variation of "all the family are well." A Washington physician who cured the ills of Jefferson's servants wrote out a bill for "Attendance on the President's Family."[43]

Like all families, this one had its share of misfortune and discord. Doctor's bills and letters reveal that servants were often incapacitated by illness.[44] In March 1807, when Jefferson was suffering from his "periodical headache" and his son-in-law was convalescing after a dangerous illness, he reported that "indeed we have quite a hospital, one half below and above stairs being sick." Lemaire was "seriously ill" and John Freeman "just getting about after a 6. weeks confinement with a broken jaw."[45] The presence of young children (of the Doughertys and the enslaved cooks) meant the dreaded diseases of infancy stalked the cellars of the mansion. A boy died in Jefferson's absence in the summer of 1802, and whooping cough carried off Fanny Hern's child in November 1808. Lemaire made several poignant entries in his account book, payments for a coffin made by Peter Lenox and other burial expenses.[46] Of at least five children born in the President's House to the Monticello cooks, only two, James and Maria Fossett, survived to adulthood.[47]

The marriages of the enslaved women felt the strains of separation. Husbands were at Monticello and wives were more than one hundred miles away, in a city with a vibrant and quickly growing African American population. Fanny Hern was able to see her husband for a day or two, at intervals. David Hern, a wagoner, journeyed alone to the Federal City twice a year, transporting plants and supplies between Monticello and the President's House. Nevertheless, as former Monticello overseer Edmund Bacon recalled, they got into "a terrible quarrel," Jefferson was "very much displeased," and Bacon was summoned to the capital to take them to Alexandria for sale. When the overseer arrived, the Herns "wept, and begged, and made good promises, and made such an ado, that they begged the old gentleman out of it."[48] Edy Fossett's husband, Joseph Fossett, made an unauthorized journey to Washington when he heard disturbing news from John Freeman or Jack Shorter, soon after their arrival with the president at Monticello in July 1806. The enslaved blacksmith left his forge and set out on foot on a road he had never before taken. Jefferson's reaction was swift. He hired a local man to follow the runaway and alerted Joseph Dougherty: "We know he has taken the road towards Washington, & probably will be there before the bearer. He may possibly trump up some story to be taken care of at the President's house till he can make up his mind which way to go; or perhaps he may make himself known to Edy only, as he was formerly connected with her." The Irishman reported the capture: "After returning from a cruise where I got wind of him I met with him in the Presidents yard going from the Presidents House. . . . I took him immediately & brot. him to Mr. Perry & has him now in jail. Mr. Perry will start with him tomorrow for Monticello." Lemaire commented on the events as well: "The poor unhappy mulatto got [i.e., Joe] was not difficult to take. He well merits a pardon for this."[49]

Jefferson's biannual migration pattern had further consequences. When at Monticello in 1803, John Freeman became engaged to Melinda Colbert, an enslaved domestic servant of Jefferson's daughter Maria Jefferson Eppes and a granddaughter of Elizabeth (Betty) Hemings. Freeman planned to ask Mrs. Eppes's permission to marry Melinda during the Monticello visit of April 1804, but Jefferson's daughter died on April 17. Her death devastated Jefferson and alarmed John Freeman and Melinda Colbert, who recognized the increased threat of separation for enslaved spouses owned by two different people. The very next day Freeman took up his pen to appeal to the grieving president, who was in the same building. In essence, he asked Jefferson to purchase them both. Jefferson did buy Freeman a few months later, but he declined to purchase Melinda from his son-in-law, explaining that he already had too many house servants "in idleness" at Monticello and, besides, "John knew he was not to expect her society but when he should be at Monticello, and then subject to the casualty of her being here or not."[50]

Relations within the free families were not entirely harmonious. Footman John Kramer left his wife and the President's House at the same time.[51] Joseph and Mary Dougherty's marital difficulties rose to such a pitch in the summer of 1807 that the coachman also left Jefferson's employ, but he returned to his wife and the presidential stables in the fall. News of their reconciliation caused Jefferson to write: "The differings between man & wife, however they may affect their tranquility, can never produce such sufferings as are consequent on their separation."[52] Back in 1802, Dougherty, also one who preferred to write his master rather than speak to him on a difficult topic, revealed some of the cracks in the solidarity of the domestic staff. After stating that "what I have to communicate to you is more than I can do when face to face," he cataloged the various misdemeanors of footman Christopher Süverman and his wife Betsy, pilfering the linens among them.[53] Jefferson's response, presumably verbal, no doubt accorded with his policy for dealing with disputes among his hired Monticello workmen: "It is my rule never to take a side or any part in the quarrels of others, nor to enquire into them. I generally presume them to flow from the indulgence of too much passion on both sides, & always find that each party thinks all the wrong was in his adversary."[54]

The presence of an enslaved African American clothed and considered as the other footmen was bound to be a source of resentment. In his very first month, footman Edward Maher was heard complaining that Jefferson "gave preference to a negro rather than to him in following you." Rapin the steward continued: "I myself heard him murmuring, saying that he would not wear the same sort of outfit as a negro wore, in speaking of the livery." Jefferson gave short shrift to these sentiments. He replied that he did not yet know Maher well enough to value him, but "the negro whom he thinks so little of, is a most valuable servant."[55] Jefferson was not distressed when Maher left his service in 1802, considering him "a very capable servant, but stands too much on etiquette. I like servants who will do every thing they are wanted to do."[56]

One Day's Round

On April 3, 1807, it is assumed that the servants did everything that was expected of them. This was a quiet day, with no open houses or dinner parties. The "fatigues of the table" were over, as the members of Congress had abandoned the capital a month earlier, and the president was about to leave for his spring break at Monticello.[57] Jefferson was an early riser, always up in time to check his thermometer at sunrise, which on this morning was just before 6:00 A.M. He marked down the dawn temperature as 32 degrees, the hygrometer at 6.8, the weather fair, and the wind from the southwest. His secretary, Isaac A. Coles, whose bedroom was a floor below in the East Room, also checked the thermometer and weather vane, noting the same results. A slightly more voluble diarist than the president, Coles described the day as "disagreeably cold."[58]

By the time these men were up and recording the weather, most of the other residents of the President's House had been on their feet for hours. At the cellar level, Etienne Lemaire rose to marshal his forces from his bed in the room below the oval drawing room. The footmen were launched on their morning tasks of carrying firewood and coal to the hearths and water to the bedrooms, and dusting and tidying on the first floor—John Freeman in the Entrance Hall and dining rooms and William Fitzjames in the drawing room, the adjacent sitting room, and Jefferson's cabinet.[59] Robert Dougherty and John Pernier resumed a perpetual round of polishing the silver, not to mention the boots of the upstairs inhabitants—besides Jefferson and Coles, Meriwether Lewis and Jefferson's son-in-law Thomas Mann Randolph.

With the domestic mechanism set in motion, Lemaire would usually have walked to the stables. On market days, Jack Shorter harnessed the cart horse to the wagon, Joseph Dougherty took the reins, and he and Lemaire set off to purchase provisions. The day before, at the Center Market, Lemaire had purchased salted beef, chickens, butter, spinach, watercress, and parsley. There was, however, no market on this day, a Friday.[60]

In the enormous room under the north Entrance Hall, the kitchen staff kept the fires burning in a fireplace, an iron range, and a stew stove. Sandy the scullion filled a scuttle with charcoal for the latter, where pots of coffee and hot chocolate sat on grates above its cast-iron stew holes. After Fanny Hern scattered corn for the hens and ducks in the poultry yard and gathered up the new-laid eggs, she met the cart of Miller the dairyman and carried in the day's milk and cream. Edy Fossett was preparing the breakfast breads, while Julien and Lemaire put their heads together to settle on a menu for dinner. Mary Dougherty was on her way to the cupboards to get linens for the breakfast table.[61]

While his servants fetched, carried, chopped, and stirred in the nether regions, the master of the house embarked on a routine that would minimize their visibility. After his session with William Conner the barber, he came downstairs to his cabinet about 6:00 A.M. and dashed off orders for books and two tons of nail rod for the Monticello nailery.[62] William Fitzjames was probably the first of the footmen to don his livery uniform, trading his behind-the-scenes cleaning role for a more ceremonial position as doorkeeper. The only known visitors were the four heads of department, who came for a "consultation" on issues of national security—the Burr conspiracy and the unpalatable Monroe-Pinkney Treaty with Great Britain.[63] This morning meeting, which extended through the dinner hour, meant that Jefferson must have missed his midday ride. But he may have mounted Wildair at an earlier hour than usual, since he saw Jack Shorter, the stable hand, paying him for a valise pad.[64] The absence of an attending servant on Jefferson's daily rides shocked Washington society and spawned numerous stories of his encounters with citizens who abused their president without realizing they were conversing with him.[65]

Even if Jefferson did not take his daily ride, there would have been activity in the stables, where Wildair, four high-blooded bay carriage horses, and the cart horse required currying and feeding. In the carriage bays were a chariot, two phaetons, a gig, and the market wagon. Jack Shorter had to clean harness and haul oats and hay. Joseph Dougherty would have been anxious to ensure that the phaeton, gig, and horses were ready for Jefferson's and Randolph's journey to Monticello four days hence.[66]

While Jefferson, James Madison, Albert Gallatin, Henry Dearborn, and Robert Smith discussed impressment on the high seas, steam rose from copper stew pans of soup and beans in the kitchen and from a copper boiler in the wash house in the west dependencies wing, where Biddy Boyle wrestled with sheets and pillow cases.[67] Julien directed Edy Fossett in putting together his specialty of the day, "partridge with sausages & cabbage a french way of cooking them." Revolving on the roasting jack before the hearth was a quarter of bear that Lemaire had purchased at market six days earlier. He was anxiously watching Fanny Hern stir an egg custard for the centerpiece of the dessert course.[68] When searching for a steward, Jefferson had specified that "honesty and skill in making the dessert are indispensable qualifications." Maîtres d'hôtel were proficient in food preparation, especially the dessert, although they were usually not expected to wield the knives and whisks themselves. Contemporary commentators extolled the presidential meals as if a single French chef were responsible, but Lemaire and Julien should get joint credit.[69]

Although Jefferson had given only one dinner party in the month since the congressional session ended, it is clear that standards of cookery and presentation had not been relaxed. Lemaire and John Freeman prepared the small dining room with their usual attention to the alignment of the tablecloth and the arrangement of the silver, china, and glass. The footmen, now all in livery for their role as waiters, brought the dishes of the first course up the stairs and placed them with a studied attention to symmetry on the table: a "ham of bacon" in the center, with a beef *bouilli*, the "quarter" of bear, the partridge dish, soup (perhaps *cressonière*, with watercress Lemaire purchased the day before), potatoes, rice, spinach, beans, lamb's-lettuce salad, and pickles disposed about it.[70] While this dining room did not have a revolving door with circular shelves for swiftly changing courses, as did the public dining room, another kind of dumbwaiter was almost certainly used—especially given the sensitivity of the business at hand. Since his residence in France, Jefferson had used these tiered tables between the diners to diminish the need for servants, "mute but not inattentive listeners," in the words of Margaret Bayard Smith.[71]

Lemaire announced dinner at 4:00 P.M., and after the president and his guests sat down at the table, the maître d'hôtel may have remained in the room, as he did for more formal dinners, "seeing that the servants attended to every gentleman but not waiting himself." On this occasion it is more likely that the footmen withdrew, leaving their job to the dumbwaiters. In any case, Jefferson liked to fill the plates of his guests himself. Servants reappeared for the transition from the first to the second course, the all-important dessert.[72] Lemaire always put the principal dessert in its place at the head of the table, on this day "a kind of custard with a floating cream on it." For the bottom of the table there were "apples inclosed in a thin toast a french dish," and "on each side four dishes & three in the middle," probably holding cakes and jellies, as on the preceding days.[73] When the nation's leaders had taken their fill, the waiters removed the tablecloth along with the dishes and brought in the wines. If the same varieties Isaac Coles had noted two days earlier, they came from four nations: Portugese Madeira, Spanish Pajarete, French Hermitage, and Italian Nebbiolo. Accompanying the wine were "olives[,] apples, oranges & 12 other plates of nuts &c."[74]

Coffee and tea were ready in the adjoining oval drawing room, so Jefferson and his fellow diners were now on their own. If they needed a servant for some special purpose—as in 1802 when Jefferson "ordered" his waterproof English greatcoat brought in for a test of its impermeability—the bell system, installed in 1801, was at hand to summon a footman from the servants' hall in the cellar.[75] There, and in the dining room, most of the household staff were dealing with the aftermath of this comparatively simple dinner party. They had dishes to wash, candles to extinguish and wicks to trim, linens and plated ware to lock up. One of the servants carried a tray to a small table with doors that "flew open" when a spring was touched. He stocked it, as usual, with "a goblet of water, a decanter of wine, a plate of light cakes, and a night-taper." When showing this convenience to a guest, Jefferson said, "I often sit up late . . . and my wants are thus provided for without keeping a servant up."[76]

Etienne Lemaire was probably the last of the household to go to bed. He had to complete the ritual of closing down the house, checking that all was in its proper place and under lock and key, the doors and windows secure. He may have also wanted to begin to organize his accounts for the last five weeks, which Jefferson would analyze before his departure.[77] Jefferson sipped his wine and transcribed the deliberations of his cabinet into his political journal at the end of a day so busy that—very unusually—he never made his afternoon observation of the thermometer. He retired in the knowledge that his household was humming along in a course very much "to [his] mind."[78] Its uniforms, the Gallic refinement of its furnishings and fare, and its reigning order provided a secure space for personal negligence and "republican simplicity." Within the elegant confines of his castle, the president could rise the next day to receive his official visitors in his faded coat and worn slippers.

After 1809

Jefferson said farewell to his household staff on March 11, 1809, when he crossed the Potomac for the last time. Stable hand Jack Shorter accompanied him through a heavy snowstorm to Monticello, while Edy Fossett and Fanny Hern, with Edy's children, made the journey more slowly in a caravan of wagons. Honoré Julien followed ten days later to spend almost three weeks helping the "two good girls," as Lemaire called them, to settle in to the new kitchen under the south terrace. Jefferson reported that Julien's "pupils are going on very well and much to our comfort and satisfaction."[79] During the years of his retirement, Monticello visitors praised the "half Virginian, half French style" of the meals they prepared.[80]

Back in Washington, the remaining servants found other places and occupations. Margaret Bayard Smith, in her glowing account of master-servant relations in the President's House, probably exaggerated when she wrote that Jefferson, "by his generous interference," helped his former servants to make "some advantageous establishment for themselves."[81] But there is no question that he parted on very cordial terms with his employees, interested himself in their futures, and on occasions made them financial contributions. He, too, had to resort to the written word to express his sentiments at the moment of parting: "My heart was so full that I could utter but the single word Adieu. indeed the enlivening idea of rejoining my family and of being once more master of my own time & actions, was lost in the moment of separation from those who had lived so long in the house with me, & served me so much to my mind." In this letter to Lemaire, he declared his attachment to his "faithful, & skilful" steward, whose "whole conduct [was] so marked with good humour, industry, sobriety & economy as never to have given me one moment's dissatisfaction."[82]

Lemaire returned to Philadelphia and prospered for a time, but his life had a "tragical" end. In 1817 he threw himself in the Schuylkill River when a friend defaulted on a $5,000 loan. Although Lemaire had a fortune equal to twice that sum, "he lost both his health and his reason."[83] An unusual number of suicides are associated with residents of the President's House of Jefferson's time, and financial worries figure in all of them. Less well known than the death of Meriwether Lewis in 1809 is that of his servant, John Pernier, who "followed his master's example" six months later by taking an overdose of laudanum. Despondent over his failure to be paid for more than a year's service to Governor Lewis, Pernier was also perhaps troubled by rumors that he was Lewis's murderer. In his last months, "wretchedly poor and destitute," he was taken in by former President's House footman Christopher Süverman, who bore the expenses of his final illness and burial. Jefferson described Süverman at this time as "a very honest man," now completely blind, who bought and sold groceries "from hand to mouth" and was "miserably poor."[84]

At the time of Pernier's suicide, Honoré Julien was making a modest but independent living on F Street selling cakes and confectionery, including, in the summer, ice cream. He also carried on a catering business. Over the years, he sent New Year's greetings to Monticello and occasionally forwarded delicacies, like canvasbacks and Swiss cheese, that were unattainable in the mountains of Virginia.[85] By 1828 his "cookshop" had been discontinued "for want of custom" and was a mere "fruit shop." His death two years later was announced in the newspaper with the comment, "His probity and worth were proverbial." He passed on his culinary skills, for his son Auguste Julien catered banquets at the President's House in the time of James K. Polk.[86] Honoré Julien's enslaved pupils, after running Monticello's kitchen for more than fifteen years, were both sold at the estate sale after Jefferson's death. Fanny Hern and her husband were purchased by University of Virginia professor Robley Dunglison. Edy Fossett and her youngest children were bought by free family members. Her husband, Joseph, who had been freed in Jefferson's will, continued to work as a blacksmith to pay for the purchase of his wife and children. The Fossetts moved about 1840 to Cincinnati, where their sons became the most prominent caterers in the city.[87]

The other slave in the President's House, John Freeman, also had to struggle for freedom and family unity. On the eve of Madison's inauguration, Freeman was again driven to take up pen and paper rather than put his case face-to-face. Jefferson wanted his slave to go with him to live at Monticello. By this time Melinda Colbert was Freeman's wife and living in the President's House, now free. Her husband considered it unsafe for her to return to Virginia, so he had refused to go. His letter included an apology and a painful concession: "Rather than disples you i will go and do the best i can . . . I shall be oblige to leave [Melinda] and the children."[88] Jefferson bowed to the inevitable. He sold Freeman to Madison, who retained him as dining room servant in the President's House. Freeman became free according to the original contract in 1815 and continued to work for the Madisons while they remained in Washington.[89] Afterward, he was a waiter at Gadsby's Hotel and a messenger in the State Department, among other unknown occupations. John and Melinda Freeman, who had at least eight children, were active in the antislavery endeavors of Washington's free blacks.

Letter of John Freeman to Thomas Jefferson, [March 2, 1809]. (Thomas Jefferson Papers, Manuscript Division, Library of Congress)

At his death in 1839, John Freeman was able to leave his family a house on K Street several blocks northwest of the President's House.[90]

Little is known of Freeman's companion of the road, Jack Shorter. In 1819 he sent word of his "present state" to Jefferson through Joseph Dougherty, his former taskmaster. After his wife had left him to go to "the western country," Shorter became "dissipated" and unable to make a living. As Dougherty reported, he "flew to me for protection. I succeeded in reforming him."[91] Dougherty's own career after his stint on Pennsylvania Avenue was a checkered one. While briefly pursuing the painting trade, he speculated in fine-wooled sheep, grazing them on the common near the President's House. When the bubble of "Merino mania" burst, he started a porter and ale bottling business but was ruined by the War of 1812.

Correspondence between the Irishman and Monticello was frequent in these first years of Jefferson's retirement, when Dougherty acted as his Washington agent, facilitating the transmission of geese, sheep, and books. Dougherty reported on the "wonderfull changes" Dolley Madison had made to the President's House,[92] and Jefferson provided numerous letters of commendation for minor government posts. One of these letters finally bore fruit in 1818, when Dougherty was appointed superintendent of buildings for the Departments of Navy, War, and State. He lost this office before the year was out, however, after being tried and imprisoned for "cowhiding"[93] Samuel Lane, commissioner of public buildings.

At the end of 1823, Dougherty was weathering very hard times, still trying to pay off debts from the war and with only a very low paying position as a ward commissioner. His wife, Mary, took it upon herself to write to her former employer, without the knowledge of her husband. Jefferson sent twenty-five dollars in response to her plea for assistance.[94] Yet in 1830, the ebullient Irishman bounded into the home of Margaret Bayard Smith and sat "talking of the dear old Man" for an hour, providing "a minute detail of Mr. J.'s distribution of every hour of the day, from sun rise until bed time." In 1819, Dougherty had exclaimed, "Oh! When shall we have another Jefferson!" And in 1830, two years before his death, he told Mrs. Smith that Jefferson's "whole life was nothing but good, . . . it was his meat and drink, all he thought of and all he cared for, to make every body happy. Yes, the purest body."[95]

Jefferson's People

Slavery at Monticello

THOMAS Jefferson became a slaveholder by inheritance. From the summer of 1757, when his father wrote "I Give & Bequeath to my son Thomas my mulattoe Fellow Sawney," he was entangled in an unjust legal and economic system that he was unable to escape or abolish. When he turned twenty-one, in 1764, he gained legal title to about thirty human beings from his father's estate. Ten years later he received 135 more after the death of his father-in-law, John Wayles. From 1770 Jefferson lived on the top of an 867-foot mountain in Albemarle County, directing the operations of a tract that grew from almost 3,000 to over 5,000 acres. John Wayles's death transformed Monticello from an ordinary tobacco plantation to the central nerve center of a far-flung economic enterprise. After the division of Wayles's estate in January 1774, Jefferson had tripled his real property, to 14,000 acres of land and 187 human beings. He now owned four major plantations in Virginia's Piedmont: Monticello, Elk Hill and Willis Creek forty miles to the east, and Poplar Forest ninety miles to the southwest. A rather well-to-do planter had instantly become one of the wealthiest men in the colony.[1] Over his long life, during which he purchased fewer than twenty slaves, Jefferson considered himself the owner of more than six hundred people—"those whom fortune has thrown on our hands."[2]

1774–1794

In April 1782, a party of Frenchmen rode up to Monticello for a three-day visit. The Chevalier de Chastellux recorded his impressions of his host, a fellow

This essay was originally published in *The Cambridge Companion to Thomas Jefferson*, ed. Frank Shuffelton (New York, 2009), 83–100.

philosophe who had "placed his mind, like his house, on a lofty height, whence he might contemplate the whole universe." Their conversation ranged widely, over literary and scientific topics, and particularly American natural history, which Jefferson was then pondering as he wrote what became his *Notes on the State of Virginia*. The epithets Chastellux used to describe Jefferson—"Musician, Draftsman, Surveyor, Astronomer, Natural Philosopher, Jurist, and Statesman"— did not include the word "Farmer."[3] Chastellux was shown Jefferson's herd of tame deer, but there is nothing in his account about corn or tobacco or enslaved laborers at work in the fields. From his eminence, Jefferson kept his eyes focused on the universe rather than on the "slovenly business of tobacco making" taking place at his feet. In these early years, he was in the midst of re-creating the ideal world he saw in the paeans to country life of Horace and Virgil. He designed his house and its surroundings with the villas of the Romans in mind. He looked down on a landscape of literary allusions, its features bearing names he had given them to evoke ancient landscapes. Unlike many Virginia plantation owners who prided themselves on being clever "crop-masters," Jefferson was so little involved in the tobacco-making process itself that he could write, after more than thirty years in the business, that "I never saw a leaf of my tob[acc]o. packed in my life."[4]

In January 1774, however, the Wayles inheritance had compelled Jefferson to pay attention to plantation management. To organize a transition he began what he called his "Farm-book," making three lists of men, women, and children and their locations: his 52 "proper slaves"; the 135 individuals inherited from Wayles; and the combined total of 187 people, many now in new locations.[5] After these arrangements were complete, Jefferson put the Farm Book away for the next twenty years, opening it very occasionally to note the births and deaths of slaves and the pedigrees of horses. Above the fray, he left the running of his planta- tions to a team of managers, including overseers at each place and intermediate functionaries—stewards and superintendents—to further protect him from the daily necessity of making enslaved workers raise a staple crop.

In this period Jefferson struggled, along with his more enlightened southern peers, to make ownership of humans compatible with new ideas and institutions, preserving conscience and principle by increasing the social distance between master and slave. He invariably used diminutives when referring to individuals: Edward became Ned, and Frances became Fanny. His views on racial inferiority pushed the blacks around him down the "scale of beings." Slaves were function- ally children, as he implied in a letter of 1789: "To give liberty to, or rather, to abandon persons whose habits have been formed in slavery is like abandoning children."[6] He could thus see himself as the benevolent steward of the African Americans to whom he was bound in a relationship of mutual dependency and obligation, the "father" of those who needed his care as well as control. In 1776, he made a census of the "Number of souls in my family," totaling 117, including his wife and daughter, his overseers, hired workmen, and their families, and 83 enslaved African Americans.[7] Here Jefferson fit the traditional patriarchal pattern, using "family" in its most ancient usage, meaning the dependents of the head of a household.

In the hands-off plantation management of the 1770s, when he exercised less direct authority over his slaves, fealty was a particular concern. His 1771 plan for a burial ground includes a pyramid of rough stone on the grave of "a favorite and faithful servant," inscribed with stanzas from English poet William Shenstone's "Inscription for an African Slave." Might Jefferson have had in mind Jupiter, still very much alive, his personal servant and constant shadow on journeys throughout Virginia—a man exactly his own age who had grown up with him at Shadwell? On one occasion when this "trusty servant" abandoned his deferential conduct, Jefferson erupted in a display of anger his family had never seen before.[8] Jefferson even devised tests for the faithfulness of his slaves. In 1774 he determined to keep a tally of his bottles of Jamaica rum to "try the fidelity of Martin," his new butler. This was Martin Hemings, part of a family often described as "faithful" or "trusty." Hemings's mother, Elizabeth (Betty) Hemings, and her children had been an important element of Martha Wayles Jefferson's domestic household as she grew up. After the death of John Wayles, said to be the father of at least six of her children, Elizabeth Hemings and her family came to Monticello and filled virtually all the serving positions in the house. Over the next half century, more than eighty of her descendants would live in slavery at Monticello. The favored status of this family is illustrated by the unusual freedom of movement Jefferson granted to her sons in this period. When not required at Monticello, Robert, James, and Martin Hemings were "at liberty" to hire themselves out to other masters and keep their wages for themselves.[9]

The Wayles inheritance marked the beginning of Jefferson's practice of shifting individuals and families among his different plantations, according to his operational needs. In the 1770s he concentrated tradesmen at Monticello, transferring almost fifty Wayles slaves there, including carpenters, blacksmiths, watermen, and a shoemaker. He then established his first blacksmith shop, hiring a free man to operate it, share its profits, and teach Barnaby, a 14-year-old smith brought from a Wayles plantation in Cumberland County. Over the next fifty years, Jefferson often engaged skilled craftsmen to stay at Monticello long enough to train enslaved men and women in their trades, making the mountaintop the site of skills in metal- and woodworking that were exceptional for its time and place.

Despite his aversion to selling human beings, Jefferson was forced to put both land and slaves up for sale in an effort to pay his enormous debts to several

British mercantile firms. (By the time of the Revolution, these debts totaled more than £5,000—three-quarters of it derived from the Wayles inheritance.) Because of Revolutionary War inflation, Jefferson's sale of 10,000 acres of inherited lands netted him, as his daughter recalled, only enough money to buy a greatcoat. Consequently, at auctions in 1785, 1792, and 1793, he sold over seventy men, women, and children—none of them from Monticello.[10] Spouses were not separated in these sales, nor were children twelve or under sold away from their parents. Jefferson additionally "alienated" almost eighty more people by gifts to family members. There were a few individual sales as well. Jefferson sold several young men with a propensity for running away, in accordance with his policy of ridding his domain of disruptive elements. He sold Robin soon after he returned to Monticello, one of the few survivors among more than twenty enslaved people who sought freedom with the British army in 1781. Nineteen men, women, and children—several whole families—left Jefferson's Elk Hill and Willis Creek plantations, while Robin, Barnaby the blacksmith, and two other young men escaped from Monticello. Most of these bids for freedom ended tragically, in death from disease contracted in the British camps.

The Revolution left an indelible mark on Monticello's residents, and its events provided stories that descended through generations of families, both free and enslaved. In light of the war's outcome, it is not surprising that in African American families all the attempts to escape slavery were forgotten. Their principal stories focus instead on the symbiotic relationship between their ancestors and the master of Monticello, with varying tales of enslaved people helping Jefferson escape from British dragoons or saving his silver. Jefferson's descendants told the same stories as evidence of a benevolent master and loyal slaves, but for the descendants of the blacksmiths, grooms, and household servants who played the major roles in the revolutionary drama, the stories honored the ingenuity and indispensability of their ancestors.

After the death of his wife in 1782, Jefferson found solace in a return to public service, turning over all his plantation operations to the management of his neighbor Nicholas Lewis. Far from his mountaintop in France, New York, and Philadelphia, Jefferson considered the fate of his slaves. While slavery continued to be the law in Virginia, he did not intend to free them, but his financial problems compelled him to consider selling or leasing them. Although they would be subject to "ill usage" in both cases, he preferred hiring them out, which would at least be temporary and would, in his view, "end in their happiness."[11] He also explored a kind of share-cropping scheme by which he would bring industrious German farmers to Virginia and establish them on fifty-acre plots "intermingled" with his slaves, whose children would thus be brought up "in habits of property and foresight."[12] Jefferson never pursued this chimerical project farther than some personal interviews on his travels in Germany in 1788. Instead, he directed his thoughts to reforming rather than ending the institution of slavery and explored ways to improve the condition of the enslaved members of his own "family," by placing them "on an easier footing."[13] As he wrote in late 1793, when he was about to be "liberated from the hated occupations of politics," "I have my house to build, my feilds to form, and to watch for the happiness of those who labor for mine."[14]

1794–1809

In the last days of June 1796, the duc de La Rochefoucauld-Liancourt arrived at Monticello in the midst of the wheat harvest, noting that even "the scorching heat of the sun" did not prevent Jefferson's daily presence. This was a new Jefferson and a new era on the Monticello plantation. For the first time, he was personally involved in its day-to-day operations, constantly in the fields, realigning their boundaries, weighing the grain they produced, or testing new machinery (including his own improved plow). This is the period—three years of retirement from 1794 to 1797—in which he called himself "the most ardent and active farmer in the state."[15]

As one who lived the Enlightenment every day of his life, Jefferson pursued the improvement of the human condition as a passionate Baconian, gathering information with the aid of his watch, ruler, and scales. He applied his measuring mind to plantation projects in a search for economy and efficiency. He enveloped his unwieldy operations in the consoling security of mathematical truths, driving a further psychological wedge between himself and the enslaved people living so close to him. His many monumental earth-moving projects, in particular, led to a lifetime of time-and-motion calculations: how many cubical yards could Phill dig and carry in a twelve-hour day or what was the daily progress of "3. hands" carving a road through the woods of Monticello?[16] At the same time that Jefferson applied a geometric grid of field boundaries to the irregular features of his mountain, he imposed Enlightenment ideals of economy and order on the people who lived there. He acquired a Chinese gong to broadcast the measurement of time across the whole plantation. His plan for a more efficient harvest in 1796 literally turned his slaves into parts of a machine. It called for assembling the necessary equipment, assigned people of all ages to a variety of tasks, and devised a means for having ever-sharp scythe blades so the mowers could cut the wheat "constantly." "In this way," he wrote of this combination of tools, carts and wagons, mules and oxen, and almost sixty human beings, "the whole machine would move in exact equilibrio, no part of the force could be lessened without retarding the whole, nor increased without a waste of force."[17]

While Jefferson's mathematical calculations and mechanistic planning reduced enslaved men, women, and children to cogs in the many wheels of a plantation machine, he remained conscious of their humanity, not forgetting to watch for their "happiness." At this time he held 155 slaves, one-third of them living on his Poplar Forest plantation. What did he actually do to improve their lives and place them "on the comfortable footing of the laborers of other countries?"[18] The food and clothing allotments he began to record in December 1794 were not notably different from those on other plantations in the Upper South; his meat allowance was even rather stingy. Everyone, regardless of age, received a weekly peck of cornmeal. Adults were given four salt herring and half a pound of salt pork or pickled beef each week; children received smaller amounts of meat and fish, according to age. The clothing allowance was a summer and winter outfit each year, with shoes for all over the age of ten and, every three years, a blanket.

Anxious to minimize "hard driving" and the use of the whip, Jefferson focused most of his attention on the conditions of labor. "My first wish is that the labourers may be well treated," he wrote in 1792, and he soon began to look outside Virginia for overseers who would be less severe than local men without sacrificing productivity. He fixed on Cecil County, Maryland, where the farmers used both free and enslaved labor and thus, in Jefferson's opinion, would "understand the management of negroes on a rational and humane plan."[19] For reasons that can no longer be recovered, this experiment with overseers from farther north failed and was never repeated. In 1796, when a newly appointed overseer did not appear, Jefferson promoted the best farmer at Monticello, his sixty-six-year-old head man, George Granger (Great George), to the highest position, the only enslaved man among almost fifty overseers hired over the years. Clearly struggling to achieve Jefferson's dual goals, Granger, "steady and industrious," made outstanding tobacco crops but was reportedly unable to "command his force" and "needs to be supported."[20]

Jefferson returned to free Virginia overseers, trying to avoid those with reputations for severity.[21] But despite his instructions to minimize corporal punishment, the whip was never banished from his fields, and some overseers gained reputations for cruelty. Disillusioned with his efforts to find managers who could unite both productivity and humanity, he declared in 1799, "I find I am not fit to be a farmer with the kind of labour we have."[22] By then he had leased out his cultivated lands and the laborers who worked them and did not take them back into his control for ten years. He gave long leases for the fields but leased the field hands and their families only from year to year, "so that I may take them away if ill treated."[23] The men and women who plowed and hoed his land would never be the "chosen people of God" of Jefferson's agrarian ideal.[24]

Jefferson was both more comfortable and more successful with another seg-
ment of the enslaved labor force. He could personally superintend the work of
his tradesmen, testing methods of management on humanitarian principles that
were being applied in reformed institutions of discipline and control, such as
schools, factories, and prisons, on both sides of the Atlantic. In Philadelphia,
Jefferson had seen the transforming effects of a new regime at the Walnut Street
Prison, where corporal punishment was dispensed with and prisoners were
treated as potentially useful members of society—as moral and rational human
beings, capable of reformation. Jefferson applied these same principles in a new
enterprise at Monticello, a nail-making factory, in which young enslaved boys
aged ten to sixteen made hand-forged nails of all sizes. In the first years of its
existence, he supervised its operations, visiting it daily to weigh the iron nail
rod supplied to each nailer as well as the nails he produced. In this way he could
monitor the efficiency as well as the productivity of the workers, by calculating
how many pounds of iron they "wasted" in the nail-making process.

A dozen teenaged boys, cooped up in a smoky shop, carrying out a boring and
repetitive task for ten to fourteen hours a day, were a management challenge.
"He animates them by rewards and distinctions," the duc de Liancourt noted.[25]
Jefferson built esprit de corps through special food and clothing rations and
improved performance by stimulating competition in a race for efficiency. He
cautioned his overseer to refrain from using the whip in the nailery except "in
extremities," describing the key to his mode of "government" as "the stimulus
of character" rather than "the degrading motive of fear." When urging restraint
in disciplining the nailers, he wrote that "it would destroy their value in my estimation to degrade them in their own eyes by the whip."[26] The youth of the nailers was an important factor. When Jefferson expanded the operation in its third
year, instead of bringing older boys from the fields to the shop, he purchased two
eleven-year-old boys and moved four others to Monticello from Poplar Forest.

Jefferson used character-building management techniques with his older tradesmen as well, encouraging a consciousness of measurable achievement and offering
financial incentives for the first time. He paid Frank, the charcoal burner, according to how efficiently he burned his coal kiln and suggested to his son-in-law
John Wayles Eppes that he have the wood for his own charcoal burner corded,
"in order to excite him to an emulation in burning it well."[27] Jefferson inaugurated an actual profit-sharing arrangement with the enslaved managers in the
nailery, and he allowed his carpenters, smiths, and charcoal burners an unusual
freedom from supervision.[28] This worried his son-in-law Thomas Mann Randolph, who expressed surprise at the results: "The thorough confidence you
place in the companies of tradesmen is less abused than I expected but I am still
convinced that being under no command whatever they will become idle and

dissipated tho' I am clear that it confirms them in honesty."[29] (He and Jefferson usually used "honesty" in its broad meaning encompassing virtue, integrity, and morality.) Randolph soon adopted the same rational management as his father-in-law, dismissing the whip from his plantation and never physically punishing slaves who showed signs of "a manly and moral character." Most overseers, in Randolph's view, "could not understand the value of character in a slave, and concluded that fear would be safer security for good conduct than any determination to do right."[30]

The character traits Jefferson wanted to instill were not so very different from those he sought in his free workmen or recommended to youthful free Virginians: honesty, industry, and sobriety, in the former, and "honesty, knowledge, and industry," for the latter.[31] Since the enslaved workmen were denied access to both alcohol and education, Jefferson's main goals for them were industry and honesty, the core virtue in his system of morality. These qualities, combined with the absolute subordination that his plantation law required, contributed to his own profit and tranquillity. Many of the nailers and tradesmen fulfilled his objectives, became "trusty servants," and were placed in charge of his house, stables, garden, and shops.

Jefferson's innovative management methods, with unaccustomed autonomy for some men, coincided with a new agricultural regime that led to decreased superintendence. On his retirement to Monticello in 1794, he launched a reforming crusade against the ravages of soil exhaustion. Tobacco was temporarily banished, replaced by wheat as the cash crop. The continuous monotonous labor of tobacco culture was superseded by the varied routine of a mixed grain and livestock operation, requiring more vehicles, draft animals, and complicated machinery. This more diversified operation called for a wide range of tasks spread widely across the plantation at different sites of activity. A single overseer could no longer closely monitor all the laborers in his charge.

The transition from tobacco to wheat culture, which demanded more land for cultivation, affected the lives of the enslaved as well as their work. Archaeological excavations at Monticello have revealed that, in the 1790s, housing patterns were transformed, as slave cabins were moved from clustered quarters near the overseer's house to scattered sites on the fringes of cultivated lands. By this time the dwellings themselves were also different. The large multifamily cabins of the 1770s had been replaced by smaller single-family dwellings. The desire of Monticello's African Americans to live independently—not just agricultural reform—undoubtedly contributed to the changes. Jefferson's policy of having houses built for enslaved women once they had children was probably active well before his statement to an overseer in 1818: "Maria having now a child, I promised her a house to be built this winter."[32]

The top of Monticello mountain was also transformed in the 1790s, becoming a construction site—as the main house was enlarged and remodeled—and a bustling village with an international flavor. House joiners from northern Ireland, a German plasterer, a gardener from Scotland, a blacksmith from Philadelphia, and other craftsmen from beyond Virginia lived and worked on Mulberry Row. Enslaved men John Hemmings,[33] son of Elizabeth Hemings, and Lewis assisted and learned from the joiners, carrying on the notable work of the joinery after their departure. Three other members of the Hemings family—Wormley Hughes, Joseph Fossett, and Burwell Colbert—received training in gardening, blacksmithing, and painting and glazing. With a near-monopoly on the household and most important trades positions, the members of this family were a kind of caste apart. Their occupations gave them the greatest access to money—through tips and work incentives—and their social separateness was reflected in their marriage choices. None of Elizabeth Hemings's twelve children, and only two of her grandchildren, found spouses at Monticello. Her grandsons Joseph Fossett and Wormley Hughes married into Monticello families, but other family members found wives in the household staffs of neighboring plantations and husbands in the local community, both free black and white.

The duc de Liancourt and other Monticello visitors saw enslaved people on the mountaintop who "neither in point of colour nor features, shewed the least trace of their original descent."[34] Elizabeth Hemings's daughters Mary, Betty, and Sally entered into long-term relationships with white men, similar to the probable one between their mother and John Wayles. In September 1802, in an article in a Richmond newspaper, James Thomson Callender blew the lid off a simmering story that spread across the country and down through decades of controversy. President Jefferson "keeps, and for many years past has kept, as his concubine, one of his own slaves. Her name is SALLY."[35] Jefferson and his family members were publicly silent on the issue, while Sally Hemings's son Madison, in 1873, stated that Jefferson was his father and had promised his mother that her children would all become free at the age of twenty-one. Privately, Jefferson's grandson Thomas Jefferson Randolph admitted that the light-skinned children of Sally Hemings and her sister Betty Brown resembled his grandfather, but he insisted that Jefferson's Carr nephews were their fathers.[36] While the father of Betty Brown's children is not certainly known, genetic testing in 1998 ruled out the Carr brothers in the case of the paternity of Sally Hemings's youngest son, Eston, indicating that a male Jefferson was his father. Science shifted opinion from doubt to belief, and most historians of the period now acknowledge that Thomas Jefferson was the father of Hemings's known children, born from 1795 to 1808. The preponderance of evidence—drawn from a combination of scientific and statistical evidence, the documentary record, and Hemings family oral history—strongly favors the existence of a long-term connection that produced at least six children. Clearly, black-white sexual encounters were quite common at Monticello. Skin tone allowed at least four slaves to vanish into free society unpursued. As Jefferson's granddaughter recalled, "Their whereabouts was perfectly known but they were left to themselves—for they were white enough to pass for white."[37]

The comings and goings of Jefferson, the Hemings men, and the free and enslaved men hired for Jefferson's major plantation and building projects had a destabilizing effect on the Monticello community. Five children of Elizabeth Hemings left the mountain between 1792 and 1796. When Jefferson left for France in the 1780s, her oldest daughter, Mary, had been leased out to local white merchant Thomas Bell, who became her common-law husband, purchased her freedom, and acknowledged paternity of their children. Martin Hemings had a falling out with Jefferson and left Monticello, his fate unknown. After accompanying Jefferson to Paris to train as a chef, James Hemings used his skills and knowledge of a wider world to achieve freedom soon after his return to Virginia. Jefferson reluctantly emancipated him after he passed his knowledge on to his brother Peter. Jefferson sold Thenia Hemings to James Monroe, possibly at her wish and to unite her with her husband. In the course of his own travels, Robert Hemings found a wife, Dolly, and persuaded her owner to help him purchase his own freedom. Both Jefferson's and Hemings's responses to this transaction reveal the striking distortions slavery produced in the feelings of the humans locked in its grip. Jefferson was angry at Hemings for behavior he considered disloyal and ungrateful, while Hemings was, according to Jefferson's daughter, "so deeply impressed with a sense of his ingratitude as to be rendered quite unhappy by it but he could not prevail upon himself to give up his wife and child."[38] Jefferson expected loyalty in exchange for the "indulgences" he had granted Hemings and could not understand that a slave might choose freedom and family over fidelity to the master.

The dynamics of the African American community shifted because of the need for extra manpower for Jefferson's most substantial undertakings, pursued while he was absent in Philadelphia and Washington as vice president and president: completion of the main house, construction of a canal and two grain mills, the leveling of an immense terraced vegetable garden, and continued road building. From 1795 to 1809 he hired up to sixteen enslaved men a year, some from as far away as Caroline and Spotsylvania Counties. This not only accentuated the imbalance of the ratio of males to females but led to unrest and frequent runaways. Even among the tradesmen, all was not tranquil with Jefferson rarely present to supervise them personally. The nail boys, growing older and more unruly, were too ungovernable for a blacksmith from Philadelphia. In 1803 the nailery erupted in violence, when Cary brought his hammer down on the head of Brown Colbert and nearly killed him. Violation of plantation rule, or "delinquency," inevitably led to separation. In this extreme case, Jefferson ordered not mere removal from Monticello but sale so far away that it would be "as if [Cary] were put out of the way by death." "So distant an exile" for the offender would be an exemplary punishment "in terrorem to others, in order to maintain the police so rigorously necessary among the nailboys."[39]

Since the time of the Revolution, there had been few recorded attempts to escape from slavery at Monticello, although there were no doubt cases of temporary absences not intended as flights to permanent freedom. During Jefferson's presidency, however, besides the hired men who tried to run back to their homes and families, two nailers and a blacksmith left the mountain without permission. The eighteen-year-old Kit was quickly apprehended and, as quickly, sold. The twenty-two-year-old James Hubbard headed north in 1805, almost reaching Washington, D.C. After several months in Fairfax County jail, he was taken back to Monticello and given a second chance. Joseph Fossett's concern was family, not freedom. He made his way to Washington because of an urgent need to see his wife, Edith, who had been transferred there to learn the art of French cookery in the presidential kitchen. Easily captured, he was brought back to Monticello, where he resumed his work in the blacksmith shop and was eventually reunited with his wife.

1809–1826

In mid-November 1813, Edward Ross rode over the Monticello plantation with Jefferson, who showed him "all his Mills, farms, Machineries, Curiosities &c. &c."[40] It was the mills and "Machineries" that dominated Jefferson's daily horseback rides of plantation superintendence. He had left the presidency in the hands of James Madison in 1809 and returned to Monticello, at last "free to follow the pursuits of my choice."[41] He took the farms back into his control but, except for a few short spells of redesigning fields and drawing up rotation plans, again lost interest in the production of his crops and increasingly turned agricultural matters over to his grandson Thomas Jefferson Randolph. Madison Hemings recalled the man he knew as his father as having "but little taste or care for agricultural pursuits" in this period: "It was his mechanics he seemed mostly to direct, and in their operations he took great interest." An apprentice carpenter, Hemings would have experienced this interest directly, as would his sister Harriet Hemings, who worked in the textile shop that Jefferson had begun to enlarge and mechanize in 1811. In the "factory" were spinning jennies with up to forty-eight spindles, looms with fly shuttles, and carding machines. Jefferson drew up complex charts of the daily tasks of his spinners and weavers, calibrating the ounces of cotton or yards of shirting they had to spin or weave according to the length of the working day, which grew from nine hours in midwinter to fourteen hours in high summer.[42]

In 1811, Jefferson designed a mill complex with a single waterwheel to drive a sawmill, gristmill and grain elevators, threshing machine and winnowers, and a hemp beater. Although he had leased out his larger mill at Shadwell, he retained control of the coopers' shops there. Seeking to increase the number of flour barrels to sell to the mill tenants, he encouraged his coopers, Barnaby Gillette and Nace, by allowing them to keep one barrel out of every thirty-one they made, to sell for their own profit. Jefferson's interest in stimulating efficiency was reflected in a new term—"premium"—he gave to the payments to his current charcoal burner, David Hern.

Designing a mechanical method of beating hemp solved a problem that had caused Jefferson to stop cultivating this staple in cloth production, because the laborious process was "so much complained of by our laborers."[43] There is plenty of evidence that Monticello's African Americans made effective use of the strategies of complaint, persistent petitioning, and artful negotiation, especially in appeals for the preservation of family integrity. Philip Hubbard ran away from Poplar Forest to Monticello to complain that the overseer was preventing him from being with his wife. Jefferson interceded to unite the spouses, at the same time granting Hubbard another favor for which he had been "long petitioning"— moving from one quarter to another, where the rest of his family lived.[44] Moses Hern, a blacksmith, persisted for years in asking Jefferson to buy his wife, Mary, a slave on another plantation. Finally, in 1807, when Mary's owner was about to remove to Kentucky, Jefferson reluctantly agreed to buy her and her sons, mentioning his strong desire "to make all practicable sacrifices to keep man and wife together who have imprudently married out of their respective families"—if the purchase could be made "with convenience."[45] In several other cases, Jefferson had to make inconvenient purchases or sales because workmen, overseers, or neighbors were about to leave the area with their enslaved property, who had "imprudently" married men and women at Monticello.

Of the almost thirty married couples that can be followed in Jefferson's Monticello records, all but one remained together until the death of one partner or the end of record keeping at Jefferson's death. Enduring unions were the rule at Monticello, a situation Jefferson fostered for the sake of the smooth and profitable running of his operation, as well as an eye to the bottom line. As he wrote on more than one occasion, "a child raised every 2. years is of more profit than the crop of the best laboring man." He offered material incentives—pots and mattress covers—to women who found husbands "at home," considering his slaves "worth a great deal more in that case than when they have husbands and wives abroad."[46] Despite his wishes, the number of "abroad" marriages was continually on the rise, from about one-third of adults under forty-five in the 1780s to almost two-thirds by the 1820s.

The work of enslaved family members was not over after their long days in the shops and the fields. They supplemented their rations and gained further access to money through work they did "in their own time." Virtually all had poultry yards, selling eggs and chickens to Jefferson's household and probably in the neighborhood. At night or on Sundays, many worked in their gardens, producing a wide variety of vegetables for Jefferson's table as well as their own. Bagwell Granger, a farm laborer, was particularly enterprising, fishing in the Rivanna River, trapping animals, growing a crop of hay as well as vegetables, and—when Jefferson inaugurated a brewing operation—cultivating a hop garden.

When they could return to their own world of nights, Sundays, and occasional holidays, Monticello's African Americans participated in a flourishing cultural and spiritual life far removed from Jefferson's observation or interference. There is evidence of both thriving Christian and African religious beliefs. John Hemmings, who was literate, and his wife, Priscilla, held prayer meetings in their cabin on Mulberry Row, while the Granger family consulted a black conjurer about their worries and ailments. A number of African Americans aspired to literacy. Two former Monticello slaves recalled learning their letters from Jefferson's grandchildren. Unlike many slaveholders, Jefferson did not try to prevent his slaves from learning to read (although there is evidence he frowned on the second stage of the learning process, writing), but he apparently took no active part in providing them with an education. As he wrote in 1808, "Letters are not the first, but the last step in the progression from barbarism to civilisation."[47]

In these final years Jefferson held more slaves than at any time since the 1780s, with a high of 230 in 1817, 140 of them living at Monticello. His most articulated thoughts on his role as a slaveholder are found in this period, when he was a magnet for letters, books, and personal appeals from authors and antislavery crusaders. In 1811 he wrote of "the moral duties which [the master] owes to the slave, in return for the benefits of his service, that is to say, of food, cloathing, care in sickness, & maintenance under age & disability, so as to make him in fact as comfortable, & more secure than the laboring man in most parts of the world."[48] A slave, as both property and human being, embodied a harsh duality in which Jefferson was able to find a kind of consolation. Steeped in the moral sense philosophy of Francis Hutcheson and other Enlightenment writers, he was certain that the "soundly calculated" self-interest of individuals (and nations) was entirely compatible with moral duties. "So invariably do the laws of nature create our duties and interests," he wrote in 1804, "that when they seem to be at variance, we ought to suspect some fallacy in our reasonings."[49] Jefferson's constant recourse to the interest-duty principle, then being applied to various institutions on both sides of the Atlantic, is revealed in letters like that to his Poplar Forest steward in 1819. He wrote that "moral as well as interested considerations" dictated mild treatment of pregnant enslaved women: "In this, as in all other cases, providence has made our interests & our duties coincide perfectly."[50]

Keeping the delicate mechanism of interest and duty in perfect equilibrium was an impossible task. Jefferson was on an inexorable collision course with both the bottom line and the demands of an institution founded on and maintained by force. Further financial reverses led him again to consider sales and leases, but when someone offered to lease Poplar Forest, Jefferson wrote that "nothing could induce me to put my negroes out of my protection." In the same year, he expressed his "scruples against selling negroes but for delinquency, or on their own request" but gratefully accepted his son-in-law John Wayles Eppes's offer of a loan of $4,000, to be "paid for" two years later in slaves in Bedford County. Since Eppes's son Francis was to inherit Poplar Forest, Jefferson was relieved that "in this way they will continue undisturbed where they always have been, without separation from their families."[51] In cases of "delinquency," however, Jefferson did not relax his severity. Moral duties were waived and malfunctioning parts of the plantation machine had to be removed. Four men who attacked and stabbed the Poplar Forest overseer in 1822 were sent to New Orleans for sale. James Hubbard's second chance ended in exile, after he ran away a second time in 1811. When he was brought back to Monticello in irons after more than a year on the run, Jefferson "had him severely flogged in the presence of his old companions, and committed to jail."[52] He had already sold him in absentia.

Men who grew up under Jefferson's supervision, exemplified his expectations, and earned his trust—all Hemingses—found a surer path to freedom. Even if he thought the cultivation of character was preparing some of his slaves for lives as free men, instilling in them the "habits of property and foresight" as in the German immigrant scheme, he did little to change their status. He freed only five men in his will: John Hemmings, Joseph Fossett, Burwell Colbert, and the brothers Madison and Eston Hemings, according to a promise made to their mother. By all accounts, the humane modifications Jefferson made to slavery at Monticello made the lot of his slaves comparatively lighter than elsewhere in Virginia. Some of them told a French visitor in 1824 that they were "perfectly happy, that they were subject to no ill-treatment, that their tasks were very easy, and that they cultivated the lands of Monticello with the greater pleasure, because they were almost sure of not being torn away from them, to be transported elsewhere, so long as Mr. Jefferson lived."[53] But his death changed everything. Jefferson's fantasy of "protection" was shattered by the magnitude of his debt, and the entire

Monticello "family" was dispersed. His white relations were forced to move away, and nearly two hundred black men, women, and children mounted the auction block. Over sixty years, Jefferson "alienated" by gift or sale more than four hundred of the six hundred people that "fortune" had thrown on his hands.

After 1826

Jefferson's death was, as Israel Gillette Jefferson remembered, "an affair of great moment and uncertainty to us slaves." He and all but five of the other Monticello slaves knew they were not to be freed and feared the sales that inevitably followed.[54] Even Joseph Fossett, who was to be free a few months later, had to watch his wife and children sold to several different bidders at the estate sale in January 1827. Fossett, whom Jefferson had described as "strong and resolute," had plenty of foresight, the characteristic Jefferson always claimed was absent in a slave.[55] The Monticello blacksmith found surrogate purchasers for some of his family members before the sale and saved the money he made by working after hours. By pursuing his trade in freedom, he was able to buy back some of his children and become a property owner. Fossett clearly had the highest expectations and ambitions for his children as can be seen in his gifts of a silver watch and a writing book to his still-enslaved son Peter.[56] The Fossett family moved to Cincinnati, Ohio, in the early 1840s, where they were successful blacksmiths and caterers as well as dynamic political, religious, and educational leaders. Joseph and Edith Fossett's great-grandson was William Monroe Trotter, famous in his time as an uncompromising enemy of discrimination and racial injustice, just one of many descendants of Monticello's enslaved families who strove to make the nation live up to the ideals of freedom and equality expressed in Jefferson's Declaration of Independence.

Perfecting Slavery

Rational Plantation Management at Monticello

O N January 5, 1794, Thomas Jefferson boarded the stagecoach in Philadelphia. Weary of political conflict, he was returning to Virginia and a retirement he expected to be permanent. Six weeks earlier he had written that soon he was "to be liberated from the hated occupations of politics, and to sink into the bosom of my family, my farm, and my books. I have my house to build, my feilds to form, and to watch for the happiness of those who labor for mine." Those who labored for his happiness were the one hundred enslaved men, women, and children who lived and worked on his Albemarle County plantation.[1] Jefferson was laying aside his battle against tyranny and barbarism at the cosmic level. On the smaller stage of Monticello, however, he still was a zealous reformer, driven by the Enlightenment beliefs that inspired his private as well as public actions. Postponing the grand project of enlarging his house, he devoted himself to perfecting the operations of his plantation in accordance with laws of physical and human nature that he considered—like any good Newtonian—universal in their application. They governed the motions of the celestial bodies as well as his treble-geared threshing machine. They applied as much to blacksmiths and carpenters as to nations.

In his three years of retirement at Monticello, Jefferson, armed with timepieces, decimalized scales, and surveying instruments, used geometry and mathematics to improve the functioning of his plantation and make the work processes in his fields and shops more economic and efficient. At the same time, in conformity with his belief in the natural law that made self-interest and moral duties

This essay was originally published in *Jefferson, Lincoln, and Wilson: The American Dilemma of Race and Democracy*, ed. John Milton Cooper, Jr., and Thomas J. Knock (Charlottesville, 2010), 61–86.

inseparable, he sought ways to "watch for the happiness" of his enslaved laborers. Freedom formed no part of this plan. Jefferson had ceased battling against slavery itself and instead devoted himself to improving the condition of slaves *within* the institution. If he could not abolish slavery, then he could use his retirement to reform it at home by applying humanitarian principles to labor management. He could experiment with new "modes of government" compatible with new ways of exercising power that were being implemented all over the transatlantic world, in governments, schools, factories, and prisons. His own plantation, and a nail shop on Mulberry Row, could be run according to "the principles of reason and honesty" that he believed were central to enlightened government.[2]

Jefferson spent the first two years of his retirement in daily contact with the Monticello plantation, crisscrossing its five thousand acres to survey new field boundaries, direct the wheat harvests, measure crops of rye, and test new agricul tural machinery. This was a new era at Monticello and a new role for its proprietor. For the very first time, Jefferson was continuously and personally involved in the plantation's day-to-day operations. Previously, he had paid so little attention to the production of his staple crop that after more than thirty years as a tobacco planter, he admitted, "I never saw a leaf of my tobo. packed in my life."[3] In the mid-1790s, however, he was, in his own words, "the most ardent and active farmer in the state," possibly even "the most industrious farmer in the world."[4] After leaving Monticello to "the unprincipled ravages of overseers" for decades, he was now dedicated to improving his plantation operations on every level, from riverside field to mountaintop workshop.[5]

Scaling down his efforts to dispel the global "cloud of barbarism and despotism," Jefferson lowered his sights to his immediate surroundings and began to tackle a host of barbarisms that were entirely agricultural.[6] His closer examination revealed a land devastated by the extractive rotation of corn and tobacco. As he wrote his friend Eliza Trist, "Never had reformer greater obstacles to surmount from the barbarous mode of culture and management which had been carried on."[7]

On the culture side, the reforms Jefferson had in mind were the elimination of "the slovenly business of tobacco making" and the restoration of the fertility of the soil through approved practices like crop rotation and the planting of soil-improving crops like red clover.[8] On the management side, he strove to eliminate waste—particularly of time and labor—from every aspect of his plantation. Although he lived in a region that had long been locked into an economic system based on the waste of both land and labor, the Enlightenment quest for economy and efficiency was second nature to him, and for the next few years, he managed to remain undaunted by the challenges he faced. He reorganized the Monticello plantation, dividing it into independent quarter farms identical in size, each "cultivated by four negroes, four negresses, four oxen, and four horses," as one French visitor recorded. Each farm had seven fields of forty acres, with the fields of the home farm laid out in an actual grid over the angular upland landscape of Monticello. Jefferson's "system," as the same Frenchman observed, "is entirely confined to himself."[9]

One of the more arresting records of Jefferson's application of rational and mechanistic approaches to plantation practices was his plan for the wheat harvest of 1796.[10] He had begun preparing for this climactic event a year earlier, after the 1795 crop had been cut and stacked. "Were the harvest to go over again with the same force," he wrote in his Farm Book, "the following arrangement should take place." His first prescription revealed problems that must have beset that harvest. It called for laying down the treading floors in advance and laying in a supply of spare scythe blades and wooden "fingers" for the grain cradles. Then he proceeded to the division of labor. To each category of worker— mowers, binders, gatherers, loaders, stackers, carters, and cooks—he assigned appropriate individuals: fifty-eight men, women, and children from the age of nine to sixty-nine.

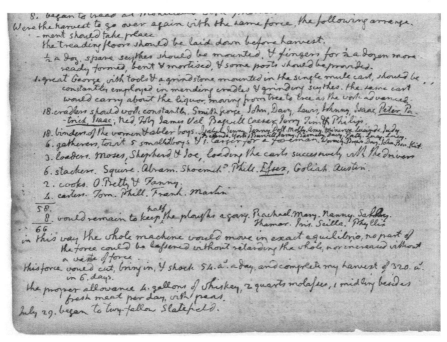

Jefferson's 1796 harvest plan, from his Farm Book. (Coolidge Collection of Thomas Jefferson Manuscripts; courtesy of the Massachusetts Historical Society)

Jefferson's "Diary of harvest" for 1796 indicates that his more-efficient plan was carried out almost exactly as he designed it.[11] Its central component was an ever sharp scythe. In the planning, he may have recalled the words of his hero Sir Francis Bacon, who had likened the "unlearned man," unable to amend his faults, to "an ill mower, that mows on still, and never whets his scythe."[12] Jefferson made the sharpening process—and thus the mowing—perpetual, by assigning to "Great George" Granger the task of advancing alongside the mowers in a mule cart, "with tools & a grindstone . . . constantly employed in mending cradles & grinding scythes." Because of Granger's continuous repairs, the "18. cradlers should work constantly." Jefferson's scheme thus did away with traditional short breaks, when scythe men stopped mowing at the signal of their leader, pulled out their whetstones, sharpened their scythes, and caught their breaths.

Jefferson's aims were clear: the elimination of idle moments, an ordered succession of interlocking tasks, and the efficiency and dependability of precision engineering. In other words, he sought to achieve the clockwork regularity of a machine. And a machine is what he called this combination of tools, carts and wagons, mules and oxen, and almost sixty human beings. At the bottom of the plan, he concluded with a flourish of Enlightenment confidence: "In this way, the whole machine would move in exact equilibrio, no part of the force could be lessened without retarding the whole nor increased without a waste of force."[13]

Even his final stipulation—an allowance of four gallons of whiskey each day—could not fuel the "machine" fast enough to achieve the speed Jefferson had predicted. The 1796 harvest of 320 acres took twelve days, instead of the estimated six, and its machinery evidently broke down at almost every step. Despite the twenty-seven scythes, the grindstone, and the repairs of George Granger, the men cut the grain at a slower rate than the year before (two acres a day instead of three). As Jefferson explained, "The wheat was so heavy for the most part that we had not more than 13. or 14. mowers cutting on an average." Even with the reduced mowing team, midway through the harvest the "pickers up" were unable to keep up with the cutters, so that eight women Jefferson had hoped could continue to drive their weeding plows through the corn fields had to be brought to the wheat field to help out.[14]

Whiskey no doubt contributed to some of the disarray. Ten years later, Jefferson called the regular allotment of ardent spirits to the laborers "an injurious & demoralising practice. They do more for a day or two but less afterwards as we see where a harvest is lengthy."[15] But liquor and the bountiful crop could not have been wholly responsible for the breakdown of the system at so many points. Two hundred years down the line, we inevitably look to the laborers, not so easy to predict and control as the laws of motion. It was common for enslaved men and women to regulate their mowing or binding speed to relieve their friends and family members. As one former Virginia slave recalled, "One could help the other when they got behind. . . . The Man what was doing the cradling would always go no faster than the woman, who was most times his wife, could keep up."[16] An inevitable conclusion is that everyone, from George Granger to the cradlers to the women and boys binding and gathering the sheaves, was engaged in collective resistance to Jefferson's all-controlling harvest machinery, which was intended to be labor saving. They found ways to save their *own* labor. And the mowing rate continued to decline over the years, despite Jefferson's use of what later agricultural writers called an "ambulatory shop."[17]

While it is a rather striking expression of how eighteenth-century gentlemen viewed people and processes in mechanistic terms, Jefferson's harvest plan was far from unique in its approach. Seventy years earlier, in a well-known letter to the Earl of Orrery, William Byrd II, of Westover, had written: "I must take care to keep all my people to their duty, to see all the springs in motion, and to make every one draw his equal share to carry the machine forward."[18] What distinguishes Jefferson from southern slaveholders of previous generations is that he considered the humanity of his slaves while reducing them to cogs in a many-wheeled machine. His return to Monticello coincided with a new mode of management that addressed his concern to "watch for the happiness" of his enslaved laborers. In an unusual experiment, he began to employ overseers from another state.

In Jefferson's view, the typical free white overseer in Virginia not only "barbarously managed" the land but was notably severe in his management of labor.[19] Family members, overseers, and former slaves recalled Jefferson as a "kind" and "indulgent" master and referred to his efforts to minimize harsh physical punishment at Monticello.[20] "I love industry and abhor severity," Jefferson wrote in 1805. In 1792 he was delighted to hear from his son-in-law that the new Monticello overseer, Manoah Clarkson, had "a valuable art of governing the slaves which sets aside the necessity of punishment allmost entirely" (a virtue that turned out too good to be true). Jefferson responded: "My first wish is that the labourers may be well treated, the second that they may enable me to have that treatment continued by making as much as will admit it. The man who can effect both objects is rarely to be found."[21]

Jefferson made one concerted effort to find men who could unite both productivity and humanity. On his regular journeys between Monticello and Philadelphia, he was impressed with the farms in Cecil County, Maryland, which had benefited from the latest approved agricultural practices. In 1792 he wrote to Jacob Hollingsworth, of Elkton, about his search for overseers: "I am anxious to provide myself from your neighborhood because the degree of farming there practised is exactly that which I think would be adopted in my possessions, and because the labour with you being chiefly by Negroes, your people of course understand the method of managing that kind of laborer."[22] Farmers in this borderland between freedom and slavery not only practiced the diversified husbandry Jefferson wished to pursue at Monticello, but, "because the labour there being performed by slaves with some mixture of free labourers," they also understood "the management of negroes on a rational and humane plan."[23]

The new regime began in late 1793 and early 1794 when Eli Alexander and Samuel Biddle moved from Elkton, Maryland, to Monticello to take up their responsibilities, Alexander on the north side of the Rivanna River and Biddle on the south, or Monticello mountain, side. This agricultural and humanitarian experiment was short-lived and never repeated. After just a few months, Jefferson described Biddle as "a poor acquisition."[24] He lasted only a year, while Alexander served for two years.[25] Jefferson's papers reveal neither what went wrong nor what, if any, were the effects of the new mode of management. At the end of 1796, Jefferson was drawn into another stretch of public service and began to lease out the quarter farms in his Monticello plantation, along with the enslaved families that lived on them. He turned his back on agriculture for the next ten years.

Consoling Jefferson through his struggle with seemingly incompatible goals was his energetic belief in the "law of nature which makes a virtuous conduct produce benefit, & vice loss to the agent, in the long run."[26] In the age-old debate over the relationship between self-interest and moral duty, Jefferson was emphatically certain: "So invariably do the laws of nature create our duties and interests, that when they seem to be at variance, we ought to suspect some fallacy in our reasonings." His confidence in this "law of nature" and its broad application is also revealed in his Second Inaugural, where he stated, "We are firmly convinced, and we act on that conviction, that with nations as with individuals, our interests soundly calculated will ever be found inseparable from our moral duties."[27]

The person of a slave, both as human and as property, was a singular embodiment of this "inseparable" combination. It is no surprise to find Jefferson harking back to the laws of nature in his role of slaveholder and plantation manager. In 1819 he wrote his steward that the high infant mortality at Poplar Forest involved "moral as well as interested considerations" and urged him to provide better treatment to the enslaved women and to "inculcate upon the overseers that it is not their labor, but their increase which is the first consideration with us." "In this, as in all other cases," he wrote, "providence has made our interests & our duties coincide perfectly."[28] For Jefferson, maximizing the efficiency of his plantation must go hand in hand with watching "for the happiness of those who labor for mine." A "happy" labor force would be the most productive and profitable.

Of course, it was no simple task to keep the mechanism of interest and duty in perfect equilibrium, and there must have been countless occasions when he had to close his mind entirely to the conflict inherent in the combination of "moral as well as interested considerations." The qualifying clause in Jefferson's letter about overseers—that his slaves might "enable" him to continue their good treatment by "making as much as will admit it"—is just one example of the mental maneuvers he had to engage in. Every decision to buy, sell, lease, or give away a slave, to punish misbehavior, or to relocate individuals tested the equation. In 1797, when his younger daughter Maria married, Jefferson wished to make her marriage settlement equal in value to her older sister's. A surviving document (obviously a fair copy made after long spells of computation) has two columns of names, thirty-one on each side, divided into males and females and listed according to their ages and thus value. Family integrity inevitably came second in this effort to calibrate human fates to make a perfect match. In this case, four children, from ten to fourteen, were separated from their families.[29]

Two of the boys made motherless by this marriage settlement worked in a shop on Mulberry Row, the site of Jefferson's most significant venture in pursuit of both his interest and his duty. For more than a year before his retirement he had been planning to add a nonagricultural activity to his Monticello operations, to provide an income "subsidiary to the farm."[30] Late in 1793, his first idea, potash production, was suddenly superseded by nail making, a process that required no skilled workers and would thus minimize the drain on labor needed in his fields. A nailery would employ only "a parcel of boys who would otherwise be idle."[31] Yet more than the efficient use of labor seems to have been at the root of Jefferson's change of mind. In Philadelphia, on December 17, 1793, he met with Quaker merchant Caleb Lownes. The next day, he placed an order with Lownes for a ton of nail rod, the imported iron product from which nails were made.[32]

Lownes was far more than an ironmonger. He is generally given credit for being the "principal agent" of penal reform in the federal city, having played a leading role in the transformation of state laws and prison management that made Philadelphia a focus of international attention for decades.[33] Philadelphia's new system of penal management was established during the years that Jefferson spent there as secretary of state. Criminals were brought in from the city streets, where they had worked encumbered by ball and chain, to a reformed Walnut Street jail that incorporated what has been called "the first penitentiary in the world."[34] There, the most hardened criminals were placed in solitary confinement, while the other inmates of the jail pursued an active regime of work from dawn to dusk—weaving and spinning, tailoring and shoemaking, stone polishing and plaster grinding, tending cabbages in the prison garden, and—by 1795—making nails. Bells sounded to mark their mealtimes and their arrival and departure from the daytime work spaces and rang every hour through the night.[35]

According to the duc de La Rochefoucauld-Liancourt, it was Caleb Lownes who initiated the change of discipline, proposing to "substitute a mild and rational, but firm treatment, in the room of irons and stripes."[36] Lownes, an indefatigable member of the prison's Board of Inspectors for a decade, wrote that "some seem to forget that the prisoner is a rational being, of like feelings and passions with themselves. Some think that he is placed there to be perpetually tormented and punished."[37]

Jefferson, like Lownes, had already absorbed the works of Beccaria and John Howard and had even engaged in prison design: the prison plan he sent home to Virginia from France in 1786 was based on a design that favored labor in solitary confinement rather than in public works and "unites in the most perfect manner the objects of security and health."[38] He almost certainly knew Lownes before they discussed the price of nail rod in December 1793, as the Quaker had been the dedicated right-hand man of Mayor Matthew Clarkson during the recent yellow fever crisis. Jefferson moved in the circles of Philadelphians, such as Benjamin Rush, who were involved in the Philadelphia Society for Alleviating the Miseries of Public Prisons. He cannot have missed what was going on at the prison just a few blocks from his Market Street residence. The elimination of corporal punishment and the importance of work, for which the prisoners were compensated, were noted by all commentators. Robert Turnbull likened the prison to a beehive when he wrote: "Such a spirit of industry [was] visible on every side and such contentment pervaded the countenances of all."[39]

Nail making apparently did not join the panoply of occupations at the prison until 1795, but Lownes, as a purveyor of nail rod, may have considered adding this trade—soon to be a staple in American penitentiaries—when he met with Jefferson at the end of 1793.[40] Whether or not the Monticello nailery was directly inspired by Lownes and the Walnut Street prison, Jefferson's methods of managing his nail makers were certainly influenced by the ideas that sustained penal reform at this time. From the 1770s, writers like Jeremy Bentham had begun to apply the principle of the junction of interest and duty to institutions of superintendence. Rational modes of management were applicable to all forms of "government," not just the purely political, and especially to institutions that involved discipline and control—prisons, poorhouses, hospitals, asylums, schools, and factories.[41] The reformed Walnut Street jail, in the eyes of its observers, incorporated elements of these other institutions. In 1798 one writer described it

as "more resembling a College than a prison," remarking that it gave "the pleasing idea of a great manufactory combining in its appearance taste with utility."[42]

From its beginning in the spring of 1794, the Monticello nailery combined
the attributes of a school and a prison, as well as a factory. For Jefferson, it was
not just an adventure of industrial entrepreneurship. It was an experimental laboratory for working out new ideas about exercising power, a place to try to manage
enslaved labor in harmony with current ideas of humanitarian reform. Stopping
short of utopian fantasy, he had joined the search for perfected social systems.
While Jefferson never explicitly described or promoted his enterprise in humanitarian terms, there are many indications that it was conceived and carried
out in the same paternal spirit as reformed institutions in the new republic,
where prisons and factories, not just academies, were being touted as "nurseries
of virtue."[43]

"I now employ a dozen little boys from 10. to 16. years of age, overlooking all the
details of their business myself," Jefferson wrote in the second year of the nailery's
operation.[44] This supervision included daily visits to the shop to weigh iron and
constant monitoring of the youthful labor force. Critical to the enterprise—as
for the Walnut Street prison—was the removal of violence from the system of
discipline. In 1801, Jefferson warned a new nailery manager to refrain from using
the whip, which "must not be resorted to but in extremities."[45] How, then, were
a dozen teenagers, cooped up in a smoky shop, to be kept at a boring and repetitive task for ten to fourteen hours a day according to the season? The duc de La
Rochefoucauld-Liancourt, who was intensely interested in prison reform, spent
a week at Monticello and must have talked with Jefferson about the nailery and
its management. His published account of his visit is disappointingly laconic:
"The children [Jefferson] employs in a nail-manufactory, which yields already a
considerable profit." But he did acknowledge the new disciplinary regime: "He
animates them by rewards and distinctions."[46]

Isaac Granger, an enslaved youth who worked in the nailery as well as the blacksmith shop, later remembered that the nailers received special meat and fish
rations and that Jefferson gave "them that wukked the best a suit of red or blue;
encouraged them mightily."[47] In keeping with the late eighteenth-century enthusiasm for the motivating power of emulation, Jefferson improved the performance
of the nailers through competition and built esprit de corps through distinctions.
The incredibly painstaking accounts that he transcribed after his daily visits to
the shop include columns of the weights of both nail rod and nails, so that he could
calculate efficiency as well as productivity. Thus he could write in 1794, "Jamey
wastes 29.83 lb. in the [hundredweight]." Sporadic computations in the accounts
reveal that as soon as a boy achieved a certain rate of "waste," Jefferson set him
a new efficiency goal. This policy seems to have been successful in steadily

Jefferson's nailery accounts, 1796. (Courtesy of the William Andrews Clark Memorial Library, University of California, Los Angeles)

improving performance. Jamey (i.e., James Hubbard), from being one of the most wasteful nail makers when he began at the age of eleven, had by age thirteen decreased his loss to 10 percent. As a group the young nailers even surpassed what was considered the "common" iron loss in the trade of 14 percent.[48]

In the case of the adult workers on the plantation, Jefferson encouraged industry through actual financial incentives. Up to the 1790s he had occasionally given his enslaved workmen what he called "gratuities," that is, gratuitous payments made without expectation or prior arrangement.[49] Henceforth, however, he began to distribute small sums of money by agreement, and with the specific aim of animating work that went beyond the ordinary. To fuel the newly established nailery, Jefferson hired a free white man, Jacob Silknitter, to produce charcoal and to train slaves in the charcoal-burning process.[50] After Silknitter left, an enslaved man, Frank, carried on the periodic charcoal-burning according to terms Jefferson penned into his memorandum book: "I am always to give Frank a half dime for every bushel to the cord of wood which his coal kilns yield. His last yielded thirty bushels to the cord: therefore paid 1.5 D."[51] In his pursuit of half dimes, Frank was producing thirty-nine bushels to the cord by the time of his third kiln. Jefferson's agreement with his charcoal burner reveals a prime objective in his ongoing battle against waste. He paid Frank not according to the quantity of charcoal he produced but according to the efficiency with which he burned it. This is an understandable goal given the staggering amounts of wood required for the charcoal kilns—as many as two hundred cords a year at the height of nailery operations.[52]

It is also another indication of the Jeffersonian blend of system and sympathy, interest and duty. In Jefferson's view, Nature had drawn "indelible lines of distinction" between whites and blacks, who were inferior in "the endowments both of body and mind."[53] Those distinctions did not, however, exile blacks from the human family. They behaved according to the same laws of human nature as whites. They had the same desire to excel, and thus their labor could be encouraged by similar appeals to reason. Jefferson made clear his expectations in a letter of 1797 to his son-in-law John Wayles Eppes. Since Eppes did not yet have a fully equipped shop, Jefferson advised him to find alternative occupations for his enslaved blacksmith: "You would do well to employ Isaac in the mean time in preparing coal for his year's work. He should have about 2000. bushels laid in. Nor will it be amiss to cord his wood in order to excite him to an emulation in burning it well."[54]

Measurement dogged every step of the enslaved men associated with the nailery, whether they were stacking wood for charcoal kilns or swinging a hammer to make tenpenny nails. Jefferson continued to keep precise records of charcoal burning—dimensions of kilns, numbers of bushels, and payments by the original formula. They show that David Hern, Monticello's charcoal burner in the years of Jefferson's final retirement, achieved a very respectable average of thirty-five bushels of charcoal to the cord of wood. And, in 1819, Jefferson began to use a new term to describe his payments to Hern: "Davy has burnt a kiln yeilding 1016. bushels which is 33.86 bushels to the cord, & makes his premium 1.70 D."[55] The word "premium" had been used for some time in the education field as well as in learned societies (Jefferson himself had earned a gold medal as a "premium" in 1806 for his moldboard of least resistance).[56] It became more common in the first decades of the nineteenth century, when the rhetoric of emulation had intensified along with the rise of agricultural societies and their attendant competitions and fairs. Agricultural journals were full of references to the need to "excite" a "spirit of emulation," and many writers voiced the opinion that premiums were the key to agricultural improvement.[57] Excellence was measurable in the charcoal-burning and nail-making operations. In trades where it was not, Jefferson focused on production rather than efficiency. He allowed his enslaved coopers to keep one of every thirty-one flour barrels they made for their own benefit and referred to their incentives as "allowances" rather than premiums.[58]

With the enslaved manager of the nailery, Jefferson entered into an almost contractual profit-sharing agreement, similar to his contracts with the free men who at times directed his textile and blacksmith shops. From 1794, head blacksmith George Granger, the son of "Great George" Granger the scythe sharpener, was in charge, combining his supervision of the nailers with his own work at the forge. Jefferson "allowed" him 3 percent of the total sales of nails. As the nailery became more productive, Granger's percentage of gross sales was reduced to 2 percent. Still, he earned about forty dollars in 1796, and again in 1797, a considerable sum for an enslaved man.[59] When Jefferson returned to public life in 1797, Granger was Jefferson's understudy as quality-control manager. The effectiveness of his management was made manifest by the state of affairs after he fell ill in 1798: the business went on "poorly," with a significant decrease in both the volume and quality of nails, and at one point nail making almost ceased altogether.[60] The nailery showed a striking profit in its first years, when George Granger was in good health, even in Jefferson's absence.[61]

Yet Jefferson's daily presence, from 1794 to 1797, was also undoubtedly a significant factor in its success. For reasons beyond economy, it was important that he carry on his works with "little boys." Even when he wished to significantly expand the nailery's operations in 1796, Jefferson did not turn to older farm laborers. He brought three eleven-year-old boys from his Bedford County plantation, Poplar Forest, ninety miles away, and, in a rare step, purchased two others.[62] That Jefferson was conducting a kind of academy on the mountaintop is also suggested by the fact that the nail boys seem to have been housed together, not with their families.[63] His corps of youthful nailers was, as Jefferson said of prospective University of Virginia students, "at that age of aptness, docility, and emulation of the practices of manhood" when lessons were "soonest learnt and longest remembered."[64] Young African Americans were rational beings, their characters as susceptible of improvement as the Pennsylvania criminals transferred from labor on the "high roads" to the confines of the reformed Walnut Street prison. Exhibiting these prisoners "as a public spectacle," Jefferson wrote, "with shaved heads and mean clothing . . . produced in the criminals such a prostration of character, such an abandonment of self-respect, as, instead of reforming, plunged them into the most desperate and hardened depravity of morals and character."[65]

As manager, schoolmaster, and warden, Jefferson focused on the characters of the enslaved teenagers in his nailery. He could harness the universal human desire to excel to turn tons of nail rod into thousands of nails. In early 1801, soon to return to Monticello for a spring break, Jefferson wrote home to enjoin mild treatment of the nailers. As they "will be again under my government, I would chuse they should retain the stimulus of character."[66] His explicit references to the molding of slave character are scarce, but there are echoes of his ideas in the words, some years later, of his son-in-law Thomas Mann Randolph, whose plantation adjoining Monticello was another laboratory for new methods of management. After hearing of the suicide of a slave on a nearby plantation, Randolph wrote a friend that he no longer needed "the old mode of government" and had long ago "dismissed the man-whip" from his own property: "I find however that the cane of a Corporal must be tolerated yet. But I allways scrupulously distinguish, and exempt, manly and moral character, when it shews itself with any steadiness of ray in the sooty atmosphere of our slave discipline." In Randolph's view, the overseer at the other plantation "could not understand the value of character in a slave, and concluded that fear would be safer security for good conduct than any determination to do right."[67]

The duc de La Rochefoucauld-Liancourt highlighted the changing attitudes toward management and discipline in this period of transition at the end of the eighteenth century, noting how a young judge of the Pennsylvania supreme court, one of the leading lights of the penal reform movement, was "less inclined" than his older colleagues "to despair of the melioration of the human character."[68] Jefferson applied similar principles to education. He described "the best mode of government for youth" in one of the founding documents of the University of Virginia: "Pride of character, laudable ambition, and moral dispositions . . . have a happier effect on future character than the degrading motive of fear." He recommended instead the "affectionate deportment between father and son" as the "best example" for tutor and pupil. This system, "founded in reason and comity, will be more likely to nourish, in the minds of our youth, the combined spirit of order and self respect, so congenial with our political institutions, and so important to be woven into the American character."[69]

Although Jefferson tried to make his plantation more politically "congenial" through the introduction of "reason and comity" into the government of his slaves, the qualities he was trying to encourage were not intended to be woven into the fabric of the American character. Reformed prisons and enlightened educational institutions restored or prepared individuals as useful citizens in a free society. The Monticello nailery, however, was a prison for life, a school for slavery, training up useful members of Jefferson's economic enterprise. Both he and his son-in-law were most concerned with the "*value* of character" in their slaves. In his letter urging restraint in corporal punishment of the nailers, Jefferson wrote that "it would destroy their value, in my estimation, to degrade them in their own eyes by the whip."[70]

Jefferson tried to minimize the "degrading motive of fear" and to instill character traits that were no different from those he—and most employers—sought in free workmen: industry and honesty. Sobriety, the third trait he sought, in vain, in free workmen was less of an issue in the case of his enslaved workers, who had little access to alcohol.[71] The inspectors of the Walnut Street prison had similar aims, according to rules drawn up in 1792: "The prisoners who distinguish themselves by their attention to cleanliness, sobriety, industry and orderly conduct, shall . . . meet with such rewards as is in their power to grant or procure for them."[72] While exciting emulation helped to achieve industry, Jefferson pursued honesty by methods that were quite unusual for the time and place. He allowed his enslaved smiths and carpenters a surprising freedom from supervision. Thomas Mann Randolph wrote his father-in-law in 1798 referring to "the thorough confidence you place in the companies of tradesmen" and expressing his fear that "being under no command whatever they will become idle and dissipated." He acknowledged the management goal he shared with Jefferson when he concluded, "Tho' I am clear that it confirms them in honesty."[73] Both Jefferson and Randolph understood "honesty" in its broad, eighteenth-century sense, as signifying virtue, integrity, and morality, not just veracity. According to Jefferson's "creed on the foundation of morality in man," it could be demonstrated "by sound calculation that honesty promotes interest in the long run."[74]

The enslaved men's greater degree of autonomy was not just a result of Jefferson's labor reforms. It was also a function of the transition, made at Monticello in the 1790s, from tobacco culture to a more diversified operation with wheat as the staple crop. Since wheat cultivation required about one-fifth the amount of labor as tobacco, more attention could be given to raising subsidiary crops and livestock. This more complex enterprise required more vehicles and draft animals, more complicated machinery, and workers with a greater variety of skills. Multiple activities that spread themselves across the entire plantation landscape were beyond the range of a single overseer. The master or overseer now had to focus on the products of his workers rather than on the labor process. Archaeological excavations at Monticello have shown that there was increased autonomy in the slave quarters as well as in the fields. On Mulberry Row, single-family dwellings replaced the larger multifamily structures of the 1770s. On the plantation, cabins that had once been clustered near the overseer's house were, by the turn of the century, moved to the fringes of the greatly expanded plow lands and scattered about on their own.[75]

It is interesting that this greater autonomy on the plantation occurred at a time when Jefferson's own vigilance was dramatically increased by his full-time presence at Monticello, from 1794 to 1797. These were the years when Jefferson monitored the performance of the nailers on a daily—even twice-daily—basis. Considered in the context of surveillance, his small Virginia mountain begins to take on the shape of a panopticon, with Jefferson, elevated above the surrounding landscape and its inhabitants, inspecting the workings of his world. Monticello thus echoes Jeremy Bentham's panopticon, an ideal prison that incorporated both the principle of the junction of interest and duty and the more infamous "inspection principle" with its "invisible eye."

At the center of Bentham's panopticon design, the warden, shielded by venetian blinds, was able to see into every cell but was invisible to the prisoners. Jefferson, in 1797, included such blinds (which, he wrote, "exclude the sight" while admitting air) in his plan for a Virginia penitentiary, and he had them added to every house he lived in. At Monticello, he had built what he called "Venetian porches," or "porticles," with louvered blinds, that adjoined his private apartments, and thus, from inside, he could see without being seen.[76]

In the preface to *Panopticon*, Bentham described his "simple idea in Architecture" as "a new mode of obtaining power of mind over mind."[77] There is no question that the African Americans within the Sage of Monticello's extensive panorama were acutely conscious of an all-seeing Jefferson and his Enlightenment optical equipment. In his recollections late in life, Peter Fossett, who was a child of eleven when Jefferson died, combined the telescope he could see every day on Monticello's North Terrace with Revolutionary War events he had heard about from older family members: "One day while Mr. Jefferson was looking through his telescope to see how the work was progressing over at Pan Top, one of his plantations, he saw 500 soldiers, headed by Col. Tarleton, . . . coming up the north side of the mountain to capture him." It is curious that Fossett chose Pantops, which means "all-seeing," as the quarter farm Jefferson was inspecting. Similarly, a black man who had worked on the construction of the University of Virginia, three miles distant from Monticello, recalled Jefferson standing in the yard, watching "we alls at work through his spyglass."[78] Jefferson's perpetual attention was also conveyed through sound as well as sight: he acquired a Chinese gong to broadcast the measurement of time "all over my farm."[79]

When Jefferson was called back into public service in 1797, his reforming experiments at Monticello came to a standstill. He leased out his quarter farms and their laborers, while the pursuit of agriculture on the home farm was so minimal that its fields grew up in broomsedge.[80] Jefferson was "overshadowed . . . with despair" because of his inability to pursue a systematic reformation of his farm and the treatment of its laborers. He admitted to a sense of defeat in his dual pursuit of profit and humanity when he wrote in 1799, "I am not fit to be a farmer with the kind of labour that we have."[81] While president, Jefferson poured his resources into rebuilding his house and pressing on with several monumental earthmoving projects: clearing roads, digging a canal for his mills, and leveling a 1,000-foot vegetable garden terrace. Enslaved men hired from other owners bore the brunt of this work, while the African American men who remained on the Monticello mountaintop carried on with their gardening, wagoning, woodworking, and blacksmithing tasks.

Work in the nailery continued but in a much-altered form. The nail boys had grown up, and it was mainly a crew of young men in their twenties who carried on the work on a reduced scale. Dependable management had ended with the death of George Granger in 1799. In 1801, Jefferson hired a free white blacksmith from Philadelphia to supervise the nailers as well as work at the forge. The highly talented but often inebriated William Stewart was unable to cope with them: "They require a rigour of discipline to make them do reasonable work, to which he cannot bring himself."[82] A shifting set of overseers, some known to be quick to use the whip, took charge, and there were episodes of violence and misbehavior.

James Hubbard, the nailer whose efficiency had risen so swiftly in the early days, became a chronic runaway, was flogged in the presence of his fellow workers, and was sold—in keeping with Jefferson's policy of removing disruptive elements from the plantation.[83] In 1803, when Jefferson was in Washington, eighteen-year-old Cary violently struck a fellow nailer, Brown Colbert, with his hammer, nearly killing him. Jefferson ordered swift plantation justice: "Should Brown recover so that the law shall inflict no punishment on Cary, it will be necessary for me to make an example of him in terrorem to others, in order to maintain the police so rigorously necessary among the nailboys." Cary's fate was that most feared by enslaved people—sale to the Deep South. If no Georgia slave trader happened to pass by, wrote Jefferson, "if he could be sold in any other quarter so distant as never more to be heard of among us, it would to the others be as if he were put out of the way by death."[84] This was the Monticello equivalent to sending a prisoner to solitary confinement, which Caleb Lownes had described as "an object of *real terror*" to all in the Walnut Street prison.[85] One incident in 1807 indicates the persistence of Jefferson's "power of mind" and the motivating force of character. Monticello overseer Edmund Bacon discovered the hiding place of several hundred pounds of nails, worth fifty dollars or more, stolen by one of the nailers. He caught the thief, who was brought before Jefferson: "I never saw any person, white or black, feel as badly as he did when he saw his master. He was mortified and distressed beyond measure. He had been brought up in the shop, and we all had confidence in him. Now his character was gone. The tears streamed down his face, and he begged pardon over and over again."[86]

On the whole, Jefferson succeeded in producing a set of enslaved artisans who were highly skilled, productive, and dependable. Several of the first occupants of the nailery became blacksmiths, carpenters, or wagoners. Others occupied the positions of butler, cooper, gardener, and shoemaker. Former nailers had charge of Jefferson's house, stables, garden, and shops. One of them, Wormley Hughes, when he was the thirty-year-old head gardener and head stable man at Monticello, was, in Jefferson's eyes, "one of the most trusty servants I have."[87]

No matter how honest and industrious they were, the Monticello tradesmen could never achieve instant liberty through good behavior, as could inmates of the Walnut Street jail, where pardons were granted to prisoners who were considered rehabilitated. Jefferson had no intention of freeing his slaves as long as slavery was the law in Virginia. He does, however, seem to have been thinking of their ultimate future in freedom, however remote. He was beginning to carry out, within the confines of Monticello, part of his plan of gradual emancipation, which included expatriation beyond the boundaries of the United States. The attributes he was trying to develop in his enslaved tradesmen are like those described in his emancipation scheme as a preparation for freedom and citizenship, even if in a distant land. The slaves were entitled, eventually, to the blessings of democracy, a word Jefferson rarely used and never in the way we do today.[88] As he wrote in 1815, "The mind . . . of the slave is to be prepared by instruction and habit for self-government, and for the honest pursuits of industry and social duty."[89]

Whether or not he was intentionally preparing them for freedom, his pursuit of the "happiness" of his slaves in conjunction with his own gave them tools to pursue their own ideas of happiness. The development of skills as well as "character" provided some of the prerequisites for freedom, a measure of personal autonomy, and the capacity for self-government. This is not to suggest that the enslaved men needed Jefferson's training to acquire such traits. But under his humanitarian management they had a broader and safer space in which to "soundly calculate" their own best interests than did many of their fellow slaves. Most of them concluded that productivity and trustworthiness were of greatest benefit to themselves and their families. And in several cases, the end result was freedom.

Jefferson apparently had considered bequeathing freedom to three of the original corps of nailers for some time. He freed butler Burwell Colbert and blacksmith Joseph Fossett in his will and recommended unofficial freedom for gardener Wormley Hughes. His granddaughter Ellen Coolidge, who had left Monticello a year before Jefferson's death, recalled that several of the slaves "knew that at his death they were to become free—he had promised it to those among them who, possessing a trade by which they could support themselves, ran no risk of falling burthens on the community, or of being reduced to unlawful means of living."[90]

In the absence of any Emancipation Acts on the state or national level, Jefferson's recipe for dealing with slavery depended, as he told Isaac Briggs in 1820, on "improving the condition of this poor, afflicted, degraded race," which would eventually end in their "equal liberty and the enjoyment of equal rights."[91] Yet the rational and moral society Jefferson imagined for Monticello remained unperfected, and it never served as a shining example to help achieve a revolution in public opinion, much less a general emancipation. Despite their humanitarian reforms, he and other more enlightened slaveholders failed to convince a skeptical world of any improvement in southern society. Two British women were among those who made this point. In 1818, Frances Wright, while acknowledging the humanity of Virginia slaveholders in their efforts to ameliorate the conditions of their slaves, considered that they were merely "gilding" rather than breaking the chains of slavery. Seventeen years later, Harriet Martineau lamented the "blunting of the moral sense of the most conscientious" of the southerners she met.[92] Soon the humanitarian rhetoric of the ameliorators would be co-opted by southerners extolling the benefits of their way of life. The cherished axiom that had consoled Jefferson in his efforts to humanize the institution of slavery was perverted to defend it. Virginia-born William H. Holcombe invoked the deity in 1860: "As the calls for the abolition of slavery became world-wide, eventually just about all Southerners would come to believe they not only had a right to own slaves, but were serving a God-given duty in owning slaves in order to improve them. . . . God has lightened our task and secured its execution by making our interests happily coincide with our duty."[93]

While Dr. Holcombe and other proslavery writers were making their cases, the flame of genuine Jeffersonian ideals was maintained largely by African Americans, plus a small band of white abolitionists. Descendants of Monticello's enslaved men and women were among those who worked steadily through the nineteenth and early twentieth centuries to make the nation live up to the ideals of its founding document, Jefferson's Declaration. The family of one of Monticello's original nailers is exemplary. Joseph Fossett had worked in the nailery from the age of fourteen. After training as a blacksmith, he was in charge of the Monticello shop for twenty years. While Fossett was freed in Jefferson's will, his wife and eight children were not, and all were put on the auction block six months after Jefferson's death. Joe Fossett availed himself of his money-earning skills as a blacksmith and his character as a man who could be trusted: he was able to persuade local white merchants to purchase some of his children until he could repay them. By mid-century, Fossett, his wife, Edith, and all but one of their children had left the world of slavery and were living in Cincinnati, where they owned a house and blacksmith shop.

It is clear that Joseph Fossett had high ambitions for his children. The importance of education, as well as social status, is indicated by his gift of a writing-book and a silver watch to his still-enslaved son, Peter. Peter Fossett and his brothers became dynamic leaders in Cincinnati's political, religious, and educational life and its leading caterers after the Civil War. And the entire family was incessantly active in opposing the institution of slavery—through the forging of free passes, the sheltering of fugitives on the Underground Railroad, the integration of streetcars, and through putting civil rights laws to the test.[94] Joseph and Edith Fossett's character emerged most strongly in their great-grandson William Monroe Trotter, the famously dedicated and uncompromising warrior on behalf of liberty and equality, who raised the ire of Woodrow Wilson in one of many spirited encounters with American presidents. In W. E. B. Du Bois's words, Trotter was "a man of heroic proportions, and probably one of the most selfless of Negro leaders during all our American history."[95] The *Philadelphia Tribune* saluted Trotter on his sixtieth birthday: "For 30 years he has been foremost among those who have borne the 'toil and heat of the day' battling unceasingly, unrelentingly for those rights guaranteed colored Americans by the Declaration of Independence."[96]

Part II

FAMILIES
IN SLAVERY

The Other End
of the Telescope

Jefferson through the Eyes
of His Slaves

IN November 1998, an assortment of historians hopped off the fence on to solid ground, joining a lonely band already there and joined by a few who had seemed firmly rooted on the other side. Since the results of Dr. Eugene Foster's DNA study became known, the staff at Monticello, too, have been shifting their positions on the issue of Thomas Jefferson's paternity of Sally Hemings's children. A deceptively simple genetic diagram excited the believers, disconcerted the nonbelievers, and galvanized many of Monticello's own fence-sitters to re-examine the evidence. A few months after the revelations, an informal telephone survey of almost forty employees (one-third of them guides) revealed that many were reading or rereading Annette Gordon-Reed's *Thomas Jefferson and Sally Hemings: An American Controversy.* It also showed that before November 1, 1998, these staff members had been about equally divided among those who accepted the Jefferson-Hemings relationship, those who discounted it, and those who were undecided. After DNA, believers almost doubled, a lone individual stated continuing disbelief, and the rest are hedging their bets.

The interpretation of Jefferson's Monticello has always relied heavily on primary sources, with which we are richly supplied—from Jefferson's own monumental archive of 65,000 documents to the abundant written testimony of family members, overseers, neighbors, and visitors. Each eyewitness account of life at Monticello is treated as a kind of sacred reliquary, from which small gems are extracted to enhance the presentation of Jefferson's daily habits, domestic character, or cultural interests. When, very rarely, a new narrative surfaces, it is immediately plundered for colorful tidbits to embellish the stories told on the mountain.

This essay was originally published as part of a Forum, "Thomas Jefferson and Sally Hemings Redux," in the *William and Mary Quarterly* 57, no. 1 (January 2000): 139–152.

Now, because of the almost seismic effect of a scientific test, we will never again read the words of Jefferson and the members of his household in quite the same way. The core feature of the Jefferson family denial—that Peter Carr or Samuel Carr was the father of Hemings's children—has been discredited by chromosomes and haplotypes. Have the accounts of Jefferson's grandchildren Thomas Jefferson Randolph and Ellen Randolph Coolidge lost some of their credibility because, in this one area, they seem to have misrepresented the truth so materially?

The strikingly articulate chronicles of Ellen Coolidge, mostly unpublished, range widely in their coverage of Jefferson's opinions, his musical tastes, and his financial tribulations. Now that our trust has been shaken, how do we interpret her expansive account of her grandfather's religious views, especially in light of her own dedicated Christianity? What about her lopsided assessment of Jefferson's daughters, comparing her mother, a paragon of intelligence and talent, to her aunt, Maria Eppes, "not remarkable for capacity or cultivation"? Although Ellen's brother Thomas, the originator of the Carr nephew thesis, was a clumsy writer, he left interesting recollections of life in the White House and at Monticello. While we would hate to do without the glimpses of plantation life and routines he provides, his post–Civil War assessment of the moral climate in Jefferson's Virginia arouses skepticism: "A married man who kept a slave concubine lost caste. An overseer who had such intercourse with married slave women or openly with single ones was dismissed. There was as much chastity among our white males as to be found in any community."[1]

Science has thus provided a worthwhile lesson in the interpretation of evidence. A genetic test has roused us from a complacent, and sometimes selective, acceptance of our favorite letters, memoirs, or travel accounts. We have been warned to read them whole, to keep in mind the context in which they were written, and to beware of favoring some elements and forgetting others that are problematic.

No account of life at Monticello has been used more selectively than that of Sally Hemings's son Madison. Historians have been inclined to accept all his statements about his genealogy except one. In their view, Madison Hemings knew the identity of his grandfather (John Wayles) but not of his father. The details he provided about his family members have been gratefully incorporated into accounts of life at Monticello, but his views of the man he considered his father have been treated with suspicion. In one case, his accurate, even perceptive, observation that Jefferson in his retirement years had "but little taste or care for agricultural pursuits" was used to undermine Hemings's overall credibility as a witness.[2]

I would like to consider in a preliminary way how Madison Hemings and other African American residents of Monticello perceived the man who viewed them as property. The voices of the enslaved community at Monticello are represented by four substantial reminiscences, a few brief statements recorded by white men, a handful of letters, and several stories that have been passed down through the generations.[3] These accounts warrant close examination and interpretation by folklorists and anthropologists as well as historians. Here I wish only to suggest the themes of trust and dependence they share and to present a perspective on the master of Monticello—the flip side of paternalism—that has hitherto been given little consideration.

In 1873, Madison Hemings lived in a rural community in southern Ohio, an area settled largely by Virginians, both black and white. Freed by Jefferson's will at the age of twenty-two, he had left Virginia for Ohio with his wife and child in 1836, after the death of his mother. There he supported his family with woodworking skills acquired in the Monticello joinery and continued to work as a carpenter and wheelwright after purchasing his own farm in 1865.[4] In spring 1873, a Republican newspaper editor, S. F. Wetmore, after conducting more than thirty interviews with white men of Ross and Pike Counties, embarked on a new set of portraits of local citizens in their own words. Madison Hemings was the first in this short-lived second series, which focused on black residents and borrowed a subtitle from Harriet Beecher Stowe for its title, "Life among the Lowly." In his introduction to the interview, Wetmore flourished some righteously indignant remarks about an institution that caused a father to deprive his son of an education. This saber-rattling introduction, the editor's political party, and the partisan response of the local Democratic paper have led some historians to suggest that the transcribed interview may have as much Wetmore as Hemings in it.[5]

In contrast to Wetmore's introduction, Hemings's account is remarkably sober, even dispassionate, and not openly judgmental. He recognized Jefferson's fame and catalogued his temperament: rarely angry, "smooth and even," "very undemonstrative." Jefferson, "the quietest of men," "was uniformly kind to all about him." Any feelings the man he called "father" might have had for his mother went unmentioned. Love and affection entered Hemings's reminiscence only in his reference to Jefferson's courtship of Martha Wayles Skelton and in his comparison of Jefferson's treatment of his Randolph grandchildren, to whom he was "affectionate," with that of Hemings and his siblings, to whom he was "not in the habit of showing partiality or fatherly affection."[6]

Some commentators have seen bitterness in Hemings's allusion to this distinction, as well as his reference to the need for "inducing" the white children (presumably those same favored grandchildren) to teach him his letters.[7] To my mind, they seem more the sober observations of a man making a realistic review of a long life. Hemings knew the Virginia of the early nineteenth century. Some men recognized their slave children or educated them beyond what society viewed as their station, but slaveholders who treated their enslaved offspring in this way were few, and most of them did not also have a legitimate family of white children and grandchildren. None of them was a former president.

Madison Hemings does make clear one attribute that, in his mind, set this white man apart from most of his southern peers. Jefferson was a man of his word. When Hemings related how Dolley Madison promised his mother a fine gift for naming her child Madison, he concluded: "Like many promises of white folks to the slaves she never gave my mother anything." He prominently featured the agreement Jefferson made with his mother to free her children when they reached age twenty-one, using the words "promise" (twice), "solemn pledge," and "treaty."[8] Jefferson kept this promise to the letter, even though it provoked considerable local gossip and entailed actions that were unprecedented at Monticello. No other nuclear slave family was freed in its entirety, and no other Monticello slave— except one runaway—was freed before the age of thirty-one.[9] Jefferson gave Madison Hemings what few sons of slave women received—a skilled trade, if not an education, and the freedom to pursue it for his own benefit.

Although he does not seem to have been as widely rumored to be Jefferson's son as his brother Eston, Madison Hemings was not averse to making known his connection to someone he called "a foremost man in the land." An Ohio census taker added an exclamatory sentence to the 1870 form: "This man is the son of Thomas Jefferson!" And in 1873 Hemings gave his interview to Wetmore, knowing it would be published in a town infamous for its treatment of blacks. Wetmore described Hemings as "an intelligent man" who "understands himself well." "If he had been educated and given a chance in the world," he continued, "he would have shone out as a star of the first magnitude." Besides Wetmore's description, only one comment on Madison Hemings's character has come down to us, through the oral history of a white family in the neighborhood. He, too, was a man who could be trusted: "His word was his bond."[10]

Another former Monticello slave echoed the theme of Jefferson's trustworthiness in the same year. Israel Gillette Jefferson, a domestic servant and postilion at Monticello, was also interviewed by Wetmore. He related one of two known versions of a story, told by the older Hemings women at Monticello, that Jefferson had "promised his wife, on her death bed, that he would not again marry." The fulfillment of this deathbed promise, also mentioned by former Monticello overseer Edmund Bacon, was of less concern to Israel Jefferson than its bearing on his confirmation of Madison Hemings's earlier account. Israel Jefferson stated that he knew Sally Hemings to be Thomas Jefferson's "concubine" and told Wetmore that he could "as conscientiously confirm" Madison Hemings's declaration that he was Jefferson's son "as any other fact which I believe from circumstances but do not positively know."[11]

Unlike Madison Hemings, Israel Gillette Jefferson was not freed by Jefferson. With the aid of his wife, a free woman of color and a seamstress, he purchased his freedom in the 1830s from Thomas Walker Gilmer, who had bought him at one of the estate sales after Jefferson's death. When Israel Gillette went to the courthouse to get his free papers, he was persuaded to take the surname Jefferson because, the clerk said, he had been "a good and faithful servant" at Monticello. Israel and Elizabeth Jefferson proceeded to Ohio and eventually settled in the same community as Madison Hemings, where both husband and wife were active in the Baptist church.[12]

Israel Jefferson, who had to make his own way to freedom and who was not the son of the master, struck a different tone in his account, which is more highly colored than that of his friend Madison Hemings. He diplomatically refrained from making direct assessments of Jefferson, except to say that he "was esteemed by both whites and blacks as a very great man." Instead, he introduced into his narrative a character who stood in marked contrast to the Sage of Monticello. The marquis de Lafayette visited Monticello in 1824, when the young Israel was a postilion. One day, from his position on one of the horses drawing Jefferson's landau carriage, Israel overheard the "great and good Lafayette" deploring the institution of slavery and the condition of slaves. Two hearts are present in this account, neither one Jefferson's. For fifty years Israel Jefferson "treasured . . . up in [his] heart" this conversation about a situation that "seemed to grieve [Lafayette's] noble heart." Jefferson is the foil to the Frenchman in this anecdote, which Israel Jefferson told in a way that required no critical commentary. He let Jefferson speak for himself, reporting his comments on ending slavery ("the time would come," but Jefferson "did not indicate when or in what manner") and educating slaves (they could be taught to read but not to write, as then they could not be "kept in subjugation")—lackluster alternatives to Lafayette's vigorous expressions on the same subjects.[13]

While Madison Hemings stated that he and his siblings "were the only children of [Jefferson's] by a slave woman," Israel Jefferson did not refer to the nature of the relationship.[14] The other two full-length accounts by former Monticello slaves are completely silent on the subject of Jefferson's relations with enslaved women, and no further comments on Jefferson's sexual habits have been found until the collection of some stories in the mid-twentieth century, passed down in branches of the Hemings family. In 1948 and 1949, Pearl Graham conducted interviews with several descendants of Elizabeth (Betty) Hemings. A descendant of Betty Hemings's oldest daughter, Mary, told her that Mary Hemings was "one of the three colored women by whom Jefferson had children." In a 1954 article in *Ebony* magazine and in interviews in the 1990s, descendants of two of Mary Hemings's children have continued to relate the family tradition that Jefferson was their ancestor. Graham also interviewed three daughters of Mary Cole Kenney, descendant of an unidentified Hemings family member. The three sisters, who grew up in Charlottesville, spoke of Jefferson's "promiscuity" and mentioned "a tradition among descendants of Jefferson's servants, that he was wont to accost one of his mistresses—a plantation washerwoman—on the paths taken by her in returning laundry to the mansion, and there compel her to submit to him." Another Charlottesville resident, who had known many of the Monticello descendants, told Graham that it was "handed down in his family traditions" that Jefferson was "unscrupulous in his sexual demands upon colored women."[15]

In contrast to the neutrality of Madison Hemings's account and the veiled criticism of Israel Jefferson's portrait, Peter Fossett presented a Jefferson fondly remembered. The eleven-year-old grandson of Betty Hemings and his mother and siblings were sold as part of the Jefferson estate in 1827; Peter's father, Joseph Fossett, was freed in Jefferson's will. Peter Fossett lived a further twenty-five years in bondage and twice failed in attempts to run to freedom. When he was interviewed by the New York *World* in 1898, he was a prominent Baptist minister and successful caterer in Cincinnati. He described Jefferson as "a master we all loved," "an ideal master" who was "kind and indulgent" and rarely punished his slaves. He commented on Jefferson's opposition to the slave trade, made much of his role in the antislavery proviso of the Northwest Ordinance, and then, startlingly, stated that Jefferson "had made all arrangements to free his slaves at his death."[16]

This claim is in no way supported by the record. Nothing suggests Jefferson intended to free more than a handful of the almost two hundred slaves he owned in his last years. When Fossett explained the financial conditions that prevented carrying out these "arrangements," he did not cite, as do some scholars today, Jefferson's improvident lifestyle or the nation's agricultural depression. Fossett told a Cincinnati newspaper in 1900, "The estate was so encumbered by [Jefferson's] generous gifts to his cherished pet, the University at Charlottesville, that all the slaves had to [be] sold." It is striking that one of the most notable achievements of Jefferson's career was remembered as the main stumbling block to freedom. Jefferson's financial commitment to the University of Virginia was actually a subscription of $1,000, paid in installments between 1818 and 1822, a major expenditure for a man with no outside income but insignificant alongside Jefferson's debts of over $100,000. Fossett's recollection might seem one man's effort to make sense of the catastrophes of 1826 and 1827, which resulted in the sale of 130 slaves appraised for almost $30,000. A similar tale, more harshly expressed, was told in another branch of the Hemings family. In 1948, Lottie Bullock, whose mother had been raised by a Hemings descendant in Charlottesville, said she was told that Jefferson had "misused large sums of money entrusted to him for the benefit of the Negroes, by applying it to the building of the University of Virginia."[17]

The implausibility of Fossett's explanation of events suggests that he could not accept a Jefferson who abandoned his slaves merely because of a personal requirement for life's luxuries or the impersonal forces of distant markets. Only a higher cause could justify such a breach of trust. Education was, next to religion, the highest cause in Peter Fossett's recollections of his life and a significant theme in other ex-slave accounts. Isaac (Granger) Jefferson, tinsmith and blacksmith at Monticello, spoke admiringly in 1847 of Jefferson's "mighty head" and his "abundance of books," describing him as rich in "larnin'" if not in property. As a child, Isaac had slept on the floor of the schoolroom and made its fire, while Jefferson's daughters and nieces pursued their educations in the same space. Madison Hemings recalled having to induce the white children to help teach him, and Israel Jefferson, who prized his memory of Lafayette's belief in slave literacy, learned to read and write in Ohio, considering "what education I have as a legitimate fruit of freedom." Mary Cole Kenney's family in Charlottesville had a tradition that a Miss Randolph, presumably one of Jefferson's granddaughters, taught the slaves at some personal risk. In Fossett's account, Jefferson makes his only appearance in connection with educating African Americans in a passive role: "Mr. Jefferson allowed his grandson to teach any of his slaves who desired to learn." A significant portion of Fossett's recollection is devoted to his secret life on the plantation of the man who purchased him at the Monticello sale. He spoke of his own strenuous, clandestine, and sometimes illegal efforts to achieve literacy, share it with his fellows in bondage, and use it to provide passports to freedom for others.[18]

Peter Fossett's rose-tinted picture of life in slavery at Monticello cannot be explained solely by his youth at the time (he was eleven when Jefferson died) or the circumstances of his 1898 interview—given to a white New York reporter two years after *Plessy* v. *Ferguson*. He was undeniably proud of his association with Jefferson and liked to quote him at length. He measured himself against his second owners by reference to his upbringing close to Jefferson: "Being with and coming from such a family as Mr. Jefferson's, I knew more than they did about many things." While Peter Fossett and Madison Hemings clearly identified with Jefferson in their different ways, Fossett's account contains traces of a less reverent view of the head of Monticello's household. When he switched from his own memories to the transmitted memories of his elders, Peter Fossett, too, provided indirect evidence of Jefferson's weakness and dependence.[19]

Fossett made that transition from memory to myth by speaking of a scientific instrument. He used a telescope to conjure up Jefferson the man of science, recalling its placement on Monticello's north terrace, where Jefferson and James Madison "spent a great deal of their time." But Jefferson's telescope did more than observe celestial bodies; it also symbolized oversight. Jefferson looked through it "to see how the work was progressing over at Pan Top, one of his plantations." This image of the monitoring manager must have been prevalent among the enslaved residents of Albemarle County. In the 1880s, a black man who had not been a Monticello slave but who had worked on the construction of the University of Virginia recalled Jefferson standing in the Monticello yard watching "we alls at work through his spyglass."[20]

Using Jefferson's fine English optical instrument as his narrative device, Fossett telescoped time, slipping smoothly from his own memories to those of his older family members passed down by repeated telling. From the images of Jefferson studying the universe and the operations of his plantation, he moved directly to the dramatic entrance on the Monticello stage of the soldiers of a foreign enemy. In Fossett's retelling of an event that had happened more than thirty years before his birth, it was while watching the work at Pantops through his telescope that Jefferson saw Banastre Tarleton's men coming up the mountain to capture him in June 1781. Isaac Jefferson, also, told of Governor Jefferson, earlier that same year, climbing to the top of his Richmond dwelling with his spyglass to look for Benedict Arnold's troops when they made their lightning raid on the state capital.[21]

The arrival of the British at Monticello in 1781 was a convergence of maximum danger, worldwide scope, and epic forces. Incidents associated with it generated the most widespread and persistent stories among descendants of Monticello residents, both black and white. The two most popular episodes are Jefferson's escape from the detachment of Tarleton's dragoons who came to Monticello's front door and the heroic actions of his slaves in keeping the family silver from falling into British hands. According to Jefferson's Randolph grandchildren, the British soldiers arrived just as "two faithful slaves," Martin Hemings and Caesar, were hiding the silver in a small cellar under Monticello's portico. "Down went the plank," shutting Caesar in the cellar with the valuables. His stay without food, water, or light lasted eighteen hours, until Tarleton's men had left the mountain. By the 1870s, this span had grown, in all family accounts, to biblical proportions— Caesar went hungry for "three days and three nights." Peter Fossett's version of the tale gave a woman the starring role; his mother's aunt hid the silver in a "potato cellar," stood over the keyhole, and faced down the British soldiers who, "with arms drawn," demanded to know the hiding place.[22]

The cast of characters is just as diverse in accounts of Jefferson's escapes. Isaac Granger, six years old when he was carried off from Richmond by British soldiers in January, missed the excitement at Monticello in June. He recalled instead Jefferson's escape from Benedict Arnold's troops, aided by John, who fetched Caractacus from the stable. Whenever he described Governor Jefferson's movements across Virginia in the early 1780s, from Monticello to Williamsburg to Richmond, he was careful to enumerate who drove the carriage, who rode postilion, and who brought the mounts from the stable. In Peter Fossett's retelling of the events at Monticello six months later, when Tarleton's dragoons were spotted coming up Monticello mountain, Fossett's maternal uncle saddled Jefferson's horse and "took him up to Carter's Mountain, where Mr. Jefferson hid in the hollow of an old tree." This less-than-heroic image shares interesting parallels with the taunts of Jefferson's political enemies, who liked to recount the tale of his hasty flight over Carter's Mountain. Both Fossett and Mary Cole Kenney repeated a further embellishment of the escape story that remains current in the Monticello neighborhood. To foil the enemy's pursuit, Monticello's enslaved blacksmith shod Jefferson's horse backwards. As Charles Bullock remembered hearing from Peter Fossett in 1900: "When Col. Tarlton and his men thought Jefferson was coming, he was going in the opposite direction." The canny blacksmith in these accounts is identified as Joseph Fossett or Peter Hemings, then, respectively, one year and eleven years old.[23]

Stories of the Revolution seem to be entirely absent among the descendants of Sally Hemings. Because he considered Thomas Jefferson his actual father, Madison Hemings may have had no need to repeat the traditions that expressed the slave response to paternalism. In the Revolutionary stories, the substitution of recognizable family members for forgotten protagonists and the embellishment with mythical elements like the reversed horseshoes reinforced their central messages. Every step of the way, Jefferson was supported by his slaves. They made the shoes for his horses, directed the course of his carriages, and kept his silver safe. Their skills and resourcefulness were essential to the safety of someone who was not just a plantation owner in Albemarle County but one of the most important men in Virginia. The British invaders, in Isaac Jefferson's recollection, wanted to clamp silver handcuffs on the elusive governor.[24]

Many of the stories magnify Jefferson's greatness and his wealth, thus making their messages even more powerful. Isaac Jefferson, who made Jefferson president during his own residence in Philadelphia in the 1790s, illustrated the luster of his owner's European sojourn with references to gilded phaeton springs and silk garments adorned with pearl buttons or gold lace. Israel Jefferson also evoked European glamour by elaborating on Jefferson's equipage, which included silver-mounted harness brought back from France. Peter Fossett remembered a house always full of company, famous people from all over the world in velvet coats and "rich silk dresses."[25]

The very opposite impression was cultivated among Jefferson's Randolph descendants. His grandson Thomas J. Randolph, responding to Israel Jefferson's 1873 reminiscences, countered that Jefferson's carriage was homemade and the French harness was twenty-five years old. He continued the poverty theme with his own example. He had worn "neither shoes, or hat, winter or summer" until he was ten years old, and his wedding coat "was made of the wool that grew on the back of his grandfathers sheep. So much for this aristocratic society." His sister Ellen, in a paper written in 1826 to explain Jefferson's pecuniary difficulties, stated that he entertained "in a style of entire simplicity": "Much has been said of the elegance of Mr. Jefferson's establishment at Monticello but there is no person of candour who has ever visited there who could not testify to the contrary." Like her brother, she cited the homespun origins of the house and its furniture, "made by the negro workmen."[26]

Another persistent story is a further illustration of the theme of Jefferson's dependence on his slaves. Sally Hemings's nephew Wormley Hughes, the Monticello gardener in Jefferson's lifetime, was interviewed by biographer Henry S. Randall in the early 1850s. Described by Jefferson as "one of the most trusty servants I have," Hughes was unofficially freed by Martha Randolph after Jefferson's death but remained an "attached and faithful" servant to the family through four generations. The conversations that Randall reports shed fascinating light on issues of mastery and control. Hughes showed Randall the path on the side of Carter's Mountain where Jefferson fled to the south and safety in 1781, the year Hughes was born. He told mainly horse stories, in which Jefferson had to apply "whip and spur" to one recalcitrant mount, was thrown over the head of another, and "rode away" on a third with the British on his tail. Jefferson's difficulty in maintaining control—whether over his horse, his enemy, or his slaves—is also present in Hughes's account of an event that has usually been cited as an example of the beloved master joyfully welcomed home.[27]

When Jefferson and his daughters returned to Monticello in 1789 after five years in France, advance word spread to the slaves, who asked for a holiday and gathered in a body at Shadwell to greet them. In an account of her father's life, Martha Jefferson Randolph recalled that the shouting, weeping slaves "almost drew [the carriage] up the mountain by hand." In 1851, Wormley Hughes told Henry Randall that when the carriage reached the Thoroughfare Gap between Monticello and the adjacent mountain, "in spite of [Jefferson's] entreaties and commands," the slaves detached the horses and dragged the carriage up Monticello to the front door. Also against Jefferson's will, on arrival at the top of the mountain, the slaves "received him in their arms and bore him to the house." Despite Martha Randolph's written account, both Randall and family biographer Sarah N. Randolph chose to accept the testimony of Wormley Hughes and other "old family servants" that the carriage had been "unhitched" and drawn up the mountain.[28]

This subtly seditious story was taken to northern Alabama in the 1840s by Susan Scott, the granddaughter of the man immured in the cellar with the silver in 1781.[29] Her owner, Jefferson's great-grandson William Stuart Bankhead, had left Virginia and resettled on a large Alabama cotton plantation. There, descendants of slave and slave owner told the very same stories, each able to interpret them in different ways. Because Susan Scott's children and grandchildren continued to work for the Bankheads until the middle of the twentieth century, the black and white versions of the stories have become almost impossible to disentangle. For the Bankheads, the silver-hiding episode and the joyful welcome of 1789 signified the loyalty of the slaves to their beloved ancestor. In 1923, William Bankhead's granddaughter wrote "A Faithful Servant" about Susan Scott's son. Her opening paragraph elaborated the "faithfulness and loyalty" theme ("Perhaps there are few instances in America where one family of servants have served the same family of masters for seven generations"), telling both the silver and the welcome stories. When the article was published in a Birmingham newspaper, the headline read: "Emancipation of Slaves During Sixties Fails to Interrupt Loyalty." Her sister exclaimed in a family interview in 1971 that she loved to tell the story of the British raid in front of Susan Scott's granddaughter and grandson, who both worked for her. When interviewed by a newspaper reporter in 1977, almost two hundred years after the event, this grandson provided a condensed account of the 1789 welcome story that conveyed his very different perspective with great simplicity. Emphasizing support rather than fidelity, he said only that "his ancestor 'carried' Jefferson up the hill to Monticello."[30]

At the same time that former Monticello slaves were formulating the tales that would perpetuate their perception of their role in Jefferson's life, his heirs developed their own version of the slave-slaveholder relationship. Jefferson had written in 1805: "The value of the slave is every day lessening; his burden on his master daily increasing." His daughter referred in 1827 to "the enormous encumbrance of those large families of negroes." In her 1826 essay accounting for her grandfather's monumental indebtedness, Ellen Coolidge explained how he had given up the profitable cultivation of tobacco "from motives of humanity," to spare the slaves "great labor and hardship." In her understanding of the situation, Jefferson's "anxiety lest his slaves should be overworked or illtreated by their overseers was carried so far, that these people did not earn enough to maintain themselves but brought him yearly still further in debt for their support." Her brother's post–Civil War recollections are particularly packed with contradictory statements. He summed up the slaveholder's dilemma in the treatment of his slaves: "Having the double aspect of persons and property the feelings for the person was always impairing its value as property."[31]

The African Americans of Monticello had a quite different view of who was the supporter and who the burden. Their accounts perpetuated the understanding that Thomas Jefferson could not do what he did alone. He needed their skills and ingenuity to preserve life and property and, by extrapolation, to pursue his scientific enquiries and his public purposes. So many symbols of support convey the impression of a Jefferson wafted through life on the arms—not to speak of the backs—of the people he held in bondage. Jefferson himself provided a metaphor for this impression. A number of Monticello guides use the image of a pillow to talk about slavery at Monticello. Jefferson's first memory, according to his grandchildren, was of being, at the age of two, "handed up and carried on a pillow by a mounted slave," as the family left Shadwell for Tuckahoe in 1745. According to Thomas J. Randolph's account of July Fourth of 1826, one of his grandfather's very last conscious acts was a wordless signal that Randolph could not interpret. It was Burwell Colbert, Jefferson's highly valued personal servant and butler, who understood his needs, adjusted his pillows, and provided the final symmetry to a life so entangled in the coils and contradictions of slavery.[32]

Free Some Day

The African American Families of Monticello

THE African Americans who experienced bondage on Thomas Jefferson's plantations were locked in a system founded on and perpetuated by law. Living inside the institution of slavery, they responded in a wide variety of ways to the enforced realities of their existence. From "trusty servants" to resourceful leaders to outright rebels, they chose different paths, different kinds of resistance or accommodation, to their situation. Their responses were part of their constant efforts to maintain family unity and cultural integrity, to achieve freedom, or to improve conditions for themselves and their children. Whether through polishing skills, pursuing religion, gaining the confidence of their owner, or running away, they struggled to maintain their humanity within a system that—even as operated by a well-intentioned owner—was profoundly inhumane.

Although Jefferson was a lifelong enemy of the institution of slavery, he was continually making accommodations to it. His spoken ideals were often in conflict with the realities of his ownership of human property. While he expressed his "scruples" against selling slaves, he sold over one hundred in his lifetime. He declared his wish to improve the living conditions of his own slaves, but worsening finances prevented him from making significant progress. Although he strove to reduce cruelty and physical punishment on his plantations, his frequent absences in public service left his overseers free to manage labor in the usual harsh manner. He encouraged the formation of stable families within his holdings, but his actions to provide for his relatives or to make his operations more efficient often led to family disruption.

"Free Some Day" was originally published in book form, with illustrations, as *Free Some Day: The African-American Families of Monticello* (Charlottesville, 2000).

To reconstruct the world of Monticello's African Americans is a challenging task. Only six images of men and women who lived there in slavery are known, and their own words are preserved in just four reminiscences and a handful of letters. Archaeological excavations are unearthing fascinating evidence of the material culture of Monticello's black families, and since 1993, steps have been taken to record the oral histories of their descendants. Without the direct testimony of most of the African American residents of Monticello, we must try to hear their voices in the sparse records of Jefferson's Farm Book and the often biased accounts and letters dealing with labor management and through the inherited memories of those who left Monticello for lives of freedom.

The stories of six families follow, linked by short sections providing general information on events and issues that affected the entire African American community at Monticello.

1774: People and Property

At the beginning of 1774, fifty-two African Americans lived and worked at Monticello. They were the slaves of Thomas Jefferson, either inherited after his father's death or born subsequently.[1] In mid-January, on the division of the estate of his father-in-law, John Wayles, Jefferson was again an heir. This legacy, which more than doubled his landholdings, included not only 10,000 acres of land but the 135 people who lived in bondage on that land. He used the occasion to inaugurate his Farm Book with a list of men, women, and children, concluding with the phrase "187. in all." He was tallying his human property, now more than triple its former total.

From the first arrival of Africans in Virginia early in the seventeenth century to the time of Jefferson's birth, the laws and demographics of slavery had changed their status from an ambiguous one with permeable boundaries to a codified system that made their condition permanent. Like other chattels, slaves could be bought and sold, given and bequeathed, and hired or leased. Their legal rights were virtually nonexistent; they could not own property, testify in court, or form conjugal relationships sanctified by law.

Over the course of his long life, Jefferson considered over six hundred human beings his legal possessions.[2] He acquired 150 slaves through inheritance and about 20 by purchase, but the majority were born into bondage on his Virginia plantations. Between 1774 and 1826, Jefferson owned in any one year from 165 to 225 slaves, the total number usually fluctuating around 200. From the 1790s, about three-fifths of them lived on his 5,000-acre Albemarle County plantation, Monticello,[3] and two-fifths at his Bedford and Campbell County plantation, Poplar Forest.

While the names of men like Sanco, Mingo, and Quash in Jefferson's 1774 list suggest the West African origin of his slaves, their native countries and the number of generations they were removed from Africa still await discovery. Jefferson's father, Peter Jefferson, had acquired his laborers from other Virginia planters in small lots of one to four. His father-in-law, John Wayles, on the other hand, had been actively engaged in the transatlantic slave trade. It is possible that among the 135 slaves Jefferson inherited from Wayles in 1774, there may have been native-born Africans, and some may even have endured the Middle Passage as recently as 1772, when the Guineaman, the *Prince of Wales,* whose human cargo was consigned to Wayles's trading firm, sailed up the James River.[4] Six years later, the Virginia assembly would enact a law, drafted by Thomas Jefferson, prohibiting the importation of enslaved Africans.

After the division of his father-in-law's estate, Jefferson left most of his recently inherited slaves on his new plantations in Bedford, Cumberland, and Goochland Counties. He brought fifteen of the Wayles slaves to Monticello, to join those who had been living in Albemarle County for most of their lives. The new arrivals included several house servants and carpenters, a blacksmith, and four watermen, who had guided canoes loaded with tobacco down the James River to market. One of the women inherited from Wayles, Suck, a cook, joined her husband, Jupiter, and thus was the first to connect the Wayles and Jefferson enslaved populations through marriage.[5]

Jupiter and Suck

The four Doric columns of the neoclassical entrance portico greet every visitor to Monticello. Formed of cylindrical blocks of quartzite, laid one on top of another and sand-painted to look like solid stone shafts, the columns were shaped by the hammer and chisel of a man whose entire life was linked with Thomas Jefferson's. For over fifty years the lives of Jupiter and Thomas Jefferson were bound together by law, for one man considered the other his property. In 1743, both were born at Shadwell, a newly opened plantation on Virginia's western frontier. As boys they may have fished in the Rivanna River, set trap lines along its banks, and shared hunting escapades in the surrounding woods. As young men they traveled the length and breadth of Virginia together and found wives on the same plantation near Williamsburg.[6]

Jefferson's choice of Jupiter as his personal servant may indicate a bond of affection that transcended their juvenile adventures. From at least 1764, when both turned twenty-one and became legally master and slave, Jupiter accompanied Jefferson on his travels and acted as his personal attendant while he studied law in Williamsburg. Jupiter probably carried out the ordinary duties of a valet, which Jefferson later described as to "shave, dress and follow me on horseback" (when traveling alone, Jefferson usually preferred to drive his carriage himself). Thus Jupiter, mounted on a horse, rode about Virginia with Jefferson, dispensing coins for ferry crossings and carriage repairs. In Williamsburg, he walked down Duke of Gloucester Street to buy Jefferson's books, fiddlestrings, and wig powder and to pay the bills of the baker, shoemaker, and washerwoman. When Jefferson was short of change, Jupiter lent him money to provide tips to other slaves, the domestic servants of his Williamsburg friends.[7]

In 1774, after ten years as a personal servant, Jupiter assumed new duties as hostler and coachman. A recently inherited slave, Robert Hemings, became Jefferson's personal attendant, and Jupiter took charge of the Monticello stables, where he was responsible for the condition of carriages, harness, and—most important— Jefferson's valuable horses. The absence of any reference to the reasons for this change of occupation leave us only with speculations. Jefferson may have preferred the attendance of the young, light-skinned Hemings—then only twelve years old. It is equally possible that Jupiter himself requested a new role. Tired of the frequent traveling and absences, he may have asked to spend more time at Monticello. He and sixteen-year-old Suck, a cook, appear together for the first time as husband and wife in the slave rolls of 1774, when she had just become Jefferson's property, part of the inheritance from John Wayles.

Jupiter had almost certainly met Suck well before this time, on his many visits to the Wayles plantation, The Forest, in Charles City County. While Jefferson courted Martha Wayles Skelton, Jupiter probably courted Suck, who was only half his age. The responsibilities of a Virginia plantation cook involved far more than the actual preparation of the main meals of the day. A kinswoman of the Jefferson household, who made frequent visits to Monticello, recalled the tasks of the cook at her own home in adjacent Fluvanna County: "The Northern housekeeper has no idea of the avocations of a cook in a southern establishment. In the first place, the wood is brought in the rough; huge unmannerly trees were to be split into manageable form by dint of axe and wedge—Then the water was not infrequently half a mile down hill, never very close at hand, for convenience was not very much considered. The butcher brought the entire animal, to be cut into orthodox pieces by the cook. . . . The Cook and his satellites made the soap, the candles, salted down and smoked the bacon, a years supply, from 80 to 100 hogs!" Despite her youth, Suck must have been capable of far more than these mundane tasks, since she accompanied the Jeffersons as cook to the governor's residences in Williamsburg and Richmond in 1780 and 1781.[8]

After 1774, while Jupiter no longer spent long weeks on the road or in Williamsburg while Jefferson attended the assembly, he was still entrusted with particularly important errands. When illness forced Jefferson to turn back on his way to the Virginia Convention in July 1774, he gave Jupiter copies of what became *A Summary View of the Rights of British America.* Jupiter carried to Williamsburg the words: "The abolition of domestic slavery is the great object of desire in those colonies where it was unhappily introduced in their infant state." Jupiter was usually the messenger chosen to carry or collect large sums of money—once as much as £40 ($133). On one occasion Jefferson wrote a debtor, "I send the bearer, Jupiter, a trusty servant express, to receive and bring any sum you may have in readiness for me." As coachman, Jupiter drove the carriage only when Jefferson traveled with his family, such as when the entire household moved to Williamsburg, and then Richmond, when Jefferson was governor during the Revolution. In 1781, when British forces raided Richmond, Jupiter probably transported Jefferson's wife and daughters to safety across the James River, while his own wife was carried off by the invading soldiers. According to the account of former slave Isaac (Granger) Jefferson, it was six months before Suck and the others seized by the British were reunited with their families.[9]

Because of his prolonged absences in public service, Jefferson had his male domestic servants trained in a second trade so that they could fill every hour with useful work. Jupiter learned stonecutting from William Rice, an indentured servant whose remaining term of service Jefferson had purchased in Philadelphia in 1775. Jefferson's 1778 account with Rice, by then a free man, reveals that Jupiter "worked on" the Monticello columns and spent several weeks transforming an irregular block of fieldstone into a smooth three-by-six-foot slab that is probably the oldest surviving grave marker in the town of Charlottesville.[10] During Jefferson's five-year absence in France, Jupiter was hired out to a local stonemason, earning £25 a year for his owner. In the flood of building projects that followed Jefferson's return to Monticello in 1790, Jupiter was busy with chisels, crowbar, and gunpowder. He used the latter in the quarry, where he raised a thousand bushels of limestone, and in the digging of a canal, where, as Jefferson's son-in-law reported in 1793, Jupiter was "constantly employed in blowing the rock."[11]

In 1777, shortly after the death of Martha and Thomas Jefferson's two-week-old unnamed son, Jupiter and Suck's first known child, Aggy, died at the age of two months. No more children are recorded until 1790, when Jefferson gave Suck and her infant son Philip to his recently married daughter Martha Jefferson Randolph. Although Jupiter was not part of this gift, the family was apparently not separated. Jupiter and Suck appear together in Jefferson's Farm Book, living on the Monticello mountaintop through at least 1797. Early in 1796, they were parted for a time when the Randolphs spent time at a plantation below Richmond. Suck left Monticello in a wagon bound for Varina, in Henrico County, where the Randolph household was established for the winter. She had just given birth to a child who apparently did not survive. Only one living child in over twenty years of marriage is a sad contrast to the large families of eight to twelve children that were more usual in the Monticello African American community. It is impossible to know if, in Jupiter and Suck's case, it was an issue of infertility, illness, or insufficient time for infant care. Jefferson, who arranged for physicians to attend his slaves in serious cases, paid fees to midwives for the enslaved women. Until the 1800s, when Rachael, a slave midwife, was brought from Poplar Forest to Monticello, Suck and the other African American women were attended in childbirth by local white women.[12]

The relationship of Jupiter and Suck's son Philip—whose full name was John Jupiter Ammon Philip Evans—and Jefferson's grandson Thomas Jefferson Randolph paralleled that of Jupiter and Jefferson. Late in life Randolph wrote that Phil Evans, "small, active, intelligent, much of a humourist, was my companion in childhood and friend through life," and he related two anecdotes that, in his view, illustrated Evans's loyalty. During the War of 1812, the twenty-two-year-old Evans traveled north to Lake Ontario with Randolph's father, Thomas Mann Randolph, and his regiment. When Colonel Randolph hastened on with his men to join Gen. James Wilkinson's army on Grenadier Island at the entrance to the St. Lawrence River, Phil Evans was left at Sackett's Harbor with three horses. Instead of taking the advice of local New Yorkers to sell the horses and seize his freedom, he set off alone to lead them to his master at the army's winter quarters over a hundred miles down the St. Lawrence the free soil of Canada visible on the opposite shore. As Thomas J. Randolph recalled, once home, Evans could be heard relating to his companions the story of his military adventures in upstate New York. In his memoir Randolph also chose to relate how, some years later, when he was dangerously injured in an affray with a brother-in-law, Phil Evans rode in search of a physician into the next county, where he was forced to make a scene to secure the doctor's attendance. When Randolph fainted from the fever that succeeded his wounds, he awoke to find that "Phil was holding me in his arms with his eyes streaming with tears."[13]

Jupiter and Philip Evans, by uniting industry and honesty with loyalty and trustworthiness, epitomized the ideal slave of Jefferson's and other southern slaveholders' expectations. And they were not unique. Jefferson's records contain frequent references to other "trusty servants" who were sent on important errands or consulted on the whereabouts of runaways. Those who earned or cultivated the master's trust were the most likely to retain their positions close to Jefferson and his family members and thus are most often mentioned in surviving records. Much is also known about slaves who generated discussion in correspondence by defying the unwritten laws of the plantation through chronic misbehavior or running away. Those who chose intermediate strategies for survival are least visible in the records.[14]

Jefferson and his grandson saw the behavior of Jupiter and his son primarily in terms of their "fidelity," a quality for which he even devised tests. When he received a shipment of Jamaica rum in 1774, Jefferson kept a tally of the bottles "by making a mark in the margin in order to try the fidelity" of his new enslaved butler, Martin Hemings. Besides the genuine attachment that was a likely ingredient of the motivations of some of the Monticello slaves, they had multiple reasons for trying to obtain Jefferson's trust. Primary were the practical considerations of survival, from fear of punishment or family separation to concern for improving conditions for themselves and their family members. Those who practiced trades, in particular, even though their work enriched their master and not themselves, could benefit their families by excelling in their craft. Several Monticello tradesmen earned money in their free time by working for local free artisans.[15]

Behavior that inspired the master's trust was also stimulated by universal human considerations of pride, integrity, and honorable behavior. Josiah Henson, a former slave from Maryland, remembered how he wished to "outhoe, outreap, outhusk, outdance, out everything every competitor." In 1825, he safely conducted his master's slaves to Kentucky rather than claiming freedom for himself and his charges as they passed down the Ohio River and were urged by black residents of Cincinnati to remain outside the borders of slavery. Henson explained his actions as a mixture of pride and a wish to act according to his belief in what was right. Philip Evans's motivations for undertaking a long solo journey through unfamiliar territory that culminated in a return to slavery in Virginia may have been similarly derived from fidelity to a trust rather than to a master. Thoughts of permanent separation from family members no doubt also affected his actions.[16]

Access to the master gave Jupiter and others like him privileges in slavery and almost their only prospects of freedom. While Jupiter himself was still a slave at his death, his son died in nominal, if not legal, freedom in New York City. When James Maury, former American consul in Liverpool, returned with his family to Virginia in 1831, Thomas J. Randolph offered Phil Evans's services to the Maurys in their travels around the state. Two years later he asked the return of "my man Phil . . . having occasion for his services as a groom." Subsequently, as Randolph recalled, Philip Evans "hired himself from me at a nominal hire" and lived the rest of his life in New York City, where he had settled in the employ of the Maurys.[17]

The steward of the Monticello stable had an exacting taskmaster. Members of Jefferson's household recalled the immaculate cleanliness that he demanded when his saddle horse was brought to him for his daily ride. He swept his white handkerchief across the horse's shoulders and, if it collected any dust, reprimanded the groom and sent the horse back to the stable. In 1795, Jefferson placed a newly acquired mule for "safe custody" in the stable, "from which Jupiter let her escape." Trusting to the mule's homing instincts, Jefferson expected her to retrace her steps to Varina, almost a hundred miles to the east. "As soon as I know of her arrival there," he wrote, "I will send Jupiter for her as a punishment for his carelessness." When the mule was apprehended by one of Jefferson's neighbors a few days later, Jupiter was spared the journey.[18]

Jupiter's side of the mule episode is unknown. Was it really carelessness that caused the mule's escape, or might Jupiter have questioned a mule's right to inhabit the space occupied by the likes of Romulus and Remus and the other blooded horses that Jefferson sought for his stable? Another story suggests Jupiter's fierce pride in his work and the positions he occupied. Jefferson's unruffled temper was legendary; his grandchildren could recall for a biographer only two instances of visible fury, one involving his coachman. After Jupiter twice refused to let a young slave sent by Jefferson take one of the carriage horses to the post office, he was summoned to the presence of his master, who was "evidently in a passion." Jupiter met a look and tone "never before or afterwards witnessed at Monticello," but he "firmly declared that he must not be expected to keep the carriage horses in the desired condition, if they were to be 'ridden round by boys.'" While Jefferson agreed with this concern, he admonished Jupiter never to use "so blunt a method of 'telling his mind.'" Jupiter had dared for a moment to cross an invisible line, stepping outside his subordinate station to challenge entrenched patterns of authority.[19]

Jupiter's pride in his position of trust may have led to his death. In the 1790s, when Jefferson was in federal office, the established pattern was for Jupiter to accompany Jefferson to and from Fredericksburg, the starting point of the public stage journey to Philadelphia. Late in 1799, when about to leave for Philadelphia, Jefferson instructed his overseer: "Jupiter is to move into the North Square cellar room . . . for the safeguard of the house." After years of being entrusted with money, children, horses, and gunpowder, Jupiter never took up this final trust—Jefferson's most valuable possession. The fifty-six-year-old slave, who was ailing, was "much disturbed" when Jefferson engaged a substitute to accompany him to Fredericksburg. Jupiter insisted on making the journey. On the second day Jefferson pressed him to stop, "but he would not hear of it." After Jefferson boarded the stage at Fredericksburg on Christmas Eve, he never saw his lifelong companion again.[20]

Jefferson left Jupiter in the care of a tavern keeper, with money for a blanket and other expenses. "Finding him self no better at his return home," wrote Martha Randolph to her father, Jupiter "unfortunately conceived him self poisoned" and consulted a doctor of his own race. It appears that Jupiter, like his African ancestors and many of his fellow slaves, believed in the supernatural origin of a lingering illness that failed to respond to the usual treatments. Inexplicable ailments or misfortunes were often attributed to the animosity of an enemy working through a conjurer, and only a conjurer had the power to remove the "fix." Jupiter traveled over twenty miles to Buckingham County to see a black doctor, who gave him a "dose" and "pronounced that it would *kill or cure*. 2 ½ hours after taking the medecine [Jupiter] fell down in a strong convulsion fit which lasted from ten to eleven hours, during which time it took 3 stout men to hold him. He languished nine days but was never heard to speak from the first of his being seized to the moment of his death."[21]

The travels of the skeptic who put his faith in human reason and the man who trusted in the magical beliefs of his ancestors were over. To several correspondents Jefferson expressed his anxiety and concern about Jupiter's illness and death, which he blamed on his "imprudent perseverance in journeying." But the cruel conflicts of the slave system were embedded in his reactions. For Jefferson, Jupiter was valuable property as well as a human being, a combination apparent in a final comment on his fifty-year companion. "I am sorry for him," Jefferson wrote his son-in-law, "as well as sensible he leaves a void in my domestic administration which I cannot fill up."[22]

1775: In Their Own Time

On Sunday, May 14, shortly after word of the battles of Lexington and Concord reached Albemarle County, Aggy and Cate walked to the top of Monticello mountain to do business with the newly elected delegate to the Continental Congress. In exchange for a pullet and two chickens, Jefferson gave each of the women a silver Spanish bit (12½¢). While for six days a week Aggy spun yarn in the textile shop and Cate worked in the fields at Shadwell, the seventh day was theirs to spend as they chose. During the sixty years of Jefferson's residence at Monticello, men, women, and children from the several quarter farms came to the mountaintop on Sundays with something to sell or something to ask. His granddaughter Ellen recalled a later period when her mother, Martha Jefferson Randolph, managed the Monticello household: "Her Sundays then were chiefly occupied with receiving colored visitors from all grandpapa's other plantations that were within walking distance. They came sometimes, to ask small favors, or complain of small grievances, to see and talk to Mistress, notice the children, and take a look at the 'great House' and all its surroundings."[23]

Ellen Coolidge neglected to mention the Sunday activity that is most apparent in the records—the regular exchange of produce and poultry for silver. A

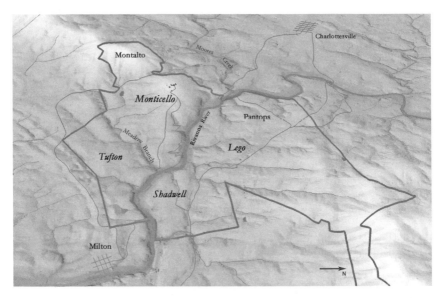

The 5,000-acre Monticello plantation. (Derek Wheeler: Thomas Jefferson Foundation, Inc.)

Monticello household account from the summers of Jefferson's presidency reveals that every enslaved family had a poultry yard, and most cultivated a vegetable plot, selling to the inhabitants of the "great house" chickens and eggs, cabbages and lettuce, cucumbers and melons. References in accounts to the sale of fish, fruit, animal skins, beeswax, and walnuts signal activities that blended recreation and labor, as families took advantage of the natural bounty of their surroundings, fishing in the Rivanna River and hunting or gathering nuts in the woodlands.[24]

Whatever the associated pleasures, it is evident that, in their free time, many of Monticello's enslaved men and women continued to work to supplement their allotments of food, clothing, and furnishings. The weekly food rations for each adult consisted only of a peck of cornmeal, a half-pound of pork or pickled beef, and four salted fish—a diet that was standard plantation fare in Virginia, although Jefferson's provision of meat was smaller than that of many of his contemporaries. The annual cloth distributions included both a summer and winter suit of clothes, plus a blanket every three years and occasional hats, socks, and "beds," burlap sacks that had to be filled with straw or leaves. Artifacts of needlework found in archaeological excavations remind us of the women's work that must have been constant to make and repair the family's clothing or to adorn and personalize the uniforms of slavery. Any furniture or household utensils, other than the occasional sifters and Dutch ovens that Jefferson distributed, also had to be made in limited free time.[25]

To acquire articles that they could not make themselves—like tea and coffee, sugar, or cloth in colors other than the standard issue—enslaved families needed money. Both written records and archaeology attest to the spirited domestic economy in the Monticello African American community. Spanish cut money and American half dimes turn up regularly in the excavations of dwelling sites, and Jefferson's memorandum books are filled with entries indicating payment for items ranging from eggs to squirrel skins. The surplus produce of vegetable gardens and poultry yards as well as hunting and fishing expeditions could be sold to the main house or taken to Charlottesville to the Sunday market. Jefferson and his family members also bought handmade items like brushes, brooms, and buckets, and money could be made by Sunday labor at supplementary tasks that were not considered part of the regular work routine or were deemed particularly arduous or unpleasant. Activities mentioned in the records include hauling and earthmoving, at a usual payment of fifty cents a day. When directing the digging of a sunken lawn at his new house site at Poplar Forest in 1807, Jefferson specified that the enslaved men should do the work "with their own free will and undertaking to do it in their own time," at the rate of a bit per cubic yard. Young men like Ned Gillette and Nace spent their Sundays cleaning the Monticello privies so that they could earn an extra dollar each month. Domestic servants and coachmen like Suck and Jupiter probably rarely had an entire Sunday at their disposal, as Suck would have had to pluck and cook the chickens bought from Aggy and Cate, and Jupiter could not neglect the horses in the stable. They, however, had access to a source of spending money that was unavailable to the artisans and farmworkers: the tips of visitors to Monticello.[26]

Thomas Jefferson told his friend Benjamin Rush that he believed in "the divine institution of the Sabbath, which he conceived to be a great blessing to the world, more especially to poor people and slaves." The customary right of Virginia slaves to spend their Sundays as they pleased was long-standing. It also had to be continually defended from masters and overseers who reckoned a tobacco crop of more importance than one of the few prerogatives a slave could claim. In 1819, when imminent frost prompted the Poplar Forest steward to cut tobacco on a Sunday, most of the laborers slipped away to Lynchburg before they could be assembled, and "a battle ensued" when one young man, ordered to assist, attacked an overseer.[27]

Jefferson's records are virtually silent on the recreational pursuits of Monticello's African Americans. Sundays, holidays, and the hours of dark provided a slave's only opportunities to mix with his fellows in song, story, or prayer. In the intervals of after-hours labor to earn money and improve their living conditions, the enslaved men and women activated a web of connections that bound them together into a community. Sunday was a time for visiting among the quarter farms of the plantation or beyond its borders, for which written permission from master or overseer was usually required. On weekends, men with wives on other plantations walked miles to see their families, and couples with vegetables to sell went to neighboring plantations or joined those from other parts of the county at the Charlottesville market. During the four-day break at Christmastime, visiting was possible between the more widely separated Monticello and Poplar Forest plantations.[28]

Sometimes the need to supplement allotments was combined with social and recreational occasions. Jefferson's grandson Thomas J. Randolph recalled his boyhood participation in moonlit expeditions of the enslaved men on the trail of possums and bee trees. One night, after the successful felling of a honey-loaded tree, the men returned to the cabin of Ben and Betty Brancher: "Old Betty had a pot of hot coffee, fried meat and eggs, and a dish of honey ready to regale the whole party. The boy [Randolph] was roused from his slumbers and seated at a little table covered with the best, while the blacks enjoyed their well earned meal around the blazing fire."[29]

The African American world at Monticello came alive after dark. "Night is their day," wrote one southerner about his own slaves. Required to spend their daylight hours laboring for another, the enslaved families took the hours of night for their own, when they gathered together to sing and dance, tell stories, or attend prayer meetings. Music and dancing were central to their lives. Animated musical scenes on the mountaintop are evoked by former slave Isaac Granger Jefferson, who as a boy was struck by the sight of Thomas Jefferson's brother Randolph, who would "come out among black people, play the fiddle and dance half the night." Excavations along Mulberry Row unearthed fragments of violins and jaw harps. Sally Hemings's fiddle-playing sons, who accompanied the dances of Jefferson's granddaughters, no doubt played in the quarters as well. In 1841 a Frenchman published a number of songs and stories he had heard from one of Jefferson's granddaughters. Besides several call-and-response songs that accompanied cornshucking or other repetitive work, this collection includes two stories told her by her "mammy." One, in the Br'er Rabbit as trickster mode, ends with the hare getting the best of a deceitful fox. In the other tale, the granddaughter thought she detected an African genesis. "Our nurse," she said, "called its evil genius the Devil; but . . . I am rather inclined to believe it must have been some African sylvan or wood spirit."[30]

While Sundays provided the best opportunities for religious expression, spirituality was an integral part of each day in the lives of enslaved African Americans, for whom the sacred and secular were intertwined. By the end of the eighteenth century, many American blacks had adopted a distinctive form of

Christianity that often went hand in hand with a belief in the supernatural forces so important to their African ancestors. The records suggest that both spiritual strands were present at Monticello. Occasional references to preachers, prayer meetings, baptisms, and Bible reading indicate the presence of a deeply felt Christian faith. No reference to a black preacher at Monticello has been found, nor are there any details about specific religious practices. One reference to a prayer meeting in a slave dwelling does suggest that the enslaved Christians at Monticello were permitted to worship without interference. Over the course of the nineteenth century, increasingly stringent laws that prohibited assembling in numbers and outlawed black preachers drove the religious gatherings of Albemarle County's African Americans into the covers of darkness and forest. Former slave Garland Monroe, born in 1848, recalled "slipping out nights to go to meeting" on the wooded slopes of Monticello mountain, from which the county patrollers would normally "keep away." If they did come, he said, the slaves "would just run down the mountainside along paths that the patrollers didn't know nothing about." This secrecy was probably not required in Jefferson's time, but the knowledge of woodland paths, navigable after sunset, had undoubtedly been expanding since the middle of the eighteenth century, when Albemarle County's African Americans began to knit their families and communities together by traveling at nighttime and on Sundays.[31]

At the same time that they embraced Christianity, Jefferson's slaves held on to the African belief in the influence of supernatural powers on everyday events. They turned to root doctors and conjurers to help them mediate between the spirit world and their daily lives, to resolve their problems and heal their ailments, to ward off evil forces or to cast spells. The reputation of one such practitioner of magic and herbal medicine was strong enough to draw at least four African Americans from Monticello twenty miles to the south. The fates of Jupiter and other influential members of the community are powerful tokens of the enduring significance of African spiritual beliefs.

George and Ursula Granger

Three members of another important Monticello family consulted the same conjurer and suffered the same fate as Jupiter. George and Ursula Granger and their son George all died within months of each other in 1799 and 1800, a catastrophe evoked in a flurry of letters between Jefferson, in Philadelphia, and his family at home in Virginia. Benjamin Franklin's grandson, Dr. William Bache, who lived near Monticello, was summoned to Ursula's case when Jefferson expressed his concern: "That a whole family should go off in the same and so singular a way is a problem of difficulty."[32]

This family had come to Monticello on a winter's day a quarter of a century before. In January 1773, Jefferson attended an estate auction fifty miles away in Cumberland County because his wife was "very desirous to get a favorite house woman of the name of Ursula." He bid £210 for Ursula and her fourteen- and five-year-old sons, George and Bagwell, a transaction that soon entailed a second purchase, that of Ursula's husband, George, for £130, from another Cumberland County plantation owner.[33]

For the next twenty-five years this family filled some of the most important positions at Monticello. Ursula Granger reigned in the domestic dependencies—the kitchen under the South Pavilion and the smokehouse and washhouse on Mulberry Row. Her son Isaac, who later took the surname Jefferson, reported that Martha Jefferson came out to the kitchen "with a cookery book in her hand and read out of it to Isaac's mother how to make cakes, tarts, and so on." Ursula also washed and ironed the clothes, supervised the preservation of the meat, and was described by Jefferson as the only person "who unites trust and skill" for superintending the annual bottling of the cider. She was also apparently called on at times to act as a wet nurse for Thomas and Martha Jefferson's children. Isaac Jefferson recalled that Martha, the Jeffersons' firstborn, was "suckled part of the time" by his mother, a memory confirmed by a letter in 1792. Jefferson stated that Martha was sickly until the age of six months, when she was "recovered almost instantaneously by a good breast of milk." This was almost certainly provided by Ursula, whose own infant son Archy, born early in 1773, did not fare so well, dying in the summer of 1774. Only three of George and Ursula Granger's children survived to adulthood.[34]

The oldest son, George, learned the blacksmithing trade from Francis Bishop, a white man hired in 1774 to operate Jefferson's first blacksmith shop and to train some of his slaves. After Bishop's departure in 1776, George and another slave, Barnaby, ran the shop until the arrival in 1781 of the hard-drinking British deserter William Orr, whose alcoholic exploits were vividly remembered by George's brother Isaac. On Orr's departure in 1783, George Granger the blacksmith took charge of the Monticello shop and directed its operations for over fifteen years. Surviving blacksmithing accounts indicate that, aside from the usual task of shoeing horses, Granger was primarily engaged in the repair of agricultural tools and the making of parts for guns and vehicles. Articles that he made in his shop included chisels and plane irons, axes and scythes, bridle bits, and spoons.[35]

When Jefferson began the manufacture of nails in 1794, the younger George Granger became manager of the enterprise and received a percentage of its profits, according to Jefferson's policy of financial incentives for his enslaved tradesmen. In 1796, for instance, he received $42 as a premium, 2 percent of the year's total earnings for the sale of nails; this amounted to about 6 percent of the profits. George and his brother Isaac, whom he probably trained, also did a brisk trade in plow chains for neighboring farmers, earning a percentage of the proceeds. In April 1798, Thomas Mann Randolph, in one of his reports to Jefferson on operations at Monticello, wrote: "I scarcely look to the Nailery at all—George I am sure could not stoop to my authority and I hope and believe he pushes your interests as well as I could."[36]

George and Ursula Granger's middle son, Bagwell, became a farm laborer, while their third son, Isaac, pursued several metalworking trades. Late in life, Isaac (Granger) Jefferson, who was born at Monticello in December 1775, recalled his boyhood tasks around the house and yard. He spoke of carrying wood and water to fireplaces and kitchen. In winter he slept in a blanket on the floor of the South Pavilion so he could rise early to make the fire for the white children who had their lessons there. One visitor to Monticello, whose arrival must have been both anticipated and dreaded by the slaves, lingered long in Isaac's memory. When Archibald Cary of Ampthill came to see his friend Jefferson, Isaac was delegated to open the three gates in the road up the mountain. If Colonel Cary found a gate closed, he sought out the boy, horsewhip in hand: "He has given Isaac more whippings than he has fingers and toes." Cary's memorable visits, during which he interfered in the kitchen, "made freer at Monticello than he did at home," and would "whip anybody," always concluded with a round of handsome tips.[37]

Isaac Granger accompanied his parents to Williamsburg and Richmond during Jefferson's terms as governor of Virginia during the American Revolution. The events of 1781 made a profound impression on the five-year-old boy, whose recollections, almost seventy years later, are dominated by his wartime memories. In January, British troops under the traitor Benedict Arnold swept up the James River and made a lightning raid on Richmond, the state capital, announcing themselves with a round of cannon fire. Jefferson made his escape on his horse Caractacus, and "in ten minutes," as Isaac recalled, "not a white man was to be seen in Richmond." The British soldiers approached the governor's mansion, with drums beating: "It was an awful sight—seemed like the Day of Judgment was come."

According to Isaac Jefferson's account, his father foiled the invaders in their search for the governor's silver, by hiding it in a bed tick. George Granger convinced the British officer that the silver, like its owner, was safely in "the mountains." After plundering Jefferson's wine cellar and meat house, Arnold's soldiers destroyed the munitions and foundry at Westham and set fire to a number of Richmond buildings. Just twenty-four hours after their arrival, they headed back toward the coast, their ranks increased by many slaves. Isaac and his mother were among them, borne along with the British wagon train to Portsmouth and, eventually, Yorktown. Isaac Jefferson said that the British treated the African Americans who had joined or been seized by the army "mighty well; give 'em plenty of fresh meat and wheat bread." Fever and smallpox broke out in the camps, however, and a "great many colored people died there." The turbulent events leading up to General Cornwallis's October surrender made an indelible impression on the young boy. As an old man he still peppered his recollections with references to the booming of the cannon and the cries of the wounded soldiers.[38]

George Granger, who may not have seen his wife and child for almost a year, probably returned to Monticello when Jefferson and the rest of the Virginia government were driven westward to Charlottesville in May by Lord Cornwallis's arrival in Virginia. Granger then again took up outdoor responsibilities that paralleled his wife's indoor duties. It is apparent that Jefferson reposed great confidence in his knowledge, often seeking his advice on horticultural and agricultural matters. During Jefferson's five-year absence in France in the 1780s, when other Monticello house servants and skilled workers were hired out to neighbors, George and Ursula Granger were "not to be hired at all." George was "reserved to take care of my orchards, grasses &c." By 1793 he was a foreman of labor, a position directly under the overseer, supervising slave laborers digging the canal for Jefferson's mills. "George, aided by Clarkson [the Monticello overseer], will be sufficient to see that the work is done, and to take all details off of your hands," Jefferson wrote his son-in-law at the time.[39]

Late in 1796, the man Jefferson called Great George rose to the highest position on the plantation. When the newly hired overseer for the Monticello and Tufton farms failed to appear in December, George Granger was appointed in his stead and became responsible for Jefferson's principal source of income. He was the one black overseer among almost fifty men who worked for Jefferson over sixty years, charged with the oversight of the farm laborers and the production of the cash crop. The beginning of Granger's three-year administration of the southern half of the Monticello plantation was the eve of its owner's return to public life after three years of retirement at Monticello. Jefferson was by then almost certain of a four-year term as vice president, an office that required part-time residence in Philadelphia.

The mantle of responsibility was transferred by December 10, when Jefferson consulted his new overseer: "Concluded with George that we will keep 12. breeding sows here." They also may have discussed the wisdom of resuming the cultivation of tobacco, abandoned at Monticello for some years in accordance with Jefferson's progressive agricultural principles. Prospects of a poor wheat crop and rising tobacco prices, and no doubt also the fact that tobacco was

Granger's "favorite crop," tipped the scales in favor of reinstating the discarded market crop.[40]

Although Jefferson's duties as vice president took him to Philadelphia only three to six months each year, he was usually away from Monticello during the seasons that were critical to a successful tobacco crop—the late winter and spring planting and transplanting times. George Granger's progress in his absence was communicated by his son-in-law, Thomas Mann Randolph. In his first year as overseer, Granger completed the summer wheat harvest successfully without Jefferson's presence and, in the fall, gathered in an estimated 6,000 pounds of tobacco. The usual procedure for the months that followed was described in the recollections of Randolph's son: "On rainy and snowy days in the winter the negroes with their overseer were sitting around fires in these tobacco houses, stripping, assorting and preparing the crop for market. This was the most important operation for its value; if negligently done deterio[rat]ing it one half." The following April, however, Jefferson heard ominous rumors that all had not gone according to the customary routine. He soon learned the truth of this report. The tobacco had been neglected over the winter, drifting snow had ruined it, and only a single hogshead (about 1,500 pounds) of George Granger's first crop as overseer was saved.[41]

Thomas Mann Randolph's periodic bulletins from Virginia are virtually the only testimony that bears on the character and abilities of one of the most extraordinary members of Monticello's African American community. In one letter, Granger is "steady and industrious," in another, "not careless in general tho' he procrastinates too much." One February, with 30,000 tobacco plants "ready" in the park, he was "absolutely wasting with care," while two months later he was "under great apprehension" about making a sufficient corn crop because of a shortage of plow horses. In June, his authority seemed to be crumbling. Randolph discovered "some instances of disobedience so gross that I am obliged to interfere and have them punished myself." In his opinion, Granger could not "command his force."[42]

George Granger was, in the words of historian Eugene Genovese, the "man between"—caught between the responsibilities of his position and the obligations of his membership in a community. His task was to produce bountiful crops by the work of his fellow slaves, some of them his own family members. His son Bagwell and his daughter-in-law Minerva were two of over one hundred bondspeople living under his regime. He had to maintain order in the slave quarters and mete out punishments and privileges, to be both judge and advocate. Enslaved men in Granger's position—as foremen, headmen, drivers, or overseers—have had a checkered reputation in ex-slave narratives and history books. Some of these men were recalled as thrashing more cruelly than white overseers, while others could give the appearance of a good whipping without actually harming the victim. Some are portrayed as identifying so strongly with their masters that they were regarded as enemy spies in the quarters. Others are viewed as successful leaders who earned the respect of management and labor alike.[43]

George Granger was, to all appearances, a man struggling with his dual roles. During Jefferson's long absences in Philadelphia, he evidently strove to exemplify Jefferson's ideal manager, one who would be both productive and humane. Jefferson's earlier experiment with overseers from Maryland, who he hoped could manage his slaves "on a more rational and humane plan," had recently failed, and he had returned to employing local men. They were enjoined to encourage industry without the use of the whip, but, as soon as Jefferson returned to Philadelphia, many seem to have resumed their usual harsh methods of management.[44]

In George Granger's first year as overseer, his counterpart on the other half of the Monticello plantation fit this mold. William Page, overseer at Jefferson's Shadwell and Lego farms north of the Rivanna River, gained a reputation as a particularly cruel manager. Thomas Mann Randolph specified the effects of the two management styles: "discontent" at Shadwell and "insubordination" at Monticello. Jefferson responded that "George needs to be supported and Page to be moderated."[45]

Despite the loss of the tobacco and some disorder in the quarters, Granger continued to retain Jefferson's confidence and remained in his post. Cooperative behavior sometimes enabled slaves to rid themselves of unpopular overseers by disrupting plantation operations. With the example of William Page across the river, however, the laborers under George Granger must have recognized the limits to which disobedience would serve their best interests. No references to further management difficulties after the summer of 1798 have been found, and agricultural affairs, too, apparently went well. Granger's failure with the first crop of tobacco was forgotten in the success of his second, a crop "so extraordinary," wrote Jefferson, "that I may safely say if there ever was a better hogshead of tobacco bought or sold in New York I may give it to the purchaser."[46]

George Granger's management ended only with his death. The burden of responsibility, fraught with its conflicting loyalties, may finally have been too much for a sixty-nine-year-old man who must have labored hard for decades before he took on a supervisory role. On November 1, 1799, after the pressing of 120 gallons of cider, Jefferson turned for advice to his experienced manager for the last time: "George says that, when in a proper state . . . [the apples] ought to make 3. galls. to the bushel, as he knows from having often measured both." The next day George Granger was dead, and in his place Jefferson hired a white man who got drunk on his employer's wine, who whipped sick slaves, who failed to distribute the blanket allotment, and who—unlike Granger—could not read or write.[47]

George Granger left a small legacy to his two surviving sons. While the laws denied slaves the right to own property, their possessions were customarily recognized by their masters. Most were able to acquire no more than some household goods and a stock of poultry, but those with greater access to money often invested in livestock. An entry in Jefferson's Memorandum Book may refer to only a part of what George Granger was able to accumulate over three years, when he was being paid an annual wage of £20 ($67). Six weeks after Granger's death, Jefferson gave his son Isaac an order on a local merchant for $11: "This is for his moiety of a colt left him by his father."[48]

It is also possible that George Granger may have been a free man at the time of his death. His son Isaac recalled that his father "got his freedom" for saving the silver during the Revolution. Although no record of manumission has been found, Jefferson did apparently have some kind of special arrangement with his headman. While Granger's wage was only half what a free white overseer received, it was still more than triple any annual "premiums" Jefferson paid to other favored slaves. George and Ursula's food and clothing allotments were also considerably larger than those for other Monticello slaves. From the dry pages of Jefferson's cloth ration lists, the Grangers emerge as imposing figures, fitting the names they were sometimes known by, King George and Queen Ursula. Jefferson had a system of allotting cloth to his slaves according to size: from one yard of linen for the youngest children to seven yards for "common sized men or women" and eight yards for "very large d[itt]o." Only George and Ursula Granger received the eight-yard allotment.[49]

Whether George Granger was freed or not, his children remained in bondage. Bagwell Granger and his wife Minerva continued to work as farm laborers, the most elusive portion of the enslaved community. They lived their lives far from the mountaintop, rarely encountering Jefferson and his family members and thus making few appearances in letters and record books. In 1796, Jefferson commented that because of his "rheumatism," he had not been able to make the two-mile journey to his Shadwell farm quarter in over a month. This couple must represent the many other men and women who labored through the seasons to produce Jefferson's market crops, raise his livestock, and execute the numerous tasks required on a plantation run on the latest and most progressive agricultural principles.[50]

It was the practice on Jefferson's farms to have "gangs of half men and half women." An inventory of tools at Lego, the farm on the north side of the Rivanna River where Bagwell and Minerva Granger lived until 1798, reflects the respective tasks of the male and female laborers. Minerva is listed as having three hoes—for hilling, weeding, and grubbing—while her husband had only two, for hilling and weeding, as well as an axe and wedges. In the growing season, their work was probably quite similar, but in the winter months Bagwell Granger and the other men took their axes to the woodlots to fell trees and split fence rails, while the women grubbed the grounds, removing rocks, roots, and briars in preparation for the passage of the plows.[51]

Like other slaveholders, Jefferson was fully conscious of a further value of his female slaves. "I consider a woman who brings a child every two years as more profitable than the best man of the farm," he wrote in 1820. "What she produces is an addition to the capital, while his labors disappear in mere consumption." Minerva and Bagwell Granger had nine children from 1787 to 1810, coming close to fulfilling Jefferson's ideal of an "addition to the capital" every second year. Expediency as well as humanitarian concerns—or, as Jefferson put it, "interest" and "duty"—harmonized in the issue of proper infant care. He cautioned his Poplar Forest overseers to allow the women "to devote as much time as is necessary to the care of their children. . . . It is not their labor, but their increase which is the first consideration with us." Nursing mothers—which Minerva would have been the greater part of the time—were allowed an extra quarter-peck of corn-meal in the weekly ration.[52]

Each morning just after dawn, Minerva Granger would have carried her hoes to the fields, leaving her youngest children at the quarters in the care of an older woman, past useful farm labor. This was probably her own mother Belinda, the oldest woman on the Lego farm. Jefferson's grandson described the daytime activities at the farm quarters: "A middle aged woman cooked for the laborers and milked a half a dozen cows and made butter. She spun two and half days task of wool in the week. The children were all brought with their nurses to her house every morning to be taken care of while their mothers were out, she employing as help all old enough."[53]

Overseeing the work of Minerva and Bagwell Granger was the notorious William Page. The narratives of former Virginia slaves are full of accounts of the cruelty of overseers and the whippings administered for transgressions as minor as arriving a few minutes late in the field or weeding too slowly. As one former slave from another Piedmont Virginia county recalled, the overseer's business was "to look after each slave in the field, and see that he performed his task. The overseer always went around with a whip, about nine feet long, made of the toughest kind of cowhide." Austin Shepherd remembered that "our overseer, thus armed with his cowhide, and with a large bull-dog behind him, followed the slaves all day; and, if one of them fell in the rear from any cause, this cruel weapon was plied with terrible force." A Frenchman, passing through the Shenandoah Valley on his way to visit Jefferson at Monticello in 1796, marveled at the sight of a master flourishing a whip in the midst of a group of workers planting peas. "He was in constant motion, threatening, snarling, turning round and round," Volney wrote. The slaves accelerated or slackened their work pace according to the direction he faced, so that Volney likened the scene to a troupe of small costumed dogs dancing on the streets of Paris to the direction of a man waving a baton. Jefferson's injunctions against physical punishment did not apparently make much of an impression on overseer William Page, the "terror" of whose name made the hiring of slaves in the neighborhood impossible for Jefferson's son-in-law a few years later.[54]

When he leased his Shadwell and Lego farms to Page in 1798, Jefferson did not lease Bagwell and Minerva Granger along with the other farmworkers resident there. He brought them to the south side of the river to live and work, a transfer from Page's harsh management to the superintendence of Bagwell's father, George Granger. This is probably when Jefferson recorded in his Farm Book: "Davy, Lewis & Abram. have done the carpenter's work of Bagwell's house in 6. days, getting the stuff & putting it together." Over the course of the eighteenth century, the increasing strength and cohesion of African American families led to a corresponding evolution of housing patterns. At Monticello, as elsewhere in the Upper South, the trend was from large structures for many unrelated people to smaller houses for single families. From the 1790s, it was usual for parents to live with their children in their own dwellings. This change is another reflection of the constant negotiation between slave and master that forged the conditions of southern plantation life. Traces of the actions enslaved people took to effect improvements in their own lives can be found in the documentary record. One woman's efforts to have a home of her own are revealed in Jefferson's instructions to an overseer in 1818: "Maria having now a child, I promised her a house to be built this winter." An English visitor to James Madison's Montpelier in 1807 noted that "each Negro family would like, if they were allowed it, to live in a house by themselves."[55]

Bagwell and Minerva Granger and their children (at this time, five) lived in a small log cabin probably very similar to the dwellings of the house servants and tradesmen on Mulberry Row on the Monticello mountaintop. These cabins were one-room structures, with lofts, ranging in size from 12 by 14 feet to 14 by 17 and 12 by 20 feet. Made of chestnut logs hewed on two sides, chinked with mud, and roofed with pine slabs, they had wooden chimneys and earthen floors. Bagwell and Minerva would have had to purchase or make for themselves any furnishings for their house, as Jefferson provided his slaves only with a few cooking utensils, mattress covers, and blankets.[56]

Bagwell and Minerva Granger's work did not end with the close of the day in the fields. Minerva had to care for and feed her children and do the washing and mending, and both tended their vegetable plot and poultry yard. They often made the Sunday journey to the mountaintop, to sell ducks, chickens, and eggs, as well as cucumbers, cymlin squash, and watermelons. Bagwell also trapped and fished to supplement his rations and to gain some spending money—on several occasions he sold Jefferson fish and, once, skins for making a bellows. In 1818, evidently spotting an opportunity in Jefferson's enthusiastic brewing operations, Bagwell Granger planted a large hop garden, earning twenty dollars for his crop of over sixty pounds of hops. He may have cultivated a grass plot as well, as he sold Jefferson hay and timothy seed.[57]

During Jefferson's absence in France, Bagwell Granger even grew a small crop of tobacco, and he might have been one of the slaves under his father's regime who, against Jeffersonian rules, planted tobacco crops in 1798. "I thank you," Jefferson wrote his son-in-law, "for putting an end to the cultivation of tobacco as the peculium of the negroes. I have ever found it necessary to confine them to such articles as are not raised for the farm. There is no other way of drawing a line between what is theirs and mine." Whether or not Bagwell Granger was one of those who tried to expand the limits of their situation to gain a new privilege, the many small clues in the documentary record convey the image of a man of skill and enterprise, continually seeking ways to better the conditions of his family.[58]

During Jefferson's presidency, Bagwell and Minerva Granger and their children were leased, with sixty other slaves, to the tenant of the Monticello and Tufton farms. For nine years John H. Craven was their master, bound by Jefferson's lease to "feed and clothe them well, [and] take care of them in sickness, employing medical aid if necessary." There was a further clause calling for revoking the lease, "should the negroes be treated with unreasonable severity, or not reasonably taken care of." One year, the family had a new food item added to their diet, when birds were substituted for the usual salted fish. In the spring of 1808 passenger pigeons passed over Albemarle County in huge numbers, darkening the sky for days. Taking immediate advantage of nature's bounty, John H. Craven reassigned his laborers to novel tasks. For days on end they netted thousands of this now-extinct bird, salted them down, and packed them in barrels.[59]

The arrangement with Craven may have entailed another move for Bagwell and Minerva's family, as the dwellings from the Monticello farm quarter were apparently relocated closer to the Tufton farm. Fourteen-year-old Ursula, the oldest daughter, was reserved from the lease to be an apprentice cook in the President's House in Washington. On her return to Monticello in 1802, she led a double life, working in the kitchen when Jefferson and his family were in residence and going back to the fields when he returned to Washington. Her experience is indicative of the permeable boundary between the worlds of the "great house" and the fields. Ursula Granger, both a house servant and a farmworker, was born into a family of agricultural laborers and married into a family of domestic servants, the Hemings family.[60]

At Jefferson's death in 1826, Bagwell and Minerva Granger and most of their nine children and many grandchildren were living at Tufton, leased at that time by Jefferson's grandson Thomas Jefferson Randolph. In the inventory of the estate, Bagwell was appraised at fifty dollars and Minerva, then only fifty-five, was declared worth "Nothing." At the 1827 and 1829 sales of Jefferson's slaves, almost the entire family was purchased back by Randolph, and they remained in bondage on his neighboring plantation, Edgehill.[61]

Only one member of George and Ursula Granger's family found freedom before he died. In 1847 in Petersburg, Virginia, the Reverend Charles Campbell sought out a man still practicing his trade as a blacksmith at the age of seventy-one. He had heard that Isaac Jefferson liked to talk of Thomas Jefferson and Monticello and was eager to record his memories. The rich recollections Campbell preserved not only are of vital interest for the study of Jefferson and life at Monticello but are almost unique records from the black perspective. Only three other, briefer, reminiscences by former Monticello slaves are known.[62]

Isaac, who apparently took the Jefferson surname after he became free, recounted to Reverend Campbell his vivid memories of the Revolution without mentioning the dreams of liberty of the black people camped with the British soldiers at Yorktown. Nor did he mention the more extended opportunity for freedom he had when he lived in a northern city in the 1790s. Fifteen-year-old Isaac Granger had probably been working with his brother George in the blacksmith shop for a time when Jefferson took him to Philadelphia to learn tinsmithing. Isaac remembered the Market Street fountain with a water-spouting goose and the impressive brick house he visited each Sunday to report to Jefferson on his progress. But he did not speak to Reverend Campbell about the antislavery beliefs of the Quaker tinsmith in whose shop he, "the only black boy," worked, nor did he say whether he became acquainted with the northern laws against slavery. Pennsylvania had enacted a gradual emancipation law in 1780 that applied only to those born after that date and entailed various forms of indenture. Congressmen and federal officeholders who brought slaves into the state were exempted from the provisions of the law. Nevertheless, the work of the Philadelphia Quakers, in particular, had made the capital city a center of antislavery sentiment and a tempting site for negotiating a change of status. It is virtually certain Isaac would have known William Gardner, a former slave of James Madison who had taken his chance for freedom almost ten years before. When Gardner refused to return to Montpelier, Madison considered it better not to force the issue, since he was "persuaded his mind was too thoroughly tainted to be a fit companion for fellow slaves in Virga." During Isaac Granger's residence in the city, Gardner, with his wife, was the secretary of state's launderer, making a weekly visit to Jefferson's house, where Isaac may have encountered him. Whether Isaac's mind also became "tainted" during several years in a free city, and what determined him to return to Monticello, and slavery, will never be known.[63]

Campbell's transcript of his conversation with Isaac Jefferson is the only source on his Philadelphia years. He began by learning to cut and solder, then to make pepper boxes and graters out of tin scraps, "so as not to waste any till he had larnt." Finally he mastered making tin cups, four dozen a day, as well as tinning sheet iron and copper utensils. Isaac then returned to Monticello to operate a tinsmithing shop, a new business that, he recalled, soon failed. He returned to work in the Monticello blacksmith shop and nailery. Isaac Jefferson's oral account is the only evidence of Thomas Jefferson's abortive tinsmithing enterprise, other than some scraps of tin found at a site on Mulberry Row along with a tin cup, probably made by the enslaved metalworker himself.[64]

For the next several years Isaac Granger moved back and forth from the forge of his brother George to the fires in the new Monticello nailery. He began his nail making during Jefferson's three-year retirement from public life, when the former secretary of state described himself as spending "half the day . . . counting and measuring nails." Jefferson's nail-making accounts reveal that he made a morning visit to the nailery to weigh the iron nail rod allotted to each nailer, returning at the end of the day to weigh the nails they produced. This meticulous monitoring, intended to measure efficiency as well as productivity, provoked diverse reactions among the largely teenaged workforce at the anvils. The twenty-year-old Isaac Granger, however, set the standard for output and efficiency. Over the first six months of 1796 he forged one thousand pounds of nails in six sizes, and he topped Jefferson's list of nailers, ranked in order of profitability according to a formula that took into account both nails produced and iron wasted. Isaac Granger earned for Jefferson the equivalent of eighty cents a day, six times the amount of the least efficient nailers.[65]

It was while making nails that Isaac witnessed an event for which he provided the only known account. In the summer of 1795 Jefferson's staunch political supporter William Branch Giles came for a visit. Isaac Jefferson later recalled that Giles was courting Jefferson's younger daughter Maria, familiarly known as Polly: "Isaac one morning saw him talking to her in the garden, right back of the nail factory shop; she was lookin on de ground. All at once she wheeled round and come off. That was the time she turned him off. Isaac never so sorry for a man in all his life—sorry because everybody thought that she was going to marry him. Mr. Giles give several dollars to the servants, and when he went away dat time he never come back no more." Isaac observed the disappointing denouement in the midst of a fourteen-hour day during which he cut and headed one thousand nails.[66]

Two years later Maria Jefferson married John Wayles Eppes, and Isaac Granger and his wife, Iris, and their two sons, Squire and Joyce, were among the thirty slaves given to the Eppeses by Jefferson as a marriage settlement. Isaac and Iris did not leave Albemarle County with their new owners, however. Jefferson's other son-in-law, Thomas Mann Randolph, needed a blacksmith and hired—and apparently later purchased—the family from Eppes. As Isaac (Granger) Jefferson remembered, he "lived with [Randolph] fust and last twenty-six or seven years. Treated him mighty well—one of the finest masters in Virginia."[67]

The account Isaac Jefferson gave to the Reverend Campbell in 1847 was a largely positive vision, focusing on childhood experiences. He spoke of the kindness of both of his masters, he wondered at the ways of foreign visitors, and his observations of Jefferson—reading, hunting, gardening, and tinkering—are fresh and authentic glimpses of rarely reported domestic activities. Some of his memories evoke an impression of a black Jefferson in the shadow of the white Jefferson, echoing enough of his characteristics to suggest what he might have been in different circumstances. Both were metalworkers, although for one it was only a hobby. Isaac Jefferson remembered the bellows and blacksmith's tools he saw in Thomas Jefferson's second-floor library, when he carried up the coal. Years later, when his own ironworking skills had been plied for almost sixty years, he recalled that "my Old Master was neat a hand as ever you see to make keys and locks and small chains, iron and brass." His memory of accompanying his father twice a day to feed the deer in the park on the side of the mountain parallels a visitor's comment on the pleasure the Sage of Monticello took in handfeeding his deer with Indian corn.

Both men were susceptible to the beauty of the mountaintop and spoke of it in similar ways. Isaac Jefferson's comment, "From Monticello you can see mountains all round as far as the eye can reach; sometimes see it rainin' down this course and the sun shining over the tops of the clouds," nearly matches Thomas Jefferson's more famous tribute to his choice of a house site: "How sublime to look down into the workhouse of nature, to see her clouds, hail, snow, rain, thunder, all fabricated at our feet! And the glorious Sun . . . gilding the tops of the mountains, and giving life to all nature!" The enslaved man was also struck by a scientific phenomenon that fascinated the free man, the "looming" of a mountain forty miles to the south. Isaac Jefferson recalled that "Willis' Mountain sometimes looked in the cloud like a great house with two chimneys to it." Thomas Jefferson liked to point it out to Monticello visitors and described its changing shapes in more geometrical terms in his *Notes on Virginia*.

"In short," he concluded, "it assumes at times the most whimsical shapes, and all these perhaps successively in the same morning."[68]

Isaac Jefferson's words, as preserved by Campbell, make no mention of his wife and children. Besides their sons Squire and Joyce, he and Iris had a daughter Maria, born after they left Monticello in 1798. Thomas Mann Randolph sold her in 1818 to the Monticello overseer, Edmund Bacon, and she may have been taken by Bacon to Kentucky when he emigrated in 1822. The fates of the sons are unknown. In 1847, Campbell described Isaac Jefferson's wife, whom he did not name, as "a large, fat, round-faced, good-humored-looking black woman."[69]

Isaac Jefferson also did not refer to the tragic events of 1799 and 1800. His brother George was the first to become ill, in 1798. At the end of November Thomas Jefferson paid ten dollars for "attendance on smith George" to "Perkins' Sam," possibly the black doctor from Buckingham County consulted by Jupiter and George's parents. George Granger the younger lingered until the midsummer of 1799, his father's death occurred in November of that year, and Ursula died some time in April 1800. Jefferson's daughter had written a few months before that "Ursula is I fear going in the same manner with her husband and son, a constant puking, shortness of breath and swelling first in the legs but now extending itself. The doctor I understand had also given her *means* as they term it and upon Jupiter's death has absconded. I should think his murders sufficiently manifest to come under the cognizance of the law." Martha Randolph's husband had similar views, referring in a letter to "the poisons of the Buckingham negroe conjuror." The motivations of the individuals who traveled to the next county to find a cure will never be known. Did they, like Jupiter, believe themselves poisoned or conjured by an enemy in the Monticello quarters? Did George Granger's role as trusted agent of Jefferson's interests provoke the jealousy and animosity of his fellow slaves? Whatever the case, the fate of this family forces us to consider the issue of solidarity among slaves and suggests that there could be conflict and dissension within an African American community living under the constraints of the institution of slavery.[70]

Some time in the 1820s Isaac Granger made his way to Richmond and then to Petersburg, Virginia, evidently as a free man. His recollections do not reveal how he obtained his freedom or acquired his new last name. Although no record of a transaction survives, Thomas Mann Randolph may have manumitted him, or he may have purchased his own freedom. When Reverend Campbell found him in Petersburg in 1847, he was still vigorous and hardworking at age seventy-one. A striking daguerrotype of him at this time, wearing the leather apron of his trade, illustrates Campbell's description: "Isaac is rather tall, of strong frame, stoops a little, in color ebony; sensible, intelligent, pleasant." When he heard of

Isaac (Granger) Jefferson (1775–c. 1850) in Petersburg in the 1840s. (Special Collections, University of Virginia Library)

Isaac Jefferson's death a few years later, Campbell added: "He bore a good character."[71]

1781: Their World Turned Upside Down

The events of the American Revolution reverberate through the accounts of former Monticello slaves and their descendants more powerfully than any others. Isaac Jefferson's recollections vividly evoke the sounds of drums and gunfire, the smoke of cannons, and the sight of the dead on the field of battle. The momentous arrival of British soldiers at the very doors of Monticello generated the most enduring of the stories transmitted through the oral tradition. For the enslaved men and women in Virginia, the war was both liberating and calamitous. It ignited the desire for freedom and expanded horizons and opportunities. But for many it brought disappointed hopes as well as disease and death.

Word of Governor Dunmore's proclamation in November 1775, offering freedom to slaves who would take up arms against their masters, passed from town to plantation. The slave communication network operated as swiftly in Virginia as in Georgia, the site of the following description that same year: "Negroes have a wonderful art of communicating intelligence among themselves; it will run several hundreds of miles in a week or fortnight." Hundreds joined Lord

Dunmore or British raiding parties in the early years of the conflict. When Virginia became a theater of war in 1781, the increased turmoil brought both harsher conditions and greater opportunities. Fears of a slave uprising led to more rigorous surveillance and more severe punishments, and some planters took their slave property westward for safety. In January, during Benedict Arnold's lightning raid on Richmond, many slaves, including some of Jefferson's, were carried off by the British troops. Four months later, when Lord Cornwallis marched his forces north into Virginia, thousands of freedom-seeking slaves joined his caravan.[72]

The movements from camp to camp must have been both disorienting and exciting for the African Americans, their fears and hopes in constant alternation. Some found new outlets for their skills, working for the British, while others must have been terrified by the culminating events of the conflict. For most, however, their bids for freedom came to a tragic conclusion at Yorktown. The experience of Jefferson's bondspeople was typical. In the summer of 1781, Lord Cornwallis made Jefferson's Goochland County plantation, Elk Hill, his headquarters. In ten days there and at Willis Creek across the James River, the British troops burned fences and barns, carried off horses and livestock, plundered the storehouses, and destroyed the growing crops. Nineteen of Jefferson's slaves—men, women, and children—left with the invaders. Seven years after the event, his anger further inflamed by a recent encounter with an arrogant George III, Jefferson spoke of the "spirit of total extermination with which [Cornwallis] seemed to rage over my possessions." The verbs he had used in 1781 to describe his slaves' behavior—they "fled to the enemy," "joined enemy," or "ran away"—were now altered to the passive tense. His human property had been "carried off" by Cornwallis, he wrote in 1788. "Had this been to give them freedom he would have done right, but it was to consign them to inevitable death from the small pox and putrid fever then raging in his camp."[73]

Jefferson's previous choice of active verbs to describe the conduct of his slaves in their encounter with Cornwallis's troops was no doubt the accurate one. They were not spoils of war but runaways in search of freedom. Two entire families from his Elk Hill and Willis Creek plantations—including nine children under twelve—had joined the British. The rest were mainly teenaged boys and young men, including four who ran away from Monticello, fifty miles farther inland. All but a possible few lost their gamble for freedom. At least fifteen of the runaways died from diseases contracted in the British camps, where, according to one observer of the scene at Yorktown, "an immense number of Negroes have died in the most miserable manner." The suffering in the months after Cornwallis's surrender, when Jefferson launched an effort to recover his human property, is captured by his biographer Henry S. Randall, who spoke to former slaves and members of the family: "Some of them were brought on blankets and mattresses in the last stages of disease, but feebly imploring that they might see Monticello again before they died." Two women and three men, brought back to Jefferson's plantations, survived the experience, only to be given away or sold within a few years of their return. Sam, Jenny, and Harry, whose fates Jefferson could never discover, may be the only runaways who achieved their freedom.[74]

The tumult of war had a lasting effect on those who did not run away. A further nine people who had remained on the plantations died from smallpox or camp fever caught from the British or the slaves who returned, and war-related disease persisted for months. Jefferson estimated his expenditures for the attendance of physicians and for retrieving his scattered property at almost £100 ($333). Jefferson's slaves also felt the economic consequences of the Revolution. Wartime inflation erased the proceeds of the sales of land he inherited from John Wayles, which had been intended to pay the large debt inherited at the same time. Five years later, Jefferson wrote: "I am miserable till I shall owe not a shilling: the moment that shall be the case I shall feel myself at liberty to do something for the comfort of my slaves." That "moment" never came, and the Wayles debt loomed over the residents of Monticello for the rest of Jefferson's life. The need to make payments on this obligation led to the sale of over seventy slaves in the 1790s and contributed to the enormous debt that compelled the sale and dispersal of the entire Monticello community after Jefferson's death.[75]

The tragic fate of the runaways, as well as the slaveholders' victory in the war, must have determined the kinds of stories that survived in the African American community at Monticello. There is no mention of the brief possibility for freedom. The most persistent tales concern the day the British came to Monticello. In the first days of June 1781, Cornwallis sent a detachment under Col. Banastre Tarleton to Charlottesville to capture Governor Jefferson and members of the Virginia legislature, who had been driven west from Richmond in mid-May. On June 4, warned of the enemy's approach by a local militiaman, Jefferson sent his wife and children to safety farther south and rode off on horseback himself only moments before the arrival of the British dragoons. This narrow escape entered the annals of Jefferson's political enemies, his family members, and his slaves. Among his enemies it was recounted as a symbol of his cowardice and ineffectiveness as war governor. For his family it became an exciting brush with danger on an international scale. For the African Americans, the story exemplified the ways in which their family members helped to foil the forces that were seeking the greatest prize in Virginia—its first executive.[76]

When memory merged into legend as the story was passed through the generations, the escape was embellished with fabulous details that emphasized its key points. In one version of the tale Jefferson, accompanied up Carter's Mountain by a slave groom, hid in a hollow tree to wait out the British, and in most versions collected in this century, the slave blacksmith cleverly shoed Jefferson's horse backwards to outwit the pursuers. While Jefferson was fleeing south, events were taking place at Monticello that would also be carefully preserved in the memories of both whites and blacks. British soldiers appeared on the Monticello lawn at the very moment that silver and valuables were being hastily hidden under the floor of one of the porticoes. As most accounts tell it, Martin Hemings, the butler, slammed down the planks, trapping the man stowing the silver in the dark hole below. There he had to remain for the eighteen hours of the British occupation. As the nineteenth century wore on, for descendants of both Jefferson and the African Americans, the original eighteen-hour ordeal assumed biblical proportions and became three days and three nights.

The descendants of the trapped man and of other enslaved families still pass on the stories of Jefferson's escape and the hiding of the silver, all peopled with a changing cast of ancestors in starring roles. The canny blacksmith was Peter Hemings or Joe Fossett (then actually only a few months old). The man trapped under the portico was variously Caesar or Jupiter or John Hemings. Peter Fossett, born thirty-five years after the events, credited his father's aunt, rather than Martin Hemings, with hiding the silver in "a potato cellar" and stated that "my mother's uncle saddled [Jefferson's] horse and took him up to Carter's Mountain."[77]

These contradictory multiple roles illustrate a larger core truth. Monticello's African Americans recognized Jefferson's importance in the world beyond Monticello, and their stories demonstrate that slaves, too, could participate in shaping world events. As told to children and grandchildren, they also reveal that Jefferson could not thwart the British alone. These most enduring tales transmit the knowledge that the entire African American community was essential to the safety and prosperity of the most important man in Virginia, not just on one day in June 1781 but throughout his whole life.

The Hern Family

In the summer of 1793, Thomas Mann Randolph wrote to his father-in-law in Philadelphia: "The Wheels you ordered were executed but in such a manner that they are not worth shoing. Davy can use the wheelwrights tools but has no rule in working: he cannot make a wheel with all the felloes in the same plane." Standing alone, this rare reference to an individual enslaved workman at Monticello conveys a message of incompetence. In Randolph's opinion, Davy's wheels were not worth shoeing, or fitting with an iron hoop tire, because the

felloes—the wooden segments of a circle that together form the wheel rim—
were out of alignment. Other references reveal that David Hern, as he knew
himself, was in fact a highly skilled woodworker. It was probably his training
rather than his ability that was inadequate in this instance, in which he was
producing wheelbarrows and their wheels, considered the most difficult variety
to make. According to one authority, it was an old saying among carpenters
and wheelwrights that "if you can make a wheelbarrow wheel, you can make
anything."[78]

It is ironic that ineptitude is the apparent message of one of the few detailed
references to David Hern, who performed a multitude of tasks over fifty years,
as a carpenter, a wagoner, and a miller. The fragmentary sources that bear on
the fortunes of Hern and his family reveal a striking array of skills that helped
to support Jefferson's building schemes and the complex operations of his plantation. Hern, at age nineteen, was one of the skilled artisans inherited by
Jefferson from his father-in-law's estate in 1774. Some of the tasks assigned to
him over the years included making gates, fences, plows, and wheelbarrows;
repairing threshing machines; and building cabins and farm buildings. For at
least two years, in 1791 and 1792, he was hired out to Benjamin Colvard, a local
carpenter. Later in the 1790s, Hern was one of the crew of carpenters that built
Bagwell and Minerva Granger's cabin in six days, including the time spent in
felling trees and hewing the logs. In 1807, overseer Edmund Bacon found a way
to save Jefferson the expense of hiring a local white carpenter, by giving a fenc-
ing task to Davy Hern. "You shall se[e] sir when you come home," Bacon wrote
Jefferson, "the work as well done as if Mr. Per[r]y had done it."[79]

David Hern's importance as a trusted workman is revealed in his assignment
to particularly delicate tasks. Jefferson considered him one of the "best hands" to
work with gunpowder to blast rock for a canal along the Rivanna River. When
that canal was completed, he worked for a time as miller at Jefferson's gristmill,
located on the Shadwell farm. He replaced a slave who had been found to be
both disobliging and dishonest. Jefferson described Hern as the "best for the
purpose," adding, "I believe he is honest: but he is addicted to drink at times."
Hern was evidently literate, as, in Jefferson's absence, Thomas Mann Randolph
was to question him occasionally from a set of written instructions listing his
tasks, to keep him to his "metal."[80]

David Hern's wife Isabel, also inherited from John Wayles, was a domestic
servant whom Jefferson thought the most suitable companion for his nine-year-
old daughter Mary on her journey from Virginia to France. He wrote from
Paris, asking his brother-in-law to send his daughter across the Atlantic accompanied by "a careful negro woman, as Isabel for instance." This request entailed
the separation of husband and wife, as Isabel Hern was taken to Chesterfield

County, where Mary Jefferson was staying with her Eppes relations. Isabel's illness following the birth of her child Edith prevented her from making the transatlantic voyage in May 1787, and fourteen-year-old Sally Hemings was sent in her place. Shortly after the departure of the ship carrying the two young girls, David Hern made the hundred-mile journey alone to Eppington to bring his wife and baby daughter back to Monticello; he was given three shillings by Jefferson's steward to pay for ferries across the James River. From then on, Isabel Hern seems to have been a farm laborer, and after a long working day, she and her husband spent some of their spare hours tending their garden plot. They sold cucumbers and potatoes as well as chickens and eggs to the "great house." Davy Hern fished in the Rivanna River and sold his catch to earn money for his family. From 1801 to 1809 Isabel and her younger children— but not her husband—were leased to the tenant of the southern portion of the Monticello plantation. Since their residence was not affected, the family was probably not separated by this arrangement.[81]

The Herns had twelve children, born from 1776 to 1801: James, Moses, Patty, Davy, Edith, Aggy, Lily, Amy, Thruston, Indridge, Thrimston, and Lovilo. Some were farm laborers, and the oldest, James (b. 1776), became foreman of farm labor at Monticello. Several were trained in particular skills and trades, some perhaps by their parents. Thrimston (b. 1799) was a carpenter who also received training in coopering and stonecutting, while Edith (b. 1787) was a household servant who learned French cookery and was head cook at Monticello for many years. Moses (b. 1779) was a nail maker and blacksmith.[82]

For some of the Herns, their valued skills, united with tenacity and persistence, helped them resist the threats to family unity that were central to the institution of slavery, even with a well-disposed master. Both James Hern and his brother Moses followed a pattern that was quite common at Monticello. Despite Jefferson's expressed desire that his slaves find spouses "at home," that is, on the plantation, they often married beyond the Monticello boundaries. Many of the men who appear in Jefferson's Farm Book lists without wives or children had families on other plantations in the county, and some may have married into the local free black community. A slave with an "abroad" spouse was thus dependent on his master's or overseer's permission for night and weekend visits, and since his family had two masters, the risk of separation was essentially doubled. If one master moved, died, or became insolvent, the fate of the couple was in the hands of the other.[83]

David and Isabel Hern's sons found themselves in this precarious situation and turned to Jefferson to prevent separation from their spouses. James Hern's wife belonged to Gabriel Lilly, Monticello overseer from 1800 to 1805. When Lilly left Monticello in the summer of 1805, Jefferson purchased from him

Lucretia and her two sons and "the child of which she is pregnant, when born" for £180 ($600). "Foreman Jim," as James Hern was known, was remembered fifty years later by former Monticello overseer Edmund Bacon for producing every year the "best lot of pork" of the several farms on the plantation, "so that the other overseers said it was no use for them to try anymore, as he would get it [the prize of extra bacon] anyway." James and Cretia Hern and their ten children lived at Monticello until 1824, when they were moved to Poplar Forest.[84]

Since there are no surviving letters about the transaction with Gabriel Lilly, we can only speculate that James Hern petitioned Jefferson to purchase his wife in the same way his brother Moses did in the same period. Moses Hern was a blacksmith and possibly the Moses who broke his leg in a wrestling contest in 1816. His wife, Mary, lived on a plantation about six miles from Monticello, the property of Jefferson's nephew Randolph Lewis. Correspondence suggests that, over several years, Moses Hern persistently asked Jefferson to purchase her. "It was always my intention to buy her whenever I could spare the money if she could be got for a reasonable price," Jefferson explained to his overseer in 1806. Finally, in 1807, when Lewis was about to emigrate to Kentucky, Jefferson reluctantly agreed to buy Hern's wife and their sons, commenting at the time: "Nobody feels more strongly than I do the desire to make all practicable sacrifices to keep man and wife together who have imprudently married out of their respective families."[85]

Like other slave owners, Jefferson recognized the value of family stability in the slave quarters and tried to discourage abroad marriages: "There is nothing I desire so much as that all the young people in the estate should intermarry with one another and stay at home. They are worth a great deal more in that case than when they have husbands and wives abroad." He offered an extra pot and mattress cover to slave women as an incentive to "take husbands at home." Other than these incentives, he seems to have intervened little in the marital relations of his slaves. Like most enslaved people elsewhere in the South, Monticello's African American men and women conducted their courtships and chose their spouses as independently as their restricted mobility permitted. They usually sought the consent of their parents, and if the master's permission was ever required at Monticello, it was probably only in the cases of those who found spouses on other plantations.[86]

Monticello's records provide no clues to the methods by which marriages were celebrated. Although slave marriages were not recognized by Virginia law, unions were validated in a variety of ways. Sometimes white ministers or black preachers officiated at weddings, or more informal rituals like the exchanging of gifts or, in the nineteenth century, "jumping the broomstick" marked this significant change of status. Whatever the ceremony, the institution of marriage, even without the sanction of the law, was of absolutely central importance in the enslaved community. In his recollections, Jefferson's grandson Thomas J. Randolph commented on the stability of slave marriages: "There was as much decency of deportment and as few illegitimates as among the laboring whites elsewhere. As many lived in wedlock from youth to age without reproach." His grandfather's records confirm this statement. Year after year, in his Farm Book, Jefferson recorded the same nuclear family units, broken only by the death of one or the other partner. Only two or three unions seem to have resulted in the equivalent of divorce.[87]

David Hern's son and namesake, known to Jefferson variously as Davy, Jr., Isabel's Davy, or Wagoner Davy, felt the pressures of separation on his own marriage. The young David Hern worked at Monticello as a nail maker, blacksmith, and charcoal burner. His major occupation, however, was driving a cart or wagon. In 1806, Jefferson decided that Davy's wife, Fanny Gillette, would begin training in French cookery at the President's House in Washington. In November Davy and Fanny made the 120-mile journey together in a cart pulled by two mules and loaded with aspen trees dug up from the Monticello grounds. As Jefferson specified to his overseer: "She must take corn for their meals, and provisions for themselves to Washington. Fodder they can buy on the road. I leave $6 with you, to give them to pay unavoidable expenses. . . . They are to go as soon as the Aspen leaves fall."[88]

The day after their arrival in Washington, Davy Hern, Jr., began the return journey to Monticello. Thereafter, every six months he drove his mule cart between Monticello and Washington, transporting letters, crates, and even horses, as Jefferson purchased new ones and retired "decayed" ones. Most of the wagoner's cargo went in the Monticello direction: seeds, nuts, and trees for its gardens and nurseries, hawthorn trees for its hedges, bells and fittings for the house, or gray geese and African hogs for Jefferson's breeding experiments. After five or six days on the road, Hern was able to spend a few days at the White House[89] with his wife and his sister Edith. Sometimes weather or other circumstances extended his stay to as much as a week.[90]

The strain of this long-distance marriage took its toll, however. In 1860 former overseer Edmund Bacon recalled that Davy and Fanny "got into a terrible quarrel. Davy was jealous of his wife, and, I reckon, with good reason." Jefferson sent for Bacon and ordered him to take the couple to Alexandria for sale: "When I got there, they learned what I had come for, and they were in great trouble. They wept, and begged, and made good promises, and made such an ado, that they begged the old gentleman out of it. But it was a good lesson for them. I never heard any more complaint of them; and when I left Mr. Jefferson [in 1822], I left them both at Monticello."[91] In the fall of 1808, Jefferson, in Washington, conveyed this message to David Hern through his overseer: "Be so good as to inform Davy that his child died of the whooping cough on the 4th day after he left." There are three poignant entries in the accounts of the presidential butler, Etienne Lemaire, noting payments for a coffin and other burial expenses for Fanny's infant. Immediately after receiving Jefferson's letter, Edmund Bacon wrote back: "Davy has petitioned for leave to come to see his wife at Christmass. He being so good a fellow I hate to deny him and probably you have some thing for him to bring a cart for." Jefferson agreed, and Davy and Fanny Hern were able to mourn their loss together for five days in Christmas week.[92]

A few months later, Davy was one of the wagoners who assisted Edmund Bacon in the caravan that transported the belongings of a retiring president from the national capital to Monticello. Three wagons, pulled by two six-mule teams and one four-horse team, carried loads of boxes and "shrubbery" from a Washington nursery. A pregnant Fanny Hern and Edith Fossett and her two children rode in the wagons. Bacon rode behind in Jefferson's carriage and was mistaken on the route back for the president himself. Part of the trip was through a snowstorm, "half-leg deep." Fanny Hern, who thereafter worked in the Monticello kitchen with Edith Fossett, was now united with her husband, and their first surviving child, Ellen, was born that summer.[93]

No Jefferson slave, other than the Hemings brothers, traveled further, on his own, than David Hern, Jr. From 1809, he continued to pursue a mixture of occupations, helping his brother-in-law Joe Fossett in the blacksmith shop or driving his mule cart. At least two more times, he took the road to Washington, once to pick up a pair of Barbary sheep and, in 1812, to get a spinning machine for the Monticello textile shop. His brother also made a solo journey to Washington, but not at his owner's bidding. Thruston Hern had been brought up to a trade, probably woodworking. In 1812, Jefferson gave him to his grandson Thomas J. Randolph. Five years later Jefferson wrote to John Barnes, his friend and financial agent in Washington: "A young negro man, named Thruston, brother to Edy, who while I was in Washington, was in the kitchen under the instruction of Mr. Julien, has escaped from my grandson to whom I had given him. He is supposed to have gone to Washington and to be lurking under the connivance of some of his sister's old friends. The bearer Mr. Wheat, my grandson's overseer, who is acquainted in that vicinity goes in quest of him. . . . It is thought best that the mission of the bearer should be known to no mortal but yourself and him, and not the least intimation of it should get out." According to Edmund Bacon, the twenty-two-year-old fugitive had taken an opportunity provided by James Madison's visit to Monticello after he retired from office. Thruston Hern left Monticello with one of Madison's wagoners, passed himself off as a servant of the ex-president, and was never recovered.[94]

When Thruston Hern chose freedom over family in 1817, David and Isabel Hern had already lost four of their children—Patty, Aggy, Lovilo, and Amy—to death. In 1819, a year full of sickness and death at Monticello, Isabel Hern died. Seven years later, David Hern and his thirty-four surviving children and grandchildren were among the 150 slaves appraised as part of the estate of Thomas Jefferson. He and his children had raised Jefferson's crops, driven his wagons, cooked his meals, built his barns, directed his laborers, and made nails, barrels, plows, and plow chains. They worked in the house, in the fields, and in the shops, a complex network of family members who crossed all social borders within the plantation and thus belied any notion of clearcut hierarchy within the African American community at Monticello. In the appraisal of the estate, the Herns were allotted values from $150 for the younger grandchildren to $500 for grandson Davy, a cooper. But David Hern the woodworker, at the age of seventy-one, was declared "worth nothing." He was one of five aged slaves for whom Thomas Jefferson Randolph received an exemption from taxes the following year.[95]

The fragmentary records that survive suggest that the Hern family members were sold to a wide range of bidders at the several auctions of the estate. Three of David Hern's children were purchased by men connected with the University of Virginia. His daughter Lily, who had spent her life laboring in the Monticello fields, was sold to a German professor of languages, along with her husband, Ben.[96]

Her brother Thrimston was sold to University proctor Arthur Brockenbrough for $600, one of the highest sums paid for a Monticello slave. This thirty-year-old man with multiple trades had worked as a carpenter and a cooper until the 1820s, when Jefferson hired him out for several years to John Gorman, a quarryman and mason. Gorman, in his own words, made Thrimston Hern into "a tollerable good stone cutter." Together Gorman and Hern had cut and installed the slate paving and stone caps and bases of the columns of Monticello's west portico. In the summer of 1823, there was a kind of family tug of war for Thrimston's talents. Jefferson's grandson needed him for the wheat harvest, while Martha Randolph, "mired" in red dirt while the portico floor was under construction, pleaded that he be allowed to remain with Gorman, who said that "he can do nothing without Thrimston." Brockenbrough purchased Thrimston Hern in 1829 to complete the stonework of Jefferson's Rotunda, saving the University twenty-five cents a foot over the prices of a Philadelphia stonecutter. The Proctor collected the payments, and Thrimston Hern constructed the steps that led from the lawn to the second floor of the University's most important building.[97]

Just before the Monticello sale in January 1827, the wife of medical professor Robley Dunglison had written to Jefferson's executor: "I have felt so much interested for Fanny as she has once lived with me, for fear she may be sent to a distance, that the Doctor has permitted me to try to obtain her at the sale as well as her youngest child, should they go at a reasonable price." The Dunglisons did purchase Fanny Hern and her youngest child, Bonnycastle, who was apparently named after another professor, Charles Bonnycastle. And it was no doubt her appeals that led to a sales invoice two years later, noting the additional purchase of her husband, "Waggoner David." Thirteen years later, Jefferson's granddaughter Virginia Trist, writing from France, asked her sister-in-law to "remember me most kindly" to "all our old servants." David and Fanny Hern were two of the eight men and women she named.[98]

The 1820s and 1830s were more difficult for David Hern's brother Moses, who had petitioned so persistently for the purchase of his wife and children. In 1819, Jefferson gave the blacksmith to his grandson Thomas J. Randolph. While his immediate fate is uncertain, it is possible he was sent to the Randolph family plantation in Bedford County, adjoining Poplar Forest. In the same year Moses and Mary Hern's eighteen-year-old son, William (Billy), who had always lived at Monticello, ran away to Poplar Forest. This puzzling destination may be explained by a desire to see his father. He was sent back to Charlottesville to jail but ran off a few months later, again to Bedford County. In the late spring of 1821, Jefferson's Poplar Forest steward wrote that "Billy is still out, and have joind. a gang of Runaways, and they are doing great mischief to the neig[h]boring stock, considerable exertions have been made to take them, but without success." A week later he reported that Billy, "still out," and his comrades took a shoat or lamb every day or two from the surrounding plantations. Billy Hern then vanished from the record.[99]

It was only in 1824 that Jefferson moved Moses Hern's wife, Mary, and their children (except for two sons, Davy and Zachariah) to his Poplar Forest plantation. The 1827 inventory of his estate includes testimony to a marriage that endured despite these dislocations: the names of two additional sons, James and Moses, born in the 1820s. The inventory was the preliminary to an auction sale that undoubtedly fragmented the family. Moses Hern's response to this crisis is captured in a local newspaper, which contained a word portrait of the fifty-three-year-old husband and father. James Brooks of Campbell County announced in the pages of the *Lynchburg Virginian* that "my Blacksmith MOSES, formerly the property of Thomas Jefferson," had run away. He described the fugitive as "about five feet ten inches high, quite stout made, rather of light complexion" and speculated that he would "likely make some stay at Mr. Joel Yancey's, Bedford . . . where he has a daughter; . . . then we suppose he will try to get to Charlottesville, Albemarle, where a great many of his family lives."[100]

1796: The Gathering

In the summer of 1796, a French traveler forded the Rivanna River and rode through a field where he found Thomas Jefferson "in the midst of the harvest, from which the scorching heat of the sun does not prevent his attendance." The duc de La Rochefoucauld-Liancourt did not mention the almost seventy other people whose activities Jefferson was directing, including all the members of the Hern family over the age of nine. Every June brought an event that drew together every able-bodied man, woman, and child from the several farms that made up the Monticello plantation. The blacksmiths extinguished their fires, the carpenters put aside their axes and planes, and the spinners left their wheels to join the farm laborers. The wagoners brought their mule teams to the field. Only the female house servants were exempted from the annual wheat harvest.[101]

In June of the previous year, Jefferson had pondered the performance of his wheat-gathering force and drawn up a plan to make the harvest of 1796 more efficient. He listed the eighteen strong men (including David Hern and his twenty-year-old son, James) who would cut the wheat with cradle scythes, the twenty-four women and boys (Isabel, Patty, and Davy Hern, Jr., among them) to gather and bind the sheaves, the three teenaged boys (Moses Hern was one) to help load the four carts, and six men to stack the cut wheat. George Granger was to be stationed at a grindstone mounted in a mule cart, "constantly employed" in sharpening and mending the scythes. Two women in their sixties, Betty and Fanny, were reserved for cooking the meals, and eight younger women—including Isaac Granger's wife, Iris—were "to keep half the ploughs agoing" in other fields.[102]

For the enslaved laborers at Monticello, the wheat harvest must have been a time of both backbreaking exertions and communal festivity. From dawn to dusk, David and James Hern, young George and Bagwell Granger, and the other cradlers—in a carefully staggered line—swung their scythes back and forth in a measured rhythm that was probably maintained by song. They cut the wheat at the individual rate of two acres a day, down from three the previous year. The women raked up the wheat and laid it in sheaves, which the boys tied and set up in shocks ready for the stackers and loaders. On these longest days of the year, the gatherers and binders were pressed to rake, bind, and tie ever faster, as a harvest operation on this scale did not permit the family cooperation possible on smaller farms. As one former Virginia slave recalled, "One could help the other when they got behind. . . . The Man what was doing the cradling would always go no faster than the woman, who was most times his wife, could keep up." A nineteenth-century British account captures the nature of the exhausting labor involved, although this harvest took place under a feebler northern sun, the cutting tool was different, and the English harvesters were paid for their efforts: "The edge of the reap-hook had to be driven by force through the stout stalks like a sword, blow after blow, minute after minute, hour after hour; the back stooping, and the broad sun throwing his fiery rays from a full disc on the head and neck. . . . So they worked and slaved, and tore at the wheat as if they were seized with a frenzy; the heat, the aches, the illness, the sunstroke, always impending in the air—the stomach hungry again before the meal was over."[103]

This was also the only time in the year when virtually the entire working population of the plantation—sixty-six people from the age of nine to sixty-nine—assembled in one place. The scene may have resembled another Virginia wheat harvest, in the 1850s, remembered by the white daughter of a plantation-owning family as "the biggest kind of frolic" for the children, black and white, who liked to watch for the rabbits and quail flushed from the grain and appreciated the special midday and evening meals spread out on long tables under the trees. After sunset brought an end to the labor, the sound of a banjo started the musical conclusion of the day and "finally the whole crowd would be singing some old-time melody." Harvest time was also one of the few occasions when whiskey was part of the Monticello slave's allotment, four gallons a day for the assembled laborers.[104]

The agricultural routine settled back into its ordinary rhythm after the harvest. The artisans returned to their shops, and the farmworkers again took up their everyday tasks at each of the Monticello farms. They plowed in the wheat stubble and, starting in September, planted the next season's crop. Jefferson had, except in occasional years when the price was high, abandoned the long and complicated process of raising tobacco, and from the 1790s, wheat was his staple crop at Monticello. His admiration for the progressive agriculture of England made him an enthusiastic advocate of crop rotation. In his rotation plan, each of the seven fields at each farm was planted in wheat twice every seven years. In the other fields, the laborers raised corn and potatoes, field peas, and the soil-improving red clover. A steady round of plowing was thus an integral part of the new agriculture. Weather permitting, the plows were in the fields every working day of the year. They came in all sizes, large ones for turning over previously uncultivated sod to small ones for weeding between corn hills. Strong young men drove the larger plows, while women and young boys guided the smaller ones.

The evolution of agriculture in Virginia at the end of the eighteenth century, when grains replaced tobacco, called for a wide array of occupations and a corresponding assortment of skills. At Monticello the multiple activities of a mixed grain and livestock operation replaced the single-minded, labor-intensive pursuit of a crop of tobacco. Along with this diversity came a need for a variety of vehicles and more complicated machinery—like threshing machines and grain drills—that demanded frequent maintenance and expertise in operation. The perpetual round of plowing meant that horses, mules, and oxen needed to be kept in top condition. It was mainly men who performed these more specialized tasks, while women remained in the fields with their hoes. John and Jerry looked after the health of the valuable mules and purebred Merino rams, while David Hern and John Hemings built the wagons and repaired the agricultural machinery. Jefferson's Farm Book and letters are filled with notations on all manner of plants and animals, as he experimented with new breeds of hogs and sheep and with fodder crops, from the standard rye and oats to the unusual pumpkins and Jerusalem artichokes. The many operations of his mathematically minded husbandry were carried out almost wholly by his enslaved labor force.

Women and children remained central to his schemes. As Jefferson wrote in 1820, "Women . . . are of real value in the farm, where there is abundance to be done of what they can do, and which otherwise would employ men." Young boys and women like Iris Granger and Tamar handled the plows, and when Jefferson introduced contour plowing to his fields, fifteen-year-old Thruston Hern used a ten-foot rafter level to make the horizontal guidelines for the plows. Jefferson later described this practice: "A man, or a boy of 12. or 15. years old, with the level, and two smaller boys to mark the steps, the one with sticks, the other with the hoe, will do an acre of this an hour." When a thirty-five-year-old crop worker asked to be sold in 1815, Jefferson described her as "a fine handy sensible [woman], a worker in the crop." Her thirteen-year-old son, he wrote, "works well at the plough already."[105]

Jefferson continued his practice of working his farms with "gangs" of men and women in equal numbers. At each of the quarter farms, the activities of the ten or twelve laborers followed the rhythm of the seasons. After the September planting of wheat, they gathered corn and field peas in October and November and spent the winter cleaning up the fields, repairing fences, or cutting firewood. Spring was the time to plant corn and peas and take a first cutting of clover. Finally, at the end of June came the climactic moment of the agricultural year.

In his harvest plan for 1796 Jefferson allotted six days for bringing in three hundred acres of wheat. The actual harvest took twice as long. Because the heavy wheat dulled the scythe blades too quickly for George Granger at the grindstone, never more than thirteen men were mowing at once. Still, the gatherers and binders fell behind the cutters so that the women at the plows had to be brought in to assist as "pickers up." It was, nevertheless, a banner harvest, "the finest . . . ever seen in this part of the country," as Jefferson wrote at the time.

By July 7 there were 546 stacks of grain surrounding the barns of the four Monticello farms.[106]

The Hubbard Brothers

In September 1805 a strapping twenty-two-year-old black man, dressed in a dove-colored waistcoat, nankeen knee breeches, a coat, and a new hat, was traveling on foot through Fairfax County, just west of Washington, D.C. Like all people of his color in a place where he was unknown, he excited suspicion. Accosted and questioned by the local jailer, he said he was a free man of Albemarle County, James Bowles by name, and produced two manumission papers and a pass to the federal city. Despite these documents, he was taken to a justice of the peace and then to Fairfax jail.

Four days in jail led to a confession. The young man on his way to Washington was actually James Hubbard of Monticello. Because of mail delays, President Jefferson did not learn of the fate of his runaway slave until a month later. He then paid a man traveling to Albemarle County twenty dollars to carry Hubbard "home." The expenses of the jailer, who tried to extract a bonus because he had run a great risk in arresting "as large fellow as he is," added a further thirty-five dollars to the costs of Hubbard's action.[107]

Although the full circumstances of Hubbard's bid for freedom will never be known, the documentary record suggests a temperament that was a rarity in the Monticello slave quarters. While there were numerous instances of men who ran away on sudden provocation and for short periods, James Hubbard's flight was evidently planned well in advance and intended to be permanent. His failure did not deter him from making a second—and possibly a third—attempt to burst the bonds of the system into which he was born. Hubbard's response to the institution of slavery was unusual, not just on Jefferson's plantations but in his own family as well.

James and Philip Hubbard, known to Jefferson as Jame, or Jamey, and Phill, were born at Monticello in 1783 and 1786, the sons of James and Cate Hubbard. The elder James Hubbard had been a waterman for Jefferson's father-in-law, John Wayles, at the Elk Hill plantation in Goochland County. Hubbard probably piloted tobacco canoes down the James River or ferried goods and livestock across it. For plantation owners, rivers provided the best means of getting crops to market. For slaves, they were important arteries of communication. Watermen carried news as well as barrels and hogsheads. At riverside plantations, they could meet and trade with many separate enslaved communities. With their boats moored together at night on a lonely stretch of river, boatmen from different parts of Virginia could exchange information or plan escape routes. James Hubbard's mobile occupation gave him an extensive acquaintance and an intimate knowledge of the James River and its fishing along the hundred-mile stretch from Elk Hill to the ports near the coast. He may also have gained a trait that was notable among watermen, an unusually independent mind.[108]

Hubbard's wife, Cate, was among the slaves Jefferson had inherited from his father. Some time in the late 1780s, the Hubbards and their children were moved from Albemarle County to the Poplar Forest plantation ninety miles to the southwest and close to the James River over one hundred miles upstream from the section James Hubbard had known so well in his youth. At Poplar Forest, Hubbard, who was also a skilled shoemaker, occupied a position of authority and trust, becoming a foreman of labor, or "headman." In Jefferson's records the Hubbard family always appears in the first place, at the top of every list he made of his Bedford County slaves.[109]

In January 1794, three days before he left Philadelphia for retirement to Monticello, Thomas Jefferson placed an order for a ton of iron with a Quaker merchant. After this shipment arrived at Monticello at the end of April, a new industry began. Jefferson had decided to manufacture nails, an operation that he hoped would provide a cash income while he pursued his efforts to bring his farms back into production. He also saw it as a way to make more efficient use of his labor force, by employing slaves who could not be fully productive elsewhere on the plantation. Even children could master the simple and repetitive process of turning long thin rods of iron into nails. As Jefferson wrote in 1795, "I now employ a dozen little boys from 10. to 16. years of age, overlooking all the details of their business myself." Virtually all the teenaged boys on the Monticello plantation became nail makers, and to bring his force up to the desired level, Jefferson turned to the families of Poplar Forest.[110]

Thus, in 1794, James Hubbard's eleven-year-old son and namesake moved into a new home, a log cabin on the side of Monticello mountain, leaving his parents and siblings behind in Bedford County. Two years later the young Jame Hubbard's brother Phill joined him in the household of Phill the wagoner and his wife Molly, who may have been relatives. Six days a week the boys rose before dawn to walk the six hundred yards to the mountaintop to take their places at the fires in the nailery on Mulberry Row.

Young Jame's performance was poor. According to Jefferson's nailery accounts, Jame Hubbard "wasted" more iron in the nail-making process than any other nailer. For every hundred pounds of iron nail rod he was given, only seventy pounds became nails. Two other boys of his age were almost as inefficient, while the rate of loss of Davy Hern, a year younger, was only eighteen pounds per hundredweight. Jame's performance improved quickly, however, for two years later he was one of the most productive and efficient nailers, making ninety pounds of nails from every hundred pounds of nail rod. In his twenties he worked with the largest size nail rod, turning out fifteen pounds of twenty-penny nails each day. He may have received some training in blacksmithing from the younger George Granger, who supervised the nailers in this period. Hubbard had at least rudimentary woodworking skills, as he was one of those released from the nailery in 1801 to wield an axe to clear land. He probably also sometimes worked with Jacob Silknitter, a charcoal burner who trained some of the Monticello slaves in his trade. The charcoal they produced, which required 100 to 150 cords of wood each year, fueled the fires of the nailery.[111]

Jame and Phill Hubbard were periodically permitted to return to Bedford County to see family and friends, usually at Christmastime. On December 20, 1806, Jame, Phill, and two other nailers with families at Poplar Forest set out on foot from Monticello, accompanying a wagon carrying cowpeas, clover seed, and chickens. They were to help Jerry the wagoner with a ram and calf also making the three-day journey and to return "home" on the evening of New Year's day. This is an interesting dispensation, in light of Jame Hubbard's actions just fifteen months before.[112]

His first attempt to escape to freedom, the previous year, had been preceded by careful preparation. Since he knew he would have to camouflage his identity as a bondsman, he needed clothing that would distinguish him from the majority of slaves, who wore a virtual uniform allotted to them by their masters. He also required papers that would convince any suspicious person that he was a free man traveling on legitimate business. These prerequisites to successful flight could only be acquired with money, which Hubbard must have saved over a long period. The records suggest an effort to accumulate funds by working in his free time. He appears in Jefferson's Memorandum Books twice before his escape, receiving payment for hauling and, in 1802, for burning charcoal.[113]

It was Jefferson's practice to encourage the efficiency of his enslaved charcoal burners by offering them a premium according to the number of bushels of charcoal they could extract, on average, from a cord of wood—at the rate of five cents per bushel. When, for instance, blacksmith Frank burned a kiln in 1799 that produced charcoal at the rate of thirty-nine bushels per cord, Jefferson gave him $1.95 (39 × $0.05), paid in "half-dimes." Jefferson's 1802 payment of four dollars to Jame Hubbard and Cary, a fellow nailer, indicates that the two youths probably burned two kilns of charcoal at a comparable efficiency rate—a better-than-average one. Each kiln required the cutting and careful stacking of about thirty cords of wood and then a painstaking round-the-clock process of maintaining constant temperature after the fire was lit. During the long nights spent monitoring the heat of the kilns, Hubbard and Cary may have talked of their longing for liberty and plotted ways to change their status from enslaved to free.[114]

Cary was not fated to continue as Hubbard's companion in conspiracy. The next year, irritated by the prank of another nailer, Cary "took a most barbarous revenge." As Thomas Mann Randolph reported, Cary came up behind Betty Hemings's grandson Brown Colbert and, with his hammer, "struck him with his whole strength," fracturing his skull. Brown survived the attack, but Cary soon felt the effects of Jefferson's swift response to the episode. "It will be necessary for me to make an example of him in terrorem to others," he wrote back to his son-in-law, "in order to maintain the police so rigorously necessary among the nail boys." He asked that Cary be sold either to a trader from the Lower South or "in any other quarter so distant as never more to be heard of among us. It would to the others be as if he were put out of the way by death."[115]

Two years later Jame Hubbard set his plan in motion. He used what money he was able to save to acquire the necessary articles of clothing. His new hat, coat, and knee breeches distinguished him from most of Monticello's male slaves, who wore coarse jackets and long trousers. Only coachmen and carriage drivers were issued greatcoats. Hubbard had procured a second coat, which he gave, along with five dollars, to the son of Gabriel Lilly, Monticello's overseer. In exchange he received a set of forged free papers that he believed would protect him in his flight to Washington. But Jame Hubbard, who never received the benefits of education, had no way of knowing what a poor bargain he had made. Wilson Lilly was barely literate himself. The precious documents the fugitive carried were "soe bad wrote and formed," according to the Fairfax jailer who apprehended him, that he was immediately spotted for a runaway.[116]

Nine years later Jame Hubbard's brother Phill also ran away, but not with the intention of leaving home and family behind. While Jame had remained a nail maker at Monticello into his twenties, Phill Hubbard had left the nailery to become a farmworker at Monticello's Tufton quarter farm. He also worked as a sawyer and assisted in building work. While Poplar Forest was under construction, Phill was sometimes dispatched from Monticello to assist the masons and plasterers there. In 1808, he spent several months excavating the sunken lawn on the garden side of the house, piling the earth he removed to make two mounds that were part of Jefferson's ornamental landscape plans. In 1812, the year he was moved permanently back to Bedford County, Jefferson suggested to the overseer that Phill Hubbard work with the plasterer, "because he understands the making mortar so well."[117]

In 1814, on Christmas day, or just before, Phill Hubbard left Poplar Forest without permission and arrived at Monticello on December 27 with a complaint. Jefferson wrote back to his Bedford County overseer: "[Phill] says, that he and

Dick's Hanah had become husband and wife, but that you drove him repeatedly from her father's house and would not let him go there, punishing her, as he supposes, for receiving him." Poplar Forest at that time was divided into two farms, Bear Creek and Tomahawk; Hannah lived at one and Phill Hubbard at the other. Overseer Jeremiah Goodman's letter of explanation does not clarify the issue. He admitted slapping Hannah several times but denied interfering in the courtship. In any case, running away to Monticello in quest of Jefferson's intercession accomplished Phill Hubbard's purpose. Not only were husband and wife united, but Phill achieved another goal. He had been "long petitioning" Jefferson to "let him go to Bearcreek to live with his family." Jefferson ordered Goodman to send Phill Hubbard and his wife to Bear Creek and then concluded: "I would by no means have Phill punished for what he has done; for altho I had let them all know that their runnings away should be punished, yet Phill's character is not that of a runaway. I have known him from a boy and that he has not come off to sculk from his work." Phill and Hannah Hubbard had a son, Dick, born in the year following the sanctioning of their union. Only four years later, however, the young father was unable to participate in the wheat harvest. "I fear [he] will hardly ever be of much service," overseer Joel Yancey wrote about the thirty-three-year-old Phill Hubbard, who was dead of unknown causes before the year was out.[118]

What is known of the contrasting motivations of the two brothers bears on the interpretation of an incident reported by Monticello overseer Edmund Bacon. Decades after the event he recalled that one day he noticed that all the eightpenny nails from the nailery were missing. Theft was a fact of life on southern plantations, and the enslaved made an ethical distinction between stealing from whites and from blacks. As reported in 1816, African American Baptists in Virginia felt that "it is no crime, in the sight of God, to steal their master's property, arguing that it is taking their own labour." Jefferson echoed this view when he wrote in his *Notes on Virginia* that "the man, in whose favour no laws of property exist, probably feels himself less bound to respect those made in favour of others." Locks were everywhere at Monticello, and keys were needed to open rooms, cellars, storehouses, shops, carriages, bookcases, chests, trunks, harpsichords, and the gate to the garden. References to theft involve Jefferson's corn cribs, charcoal sheds, poultry yard, washhouse, wine cellars, and even his bedroom.[119]

Edmund Bacon suspected one of the nailers, who, charged with the theft, "denied it powerfully." Later, however, Bacon spotted some muddy tracks that he followed to a tree in the woods, in which he found a box containing several hundred pounds of nails. After the discovery, the offender "was mortified and distressed beyond measure. He had been brought up in the shop, and we all had confidence in him. Now his character was gone. The tears streamed down his face, and he begged pardon over and over again." Jefferson was surprised by this misbehavior in "a favorite servant" but did not have him punished. According to Bacon, Jefferson's indulgent treatment caused the repentent thief to determine "to seek religion till I find it," and soon afterward he applied for a permit to be baptized. Bacon remembered this man as "Jim Hubbard," but his final remark—"He was always a good servant afterwards"—certainly suggests a mistaken memory. The hoarder of nails must have been another nail maker, possibly even Jame Hubbard's brother Phill. Three hundred pounds of nails with a market value of almost fifty dollars would have been a very tempting prize for someone saving for freedom, but there is no way Bacon could have remembered Jame Hubbard as "a good servant afterwards."[120]

After his first ill-starred attempt to escape, Jame Hubbard was apparently only biding his time and conserving his resources. Late in 1810 or early in 1811, he again left Monticello, this time heading west instead of north. While the timing of his first flight in 1805 may have been precipitated by the arrival of a new overseer, his destination was probably influenced by the presence at Monticello of two black servants from the White House—one a free man and the other with ten more years to serve on a contract for freedom. Jack Shorter, a hostler, and John Freeman, a dining room servant, usually accompanied Jefferson back to Monticello for the long summer vacation. Shorter and Freeman, as well as Ursula Hughes and Edith Fossett, apprentice cooks in the White House kitchen, would have shared their knowledge of the African American community, both free and enslaved, in Washington. Confident in his camouflage clothing and his forged free papers, Hubbard no doubt thought that the network of urban blacks in the federal city offered the best chance for refuge or assistance in reaching the free states of the North.[121]

For his second attempt, however, Jame Hubbard chose a different direction. The Christmas holidays, the longest period without work in a slave's year, were often used by escaping slaves to cloak their unauthorized movements. During this four- to seven-day release from daily routine, many African Americans were on the move. Children visited parents, and husbands and wives visited spouses on other plantations. Hired men and women returned home at the end of their period of service. In this shifting, unsettled atmosphere, Jame Hubbard undertook his journey southwest to Lexington, seventy miles from Monticello. While he may have made his way across the Blue Ridge Mountains by road and woodland track, it is equally possible that he used a method of travel associated with his father's former life on Virginia's waterways. Because of his many trips between Monticello and Poplar Forest, the younger Hubbard knew the best routes to the James River. The independent community of boatmen could then have assisted him in reaching Rockbridge County, through the Blue Ridge along the passage carved by the river.

For over a year, Jefferson had no idea where his rebellious slave had gone. Soon after this second desertion, however, he took measures to divest himself of such a disruptive element. He sold Hubbard, in absentia, to Reuben Perry, one of his hired carpenters. As Edmund Bacon recalled, Jefferson's "orders to me were constant: that if there was any servant that could not be got along without the chastising that was customary, to dispose of him." An early runaway, Sandy, a shoemaker and carpenter who absconded in 1769, was sold within three years. The two surviving runaways from Monticello during the Revolution were both sold soon after their return. In 1804, Jefferson took measures for the sale of Kit even before he was recaptured and jailed. Jefferson wrote in 1820 that he had "scruples against selling negroes but for delinquency, or on their own request." Jame Hubbard had crossed the line, entering the category of "delinquency" or persistent violation of the rule of the plantation. Jefferson wished to have nothing more to do with the twenty-eight-year-old runaway.[122]

Nevertheless, in 1812, he spent seventy dollars in efforts to recapture him because, according to his contract with Perry, he would receive two hundred dollars more in payment if Hubbard were recovered. When, in March, Jefferson learned that the fugitive had been living in Lexington for over a year, he sent in pursuit a man who arrived "five days after Hubbard had run off from there, having committed a theft." The man set off a second time, stimulated by a premium of twenty-five dollars. This time "he got upon his tract, and pursued him into Pendleton county, where he took him and brought him here in irons."

When Jame Hubbard was brought back to Monticello from the mountains of what is now West Virginia, Jefferson decreed another kind of exemplary punishment in addition to that meted out to Hubbard's nail-making companion Cary nine years before: "I had him severely flogged in the presence of his old companions, and committed to jail." Jefferson strongly advised Perry to sell the runaway, and he urged that he be sold "out of the state," expressing his view that "the course he has been in, and all circumstances convince me he will never again serve any man as a slave. The moment he is out of jail and his irons off he will be off himself."[123]

No further word of Jame Hubbard's fate has been found. An advertisement placed in the Virginia papers by Reuben Perry shortly after he ran off in 1811 confirms the impression of a character that was probably not soon forgotten at Monticello. Jame Hubbard was a perfect match for John Hope Franklin's profile of a runaway as young, strong, and black: "RANAWAY, from his plantation, in Albemarle, a negro man called JAMES HUBBARD . . . 27 years of age, about six feet high, stout limbs and strong made, of daring demeanor, bold and harsh

RANAWAY, from his plantation, in Albemarle, a negro man called JAMES HUB-
BARD, of the property of the Subscriber, living in Bedford, a Nailor by trade, of 27 years of age, about six feet high, stout limbs and strong made; of daring demeanor, bold and harsh features, dark complexion, apt to drink freely and had even furnished himself with money and probably a free pass ; on a former elopement he attempted to get out of the State Northwardly, and was taken and confined in Halifax Jail for some time, being then the property of Thomas Jefferson, and probably may have taken the same direction now ; whoever apprehends the said slave, and delivers him to the Subscriber in Bedford county, or into the Jail of either Albemarle or Bedford, shall receive Forty Dollars in addition to what the law allows.

REUBEN PERRY.

April 12.   w4w

Advertisement from *Richmond Enquirer*, 12 April 1811.

features, dark complexion." A further line confirms the impression that, for Hubbard, achieving freedom was his life's work. Perry stated that the runaway "had even furnished himself with money and probably a free pass."[124]

1807: Force and Resistance

Sometime in May 1807, John Craven, tenant of Jefferson's farms south of the Rivanna River, met a black man at a spring on the mountain adjacent to Monticello. When the man failed to give a satisfactory account of his presence there, Craven "took hold" of him as a suspected runaway slave and started for the town of Milton. After a half mile, the black man, whose name was James, told Craven he had taken some pork and cornmeal from the storehouses of Jefferson's overseer Edmund Bacon. They turned around and walked instead to James's "den in the mountain," where Craven found three pieces of bacon and a bag of meal. A few days later, Edmund Bacon encountered James in chains outside a house in Milton and, again, James spoke of breaking into Bacon's smokehouse. These unaccountable confessions—apparently voluntary—were enough to convict James of burglary two months later. He was sentenced "to be hanged by the neck at the Public Gallows" in Charlottesville on the second Friday in September.[125]

James, as it turned out, belonged to Martin Baker of neighboring Orange County, and his "den" was located on Jefferson's land. His drama, which unfolded through the summer of 1807, is a striking emblem of the forces of law arrayed against a Virginia slave. That he chose for his refuge a remote corner of the

Monticello plantation, over thirty miles from home, suggests that he was one of the slaves Jefferson had hired from Baker the previous year. James may have had friends, or even a wife, among Monticello's African American residents, who would thus have been vividly aware of his situation after his apprehension and very probably before that. It is virtually certain they would have known of his presence and may even have assisted him by providing food and information.[126]

The violence that was a part of daily life in Virginia was reflected in its legal code. The increasingly humanitarian climate at the end of the eighteenth century led to gradual reform of the statutes on crimes and punishments. Because of the need to protect the system of slavery, however, the laws still fell especially hard on the enslaved. James's sentence shocks us today, but stealing was still a capital crime for slaves; for whites, crimes against property had not been capital offenses since 1796. While only fifty free Virginians were executed in the eighty years from 1785 to 1865, ninety-eighty Virginia slaves were hanged just in the decade of James's case. In 1809, when Jefferson's baggage was plundered by enslaved James River boatmen, he expected that the thieves would "doubtless be hung for it." "Some such example," he continued, "is much wanting to render property waterborne secure."[127]

Once James had been found guilty of burglary, the local justices that convicted him had only one option: a sentence of death. Since 1801, however, a law, which Jefferson had endorsed, permitted the governor and Council to commute death sentences to transportation. Thenceforth, almost 90 percent of slaves convicted of stealing were spared the gallows. James was among almost one thousand enslaved Virginians who were removed from the state rather than executed over the course of the nineteenth century, a fate that he may or may not have viewed as preferable to death. He was taken out of Virginia, probably to Florida or another location in Spanish territory, and sold.[128]

Monticello's African Americans were acutely aware of the mechanisms of Virginia justice that safeguarded the institution of slavery and treated the enslaved as property rather than humans. They had encountered or at least heard tales of the patrollers who were paid by the Albemarle County court to police the plantations at night or on weekends, breaking up unlawful assemblies or arresting those without passes.[129] Those who tried to run away were familiar with sheriffs and jails, and a few men had actual experience of the courts. In 1824 a Monticello carter named Isaac was tried and acquitted for the murder of his wife, Sucky, who languished for a month after being struck in the temple by a hoe. Hercules, a Poplar Forest slave, had at least three brushes with the law. In 1813, at the age of nineteen he was jailed after running away. Jefferson recommended leniency to his overseer, believing that "it is his first folly in this way." Six years later Hercules was called before the local magistrate and accused, along with a black doctor, of poisoning, the suspected cause of many deaths among the Poplar Forest slaves. Although the evidence was not strong enough to send them to jail, Jefferson's steward believed Hercules deserved hanging. In 1822, Hercules was involved in an incident that led to a full-fledged court case. He and two other Poplar Forest slaves attacked the overseer and were charged not only with stabbing and intent to kill but with "wickedly and feloniously having consulted upon the subject of rebelling and making insurrection against the law and government of . . . Virginia." Hercules and Gawen were found not guilty, while Hannah's Billy, who had wielded the knife, was sentenced to burning "in the left hand" and thirty-nine lashes for all counts except conspiracy.[130]

When the legal system failed to mete out sufficient punishment, Jefferson enacted his own form of plantation justice. Malfunctioning parts of his plantation machine had to be removed, and those who remained had to be given an object lesson in how to survive the system. Like Jame Hubbard, the three Poplar Forest rebels were probably whipped before their companions. They were almost immediately transported to the Deep South, "sent as an example to N. Orleans to be sold." Before Jefferson could recover their value by sale, the infamous climate took its toll. In Louisiana all three became "very sick." Hercules and Gawen died, while Billy ran away after his recovery and found himself in jail again in New Orleans. Because of the comings and goings of workers and wagoners, as well as the number of families with members at both plantations, the impact of this news, the most dreaded by enslaved African Americans, would have also been felt ninety miles away at Monticello.[131]

Edmund Bacon recalled that Jefferson "could not bear to have a servant whipped, no odds how much he deserved it." It seems clear that the harsh physical punishment that was customary in Virginia was tempered at Monticello. "I abhor severity," Jefferson wrote in 1805, and former slave Peter Fossett remembered that Monticello slaves "were seldom punished, except for stealing and fighting." Whips and brutality were by no means unknown at Monticello, however, as previously mentioned cruel overseers and exemplary whippings attest. Still, conditions were probably better at Monticello than on most other plantations in the state, particularly when Jefferson was in residence.[132]

Monticello's African American residents well knew that those with a persistent dream of freedom were not given a second chance. Repeated violation of plantation rule, or "delinquency," inevitably led to separation. As they watched the flogging of Jame Hubbard or saw Cary taken away by a Georgia slave trader, they developed their own strategies for contending with the system that shackled them. Theirs was a daily struggle against the indignities of slavery, and they undoubtedly practiced many of the forms of day-to-day resistance that were universal in the South. Slaves collaborated to set their work pace, to improve their working conditions, and to maintain their customary rights. Ingenuity and cooperation could lessen the workload. A woman might "lose" the hoes one morning to save herself and her friends from some of the day's grubbing. Another farm laborer would slow his rate of weeding if a friend was feeling poorly. Monticello's African Americans became masters of the art of complaint and negotiation. Jefferson gave up the cultivation of hemp for a time because breaking and beating it was "so much complained of by our laborers." A group of Poplar Forest farmworkers slipped off to Lynchburg on a Sunday, before the overseer could force them to gather the tobacco crop. The Herns, the Gillettes, and the Hemingses knew that the acquisition and exercise of skills that made them valuable to their master increased their bargaining power as well as giving them access to material goods.[133]

While protecting their right to their "own time," as the Poplar Forest farmworkers did, Monticello's African Americans resisted the dehumanizing effects of the institution of slavery by filling this time with creative expressions of a rich culture. Bountiful gardens, bright pieced quilts, and rhythmic songs were far more than methods of nourishment, keeping off the cold, or marking the swing of a scythe. They were part of a cultural and spiritual life that flourished independent of masters and forced labor. On the same wooded mountain where the fugitive James had his hideaway, enslaved people fifty years later gathered to listen to their preacher, safe in their knowledge of ancient routes of communication, should patrollers interrupt their worship.[134]

The Gillette Family

On June 3, 1844, a forty-three-year-old man appeared in the Albemarle County courthouse to obtain a document that would officially recognize his new status of freedom. Israel Gillette produced evidence of his emancipation by his wife Elizabeth. The clerk of the court recorded his age, his height (five feet four inches), and his "light complexion" and then asked him by what surname he chose to be known. As the former slave remembered thirty years later, "I hesitated, and he suggested that it should be Jefferson, because I was born at Monticello and had been a good and faithful servant to Thomas Jefferson. Besides, he said, it would give me more dignity to be called after so eminent a man. So I consented to adopt the surname of Jefferson, and have been known by it ever since."

Israel Jefferson left the courthouse with a piece of paper that, as long as he kept it safely at hand, would protect him from arrest as a runaway slave in parts of the South where he was not known. He needed his free papers because he and his wife were about to leave the state of Virginia for the Northwest. In Israel

Jefferson's opinion, freedom in a slave state was only nominal: "When I came to Ohio I considered myself wholly free, and not till then."[135]

Israel Jefferson's recollections, recorded in Ohio in 1873, are the only source of our knowledge that all the other members of his family bore the surname Gillette. His parents, known throughout Jefferson's records as only "Ned" and "Jenny," knew themselves as Edward and Jane Gillette. Edward Gillette, the son of Gill and Fanny, was inherited by Jefferson from his father, while Jane, Aggy's daughter, was part of the inheritance from John Wayles. Both worked as farm laborers. In the June wheat harvests Ned Gillette joined the men who mowed the grain with cradle scythes, while Jane was part of the team that gathered and bound the cut sheaves. Gillette also drove one of the Monticello carts and in 1822 transported rocks from Shadwell to the site of the milldam, three-quarters of a mile up the Rivanna River. Jefferson compiled a chart of the number of journeys made by each mulecart and oxcart, noting that the carters were assisted in loading the stone by some "small boys and girls." In twenty days in August sixty-two-year-old Ned Gillette loaded and hauled 380 cartloads of stone.[136]

Edward and Jane Gillette had twelve children: Lucy, Barnaby, Edward, Fanny, Richard, Gill, Priscilla, James, Agnes, Israel, Moses, and Susan.[137] They lived at the Monticello farm quarters a mile from the mountaintop, and there, in 1800, their house and its contents were consumed by fire. Jefferson wrote from Philadelphia to his overseer, "As I understand Ned lost every thing in his house, and of course his bedding, give him three new blankets, and a hempen roll bed." During the eight years of Jefferson's presidency, from 1801 to 1809, the whole Gillette family was leased, along with the other Monticello farmworkers, to John H. Craven, tenant of the southern half of the plantation. In 1806, when the slave miller at Jefferson's gristmill proved incompetent, Jefferson considered possible replacements, writing to his overseer that "the black person among my own in whom I have the most perfect confidence is Ned. But he will not be subject to me for 3 years to come." Ned Gillette's son Gill was equally reliable. In 1820 he was the "sober and trusty servant" sent to Buckingham County to collect a check for $3,500 and carry it to Richmond for deposit. In a letter to his son-in-law John Wayles Eppes, Jefferson explained his instructions to Gill Gillette: "The bearer is charged with special care of your letter as containing a paper of great consequence to me, and not to trust it to any pocket, but to sew it inside of his waistcoat, and not to pull that off at night." The check Gill sewed into his waistcoat was payment for the sale to Eppes of men, women, and children from Poplar Forest.[138]

The Gillette family, who had a wide array of skills, combined ability and enterprise. The seven sons worked in the house, on the farm, and in the nailery, drove wagons and carriages, made barrels, and cared for horses. Three of the daughters were cooks or nurses. Scattered references to Edward Gillette show that, from an early age, he used his evenings and Sundays to better the conditions of life for himself and his family. At the age of sixteen he earned money cleaning chimneys and four years later, sold two squirrel skins to Jefferson. During the years of Jefferson's presidency, he and his wife sold chickens, eggs, cucumbers, and melons to the main house. His children also worked in the family poultry yard and vegetable plot; fifteen-year-old Gill raised and sold Muscovy ducks. One year Gill and his brother Dick, then in their twenties, sold Jefferson a barrel of tar. If, as seems quite likely, they produced the tar themselves, the fourteen dollars they earned had entailed gathering fallen pinewood on the eastern fringe of the Monticello plantation (a cord per barrel of tar), digging a large trench for a kiln, and watching their fire over many days and nights. Moses Gillette, a cooper, used his free time to make pails and firkins, selling some to Jefferson's family. For twelve years Edward, Jr., a farmworker, earned a dollar a month cleaning the Monticello privies.[139]

Barnaby Gillette worked in the nailery from age eleven to fifteen, leaving his anvil for several years during shoemaking season to learn that trade from Shoemaker Phill. His principal trade, however, was coopering. He worked in the shop adjacent to Jefferson's merchant mill at Shadwell, supplying the mill tenant with flour barrels. At the age of thirty he struck a deal with Jefferson, who wrote in his Memorandum Book in 1813: "Promised Barnaby to give him one barrel out of every 31. he sends to the mill." Subsequent payments indicate that the enslaved woodworker was producing seven to eight flour barrels a day, well over the six barrels Jefferson considered a cooper's daily task. When, at the end of June 1821, Barnaby collected one-thirty-first "allowance" for the 1,203 barrels he had made thus far that year, he took Jefferson's order for thirty-nine barrels to the mill. Rather than taking delivery of the barrels themselves, he would have received their monetary value from the miller. At this rate, Gillette—and the other cooper, Nace—could earn as much as forty dollars a year, a greater regular supply of cash than any other Monticello slave was able to acquire in this period. Both coopers were also occasionally sent to Poplar Forest to make hogsheads, twice the size of flour barrels, for the tobacco crop there.[140]

Barnaby Gillette also trained a number of young men in his trade, including his brother Moses and Thrimston Hern. When Hannah's Billy was found "too ungovernable" to work with John Hemings at Poplar Forest, Jefferson had him sent to Monticello and placed under Barnaby Gillette's management and instruction in the cooper's shop. Gillette had no more luck with the unruly eighteen-year-old than Hemings had, and within three months Billy was sent back to Bedford County to "go into the ground," that is, become a farm laborer.[141]

Barnaby Gillette and his first wife, Lily Hern, from whom he later separated, had three children; his second wife was Milly, who died in 1819. In the summer of that year a "nervous" or "malignant" fever swept through the slave quarters at Monticello. Sixteen "working hands" were sick at one time in June, and the Tufton farm, where several of the Gillettes were living, was particularly hard hit. Milly and a three-year-old boy were apparently the only deaths; James Gillette was quite ill but survived. Contagious fevers and dysentery in the summer and measles and whooping cough at any season were probably the most dreaded illnesses for Monticello's African American parents. Priscilla Gillette and Cretia Hern both lost infants to whooping cough in March 1814. In the summer of 1815, "an epidemic dysentery" caused Jefferson to remark that he had never known so much sickness since he began living at Monticello: "All the houses of the negroes are mere hospitals requiring great and constant attendance and care."[142]

The Gillette family seem to have had vigorous constitutions. Ned and Jenny lived at least into their sixties, all of their children reached adulthood, and only one reference has been found to an illness requiring a doctor's visit. Dr. Thomas G. Watkins went to Tufton on New Year's Day 1821 "to see negro Gill." Despite his skepticism about doctors, Jefferson always had local physicians on call for his slaves, spending from forty to sixty dollars a year for medical attendance. When the African Americans on Jefferson's plantations consulted black doctors or conjurers, their actions may indicate a lack of confidence in white medicine as well as the persistence of African belief systems.[143]

Jefferson believed that physicians were necessary only in certain circumstances. As he wrote to an overseer in 1811, "In pleurisies, or other highly inflammatory fevers, intermitting fevers, dysenteries, and venereal cases, the doctors can give certain relief; and the sooner called to them the easier and more certain the cure, but in most other cases they oftener do harm than good. A dose of salts as soon as they are taken is salutary in almost all cases, and hurtful in none. I have generally found this, with a lighter diet and kind attention restore them soonest." For illnesses not warranting a doctor's visit, Jefferson, like other plantation owners, kept on hand a good supply of sugar, molasses, and Epsom salts. He was not an enthusiast for bleeding and inserted the clause "Never to bleed a negro" in his contracts with overseers. While he did not ban this much-abused practice entirely, he believed that the lancet should "never be used without the advice of a physician."[144]

One disease Monticello's families did not have to fear after 1801 was smallpox. Jefferson, an early advocate of inoculation, became an actual vaccinator after the development of Edward Jenner's method of using cowpox vaccine. In 1801 he used a lancet to treat the black residents of Monticello: "I inoculated about 70 or 80 of my own family," from adults to infants at the breast. One or two people had sore arms and a dozen had slight fevers, but "none of them changed their regimen, and few intermitted their ordinary occupations." Another mass vaccination took place in the spring of 1826, when Jefferson treated the children between two and ten, including six Gillette grandchildren. This procedure was less successful. As Jefferson noted of his vaccination efforts, "Not one took."[145]

While Priscilla Gillette was apparently a farmworker like her parents, three of her sisters became domestic servants. Lucy and Fanny, mentioned earlier as the wife of David Hern and trainee cook at the White House, were both cooks. Lucy was given in 1797 to Maria and John Wayles Eppes, and Susan (Sucky) later became the property of their son Francis Eppes. The fourth sister, Agnes, worked in a space that, like the Monticello kitchen, was the realm of women and children. In 1815 she appears in a Farm Book list of ten other teenagers and three women working in the "factory," Jefferson's word for the spinning and weaving operations that he had begun to expand and mechanize in 1812. He had a new structure built on the north side of the Rivanna River at the Lego farm, hiring a white weaver to make the equipment and train slaves in its use. Yarn was spun, not just on spinning wheels but on spinning jennies of the kind patented by Englishman James Hargreaves in 1770. Jefferson wrote a friend in 1813 that he had "three spinning Jennies agoing, of 24. and 40. spindles each which can spin 11. pounds of coarse cotton a day, and our looms fixed with flying shuttles, which altho' they do not perform the miracles ascribed to them, do, I think, double the effect of the common loom."[146]

By 1815 the operation had been moved across the river to the Monticello mountaintop. Cretia Hern worked the many spindles of the jenny to spin cotton, fourteen-year-old Harriet Hemings spun wool, and seventeen-year-old Agnes Gillette and two fifteen-year-old girls were charged with spinning hemp, which was mixed with cotton for the clothing of slave children. The young girls learned to spin on smaller machines. A fifteen-year-old was brought from Poplar Forest to the factory for training. Jefferson reported on her progress: "Maria is becoming a capital spinner. She does her ounce and a half a day per spindle on a 12. spindle machine and will soon get to 2. ounces which is a reasonable task. She learnt from a girl younger than herself, in 4. or 5. days." Agnes Gillette's task per spindle can be viewed in a chart Jefferson penned in his Farm Book. It shows the daily task for the weavers, spinners, and carders, growing with sunlight, from nine-hour days in midwinter to fourteen-hour days in midsummer. Agnes's task almost doubled over the course of the spring, from one and a quarter pounds per spindle in January to two and a half pounds in June.[147]

Agnes Gillette, whom Jefferson gave to his newly married grandson, Thomas J. Randolph, in 1816, may well have been the woman who recalled her days in

Jefferson's chart of textile workers' tasks, ca. 1815. (Manuscripts Division, Department of Rare Books and Special Collections, Princeton University Library)

the factory more than half a century later, when she still lived a few miles from Monticello. Randolph's sister Ellen wrote her niece in 1876: "I remember at one time after the introduction of the spinning Jenny that we had a sort of manufacturing establishment in an out building at Monticello, when work used to be weighed out and in my mother's presence and partly with her own hands. When I was last at Edgehill one of the very old women remaining there who welcomed Mrs. Trist and myself with great delight reminded us that she had been one of the spinners employed in those days. 'Oh,' she said, 'we were so bad, so troublesome, I wonder how mistress had the patience to bear with us as she did.'" Four teenaged boys, one of them Agnes Gillette's younger brother Israel, also worked in the textile shop as carders and no doubt contributed to an atmosphere that occasionally erupted in high spirits and mischief. It is apparent, however, that the textile workers remained productive. In the summer of 1815 Jefferson told a friend: "I make in my family 2000. yds. of cloth a year, which I formerly bought from England, and it only employs a few women, children and invalids who could do little in the farm."[148]

It may have been Fanny Gillette's presence in the Monticello kitchen that led Jefferson to place her younger brothers James, Gill, and Israel in the youthful corps of domestic servants in the house. In 1873 Israel Gillette Jefferson recalled his boyhood in the recently completed dwelling, making fires, dusting and polishing, and running errands. He did not speak of his tour of duty as a scullion in the kitchen. Thomas Jefferson's grandson Thomas Jefferson Randolph, also in 1873, remembered Israel's complaints of treatment by one of the Monticello cooks, who "in chastising him [had] given him a scratch on the head." That punishment evidently left the scar, "on the brow of the right eye," that was recorded for posterity in his 1844 free register in the county courthouse.[149]

The three Gillette boys combined their role as house servants with more energetic duties in the stable and on the road. In December 1813 they and two carters, Jerry and Isaac, were the only slaves to receive a greatcoat as part of their clothing allotment. A few months later, John Hemings and Joseph Fossett completed construction of a new carriage designed by Jefferson. This landau, which evoked some unfavorable comment among Jefferson's friends, featured a convertible top that Israel recalled many years later: "When the weather was pleasant the occupants could enjoy the open air; when it was rainy, they were protected from it by the closing of the covering, which fell back from the middle." This controversial vehicle required four horses, which in turn necessitated two postilions to ride the near horse of each pair. James and Israel Gillette were chosen to ride postilion on the landau's maiden journey, ninety miles south to Poplar Forest. Jefferson wrote back to Monticello to reassure his daughter of the safety of the new equipage: "My journey was performed without an accident. The horses and postilions performed well. James will be an excellent driver, and Israel will do better with more strength and practice. You will always be perfectly safe with their driving." Seven years later, when their older brother rode postilion on another spring journey to Poplar Forest, Jefferson's granddaughter reported that "the roads for the greater part of the way were so bad that Gill once stopped and said he thought if he ventured any farther we should certainly be upset, and once Burwell was obliged to dismount and hold up the carriage to prevent its going over."[150]

For Jefferson's two or three annual visits to Poplar Forest, Israel Gillette made the journey as postilion and continued his household tasks on his arrival there. In the summer of 1819, when the butler, Burwell Colbert, fell ill, the understudy took center stage. Jefferson's granddaughter Ellen reported to her mother that "Israel has shone, during B's illness. Has kept himself as clean and genteel as possible, and in the pride of being chief waiter has followed Miss Edgeworth's rules of doing every thing in its proper time, putting every thing to its proper use, and every thing in its proper place, with as much exactness, as if he had studied them with every desire of edification. Grandpapa is quite delighted."[151]

The year 1824 provided Israel Gillette's most vivid memory of his life at Monticello. In November, partway through a triumphal tour of the United

States, the Marquis de Lafayette came to visit his friend Jefferson. In a still moment on one of their daily rides in the landau, Israel listened to a conversation between the two old men and "treasured it up in my heart." Fifty years later Israel Gillette Jefferson repeated to a reporter Lafayette's never-forgotten words, "No man could rightly hold ownership in his brother man." The "great and good" Lafayette was grieved, after his lifelong dedication to the American cause of freedom, to see so many still in bondage. Jefferson's response, as Israel remembered it, reflects an enlightened statesman's personal entanglement in an unjust system: "[Jefferson] thought the time would come when the slaves would be free, but did not indicate when or in what manner they would get their freedom. He seemed to think that the time had not yet arrived."[152]

Jefferson's death in 1826 "was an affair of great moment and uncertainty to us slaves," said Israel Gillette Jefferson nearly half a century later. After recalling the handful of men whose freedom had been provided for, he noted that "all the rest of us were sold from the auction block." The sales included Israel's parents, both in their sixties, even though his father was valued at fifty dollars and his mother was "worth nothing" in the eyes of the appraisers. Nine of their children and twelve grandchildren also stood on the block. The estate sales of 1827 and 1829 dispersed this family in at least ten different directions; the purchasers of the other family members, including Edward Gillette himself, are not certainly known. Susan (Sucky) Gillette escaped immediate sale but was nevertheless separated from her family. Relocated by Jefferson to Poplar Forest in 1824, she became the property of his grandson Francis Wayles Eppes. When the Eppeses left Virginia in 1829, Sucky Gillette, a nurse to their children, traveled with them in the wagon train to northern Florida.[153]

Israel Gillette was sold to Thomas Walker Gilmer, who became a congressman and, briefly, secretary of the navy. When Gilmer was elected to Congress in 1841, he wished his slave to accompany him to Washington, "but I demurred," recalled Gillette. "I did not refuse, of course, but I laid before him my objections with such earnestness" that Gilmer offered to consider selling him his freedom. The sum Gilmer had paid in 1827, $500, was agreed upon, and Israel Gillette became a free man. Thomas W. Gilmer was killed in 1844 in a gun explosion on the U.S.S. *Princeton*, a fate that caused Israel to note in his 1873 recollections the timeliness of his bargain for freedom: "Had I gone to Washington with him it would have been my duty to keep very close to his person, and probably I would have been killed also, as others were."[154]

Israel Jefferson first married Mary Ann Colter, a slave belonging to someone other than Jefferson or Gilmer. The fates of their four children were thus beyond his control, and they took what he called "the usual course" of the enslaved. "I do not know where they are now, if living," he said in 1873. After Mary Ann's death, he vowed never to marry another woman in bondage. About 1838 he married a free woman of color, Elizabeth Farrow Randolph, a seamstress who helped provide the purchase money for his freedom. In the mid-1840s they made their way to Cincinnati, Ohio, where Israel Jefferson worked as a waiter, at first in a private home and later on a steamboat. Some years later he, his wife, and her children moved ninety miles east to the rural community near Chillicothe where Madison Hemings and other former Virginia slaves lived. Both Israel and Elizabeth Jefferson were active members—he as deacon and treasurer—of the local congregation that became Eden Baptist Church, which played a key role in the safe passage of fugitive slaves through the unfriendly southern portion of Ohio.[155]

Israel Jefferson returned several times to Monticello, probably to see family members, both before and after the Civil War. On his last visit, in 1866, he saw Thomas Jefferson Randolph, still paying off his grandfather's debts and stripped by the war of all but his land and "one old blind mule." As he remembered this encounter in 1873, Israel Jefferson said: "I then realized more than ever before, the great changes which time brings about in the affairs and circumstances of life."[156]

1824: Connecting Worlds

"There was never such a time in Virginia as during the visit of Gen. Lafayette," said Peter Fossett in 1898. Many witnesses to the Marquis de Lafayette's arrival at Monticello in November 1824 left accounts of the affecting scene on the east lawn. They described the arrival of a cavalcade of carriages and the emotional embrace of the two elderly patriots, who had not met in thirty-five years. The account of Fossett, who was a nine-year-old slave at the time, is the only one to refer to the African Americans present. "I well remember the visit of Gen. Lafayette to Monticello," he told a New York reporter. "The whole place was in gala array in his honor. He was met at Red Gate and escorted to Monticello by the Jefferson Guards and the Virginia Militia. The latter consisted of all the school boys in the county, who had been drilled for the occasion, armed with sharp pointed sticks tipped with pikes. The meeting between Jefferson and Lafayette was most affectionate. They fell into each other's arms with these words: 'My dear Lafayette,' 'My dear Jefferson,' and wept. . . . Even the slaves wept."[157]

The next day the enslaved workers were given a holiday for the "grand procession" to the University of Virginia. Peter Fossett was not the only African American to recall the precise seating arrangement in Jefferson's landau carriage.

At the end of the century, his cousin Robert Scott, who had lived in 1824 with his free family on Charlottesville's Main Street, told of seeing the Monticello equipage pass in front of his house, its four bay horses no doubt ridden by the Gillette brothers. He could remember Jefferson's red waistcoat and the position of the other occupants—Lafayette and ex-presidents James Madison and James Monroe. In Scott's opinion, "Mr. Jefferson was by far the most distinguished looking of the four."[158]

The indelible figure of the Marquis de Lafayette thus appears in the recollections of three African Americans connected with Monticello. Through the stories they chose to tell, Fossett, Scott, and Israel Gillette Jefferson demonstrate their understanding of Jefferson's position not just in the nation but in the wider world. His international standing, and their association with it, remained important to them. It is also striking that each of the storytellers spoke about issues of education, in one case directly connected to Lafayette's visit. The overheard conversation that Israel Jefferson "treasured up" in his heart included Lafayette's recommendation that slaves be educated. He heard Thomas Jefferson agree that slaves should learn to read but not to write. If taught to write, Lafayette's host said, slaves could forge free passes and "no longer be kept in subjugation." In this period, when reading and writing were taught separately, the student usually fully mastered reading before proceeding to learn to write.[159]

Jefferson's role in the education of his slaves remains a mystery. His lifelong efforts on behalf of education for white Virginians were certainly not matched by a parallel concern for schooling for blacks. There is no indication that he set up schools for his slaves at Monticello or played an active role in their education. On the other hand, he apparently did not prohibit them from learning their letters, as did a good many of his fellow slaveholders. Educated African Americans were considered a danger to the status quo, and the pervasive opposition to instructing slaves stifled educational efforts by more enlightened white Virginians. Particularly after Gabriel's aborted revolt in 1800, legal barriers to black education became progressively harsher, culminating in an 1831 law that proscribed schools for free blacks and penalized whites for teaching them.[160]

During Jefferson's lifetime, and even afterward, it was not strictly illegal in Virginia to teach slaves to read and write, as long as the instructor was neither paid nor a free black. The climate of hostility and the symbolic power of the legal restrictions were so potent, however, that a widespread belief that teaching slaves was against the law persists to this day. An oral account collected in this century mentions Jefferson's granddaughter as a teacher of young blacks on the mountaintop, at risk to herself because it was "a crime." Interestingly, it is only the accounts of African Americans that mention Jefferson's educational role. Robert Scott, Mary Hemings's grandson, said that Jefferson "had encouraged [his father] to have his children educated." The Scotts, who were part of Charlottesville's free black population, attended white schools. In the case of their relatives in bondage at Monticello, however, there is little sign of Jefferson's encouragement. Peter Fossett's account, which states that Jefferson "allowed his grandson to teach any of his slaves who desired to learn," suggests a more passive role. Madison Hemings talked of learning to read by "inducing the white children," presumably Jefferson's grandchildren, to teach him, and in 1819, one of Jefferson's granddaughters expressed a wish to educate a young slave girl who had lost her mother.[161]

These references indicate the active sharing of knowledge between white and black young people at Monticello. There was a surprising level of literacy among Monticello's enslaved families, especially the artisans, so it is also possible that despite the silence of the documents on this point Jefferson had some of his tradesmen taught their letters. In his absences, he left written instructions for several tradesmen and overseer George Granger. John Hemings read the Bible to his wife and wrote a number of letters to Jefferson about his progress in the construction of Poplar Forest. James Hemings left a written inventory of the Monticello kitchen, and some of the blacksmithing accounts kept by Peter Fossett's father have survived. Also in the Jefferson archive is a letter from Hannah, a house servant at Poplar Forest, although it is possible it was written by someone else at her dictation.[162]

There were also undoubtedly enslaved teachers at Monticello, passing knowledge from parent to child or sister to brother. Literacy was a communal benefit in the slave quarters. Access to knowledge of national events in newspapers or to the consolations of the Bible was shared among the members of the African American community. Educated slaves were mediators between the black and white worlds, who could win advantages for their families and, in some cases, even freedom. An artifact unearthed in archaeological excavations below Mulberry Row attests to the hunger for education at Monticello. It is a triangular fragment of slate, bearing cursive letters that are apparently part of a verse. The writer probably had only the hours of darkness to practice his letters and found a piece of locally available stone that saved him the purchase of pen and paper. The flourish of the capital *B* evokes a writing lesson at the hearth of a log cabin two centuries ago.

Despite the cooperation of some of Jefferson's family members and the exertions of some of the enslaved, reading and writing were inaccessible to the majority of Monticello's African Americans. Israel Gillette Jefferson mentioned that his own struggle to learn to read and write did not begin until he was in his forties, when he reached freedom and Ohio. "My duties as a laborer would not permit me to acquire much of an education," he said in 1873, but he considered "what education I have as a legitimate fruit of freedom."[163]

Peter Fossett's nostalgic recollections of his childhood at Monticello suggest other ways in which blacks and whites interacted on the mountaintop: "As for the social enjoyment of the men of those days the people of this time do not begin to come up to it. Weddings, parties, barbecues and the like, even the slaves participated in." The house was always "full of company," he recalled, Europeans as well as Americans. During Lafayette's visit in 1824, as Jefferson's great-granddaughter heard, the two elder statesmen sat long at the dinner table, recounting shared memories of the early days of the French Revolution: "So animated did they become, with such eloquence did they speak, that, carried away by the enthusiasm of the moment, the rest of the company involuntarily left their seats at the table and grouped themselves around the two sages, that they might not lose one of the eloquent words which fell from their lips." The boys serving as waiters and Monticello butler Burwell Colbert, who would later own engravings of both Jefferson and Lafayette, probably also listened intently to some of these stories.[164]

Lafayette's visit also featured music that brought together white Jeffersons and free and enslaved blacks. Mary Hemings's Scott grandsons were called from Charlottesville to Monticello to play for the occasion and may have been joined by some of their Hemings cousins. When Jefferson's daughters organized weekend dances in the 1820s, they turned to young Beverly Hemings to provide the music. He and his brothers had learned to play the violin and call the figures of favorite dances. Also living on the mountaintop in the first decade of the century were some fiddle-playing Irishmen, hired in the reconstruction of the house. While it is not known exactly how musical skills and melodies might have been passed among slaves, hired workmen, and Jefferson family members, it is interesting to note that one tune, at least, was played by both Jefferson and his slave, who was also probably his son. A manuscript survives on which the master of Monticello has written out the Scottish dance tune "Moneymusk." Sally Hemings's son Eston, described as a "master of the violin," was known for playing this tune at dances in southern Ohio in the 1840s.[165]

It was in the main house, where Sally Hemings and her relations worked, that the daily lives of black and white were most inextricably linked. There, intimate secrets as well as knowledge, stories, and music must have been shared. Monticello's domestic servants, almost all members of a single family, had the greatest opportunity to learn from and influence Thomas Jefferson and his children and grandchildren.

Elizabeth Hemings and Her Family

One August day in 1831, a man with exceptional talents as a carpenter was working in an unfamiliar medium. John Hemings was seen by one of Jefferson's granddaughters "cutting a headstone" to place on the grave of his wife, Priscilla. In the 1950s the piece of slate he shaped came to light wedged in a small tree on the side of Monticello mountain. Close to the site of its rediscovery is a flat stretch of ground, with only scattered depressions in the soil to mark it as a graveyard. It is most probably here that John Hemings's mother, Elizabeth (Betty) Hemings, and some of her children and grandchildren lie buried, still on the mountain where, for half a century, they played such an important role.[166]

The House

Over the course of Jefferson's lifetime, five generations of the family of Betty Hemings—more than eighty people—lived and worked at Monticello. At the time of his death, one-third of the 130 African Americans who were listed as part of his Albemarle County estate belonged to this one family. When they left Monticello, Betty Hemings's children and grandchildren took with them artifacts associated with the house and its residents, among them a small cast-metal bell of the type used to summon servants. One of their descendants gave it to Howard University in 1949, and it now sits on a table in a sitting room at Monticello. According to the story that accompanied the bell as it passed through generations of women, Thomas Jefferson's dying wife, Martha, gave it to Betty Hemings or one of her children. As she lay on her deathbed in 1782, Martha Jefferson was surrounded by her female relatives. She was attended in her long illness by her half sisters and sisters-in-law as well as by Betty Hemings and her daughters, some of whom also considered themselves Martha Jefferson's half sisters. Decades later, the women of the Hemings family still told the story of the final scene in the sick chamber. Monticello overseer Edmund Bacon said that Betty Hemings and her daughters "often told my wife that when Mrs. Jefferson died they stood around the bed" and heard Jefferson promise never to remarry. A former Monticello slave, Israel Jefferson, also heard them tell the tale of this deathbed promise.[167]

Martha Jefferson had grown up in the midst of Hemingses, domestic servants in her father's house. Betty Hemings was the one constant maternal presence in her life, shadowed by the deaths of a mother she never knew and two stepmothers. Betty Hemings's grandson Madison Hemings stated that she was the daughter of the captain of an English trading vessel and a "full-blooded African" woman, a Virginia slave. Her birthplace is not known, but by 1746, when

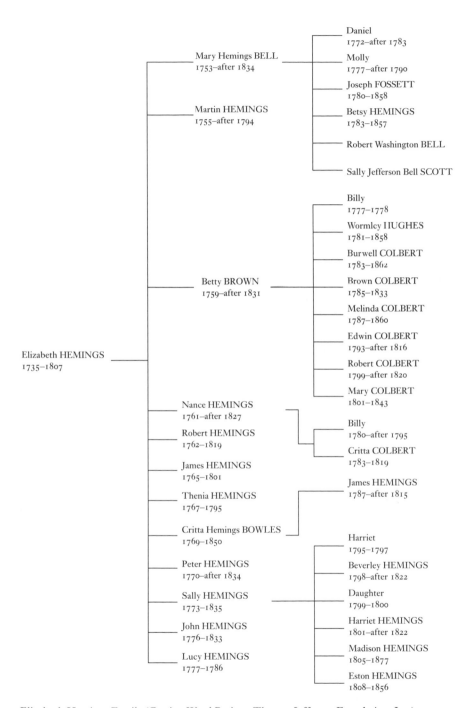

Elizabeth Hemings Family (Getting Word Project; Thomas Jefferson Foundation, Inc.)

she was about eleven, she was the property of Francis Eppes IV of Bermuda Hundred in Chesterfield County. In that year title to Betty and other slaves passed to John Wayles of The Forest, Charles City County, on his marriage to Martha Eppes, Martha Jefferson's mother.[168]

Madison Hemings also stated, in 1873, that his grandmother became John Wayles's concubine after the death of his third wife in 1761 and that six children were born to them: Robert, James, Thenia, Critta, Peter, and Sally. Neither Jefferson nor any of his family left any known reference to this relationship, on which there is only one other comment from someone close to the Monticello household. Isaac (Granger) Jefferson, the former Monticello blacksmith, recalled that "folks said that these Hemingses was old Mr. Wayles's children." Whoever their father was, he was almost certainly a white man. Isaac Jefferson described Betty Hemings as "a bright mulatto woman" and her daughter Sally as "mighty near white."[169]

Betty Hemings and her children appear throughout Thomas Jefferson's Memorandum books in the early 1770s, the recipients of tips on his visits to The Forest in the years of his courtship and marriage. Then, after John Wayles's death in 1773 and the partition of his estate in 1774, this family of very light-skinned slaves, familiar to both Martha and Thomas Jefferson and fully trained in household work, arrived at Monticello. Whereas Ursula Granger reigned supreme during her lifetime in the kitchen, smokehouse, and washhouse—the outdoor dependencies—Betty Hemings and her older children took charge inside the house. Their duties, seldom specifically described, ranged from cleaning and sewing, or acting as personal maids and valets, to superintending the entire domestic staff. Betty Brown, Betty Hemings's second daughter, and her sister Critta were housemaids. As Jefferson mentioned in 1793 that Critta Hemings was "oftenest wanted about the house," she was probably the equivalent of a house parlor maid. In 1802, Jefferson's builder lamented her absence, as "there is no person to undertake" the washing of the floors in the recently plastered rooms. Several of Betty Hemings's daughters were skilled with the needle. Her oldest child, Mary, was a seamstress; Betty Brown attended to the mending; and Sally Hemings was described by her son as a chambermaid and seamstress.[170]

Betty Hemings's oldest son, Martin, was the Monticello butler, and his brother Robert (Bob), at the age of twelve, replaced Jupiter as Jefferson's personal attendant. From 1775 Robert Hemings traveled all over the eastern seaboard with his master and received instruction in barbering in Annapolis; when Jefferson embarked from Boston for France in 1784, Hemings returned to Virginia alone, entrusted with three valuable carriage horses. His brother James also acted as a manservant. Betty Hemings's grandson Burwell Colbert inherited his uncles' mantles, becoming both butler and personal servant to Jefferson during the years of his final retirement.[171]

Jefferson's public service affected the lives of his domestic servants in significant ways. In his two years as Virginia governor, Mary Hemings and Betty Brown and their children, part of the domestic household in Williamsburg and Richmond, were caught up in the turbulent events of the Revolutionary War and carried off by the British troops. In peacetime, Jefferson's prolonged absences brought about both an increase in mobility and a reduction of labor. Robert, James, and Martin Hemings all were at times permitted to hire themselves out to other masters and keep their wages for themselves. During Jefferson's absence in France, Martin Hemings worked for James Monroe, who wrote in 1786, "I have Martin attending on me, being inform'd by him he was at liberty to engage for himself." Whenever Jefferson was ready to return to Monticello, he sent out a summons to the mountain. In the summer of 1792 he wrote a friend: "If you should know any thing of my servants Martin or Bob, and could give them notice to be at Monticello by the 20th. I should be obliged to you."[172]

A tour of duty for Jefferson meant a spell of inactivity for Betty Hemings and her daughters. Overseer Edmund Bacon remembered that they remained at Monticello during the presidential years: "I was instructed to take no control of them. They had very little to do. When I opened the house, they attended to airing it." Jefferson's vacations changed the scene entirely. A house servant was at a master's beck and call, night or day, Sunday or weekday. And after Jefferson's retirement in 1809, when Martha Randolph and her family moved permanently to the mountain and the steady stream of pilgrims to the home of the Sage of Monticello became a torrent, the lives of the house servants must have been extraordinarily busy ones. Long visits of Randolph kin, surprise arrivals of traveling Europeans, and the usual hospitality extended to friends and neighbors made the work of the household staff a perpetual round. Beds had to be made and fires laid. There were meals to be served, guests to be satisfied, and children to be cared for. At any time of day or night, the domestic servants might be fetching or carrying, cleaning or polishing, washing or mending. Anonymous figures pass through the accounts of Monticello visitors like shadows, victims of the passive voice. Dinner "was served," tea or toddy "was brought," fires "were lighted," and a "servant" brought candles or waited to receive orders.[173]

Almost all of the "servants" ringing bells, building fires, or serving dinner were Betty Hemings's children or grandchildren. Jefferson's grandson Thomas Jefferson Randolph remembered that "Mr. Js Mechanics and his entire household of servants with the exception of an under cook and carriage driver consisted of one family connection and their wives. . . . It was a source of bitter jealousy to the other slaves, who liked to account for it with other reasons than the true one; viz. superior intelligence, capacity and fidelity to trusts."[174]

It is clear that the Hemings family members lived a distinctly different life from other Monticello slaves and seem to have been, in effect, a caste apart. Betty Hemings and her daughters were spared the annual task of helping to harvest the wheat, when virtually every other able-bodied person was drafted. Her sons were exceptional as the only slaves allowed to hire themselves out to other masters for their own benefit. As house servants, whose tasks were performed within view of Jefferson's family and Monticello visitors, the Hemingses received clothing that distinguished them from the rest of the enslaved community. In the 1790s the three "housemaids," Critta, Sally, and Mary's daughter Betsy, were clothed in muslin, Irish linen, and calico "of different patterns," while the other female slaves received a uniform allotment of osnaburg, the coarse brownish linen issued to slaves all over the South. The fieldworkers wore baggy stockings of woven cloth, while the house servants received knitted stockings that fit well. Martin, Robert, and James Hemings also received special apparel, some of it custom tailored, and occasionally Jefferson's cast-off clothes. In 1792, Jefferson wrote his daughter that instead of the promised new suit of clothes, he was sending Bob Hemings "a suit of superfine ratteen of my own, which I have scarcely ever worn."[175]

Betty Hemings's grandson Peter Fossett's recollections of his childhood reflect the distinct separateness of his mulatto family: "A peculiar fact about [Jefferson's] house servants was that we were all related to one another, and as a matter of fact we did not need to know that we were slaves. As a boy I was not only brought up differently, but dressed unlike the plantation boys." The social stratification suggested by this account is especially apparent in the marital choices made by the Hemingses. None of Betty Hemings's twelve children and only two of her more than twenty grandchildren married within the Monticello African American community. Peter and John Hemings found wives in the enslaved domestic households of Jefferson's daughter and son-in-law, while Robert Hemings's wife was a slave belonging to a Richmond doctor. Mary Hemings became the common-law wife of a well-respected white merchant, and her sister Critta's husband was Zachariah Bowles, a free black farmer. The fathers of the children of Betty Hemings's daughters Betty Brown, Nance, and Thenia are not certainly known, while the issue of uncertain paternity made her sixth daughter the most famous enslaved woman in the United States.[176]

On September 1, 1802, James Thomson Callender announced in the pages of the *Richmond Recorder* that "it is well known that the man, whom it delighteth the people to honor, keeps, and for many years past has kept, as his concubine, one of his own slaves. Her name is SALLY." The story was immediately taken up by Federalist editors, and as it spread in the form of prints and doggerel, a young woman about whom little is known became a distorted figure incorporating extreme racial stereotypes. Over the next two centuries Sally Hemings, her name always linked with her owner's, became part of popular and scholarly debate over slavery and the American political system. Abolitionists and foreign critics of the United States, to further their causes or make their cases, harped on her alleged liaison with the man who was a convenient personification of the profound contradictions in American society.[177]

Lost in the clouds of debate was Sally Hemings herself, who spent her entire life in legal bondage. The dry records of Jefferson's Farm Book, occasional references in letters, and the recollections of one of her sons provide the few details known about her life. Betty Hemings's daughter was born in 1773, probably at the Charles City County plantation of her alleged father, Jefferson's father-in-law, John Wayles. She came with her family to Monticello about 1775 and, by 1787, was living at the Chesterfield County home of Elizabeth Wayles and Francis Eppes, who had taken charge of their niece Mary (Polly) Jefferson during Jefferson's absence in France. Sally Hemings's presence at Eppington rather than Monticello suggests that she was Polly's maid, acting as an assistant "nurse" and companion to the young girl five years her junior.[178]

Jefferson, anxious to have his daughter with him in Paris, asked the Eppeses to send her across the Atlantic attended by "a careful negro woman" who had had smallpox. He suggested David Hern's wife, Isabel, adding that she could make the return journey to Virginia immediately after landing in Europe. After long delays because of the vagaries of the mail, seasonal requirements for safe ocean travel, and Polly's reluctance to leave her relations, preparations for the voyage were made in the spring of 1787. Because Isabel Hern was ill after the birth of her daughter Edith, Sally Hemings, then only thirteen or fourteen years old, was selected to fill her place. A very apprehensive Polly Jefferson was taken on board the ship at Bermuda Hundred on the Appomattox River and distracted by her cousins until she fell asleep. She awoke to find the *Robert* under sail and the only familiar face that of her young nurse.[179]

This transatlantic voyage made a deep impression on the enslaved girl. Monticello overseer Edmund Bacon recalled that he had often heard Sally Hemings talk about the time "they crossed the ocean alone." After a calm passage, the two voyagers reached London, where they stayed two weeks with John and Abigail Adams, in their house in Grosvenor Square. As the Jefferson-Adams correspondence is silent on the issue of Sally's return to Virginia, it is probable Polly Jefferson refused to entertain the possibility of being separated from her companion since infancy—the one constant in the traumatic transition from one hemisphere to another. Mrs. Adams noted that Sally Hemings "seems fond of the child and appears good naturd," but, in her opinion, the young slave who had shared the terror and excitement of the ocean voyage with her charge "wants more care than the child, and is wholy incapable of looking properly after her, without some superiour to direct her." Five weeks in the company of "men only" had made Polly (and no doubt Sally, too) "as rough as a sailor." As they both had clothing "only proper for the sea," Mrs. Adams outfitted them with new wardrobes: calico and Irish linen for two short gowns and aprons for Sally Hemings, and, for Polly Jefferson, a half-dozen frocks of "Irish Holland" and lace-trimmed muslin.[180]

Escorted by Jefferson's French butler, the two girls arrived in Paris on July 15, 1787. Polly Jefferson immediately joined her sister, Martha (Patsy), at the Abbaye de Panthemont, a fashionable convent school with a number of English as well as French students. It is not known whether Sally Hemings lived at the convent or at the Hôtel de Langeac, Jefferson's residence on the Champs-Elysées. It was not uncommon for the servants of boarding students to continue to attend their mistresses in the Abbaye, and some of the Jefferson sisters' schoolmates knew Sally well enough to send her greetings in their correspondence. Since she received an occasional wage (two dollars a month, a bit less than Jefferson's French scullion), Sally Hemings must have been performing some domestic tasks as well as beginning to acquire the finer skills of a lady's maid, particularly those related to the maintenance of the wardrobes of Jefferson's daughters. Needlework and the proper techniques for washing delicate fabrics were two necessary accomplishments. A five-week stay with Jefferson's launderer in 1789 may have been part of this training.[181]

Little can be recovered of Sally Hemings's life in the French capital. Like both Thomas Jefferson and his daughter Patsy, for whom the years in Europe were always a primary topic of conversation, she must have often talked about her experiences. A few months after her arrival, she had to undergo the unpleasant procedure of inoculation against smallpox, something Jefferson took pains to arrange for slaves in regular contact with his family. She was treated by a member of the Sutton family, famous for their improved techniques and endeavors to spread the benefits of inoculation, especially among the poor of England. The Suttons' method reduced the risks and shortened the expense and duration of treatment. Nevertheless, Jefferson paid Dr. Sutton the considerable sum of 240 livres (forty dollars) and Sally had to spend several weeks in isolation somewhere outside the city during her convalescence. In later years, after the development of the safer and simpler Jennerian method of vaccination, Jefferson would himself use a lancet and a bit of cowpox to protect Sally's children and others at Monticello against this dreaded disease.[182]

Sally Hemings's brother James, working in the kitchen of the Hôtel de Langeac, was no doubt a welcome presence in alien surroundings. She must have benefited from his knowledge of the community of domestic servants in aristocratic Parisian households, some of them undoubtedly former slaves from the French colonies. In 1786, according to Jefferson's report, James Hemings "has forgot how to speak English, and has not learnt to speak French." By the time of his sister's arrival, however, he was eager enough to associate with the local inhabitants to hire a Parisian to give him lessons in French grammar. Sally, eight years younger than her brother, probably achieved a greater fluency. Her son recalled that after two years in Paris "she was just beginning to understand the French language well."[183]

In the winter of 1788–1789 Patsy Jefferson, now almost seventeen, began to go out in Parisian society and to attend a number of aristocratic balls. Sally Hemings would certainly have helped to dress her for these occasions, but it is also likely that she sometimes accompanied her. Jefferson greatly increased his expenditures for Patsy's clothing in this period, at the same time spending over thirty dollars on clothes for Sally Hemings, who would have also needed a better wardrobe for this new milieu. While Patsy Jefferson danced with the Comtes de Fronsac and Polignac, her maid heard the first rumblings of a rising new order. Sally Hemings was in Paris for the storming of the Bastille and the procession a few days later that brought a chastened Louis XVI to the city under the escort of the National Guard and sixty thousand citizens flourishing swords, scythes, and pruning hooks. Patsy Jefferson, who had a fine vantage point at an upper window for this historic event, often told her children of the moment she heard a sound "like the bellowings of thousands of bulls." It was the Parisian crowd shouting, "Lafayette! Lafayette!" When the Marquis rode by at the head of the cavalcade, he looked up and bowed to the American minister's daughter. At a party a few weeks later, a young officer of the Guard pinned the newly launched tricolor cockade to Patsy's dress, a memento she preserved for the rest of her life. Nothing is known of what souvenirs were saved by Sally Hemings, who must also have been a fascinated observer of some of these revolutionary events.[184]

In the fall of 1789, Jefferson booked passage home to Virginia for the five members of his household. He asked for "births for a man and a w[o]man servant, the latter convenient to that of my daughters," confirming that Sally Hemings was acting as "lady's maid to both sisters," as Jefferson's granddaughter described her. Unaware of his appointment as George Washington's secretary of state, Jefferson intended to stay in the United States for only six months and planned to return to Paris without his daughters, eager to see the sequel to the "first chapter of the history of European liberty." The plans of Sally and James Hemings are not similarly preserved in diplomatic correspondence, but their interest in remaining in or returning to France went far beyond the political fates of Frenchmen. In the words of Sally Hemings's son, Jefferson "desired to bring my mother back to Virginia with him but she demurred. . . . In France she was free, while if she returned to Virginia she would be re-enslaved. So she refused to return with him."[185]

The ancient maxim recognizing the freedom of any slave who set foot on French soil was not codified until the French Revolution. As the customary law of the land, its operation in the cases of slaves brought into the country by their masters was complicated by a variety of edicts and declarations. A slave with a master unwilling to release him had to go to court to gain his freedom. If Jefferson had opposed their wishes to claim their freedom, Sally and James Hemings would have had to petition the Admiralty Court, hire lawyers, and pursue a lawsuit. Nevertheless, had they insisted on remaining in France and living as free citizens, Jefferson could probably not have stopped them. Since the 1760s, all freedom suits had been successful, and it is virtually certain that Sally and James Hemings would have learned of their rights and opportunities. In Paris on the eve of revolution, antislavery crusaders added their voices to a public forum simmering with intense discussion of the issues of liberty and tyranny. The Hemingses and their acquaintances among other black domestic servants in the capital city must have heard and talked of new notions of the rights of man.[186]

Sally Hemings and her brother both chose to leave France. Her son Madison Hemings maintained that Jefferson "induced" her to return with promises of "extraordinary privileges" and freedom for her children when they reached the age of twenty-one. These "extraordinary privileges" are not visible in the lists of Jefferson's Farm Book, almost the only source on her subsequent life at Monticello. In it he recorded, just as he did for his other slaves, the births of Sally Hemings's children, the clothing she and other "house-maids" received, and her meat and cornmeal rations—the usual allotment. Madison Hemings's recollections, the other main source, describe his mother's duties at Monticello, which included taking care of Jefferson's chamber and wardrobe and "such light work as sewing, &c." On her return to the mountain in 1789, she probably lived in a stone dwelling on Mulberry Row, built in the 1770s for free white artisans working on the construction of the main house. After the workmen's departure in 1784, this stone building, which survives intact although somewhat altered, was occupied by some of the house servants. Letters reveal that Sally's sister Critta lived there with her son until 1793, when they were transferred to one of the new 12-by-14-foot structures between the stone house and the stable. Sally Hemings, too, may have moved into one of these long-vanished log cabins, which had wooden chimneys and earthen floors.[187]

A reference by Jefferson's grandson, conversing with Henry S. Randall in the 1850s, to a "smoke blackened and sooty room in one of the collonades," suggests that Sally Hemings later lived in one of the "servant's rooms" under the South Terrace of the main house. This dependency wing, completed by 1808, contained three small rooms as living spaces. The head cook—at first Sally's brother Peter—lived in the room nearest the kitchen (10½ by 14 feet), and the other two (almost 14 feet square) were probably occupied by Critta and Sally Hemings. Built in stone, brick, and wood into the side of the hill, these rooms were considered by overseer Edmund Bacon as "very comfortable, warm in winter and cool in the summer."[188]

Despite her long association with Polly (after 1789 known as Maria) Jefferson, Sally Hemings was not one of the thirty slaves given by Jefferson to his daughter on her marriage to John Wayles Eppes in 1797. Nevertheless, two years later, Jefferson still linked her name with his daughter's. In a letter of December 1799 to his son-in-law, he reported that "Maria's maid produced a daughter about a fortnight ago, and is doing well." This birth occurred nine months after Jefferson's return to Monticello from a tour of duty as vice president in Philadelphia. It was no doubt the timing of this birth and the births of Sally Hemings's other children, as well as their striking resemblance to the master of Monticello, that led to the gossip that James Thomson Callender heard in Richmond and published in the *Recorder* in 1802. It was seventy more years before her son Madison's version of events was recorded. He told an Ohio newspaperman in 1873 that his mother "became Mr. Jefferson's concubine" in France, returned pregnant to Virginia in 1789, and had a child that "lived but a short time."[189]

Sally Hemings lost two more children in infancy, both daughters. Her daughter Harriet and sons Beverly, Madison, and Eston lived to adulthood. "My brothers, sister Harriet and myself, were used alike," Madison Hemings recalled of his childhood in 1873. "We were permitted to stay about the 'great house,' and only required to do such light work as going on errands. . . . We were free from the dread of having to be slaves all our lives long, and were measurably happy. We were always permitted to be with our mother, who was well used." A consistent and enduring family tradition among the descendants of Thomas C. Woodson maintains that the child born soon after Sally Hemings's return from France survived to adulthood and that Woodson was that child. It has not yet been possible to link Woodson with Hemings and Jefferson through the historical record, and scientific studies in 1998 and 2000 found no genetic relationship between Woodson and Jefferson.[190]

In accordance with his general policy of not responding to political attacks on his character, Thomas Jefferson made no public comment on the alleged relationship with Sally Hemings, nor has any private reference to it been found in his papers—with the exception of one oblique allusion that has been interpreted by some historians as a denial. Sally Hemings's observations on the topic can only be inferred from the recollections of her son. Jefferson's daughter Martha and her children stated their firm disbelief in such a relationship, making their denials privately. Martha Jefferson Randolph's son assigned the paternity of Sally Hemings's children to one of Jefferson's Carr nephews, a conclusion contradicted—at least for the youngest Hemings, Eston—by genetic testing in 1998. Thomas Jefferson Randolph also provided one of only two known descriptions of the woman at the center of the controversy, telling Jefferson's biographer that Sally and her sister were "light colored and decidedly good looking." Isaac Jefferson, the other source, remembered Sally Hemings as "mighty near white . . . very handsome, long straight hair down her back."[191]

Visitors to Monticello in 1796 were surprised by the appearance of some of Jefferson's slaves. The Comte de Volney saw enslaved children "as white as I am," while the duc de La Rochefoucauld-Liancourt exclaimed, "I have even seen, and particularly at Mr. Jefferson's, slaves who have neither in their color nor features a single trace of their origins." Since Sally Hemings's child[192] was at this time a babe in arms, they may have been referring to children of her sisters Mary, Betty Brown, or Critta. However light-skinned these children might have been, they still inherited their condition of slavery from their mothers. The Virginia law that, until 1910, declared that a person with more than three-quarters white ancestry was not black applied only to free persons.[193]

There is no way to recover the true circumstances surrounding the acts that produced so many nearly white slaves at Monticello. The extreme imbalance of power in a slave society made the whole idea of consent, when it concerned a female slave and a free white man, especially if he owned her, an absurdity. Nevertheless, it is apparent that interracial sex in Virginia and elsewhere in the South took every form from the most cruel exploitation to the most enduring affection. A very speculative case might be made for reading the nature of the Hemings women's relationships in the surnames taken by their children. For example, Betty Hemings's son John was the child, according to his nephew, of Joseph Neilson, a white workman at Monticello; John kept the surname Hemings[194] rather than Neilson. Was Betty Hemings's encounter with Neilson more exploitative than that of Mary Hemings and William Fossett, another white workman at Monticello? Mary's son Joseph always used the surname Fossett. The surnames borne by her nephews Burwell Colbert and Wormley Hughes may also indicate their paternity. In the case of Sally Hemings's children, open use of the Jefferson surname would, of course, have been taboo at Monticello, although at least one of her sons did adopt it later in freedom.[195]

The temptation to turn to such scanty and ambiguous clues for information on this issue highlights the mystery that will probably always remain in the absence of testimony of the women involved. Whites often explained the mulattoes that surrounded them by pointing to the habits of overseers, as the duc de La Rochefoucauld-Liancourt heard when visiting Monticello in 1796. Jefferson's granddaughter Ellen Randolph Coolidge blamed the resident "Irish workmen" at Monticello, as well as "dissipated young men in the neighborhood," and former Monticello overseer Edmund Bacon recalled that the schoolmates of Jefferson's grandson were "intimate with the negro women."[196]

We will never know who might have welcomed the privileges that came with the attentions of a wealthy plantation owner or who was unable to repel the advances of an intemperate youth, a vicious overseer, or an importunate master. What is certain, however, is that the sexual morality of some women in slavery at Monticello, as elsewhere, was violated and that all of them were painfully at the mercy of the natures of the white men in their vicinity, whether artisan, overseer, or aristocrat. The moral climate of Monticello in Jefferson's absence is captured in a letter of one of his hired workmen. In 1804 house joiner James Oldham, a free white man, complained bitterly of his treatment by overseer Gabriel Lilly and then proceeded to enumerate Lilly's transgressions. The overseer embezzled flour and pork, got "Beastly drunk" with his cronies on Jefferson's wine, and was excessively harsh in his punishments. In a letter to Jefferson, Oldham described a recent example: "The Barbarity that he maid use of with little Jimmy was the moast cruel. To my noledge Jimmy was sick for thre nights and the moast part of the time I raly thot he would not of liv'd. . . . I inform'd Lilly the boy was not able to worke and Beg'd him not to punnish him, but this had no affect. He whip'd him three times in one day, and the boy was raly not able to raise his hand to his Head."[197]

"Little Jimmy" was seventeen-year-old James Hemings, son of Critta Hemings the housemaid. "The severe treatment which he experienced" caused him to run away from Monticello and take up life as a boatman on the James River between Richmond and Norfolk. About six months after his flight, young Hemings was apprehended in Richmond, and negotiations for his return were pursued through Oldham, who now lived there. Jefferson, who said he "could readily excuse the follies of a boy," promised "an entire pardon" and removal from Lilly's management if Hemings returned to Monticello. Just before he was to board the stage back to Charlottesville, James Hemings vanished up the James River, never to appear on the Monticello slave rolls again. He is no doubt one of the three young men that Jefferson's granddaughter Ellen Coolidge mentioned in a letter to her husband in 1858: "It was [Jefferson's] principle . . . to allow such of his slaves as were sufficiently white to pass for white men, to withdraw quietly from the plantation; it was called running away, but they were never re-claimed." One of the other young men and the "one girl" who gained their freedom in the same way were Sally Hemings's children Beverly and Harriet. Both left Monticello soon after their twenty-first birthdays, possibly together. Overseer Edmund Bacon remembered that, at Jefferson's request, he provided Harriet with travel funds and put her on the stage to the North. According to their brother, Beverly and Harriet Hemings lived the rest of their lives as white people.[198]

Spurred by the further confirming evidence of DNA testing in 1998, histori-ans will continue to contemplate the nature of the probable relationship be-tween Sally Hemings and Thomas Jefferson as well as the meaning of family at Monticello. Renewed interest in these topics will, it is hoped, begin to shed more light on Sally Hemings as a full human being rather than as a two-dimensional symbol in an ongoing debate about American institutions and society. While the dynamics of the relationship at its outset, and the degree of affection involved, will remain mysterious, all evidence tends to support the impression of an en-during connection. The pattern of births and Madison Hemings's statement that he and his siblings were "the only children of [Jefferson's] by a slave woman" indicate that the bond was also monogamous, at least on Sally Hemings's part. Even her contemporaries who denied that Jefferson was sexually involved with her never claimed that her children had more than one father, and she was never described as promiscuous by anyone who knew her. A recent statistical study of the intersecting patterns of the births of her children and Jefferson's presence at Monticello concluded that there was a one percent chance that the father of her children was someone other than Jefferson (or a man with an identical pattern of arrivals and departures).[199]

It is the fate of her children that reveals most about Sally Hemings. No other enslaved woman at Monticello achieved what she did—the freedom of all of her children, at an age when they could set the courses of their lives. Madison Hemings's allusions to the promises Jefferson made to his mother to persuade her to leave France evoke a woman who, although limited by her race and condi-tion, exercised a measure of control over her own destiny. The several refer-ences to Jefferson's "promise," "treaty," and "solemn pledge" even suggest Sally Hemings's strength and agency at other times in her life, condensed for the sake of transmitting a story into the single negotiation over the return to Virginia. In Madison Hemings's account, his mother's actions were driven by concern for the welfare of her children, and other evidence confirms the impression of a family tightly knit around a respected parent.[200]

Sally Hemings was only one member of her family with access to Thomas Jefferson, who was the dispenser of money, privileges, and most important, freedom. The first to persuade a reluctant Jefferson to grant him his freedom was her brother Robert, who received his manumission papers at the age of thirty-two, on Christmas Eve in 1794. In the years that he hired himself to other masters when Jefferson was absent in public service, Bob Hemings had found a wife, Dolly, an enslaved woman in the household of a doctor for whom he worked. Wishing to live permanently with his family in Richmond, he negotiated an arrangement whereby he, in essence, bought his own freedom. The doctor advanced the purchase price, which Hemings repaid in work by 1799. Jefferson, who felt that his bondsman had been "debauched" from him, expressed his anger at the arrangement. Martha Randolph saw Hemings in Richmond a few weeks after he left Monticello and reported to her father that the newly freed man "expressed great uneasiness at having quitted you in the manner he did" and "seems so deeply impressed with a sense of his ingratitude as to be rendered quite unhappy by it but he could not prevail upon himself to give up his wife and child." Robert Hemings was one of eleven Monticello slaves known to have gained their freedom in Jefferson's lifetime or in his will—all of them Betty Hemings's children or grandchildren.[201]

The Dining Room

Martin Hemings was the Monticello butler for twenty years, memorialized in a Jefferson family story for his vigorous behavior in the face of the British dragoons in 1781. One of them clapped a pistol to his chest and threatened to fire unless Hemings revealed which way Thomas Jefferson had fled. Biographer Henry S. Randall recounted the story as he had heard it from Jefferson's Randolph granddaughters: "'Fire away, then,' retorted the black, fiercely answering glance for glance, and not receding a hair's breadth from the muzzle of the cocked pistol." The granddaughters also told Randall of Martin Hemings's "gloomy, forbidding deportment" and recalled that he "would voluntarily suffer no fellow-servant to do the least office for his master; he watched his glance and anticipated his wants, but he served any other person with reluctance, and received orders from any other quarter with scarcely concealed anger." It was perhaps these latter characteristics that led to a falling out between master and servant and, in 1792, a mutual wish to part. As Jefferson wrote at the time, "Martin and myself disagreed when I was last in Virginia insomuch that he desired me to sell him, and I determined to do it, and most irrevocably that he shall serve me no longer." There is no record of a sale, however, and the fierce son of Betty Hemings vanishes from Jefferson's records after 1794.[202]

Shortly after Martin Hemings first came to Monticello in 1774, Jefferson used the arrival of fifty-eight bottles of Jamaica rum to test his new butler. He wrote in his Memorandum Book: "Note I shall keep a tally of these [bottles] as we use them by making a mark in the margin in order to try the fidelity of Martin." Hemings survived this scrutiny and was entrusted with the keys for two decades, following Jefferson to Williamsburg and Richmond to run the household during his governorship. At the end of the Revolution Jefferson sent Martin Hemings to the coast in search of slaves scattered by the British army's advance through Virginia. George Wythe wrote his friend Jefferson on the last day of 1781: "I desired Martin to take the roan horse then in good plight to assist him in carrying home the servant he recovered in my neighbourhood."[203]

In the years of Jefferson's final retirement after 1809 it was Martin Hemings's nephew Burwell Colbert who kept the keys and regulated the contents of the locked rooms below stairs: the wine and spirits in the cellars, the imported food staples in the ware room, and the valuable china and silver in the storerooms and sideboard. The man described by overseer Edmund Bacon as "the main, principal servant" at Monticello was responsible for both the running of the household and the upkeep of the house. He supervised the activities of the housemaids, waiters, and porters and was himself chief waiter, setting out and removing the main courses at the dinner table. He saw to the ringing of the bells that announced breakfast and dinner and responded to the bell system that rang in the cellars, activated by Jefferson or his family members in bedroom and parlor. Colbert also apparently acted as Jefferson's personal servant, as his uncles had before him. When Jefferson made his periodic extended visits to Poplar Forest, Colbert accompanied him, leaving domestic affairs at Monticello in less capable hands. "You know we never have the comfort of a clean house while Burwell is away," wrote one resident.[204]

Burwell Colbert had started his working life, at the age of ten, in the Mulberry Row nailery. He was at that time one of the least efficient workers, but he quickly improved and rose to be foreman of nailers. When Jefferson was at home, Burwell divided his time between the nailery and the house, where he probably helped in the kitchen and dining room. In 1805 he evidently received training from a free workman hired to paint the recently finished rooms of Monticello, for in 1806 Jefferson wrote his overseer that "Burwell paints and takes care of the house." He spent much of the winter of 1808–1809, while Jefferson was absent in Washington, on the roof of the house, painting the Chinese railing and the more than 250 balusters of the balustrade. In 1814 Burwell Colbert completed a painting task demanding particular skill—the landau carriage built by his relations John Hemings and Joseph Fossett. Like other skilled painters, he was also a glazier. On one of his trips to Poplar Forest, he glazed some of its windows while continuing to run the household and attend to Jefferson's needs.[205]

It is evident that Burwell Colbert occupied a special place in Jefferson's affections as well as in the household. At age seventeen, while working in the nailery, he had been singled out by Jefferson as the one nailer to be "absolutely excepted from the whip alltogether." While he was still in his twenties, Jefferson began to give him an "annual gratuity" of twenty dollars; his uncle John Hemings was the only other slave to receive a similar allowance. Edmund Bacon recalled of Colbert that "Mr. Jefferson had the most perfect confidence in him. He told me not to be at all particular with him—to let him do pretty much as he pleased, and to let him have pocket money occasionally, as he wanted it."[206]

It was Bacon who remembered a scene in the Monticello dining room, the main theater of Colbert's activities, that illustrates how access to the inner circle could bring problems as well as privileges. Charles L. Bankhead, husband of Jefferson's granddaughter Anne Randolph, "was very drunk and made a great disturbance, because Burwell, who kept the keys, would not give him any more brandy." The noise of the fracas drew Bankhead's father-in-law, Thomas Mann Randolph, to the room and, in the moments that followed, he seized an iron poker and knocked Bankhead down "as quick as I ever saw a bullock fall." Randolph felled his son-in-law with a blow that "pealed the skin off one side of his forehead and face." An account by another Monticello resident suggests that Burwell Colbert might have been a victim in this or another incident. Ellen Randolph Coolidge wrote in 1856: "I remember the distress of my grandfather when one evening, after he had retired to his room, this wretched castaway [Bankhead], in a fit of drunken fury, insulted, reviled and at last struck the excellent, faithful Burwell, the trustworthy and affectionate servant whom his master had always treated like a friend. That Burwell should have received a blow, should have been outraged under his master's roof, and the author of the outrage the husband of one of his own granddaughters seemed to produce upon my grandfather an effect more painful than I can well describe." In any case, because he conscientiously carried out the responsibilities of his position, Burwell Colbert was at least once subject to the violence of one of Jefferson's relations.[207]

Jefferson's grandson Thomas J. Randolph remembered that Colbert was the only person, besides the maid who cleaned the room and made the bed, who ever entered Jefferson's bedroom, to which he brought wood and water during the family breakfast. He accompanied Jefferson on his overnight visits to friends or on journeys to Richmond and to Poplar Forest. It was at the latter place, in 1819, that a series of calamities caused Jefferson's granddaughters to provide the fullest surviving accounts of Colbert. Their letters home to Monticello depict a disastrous summer for both Jefferson and his enslaved servant. Jefferson suffered the "severest attack of rheumatism" of his life and learned of impending financial ruin when a friend's insolvency brought in its train a new debt of $20,000. Burwell Colbert became dangerously ill with a bowel complaint. Ellen Randolph reported the family's state of acute fear and concern "for the life of a servant so faithfull, so attached and so usefull to my dear Grand father," also noting that "I never saw any body more uneasy than Grand papa, and his constant anxiety [convinced] me still more of his extraordinary value for Burwell."[208]

Jefferson and his granddaughters were not the only witnesses of Colbert's suffering. His uncle John Hemings, at Poplar Forest to work on the house, "nursed him constantly with the greatest care and attention" and gave him a warm bath that may have saved his life. Some weeks later, when Colbert had returned to his household and glazing tasks, he learned of the death at Monticello of his wife. According to Ellen Randolph, "Burwell as you may suppose is overwhelmed with grief. I have not seen him since he heard the news which was last night, but although he did not shew himself, he came out early in the morning and did all his business as usual. He did not lay by and send us the keys as I expected he would, and I am very glad of it for the want of employment would only leave him more time for the indulgence of his grief; which is so sincere as to excite the greatest degree of sympathy."[209]

Critta Colbert was her husband's first cousin. Jefferson had given her mother, Nance Hemings, to his sister Anna on her marriage to Hastings Marks in 1785. When expanding his textile operations ten years later, Jefferson embarked on negotiations to repurchase Nance, who was a skilled weaver. "She wishes me to buy her children," he wrote, "but I would not purchase the boy; as to her youngest child, if she insists on it, and my sister desires it, I would take it." As it turned out, Jefferson bought neither of Nance's children. Billy apparently remained on the Marks plantation in neighboring Louisa County, while Critta was purchased by Jefferson's son-in-law Thomas Mann Randolph. In 1809, she moved with the Randolphs to Monticello, where she was a nursemaid to Jefferson's grandchildren.[210]

Only thirty-six at the time of her death, Critta Colbert left eight motherless children. It was common in southern households for slaveholders to give the daughters of privileged domestic slaves to their own daughters, as John Wayles apparently gave Burwell Colbert's mother, Betty Brown, to Martha Wayles Jefferson. According to Ellen Randolph, several of Burwell and Critta Colbert's daughters had already been "disposed of" in this way to Jefferson's granddaughters. After learning of Critta Colbert's death, Ellen asked her mother for young Martha Colbert, adding, "I am more than ever anxious to have it in my power to befriend, and educate as well as I can, one of these children." Martha, who remained the property of Martha Randolph, was raised by her great-aunt Critta Hemings Bowles. The all-encompassing demands on the time of enslaved nurses, which often led to unavoidable neglect of their own children, is suggested by Ellen Randolph's further comment. It shows that she was only vaguely aware of the identities of the children of two of the house servants she knew best: "If I remember right Martha is a little sprightly black-eyed girl, whom I have often noticed with pleasure."[211]

Both Martin Hemings and Burwell Colbert gave twenty years of service in the household position of greatest responsibility. Martin Hemings's lot was very different from that of his nephew, who apparently never incurred Jefferson's displeasure. On March 27, 1826, in a codicil to his will, Jefferson wrote: "I give to my good, affectionate, and faithful servant Burwell his freedom, and the sum of three hundred Dollars to buy necessaries to commence his trade of painter and glazier, or to use otherwise as he pleases." He also directed that Colbert be given life tenancy of a "comfortable log-house" and an acre of land. Three months later Burwell Colbert, whose mother was at the deathbed of Martha Jefferson, attended the dying Thomas Jefferson. Four hours after midnight on July 4, Jefferson's last words were not "This is the Fourth?"—as posterity remembers—but instructions to his servant, made in "a strong and clear voice." At ten, no longer able to speak, Jefferson "fixed his eyes intently" on his grandson, who failed to understand his need. Burwell Colbert recognized and acted on the dying man's desire to be raised higher on his pillows. Three hours later Thomas Jefferson died.[212]

The Kitchen

Late on the night of July 4, 1784, Betty Hemings's nineteen-year-old son James sailed from Boston harbor on a new merchant ship bound for Europe. During a placid three-week crossing, the passengers on the *Ceres*, who also included Thomas Jefferson and his daughter Martha, caught cod on the Grand Banks and watched the movements of seabirds, sharks, and whales. After landing on the Isle of Wight and transferring to a cross-channel vessel, the trio from Virginia disembarked at Le Havre. Jefferson there gave James Hemings the equivalent of twelve dollars "to bear expences &c. to Rouen." If Hemings was being sent ahead to prepare the way for his master, his solo journey through new and strange surroundings was both successful and frugal. He was able to hand back half the money when he rejoined Jefferson at Rouen.[213]

As a boy James Hemings had captured mockingbirds for Jefferson when he was courting Martha Wayles Skelton. He then served as Jefferson's valet and traveling attendant. Now he had been selected to accompany Jefferson to France for the "particular purpose" of receiving training in the art of French cookery. Soon after his arrival in Paris, Hemings began his apprenticeship with Monsieur Combeaux, a *traiteur*, or caterer, who provided Jefferson's meals until he hired a female cook at the end of 1785. Hemings then studied with Jefferson's cook, as well as with a pastry chef and a chef in the household of the Prince de

Condé. By the summer of 1787, while continuing his training, James Hemings commenced his career as *chef de cuisine* in Jefferson's house on the Champs-Elysées. He received a wage of twenty-four livres (four dollars) a month—half the wage of the *cuisinière* who had preceded him.[214]

The moment James Hemings set foot on French soil, he became a free man—in theory. His freedom was only an abstraction until he took measures to claim it, and had he claimed his freedom, Jefferson would have had no choice but to acquiesce. Yet five years later he boarded another transatlantic vessel for the journey back to Virginia, where he had no legal rights. James Hemings, as well as Thomas Jefferson, breathed what Henry Adams called "the liberal, literary, and scientific air of Paris" in a period of revolutionary ferment. In March 1789 Jefferson had written: "The frivolities of conversation have given way entirely to politics—men, women and children talk nothing else: and all, you know, talk a great deal." By allotting a portion of his small salary for French lessons, Hemings had equipped himself to take part in these political discussions. While his views at the time have not been preserved, later developments strongly indicate that Hemings also talked to Jefferson about the issue of his own liberty and that his return to Virginia was part of an understanding about his eventual freedom or an interim quasi-free status.[215]

Back in the United States in 1790, James Hemings accompanied Jefferson to New York City and then Philadelphia, where he took charge of the kitchen and carried out some of the duties of butler in his daily forays to the market for provisions. In 1791, he filled his old position as a riding valet during Jefferson and James Madison's monthlong tour of New York State and New England. Living and traveling in states where, although there were still slaves, slavery itself was illegal, Hemings had his best opportunities to take freedom without Jefferson's consent. The possibility that Hemings might become a runaway would always have been part of this well-traveled chef's bargaining power. One indication of an agreement made in France is Hemings's wage, now comparable to that of a free servant. He also received—and probably petitioned for—annual raises, another sign of continued negotiation. In the fall of 1793, when the secretary of state was preparing to retire from public life, the inevitable break came. After years in the metropolises of Europe and America, James Hemings did not share Jefferson's yearnings for the rural retirement of Monticello. Master and slave struck a bargain in the midst of a yellow fever epidemic that took the lives of over four thousand Philadelphians. The contract Jefferson drew up stipulated that, as he had been "at great expence" in having his slave trained in "the art of cookery," Hemings would return to Monticello to pass his art on to another before receiving his freedom. So for more than two additional years Hemings produced French meals in the kitchen in the basement of Monticello's South Pavilion. At his side was his younger brother Peter, to whom he transmitted a decade of knowledge and experience.[216]

In late February 1796, James Hemings completed an inventory of the utensils in the Monticello kitchen and left the mountain with his free papers and thirty dollars in hand. While Philadelphia was his immediate destination, the terminus of his first journey as a free man may have been Paris. A year later, he was back in Philadelphia, from which Jefferson wrote his daughter: "He tells me his next trip will be to Spain. I am afraid his journeys will end in the moon." This letter also hints at a periodic problem with drink that may have contributed to his death four years later.[217]

In February 1801, Jefferson learned that he would be setting up house in a city again, this time in Washington. Knowing that Hemings "made his engagements such as to keep himself always free to come to me" and assuming his former slave would find a position as presidential chef acceptable, Jefferson opened negotiations through an intermediary. Correspondence between the president and William Evans suggests that Hemings, who was then working as a cook in a Baltimore tavern, was uncomfortable with this method of communication. More of a summons than an invitation, it may have reminded him of the days of slavery in Virginia, when Jefferson would recall him to Monticello from engagements made during his months of mobility in Jefferson's absences. Despite hearing that this free, and literate, man wished for "a few lines of engagement . . . with your own handwriting," Jefferson never wrote to his former slave. He chose to attribute Hemings's reluctance to take up the post to an attachment he might have formed in Baltimore.[218]

Ruffled feathers must have been smoothed over by the summer, when James Hemings came to Monticello to run the kitchen during Jefferson's long vacation, at a wage of twenty dollars a month—more than twice his previous wage. When he left in September, his mother and siblings never saw him again. A month later, word came to the White House through the grapevine connecting the black communities of Baltimore and Washington that the thirty-six-year-old Hemings had "committed an act of suicide." Jefferson heard that his former chef "had been delirious for some days previous to his having commited the act, and it is as the General opinion that drinking too freely was the cause." Jefferson then wrote to his head builder at Monticello to inform Betty Hemings and the rest of her family of her son's "tragical end."[219]

Four of James Hemings's recipes—for Snow Eggs and three kinds of dessert creams—survive in the Jefferson-Randolph family papers. They were probably also prepared by Peter Hemings, who was Monticello's cook after his brother's departure. Peter Hemings never worked in the kitchen of the White House, where Jefferson installed instead a Frenchman, Honoré Julien, who had been chef to George Washington in Philadelphia. But Betty Hemings's fourth son, who later became a very skillful brewer, had some specialties that Julien could not compete with. The characteristic blend of French and Virginian cooking traditions that became well known at Monticello is evoked in a request Jefferson sent home from Washington in 1802 for a recipe for "muffins in Peter's method." "My cook here cannot succeed at all in them," he wrote, "and they are a great luxury to me."[220]

In 1821 Jefferson wrote to a friend, "I envy M. Chaumont nothing but his French cook and cuisine. These are luxuries which can neither be forgotten nor possessed in our country." His lifelong search for surrogates expanded the horizons of other slaves besides James Hemings. During his presidency, Jefferson brought three women from Monticello to Washington for training in Honoré Julien's kitchen. Bagwell and Minerva Granger's daughter Ursula remained less than a year, but Edith Hern Fossett and her sister-in-law Fanny Gillette Hern both spent a number of years at the White House. They received a small monthly gratuity but not a regular wage. The rest of the domestic household in the White House included, besides chef Julien, a French butler, an Irish coachman and his family, and two other African Americans, Jack Shorter and John Freeman.[221]

Edith Fossett, who married a grandson of Betty Hemings, had almost seven years of culinary training in Washington. In the White House kitchen, below the entrance hall, she participated in the preparation of meals that struck Jefferson's guests by their elegance and abundance, enhanced by fine imported wines and unusual desserts. "Never before had such dinners been given in the President's House," recalled one Washington resident. "The dinner was excellent," wrote Benjamin Latrobe, "cooked rather in the French style (larded venison), the dessert was profuse and extremely elegant." One of the desserts, described as "balls" of ice cream "inclosed in covers of warm pastry," elicited more comments than any other dish. In her years in Washington Edy Fossett may have encountered some of the exotic visitors to the presidential mansion, from a Turkish envoy in turban and purple pantaloons to the Osage chiefs swathed in blankets and wearing moccasins. Her monthly two-dollar gratuity would have enabled her to participate to some degree in the life of the new city. She also unquestionably made friends in the growing community of free blacks as well as slaves. When enlisting assistance in recovering Edy's runaway brother Thruston Hern years later, Jefferson noted that he had probably gone to Washington, where he was "lurking under the connivance of some of his sister's old friends."[222]

In March 1809, Thomas Jefferson retired to Monticello for the last time. Edith Fossett and Fanny Hern and their children made the eight-day journey back to Monticello with the wagon train led by overseer Edmund Bacon and

David Hern. Master chef Honoré Julien soon arrived for a two-week visit to help set up the Monticello kitchen, now relocated under the south terrace. Like the White House kitchen, it was equipped with iron stew holes mounted in a brick base, a built-in precursor to the kitchen range. Jefferson's Washington butler, Etienne Lemaire, was certain Edy and Fanny, who were "good girls," would succeed in the plantation kitchen: "I am persuaded they will give you much satisfaction."[223]

The young cooks were reunited with their husbands, and it was probably the Fossett family—as Edy was head cook—who took up residence in the 10-by-14-foot room adjacent to the kitchen, recently vacated by Peter Hemings. The pace at Monticello was probably little slower than at the White House. Edith Fossett's son recalled "the streams of visitors" and "the merry go round of hospitalities" during Jefferson's final retirement. Breakfast at eight or nine entailed the early baking of fresh breads. The peak of activity occurred between breakfast and the late-afternoon dinner, with preparation of vegetables from the garden, roasting and stewing of meats, and the making of desserts, probably much less elaborate than those in Washington. Ice cream was a Monticello favorite, so there would have been trips to the ice house and the patient turning of the ice cream freezer. Edy Fossett and Fanny Hern were assisted by young boys, like Fanny's brother Israel Gillette, who kept the kitchen supplied with firewood and water and performed a scullion's tasks of peeling, slicing, and dishwashing.[224]

While no particular descriptions of Monticello meals survive, Jefferson's guests regularly praised the fare during Edith Fossett's regime. "The dinner was always choice, and served in the French style," wrote Bostonian George Ticknor. Daniel Webster recorded in 1824 that "dinner is served in half Virginian, half French style, in good taste and abundance." And Margaret Bayard Smith called attention to the "excellent muffins."[225]

The Shops

In July 1806 Jefferson was startled by the action of one of his most trusted slaves five days after he returned to Monticello from Washington for his summer vacation. He wrote to his Irish coachman at the White House: "I send Mr. Perry in pursuit of a young mulattoe man named Joe, 27. years of age, who ran away from here the night of the 29th. inst[ant] without the least word of difference with anybody, and indeed having never in his life recieved a blow from any one." The runaway was one of the blacksmiths, Joseph Fossett. The president was slow to understand that his tradesman was not running from Monticello and mistreatment but to Washington and Edith Hern. Almost four years had passed since fifteen-year-old Edy had become a trainee cook in the White House. Jefferson spoke of Joe Fossett as "formerly connected" to Edy, but in all probability they were husband and wife, separated by Jefferson's desire to have his slaves taught the arts of French cookery.[226]

Joe Fossett evidently heard disturbing news about his wife or his young son, James, from the black servants, John Freeman and Jack Shorter, who accompanied Jefferson from the White House to Monticello. Fossett, whom Jefferson described as "strong and resolute," successfully accomplished the 120-mile journey to Washington in four days or less, but his adventure was short-lived. On August 3 Jefferson's coachman "met with him in the Presidents yard going from the Presidents House" and "took him immediately." The French butler at the White House commented on this part of the drama: "The poor unhappy mulatto Joe was not difficult to take; he certainly merits a pardon for that." After a night in jail, Fossett was taken back to Monticello, where he had to wait another three years for Jefferson's retirement and Edy's return.[227]

Joseph Fossett was the son of Mary Hemings, Betty Hemings's oldest child. He was born in November 1780 in the Governor's residence in Richmond, where his mother and other household slaves from Monticello lived, and thus was carried off with them three months later by the British troops after Benedict Arnold's raid on the capital. From the age of six to twelve, when his mother was hired to a Charlottesville merchant during Jefferson's absence in France, Joe lived on Main Street in the town. In 1792, Mary Hemings asked to be sold to Thomas Bell, the merchant who was now her common-law husband. Jefferson gave his superintendent "power to dispose of Mary according to her desire, with such of her younger children as she chose." Jefferson sold only Bob and Sally, Mary and Thomas Bell's children, who remained with her in Bell's house in Charlottesville. He was apparently unwilling to sell her older children, twelve-year-old Joe and nine-year-old Betsy. Joe and Betsy returned to live in slavery at Monticello, while their mother and half siblings lived in freedom in Charlottesville and inherited Thomas Bell's considerable estate. Mary Hemings Bell remained a presence in the lives of her still-enslaved children and grandchildren, and there is every indication that this separation caused no lessening of the ties that bound this family together.[228]

In 1794, Joe Fossett was one of nine "little boys from 10. to 16. years of age" who began to work in the new nailery on Mulberry Row. According to Jefferson's daily analysis of nailery operations, he "wasted" only nineteen pounds of iron per hundredweight in the nail-making process, an efficiency rate better than the twenty-two-pound average. Like some of his cousins, he divided his working days between the nailery and the main house, where he made fires, fetched wood and water, ran errands, or waited at table. At sixteen, his life as a household servant came to an end when he started to learn the blacksmithing trade from George Granger while continuing to work part-time as a nailer. In April 1796,

Joe Fossett was the third most profitable nail maker, earning for Jefferson an average daily profit of sixty cents, and in 1800 he became a foreman in the nailery.[229]

In 1801 Joseph Fossett had a new teacher, a blacksmith Jefferson had engaged in Philadelphia. For six years William Stewart crafted fine ironwork, trained Fossett and other Monticello smiths, and, too frequently for Jefferson, deserted his forge for drinking sprees that left the business of the blacksmith shop in the hands of Joe Fossett. From 1807, when Stewart was finally fired, until 1827, Fossett ran the shop, to which local farmers came to have their horses shod and their plows and hoes sharpened. He also made garden forks, spikes for a dam, and all the metal parts of an elaborate carriage Jefferson designed in 1814. Fossett was allowed to keep one-sixth of the money earned for work "in his own time." In 1824, for instance, he received $7.33 when a local carpenter paid for $44.00 worth of work done in the shop. He earned most of his extra money from making plow chain traces and plating saddle trees. Overseer Edmund Bacon described Fossett as "a very fine workman; could do anything it was necessary to do with steel or iron."[230]

Joe Fossett's cousin Wormley Hughes, the oldest son of Betty Hemings's daughter Betty Brown, was born in March 1781, probably in a British internment camp, as his mother was apparently one of the house servants carried off from the Governor's palace two months before. It is possible that Wormley Creek, at Yorktown, had some influence on his interesting given name. His surname, learned from the 1850 census, is more mysterious. His younger half brother Burwell used a different name, Colbert, suggesting that their surnames may derive from their unidentified fathers. Since many reasons governed the adoption of last names by enslaved men and women, it is impossible to be certain. What is significant is that surnames were widespread, possibly even universal, in the Monticello community and were an important part of African American identity, usually either unknown to or ignored by slaveholders.[231]

After the upheaval of the Revolution, Wormley spent his boyhood years very much as did his cousin Joe, dividing his time between the nailery and the main house, where he was a "door-yard servant," fetching horses, greeting visitors, or running errands. At the age of thirteen he was the second most efficient nailer. When he was nineteen, he and Joe Fossett were employed, with auger and gunpowder, in blasting rock for Jefferson's interminable canal-building project. Wormley Hughes also learned gardening skills, probably from Robert Bailey, a Scotsman who came to Monticello in 1794 to assist in laying out the ornamental grounds. By at least 1806, Hughes was Jefferson's principal gardener.[232]

References to Wormley Hughes's gardening activities are frequent in Jefferson's correspondence as president. He planted seeds, bulbs, and trees sent back from Washington; prepared and planted flower beds; took up bulbs for the winter; and spread dung in the vegetable garden. In the fall of 1807 Jefferson sent his overseer instructions for seeds of the cucumber magnolia and mountain laurel: "Wormley must plant [them] in the Nursery. And he must plant the Pitch pine in the woods along the new road leading from the house to the river, on both sides of the road. He is to lay the seed on the ground and scratch an inch of earth over it." Jefferson's granddaughter Ellen remembered that Wormley Hughes, "armed with spade and hoe," assisted Jefferson, who "carried the measuring-line," in laying out the flower beds on Monticello's west lawn.[233]

Since gardening was a seasonal activity, Jefferson's perpetual quest for efficiency in his plantation operations meant that Wormley Hughes, like other Monticello slaves, was trained in a variety of skills so that he could turn to alternative work if weather or other circumstances interrupted his labor. Hughes seems to have performed an unusually broad range of tasks. He continued to make nails until at least 1809, and in 1801, he was temporarily detached from the nailery to fell trees in a new field. He was often engaged in clearing roads and paths and helped to dig the sunken fence, or ha!ha!, that surrounds Monticello's west lawn.[234]

Wormley Hughes also became, like Jupiter, chief hostler in the Mulberry Row stables. He was responsible for the stable equipment as well as the care and provisioning of the horses. Jefferson's biographer Henry S. Randall recognized Hughes's love of horses in a conversation in 1851: "He could distinctly remember and describe the points, height, color, pace, temper, etc. of every horse as far back as Arcturus, which Mr. Jefferson brought home from Washington." Hughes also pointed out to Randall the rock outcrop that caused Jefferson's horse to shy and the ford where his master was thrown over his horse's head. During Jefferson's retirement years, Hughes often drove a carriage or cart, taking family members to and from Monticello or transporting valuable goods. In 1810, when Hughes drove Jefferson's young grandson home to Eppington in Chesterfield County, Jefferson wrote that "I shall dispatch Francis tomorrow morning in the care of one of the most trusty servants I have."[235]

Wormley Hughes's marriage to Ursula, a granddaughter of George and Ursula Granger, linked two important Monticello families as well as the worlds of the fieldworkers and the house servants. Born in 1787 to Bagwell and Minerva Granger, Ursula grew up in the farm quarters at Lego and Tufton. When she was fourteen Jefferson took her to Washington for training as a pastry cook at the White House. After only a year there, she returned to Monticello in 1802 and thereafter lived a double life, working in the fields during Jefferson's absences in the nation's capital and returning to the house—and probably the kitchen—during his vacations. Her duties during Jefferson's final retirement are not known.[236]

More is known about Wormley Hughes's uncle John Hemings[237] than perhaps any other member of the African American community at Monticello. He left behind to speak for him a dozen letters and his own handiwork—chairs, cabinets, arches, and mantels. He also frequently appears in the letters or recollections of Jefferson and his family members. Hemings was born on April 24, 1776, Betty Hemings's youngest son. According to his nephew Madison Hemings, his father was Joseph Neilson, an English carpenter hired by Jefferson in 1775. Apparently a fieldworker as a child, John Hemings began to pursue his trade as a woodworker at the age of fourteen, first as one of a "gang" of what Jefferson called "out-carpenters." They spent their days "out" in the woods and fields, felling trees for firewood, fences, and charcoal, and hewing logs for building. They also erected the barns, granaries, and other log structures on the plantation. John Hemings was one of the men who, in 1792, built the log dwellings on Mulberry Row that were inhabited by his sisters.[238]

In 1793, when he was planning to remodel his house, Jefferson hired a skilled white joiner named David Watson, a prodigious drinker who in one month bought from Jefferson ten gallons of whiskey. Former slave Isaac Granger Jefferson remembered that Watson "drank whiskey; git drunk and sing; take a week at a time drinkin' and singin'." John Hemings became Davy Watson's apprentice, "for the purpose of learning to make wheels, and all sorts of work." Hemings's major training began in 1798 when a recent immigrant from County Antrim in northern Ireland came to Monticello. James Dinsmore was a house joiner of exceptional skill, and Hemings became his principal assistant in completing the decorative interior woodwork in the remodeled Monticello house. Of the craftsmanship of this team of Irishman and African American, Jefferson wrote, "There is nothing superior in the US."[239]

After Dinsmore's departure in 1809, Hemings took charge of the Mulberry Row joinery. Overseer Edmund Bacon remembered him as "a first-rate workman—a very extra workman. He could make anything that was wanted in woodwork." Called on for the more difficult plantation carpentry tasks, Hemings repaired the threshing machines and spinning jennies and made the plow frames for Jefferson's innovative moldboard "of least resistance." In 1814 he made all the wooden parts of Jefferson's landau carriage, and after 1815, he periodically went to Poplar Forest to make and install the doors, windows, and decorative woodwork. It was this work that generated a dozen surviving letters in John Hemings's hand between 1819 and 1825. Jefferson asked Hemings to make weekly reports on "exactly what work is done, and what you will still have to do." Hemings responded with accounts of his progress on the architraves of the skylight or the Chinese railing on the roof: "I am at worck in the morning by

Letter of John Hemings to Thomas Jefferson, September 28, 1825. (Coolidge Collection of Thomas Jefferson Manuscripts; courtesy of the Massachusetts Historical Society)

the time I can see and the very same at night." In 1819 he stayed up all night tracing the sources of roof leaks. While Jefferson's letters to this highly skilled workman have no complimentary closings, except for an occasional "farewell" or "I wish you well," Hemings closed each of his letters with a stock phrase of the day: "I am your servant John Hemmings," sometimes inserting the adjective "faithful," "humble," or "obedient" before "servant."[240]

John Hemings, who was fully trained in cabinetmaking as well as house joinery, also made a great deal of furniture, including bedsteads, Venetian blinds, dressing tables, and a writing desk for Jefferson's granddaughter Ellen Randolph Coolidge. The loss of this fine piece at sea caused Hemings a despair that Jefferson compared to that of Virgil, had "his Aeneid fallen a prey to the flames." A number of pieces now on display in the Monticello house, because of their style or probable date, were almost certainly made by Hemings. Jefferson was so attached to the comfort of a campeche, or "Siesta," chair he received from New Orleans by 1819 that he had Hemings make several copies for himself and his friends. Each captured the basic form of the original but had details and decorative elements that were undoubtedly Hemings's own creative interpretation of his instructions. Even in the twentieth century, Jefferson's descendants spoke of the work of John Hemings. One sewing table came down through the family with the tale that Hemings had used for it part of a stock of wood he was saving for "old Master's coffin."[241]

John Hemings, perhaps more than any other member of his family, allied himself with his "old Master" and his household. He is one of the few slaves to appear in stories passed down by Jefferson's grandchildren. They often visited "Daddy," as they called him, in the Mulberry Row joinery and begged him for nails and bits of wood or asked him to make a box for their flowers or drawings. His reported reply was: "Yes, yes! my little mistises, but Grandpapa comes first! There are new bookshelves to be made, trellises for the roses, besides farm work to be done." He was especially fond of Jefferson's youngest granddaughter, Septimia Randolph. When Septimia was almost three, as he told her older sister, "he had cried for about five miles of the road after taking leave of her" to go to Poplar Forest. A letter survives, written by Hemings in 1825 from Poplar Forest to an eleven-year-old Septimia. After inquiring about her grandfather's health and sending love to her brothers, he concluded: "I am in hope I shal be able to com home by the 25 of November if life last. I am Your obediente servant John Hemmings." Cornelia Randolph wrote back to Monticello from Poplar Forest in 1816, asking her sister to send "a little English dictionary" she had received some years before from her mother: "I intended to give it to Daddy but could not bring it with me."[242]

"Daddy" Hemings's association with his master's family was doubly close as his wife was "mammy" to Jefferson's grandchildren. Priscilla Hemings belonged to Jefferson's daughter and son-in-law Martha and Thomas Mann Randolph and thus, from 1790 to 1809, lived across the Rivanna River up to three miles from the mountaintop. From 1809, when the Randolphs moved to Monticello permanently, she was able to live with her husband. She evidently accompanied Martha Randolph and her children to Washington in 1802 and 1806. A Randolph great-granddaughter recalled hearing about "the good Priscilla, who presided over the nursery through so many long years. At the White House we may picture her a tall and comely young woman watching over the children in the nursery or as they played in the East room." Former overseer Edmund Bacon also remembered Priscilla Hemings: "She took charge of all the children that were not in school. If there was any switching to be done, she always did it. She used to be down at my house a great deal with those children. . . . They were very much attached to their nurse. They always called her 'Mammy.'" When her husband went to Poplar Forest, Priscilla Hemings maintained contact through Jefferson's letter-writing daughter and granddaughters. Ellen Randolph wrote from Monticello: "Aunt Prisilla begs to be remembered to the young ladies—and that they will inform John H of her *well doing and constant recollection.*"[243]

John and Priscilla Hemings shared a religious life, and there is a reference to a "prayer meeting" actually at their house. John Hemings's literacy enabled him to read prayers to his wife, something he did on the night she died in 1830. Jefferson's granddaughter Cornelia memorialized her: "We were all much

afflicted; she has always been a kind nurse to us, and shewed a never tiring desire to serve us ever since we left Monticello. . . . There were a thousand little
attentions she paid us, and some very troublesome to herself."[244]

John Hemings showed his allegiance to Jefferson in 1821 when he informed on
a Poplar Forest slave. "Above all things on earth I hate compla[i]nts," he began,
driven to write by the refusal of Nace, the foreman, to provide him with vegetables. Nace "takes every thing out of the garden and carries them to his cabin and
burys them in the ground." While the foreman told Hemings that they were for
Jefferson's use, "at the first oppertunity," as Hemings heard from other Poplar
Forest slaves, Nace carried the vegetables to sell at Lynchburg market. While the
view that most house slaves were plantation spies is exaggerated, Hemings's tale
bearing is an indication of the fissures that the system of slavery deepened in a
community subject to the social divisions normal to any human society. John
Hemings benefited from the daily contacts with his master in their close working
relationship. He was the only Monticello slave, other than his nephew Burwell
Colbert, to receive an annual gratuity of twenty dollars "as an encouragement."
He also had the unusual perquisite of being able to select his own clothing,
receiving a credit at the local store instead of the regular allotment.[245]

The greatest privilege John Hemings and some of his relations gained from
their association with Jefferson was their freedom. Like Burwell Colbert, John
Hemings and Joseph Fossett were both freed by Jefferson's will and given the
tools of their trades and life tenancy of a log house and an acre of land. Hemings
was also allowed the "service" of his two apprentices, his nephews Madison and
Eston Hemings, until they reached the age of twenty-one, when they too would
be freed. On July 4, 1826, John Hemings took the piece of wood he had been
saving and began to make Thomas Jefferson's coffin. A year later, he and Joseph
Fossett became free men.[246]

1827: Dispersal

On a bitterly cold day in January, the dismantling of Monticello began.
The house was unoccupied. Jefferson's daughter Martha Randolph had gone
to Boston to visit a daughter, and her other children had moved to a small
house on another part of the plantation. The women of the family stayed at
home while crowds of people made their way to the mountaintop, drawn by
newspaper advertisements offering household and kitchen furniture, articles
"curious and useful," farm equipment, crops and livestock, and "130 valuable
negroes."[247]

Six months of preliminaries led up to this moment, brought about by the
enormous debt left by Jefferson at his death. His executor and grandson, Thomas

Jefferson Randolph, assumed the burden of responsibility for repayment of obligations in excess of $107,000. Respected local men were called in to assess the property on the Monticello plantation, which included the two quarter farms, Lego and Tufton, as well as the home farm. The appraisers assigned modest figures to the horses and mules, cattle, vehicles, axes and saws, hoes and plows. The 126 men, women, and children in the three inventories accounted for 90 percent of the $31,400 total appraised value of Jefferson's Albemarle County property (land and furnishings were not part of these inventories). In his advertisements Colonel Randolph described the slaves as "the most valuable for their number ever offered at one time in the State of Virginia." Before the sale, he turned down several offers to purchase them, one from a man wishing to acquire fifty people to settle a cotton plantation in upland Georgia.[248]

Despite the severe weather, bidding was brisk over five days, and even old chairs losing their stuffing brought good prices. The slaves, in particular, were bought for amounts averaging 70 percent more than their appraised value. Half a century later Thomas J. Randolph, recalling the "sad scene" he witnessed, likened it to "a captured village in ancient times when all were sold as slaves." His sister Mary, who stayed two miles away at Tufton during the sale, wrote her sister the following week: "Thank heaven the whole of this dreadful business is over, and has been attended with as few distressing occurrences as the case would admit. . . . You may imagine what must have been the state of our feelings, such a scene passing actually within *sight* and every hour bringing us fresh details of everything that was going on."[249]

The feelings of those most affected by "this dreadful business" were preceded by years of anxious speculation. The account of a Frenchman who visited Monticello in 1824 suggests an acute awareness of Jefferson's declining health and fortunes and of the probable consequences of his death. Auguste Levasseur spoke to several African Americans on the mountaintop. "They cultivated the lands of Monticello," they told him, "with the greater pleasure, because they were almost sure of not being torn away from them, to be transported elsewhere, so long as Mr. Jefferson lived." His death, of course, changed everything. Creditors content to collect their annual interest when Jefferson was alive began to call in their loans. Over the next five years, in sale after sale, furnishings, books, paintings, land, and the humans who lived there were dispersed. Finally, the house itself was sold in 1831.[250]

The state of mind of the African American men and women is preserved in the recollections of Israel Gillette Jefferson, who remembered Jefferson's death as "an affair of great moment and uncertainty to us slaves." The perspective of children, protected by their parents from worried discussions, is captured in the memories of Peter Fossett, who was eleven years old at the time of the sale. Noting the striking coincidence of the deaths of Jefferson and John Adams on the same day, he told a reporter that "sorrow came not only to the homes of two great men who had been such fast friends in life . . . but to the slaves of Thomas Jefferson. . . . Born and reared as free, not knowing that I was a slave, then suddenly, at the death of Jefferson, put upon an auction block and sold to strangers."[251]

Israel Jefferson recalled that Thomas Jefferson provided for the freedom of only seven slaves: "All the rest of us were sold from the auction block." The seven that were spared the block that haunted the memories of Fossett and Gillette were all children or grandchildren of Betty Hemings, and all had apparently discussed their approaching freedom with Jefferson. In his will Jefferson freed Burwell Colbert, Joseph Fossett, and John, Madison, and Eston Hemings, petitioning the Virginia legislature to exempt them from the 1806 law requiring freed slaves to leave the state. In the case of Wormley Hughes and Sally Hemings, it seems that Jefferson recommended them to the care of his daughter, who unofficially freed them. Jefferson's biographer Henry S. Randall wrote of Hughes: "His manumission, in case he should desire it, was orally recommended to Mrs. Randolph." In her 1834 will, probably intended to invest a verbal act with quasi-legal weight, Martha J. Randolph asked her heirs to give "Sally and Wormley" their "time." "If liberated," she wrote, "they would be obliged to leave the state of Virginia." "Giving time" was a common method of granting virtual freedom while avoiding the rigors of the 1806 removal law. Although Sally Hemings and Wormley Hughes evidently never had their own free papers, their freedom was sufficiently recognized in Albemarle County for them to be listed in censuses as free people of color.[252]

Burwell Colbert, bequeathed immediate freedom by Jefferson, was the only member of his family and community to attend the 1827 dispersal sale as a purchaser. He spent over fifty dollars, buying a carving knife, tea china, and portrait engravings of Thomas Jefferson and the Marquis de Lafayette. His most expensive purchase was a mule, for thirty-one dollars. The fates of his children, the property not of Jefferson but of the Randolphs, were not then at risk. Nor did Sally Hemings have to consider life apart from her sons. Every other enslaved parent, however, knew that the chance of lifelong separation from a child was very real. Slave traders from the Lower South undoubtedly attended this well-publicized sale, and it may have been the prestige of the event that helped to moderate the extent of dispersal of the enslaved families. The consequent large crowd of bidders and the inflated prices neutralized the effects of the traders. "The negroes with one exception I believe," wrote Mary J. Randolph, "are all sold to persons living in the state, many of them in this neighbourhood or the adjoining counties, and most of them I believe also, are well and satisfactorily placed, as much to their own wishes as they could be in leaving our estate."[253]

While fears of exile to Georgia or Louisiana were allayed, the fragmentation of families by the sale was undiminished. Wormley Hughes and Joseph Fossett, whose freedom would not become effective until the next July Fourth, had to watch their wives and children sold to many different bidders. The customary practice in Virginia at this time was for slaves to be sold "in families," a term that had a limited definition when applied to human property. Usually, husbands were sold together with wives and mothers with their youngest children. Teenagers, as well as single adults, however, were often sold separately from their parents and siblings, since, in the slave economy, childhood ended at about age ten. The fragmentary records of the Monticello sale indicate that several eight- and nine-year-olds, in addition to the children over ten, were sold separately from their families.[254]

Such was the case for the Fossett and Hughes families, as eight-year-old Isabella Fossett and nine-year-old Caroline Hughes were, like their older siblings, put on the auction block by themselves. The total spent for Joe Fossett's wife and four of their seven children was $1,350, far more than he could have accumulated from his percentage of the income of the blacksmith shop. Three men bid a total of $2,125 for Wormley Hughes's wife and eight of his children. David Hern and his children and grandchildren were sold to at least eight different men, while more than seven new owners claimed members of the Gillette family. The few surviving receipts of the 1827 sale and an account of a further sale of thirty slaves in 1829 reveal the purchasers of two-thirds of the 126 people listed in the inventories of the Monticello plantation. Letters and recollections also tell us that both before and after the inexorable machinery of the estate sale dispersed an entire community, fathers and mothers, and husbands and wives, did what they could to keep their families together.[255]

Leaving the Mountain

1831

The inscription that John Hemings chiseled into the piece of slate destined to mark his wife's grave reads: "The sed[256] is placed at the hea[d] of my dear affectionat[e] wife Priscilla Hemmings departed this life on Friday the 7th of May 1830 ag[e] 54." It was late August 1831 when Jefferson's granddaughter Cornelia rode to Monticello and found Hemings cutting the stone, over a year after his wife's burial. Cornelia Randolph also provided the report of Priscilla Hemings's sudden death, in May 1830:

> She had been complaining of headach several days and one day had a prayer meeting at her house. Seeing her husband troubled she asked him how he

Tombstone carved by John Hemings for his wife Priscilla (1776–1830). (Thomas Jefferson Foundation, Inc.)

could bear a greater misfortune if he was distressed by a small one; that night he read prayers to her and they went to bed. During the night she groaned and he asked her if she was worse. She said no but that her head ached a great deal; she told him also to look under the looking glass and he would find something he would care for; he thinking it was a paper of seed he had lost thought no more about it. At last she uttered an exclamation calling god, gave a deep sigh . . . and was still and silent. He thinking she had gone to sleep, dozed himself, but being uneasy he soon awoke and shaking her found she was dead on his arm. He arose and called up the servants in the next house but she was stiff and cold. Some days after, recollecting that she had told him to look under the glass he did so and found a bundle containing a black cravat, crepe hat band and a lock of her hair.[257]

Over a year later, it was this aspect of his wife's death that still haunted the grieving man: "The servants . . . say . . . that all the things he tells about her knowledge of her approaching end and the speeches she made on the occasion are mere romancing or else that he misunderstood her and imagined what was not really so." Hemings still talked "incessantly" of Priscilla's sickness and death, "detailing the minutest circumstances and with his odd manner and gesticulation." The "servants" also reported that he had taken to drink—something he "positively" denied—and, most ominously, "he has given up work and does nothing I believe."[258]

If John Hemings, the master workman of Monticello, no longer pursued his trade, then the underpinnings of his world were truly shattered. The two fixed points of his life—his wife and the man who called forth his talent—were both gone. Monticello had been sold, and its new owner was shortly to take possession. Hemings had his freedom, but only after he had given to Jefferson the most productive years of his life. He was fifty-one when he became free, with failing eyesight and poor health. Little is known about his working life in the years after Jefferson's death, although scattered references in letters indicate that he continued to carry out miscellaneous woodworking tasks for the Randolph family. He apparently never worked at the University of Virginia, the most likely site for his skills.[259]

On the very day when John Hemings was carving his wife's gravestone, Nat Turner was waiting for the cover of darkness. Late that night Turner would launch the bloody revolt whose repercussions would lead to intensified oppression of African Americans in Virginia. The shock waves from Southampton County soon reached Charlottesville. Thomas Jefferson Randolph's wife Jane wrote her sister that the "horrors" in Southampton had increased her fears "to the most agonizing degree." Her mother-in-law, Martha Jefferson Randolph, however, was confident that the slaves that surrounded her could be trusted: "Here there has never been the least alarm or disturbance. Our negroes have applied freely to the boys for information, cursing the folly and wickedness of the wretches, but I have scribled away upon a disgusting subject and one that has excited much horror but no fear." In October Mrs. Randolph reported to her son-in-law in Boston that the laws restraining blacks were now "more exactly enforced and they are denied the liberty of social intercourse by the restrictions with which it is hampered. No meetings, no night visiting, and upon those plantations which are at all disorderly, harassed with the night visits of the patrol, besides being watched at every turn." It was no doubt this climate of increased vigilance that caused John Hemings, for the first time since his manumission, to observe the law that required free blacks in Virginia to register with the county court. On September 16, he entered the courthouse, stated his name and age, and was examined and measured. The clerk recorded that he had a "light complection," that he had a small scar on his right wrist, and that he stood a shade over five feet five and a half inches tall.[260]

His nephew and former apprentice Madison Hemings, five feet seven and three-eighths inches tall, registered with him. Madison and Eston Hemings, who, according to his free register, was six feet one inch tall, had set up a household with their mother in Charlottesville, first in a rented house and, in 1830, in a house they bought on West Main Street, not far from the University. Both pursued their trades as carpenter, and Eston Hemings evidently began what would be a notable career as a professional musician. Without official freedom, Sally Hemings could not safely travel beyond the boundaries of Albemarle

County. It was only after her death, in 1835, that the Hemings brothers determined to leave a state that was increasingly hostile to free blacks. They sold their Charlottesville property and moved with their wives, both free women of color, to southern Ohio.[261]

Madison Hemings worked in the building trade in Ross and Pike Counties and owned a sixty-six-acre farm at the time of his death in 1877. Eston Hemings purchased a house in Chillicothe for one thousand dollars and led a dance band that played for balls all over southern Ohio. At midcentury he set in motion the metamorphosis previously adopted by his siblings Beverly and Harriet. He and his family moved to Wisconsin, where they changed their surname to Jefferson and lived as white people.[262]

John Hemings did not have his nephews' youth to spend on freedom. In 1833 he died suddenly, like his wife Priscilla. Martha J. Randolph wrote her daughter Septimia, Hemings's favorite, about "your poor Daddy's" death: "We ought not to regret it, for old age to him would have been a season of such suffering that his best friends ought to have wished to see him taken as he was from a life which had become a very unhappy one from his losses and his habits of drink and idleness. His liberty poor fellow was no blessing to him."[263]

1837

On September 15, 1837, Joseph Fossett entered the courthouse, a block from his blacksmith shop on Charlottesville's Main Street. "Know all men," wrote the clerk in the county deed book, "that I Joseph Fossett of the County of Albemarle and State of Virginia have manumitted, emancipated and set free, and by these presents do manumit, emancipate and set free the following negro slaves." The deed of manumission, which named Fossett's wife, Edith, five of their children—two born since the 1827 sale, and four grandchildren, continues: "I hereby declare the said Eady, Elizabeth Ann, William, Daniel, Lucy, Jesse, James, Joseph, Thomas and Maria Elizabeth to be entirely liberated from slavery and entitled to all the rights and privileges of free persons with which it is in my power to vest them." It concludes with the ages, heights, and complexions of Fossett's ten family members.[264]

Years earlier Joseph and Edith Fossett must have been painfully aware of the worsening condition of Jefferson's finances after the agricultural depression of 1819. The Monticello kitchen and blacksmith shop would have been important sites for the exchange of local gossip and discussion of the aging master and his family. Since slaves were particularly vulnerable to separation at the death or financial failure of their masters, Monticello's African Americans must have listened intensely in dining room or stable and talked often among themselves about the future. Some even approached Jefferson with their concerns. The recollections of Thomas Jefferson Randolph suggest that his grandfather spoke of his intentions to the five men to whom he bequeathed freedom. Joe Fossett knew, therefore, that he would become a free man after Jefferson's death. He also no doubt knew that his wife and their children would remain in bondage.[265]

Fossett was also probably more realistic about the fate that might befall his family than Jefferson himself, whose will suggests that he died in expectation of a financial rescue that would have prevented an outcome like the Monticello sale in January 1827. It is apparent that the blacksmith, who would not become free until a year after Jefferson's death, prepared for the worst by enlisting the aid of family members and acquaintances in the neighborhood. He evidently sought out local white men to purchase his children on his behalf. "My father made an agreement with Mr. Jones," Peter Fossett told a reporter in 1898, "that when he was able to raise the amount that Col. Jones paid for me he would give me back." Peter's sister Elizabeth Ann was bought by merchant John Winn. Since she soon became her father's property and Winn became a creditor of the Fossett family, this purchase was also presumably based on a mutual agreement. In the case of his wife and youngest children, Joseph Fossett could rely on the support of his own mother, now living in Charlottesville with her daughter and son-in-law Sally Bell and Jesse Scott, in the house left them by Thomas Bell, who had acknowledged his two children by Mary in his will. Thus it was Joe Fossett's brother-in-law Jesse Scott, a free man of color and well-known local musician, who came to the sale and, for $505, purchased Edith and the youngest Fossetts, six-year-old William and three-year-old Daniel.[266]

The profits of the Bell store, and the credit the Bell and Scott property made possible, were insufficient to secure the safety of the entire Fossett family. Jefferson had given the oldest child, James, born in the White House, to his grandson Thomas J. Randolph in 1812. Since seventeen-year-old Patsy, bought by University of Virginia professor Charles Bonnycastle, ran away soon after the sale, it is unlikely that her purchase was the result of an agreement with her father. The purchasers of her sisters Maria and Isabella are unknown.[267]

Joe Fossett's emancipation of part of his family in 1837 signals his intention to leave the land of slavery. Because of the 1806 removal law, he had been compelled to keep them in the safety of bondage for ten years, until plans were laid for resettling in the free state of Ohio. During those years he pursued his trade as a blacksmith, in 1831 purchasing a lot and shop on Charlottesville's Main Street. When the Fossetts left Charlottesville for Ohio in 1837, their son Peter did not accompany them. John R. Jones, who had purchased the eleven-year-old boy at the 1827 sale, failed to keep his promise and refused to sell Peter to his father.[268]

After Peter Fossett parted with his family, he may have reviewed a childhood he later described as "one ray of sunshine—little to do, every one kind, a master we all loved, and so many famous people and wonderful sights that are all a part of the country's history now." His memories of his tasks at Monticello included ordering Jefferson's horse Eagle from the stable or, at the summons of a bell, opening the gate for arriving visitors. He claimed that his upbringing differed from that of boys in the farm quarters, and his clothing, too, distinguished him from other plantation slaves. His grandmother Mary Hemings Bell gave him a suit of blue nankeen cloth and a red leather hat and shoes. Using his earnings in the blacksmith shop, his father added a silver watch to this striking outfit.[269]

Shortly after his eleventh birthday, however, Peter Fossett's carefree childhood came to an end. "I knew nothing of the horrors of slavery till our good master died, on July 4, 1826," he told a newspaper reporter in 1900. The bargain Peter's father made with John R. Jones also included a promise to let Joseph Fossett teach his son the blacksmithing trade and to allow Jones's sons to continue Peter's education, begun at Monticello with one of Jefferson's grandsons. Peter Fossett's first recognition of the worth of his new owner's word came when Jones found him with a book, almost certainly Noah Webster's famous *American Spelling Book*. Peter was "kneeling before the fireplace spelling the word 'baker,'" a momentous occasion for every American who learned to read with Webster's "blue-back" speller, since it marked the transition to two-syllable words, after twenty-nine previous lessons on monosyllables. Colonel Jones threw the speller in the fire and promised thirty-nine lashes if he ever caught his slave with a book in his hand; he also threatened his sons with punishment if they provided instruction. The Jones brothers persisted in their teaching, however, and Peter Fossett persevered with his learning. He remembered an evening by the dying coals of a fire for his bath, when he practiced his letters in a copybook his father had given him and wrote out the phrase "Art improves nature."[270]

Soon Peter Fossett was passing his knowledge on to his fellow slaves. The son of one of his students heard stories of Fossett's nighttime lessons by the light of pine knots, in a remote cabin on the Jones plantation. "All the time I was teaching all the people around me to read and write," Peter Fossett recalled at the end of his life, "and even venturing to write free passes and sending slaves away from their masters." His secret writing skills succeeded in freeing his sister Isabella, who made her way to Boston using free papers forged by her brother.[271]

His efforts on his own behalf were not so effective. As he remembered his feelings on the departure of his family, he declared in 1898, "My parents were here in Ohio and I wanted to be with them and be free, so I resolved to get free or die in the attempt." His first bid for freedom ended in recapture. After his second attempt to run away, in 1850, he "was caught, handcuffed, and taken back and carried to Richmond and put in jail. For the second time I was put up on the auction block and sold like a horse." On this occasion his own brother-in-law, a free man of color named Tucker Isaacs, was arrested for "falsly, wilfully and feloniously forging and counterfeiting a certain register of freedom" for his runaway relative. Since Isaacs was found not guilty, it was probably actually Peter Fossett himself who tried to write himself, as well as his fellows in bondage, into freedom.[272]

Accounts of the second auction vary, but it is apparent that family members and friends banded together to purchase Fossett out of slavery. After thirty-five years in bondage, he was able to cross the Ohio River to join his parents and siblings in the city of Cincinnati. His seventy-year-old father, with two of Peter's brothers, continued to pursue the blacksmithing trade and owned property there worth $1,500. Peter Fossett at first had a double career as a whitewasher and a waiter, working in the homes of Cincinnati's white elite. By the 1870s he had established his own catering company, with a notable collection of china, linen, and silver purchased from a retiring caterer. Fossett's firm, in which other family members participated, was described as "the most prominent" catering establishment of the period, and Fossett himself as "the indispensable major domo at wedding feasts and entertainments." It seems probable that some of Edith Fossett's French recipes from her years in the White House and Monticello kitchens might have been prepared and served by her sons at the banquets of the city's wealthy residents.[273]

In 1854 Peter Fossett married Sarah Mayrant Walker, a former slave who had learned the finer points of hairdressing and scalp care in Louisiana. The Fossetts were both active in community affairs. Peter Fossett, who had arrived in the city shortly after the establishment of free schools for blacks, was soon on the board of directors for the western district schools. He was a member of the University Extension Society and the National Prison Reform Congress. His wife's favorite charitable work was a local orphanage, which she helped manage. Now that he had attained his own freedom, Peter Fossett did not forget those still enslaved in the South. He served as a captain in Cincinnati's Black Brigade during the Civil War, and he and his wife were both noted for their work with Levi Coffin in the Underground Railroad.[274]

While living in the household of the Joneses, who were ardent Baptists, Peter Fossett had listened to the theological discussions of visiting itinerant preachers and followed with interest the controversy that divided Baptist congregations all over the South in the 1830s. Fossett recalled the struggle over this issue in Charlottesville, after "two eloquent young preachers" tried to turn the local congregation toward the beliefs of the Campbellites, who in this century term themselves Disciples of Christ or Christian Churches. "The people belonging to the church had a church meeting which lasted for a week, day and night," Fossett told a reporter in 1898. Continuous tie votes were finally broken after the words of the "young hero" Robert Ryland, chaplain of the university, convinced one man on the fence to cast his lot with the "regular Baptists." Peter Fossett attended the weeklong revivals at country churches in this period of the Second Great Awakening. "It was during one of these meetings that I was convicted of my sins from a sermon preached by Cumberland George," he recalled. "I was converted at a two weeks' meeting at Piney Grove," a Baptist church south of Charlottesville.[275]

On his arrival in Cincinnati, Fossett joined the black Union Baptist congregation, where he was both clerk and trustee. Energetic in Baptist organizational work, he assisted Rev. Wallace Shelton, pastor of Zion Baptist Church, in founding churches all over southern Ohio. His travels on behalf of the church took him ninety miles east to Chillicothe, where his sister and brother-in-law Elizabeth Ann and Tucker Isaacs had settled. The Isaacs home was a well-known stop on the Underground Railroad, and stories are still told in the neighborhood of the light that shined from their farmhouse as a beacon to fugitive slaves.[276]

Finally, in 1870, Peter Fossett was ordained a Baptist minister and organized a new congregation in Cumminsville, just north of the city. Eight years later, First Baptist Church was constructed, largely funded by Fossett and his wife. While the original building no longer stands, the congregation flourishes nearby, their founder's photograph prominently displayed in the vestibule of the new church. Reverend Peter Fossett led his Baptist flock for over thirty years and was described by one author as "the greatest exemplar, expounder and disciplinarian of that doctrine in this state."[277]

In 1900, the members of Reverend Fossett's church and others helped him satisfy a long-held wish to return to the scenes of his childhood. He traveled to Virginia and was driven up Monticello mountain by the son of the fellow slave he had taught to read. The man who had left Monticello over seventy years before from an auction block entered the house by the front door and was welcomed by the current occupants, Jefferson Monroe Levy and his sister, "with most gracious hospitality." "All was so changed," he reported sadly, but it brought back memories of a happy boyhood in an "earthly paradise," animated by streams of famous and foreign visitors. The rooms still echoed in his mind with the rustle of silk, the laughter of women, and the sounds of the harpsichord, and "I could see Mr. Jefferson, stately and gray-haired." The reporter noted Fossett's esteem for the author of the Declaration of Independence: "He can quote his words by the hour." Six months after his return from Monticello this "widely known and respected resident of Cincinnati" died, mourned at his funeral by fifteen hundred people, both black and white. His tombstone in Union Baptist Cemetery, like Jefferson's in the form of an obelisk, bears inscriptions for Rev. Peter Fossett, his wife, and his parents, Joseph and Edith Fossett, who had worked unremittingly to maintain their family's unity.[278]

1850

In the summer of 1850, John J. Winn, the Albemarle County census taker, stopped at a dwelling on the Shadwell plantation, Thomas Jefferson's birthplace. Winn enumerated the residents of this house: sixty-six-year-old Burwell Colbert, who gave his occupation as "painter"; his forty-five-year-old wife Betsy; their three daughters Sarah, Caroline, and Melinda; and Colbert's half brother, sixty-nine year-old Wormley Hughes.[279] After the 1827 Monticello sale, butler Burwell Colbert had pursued his trade as a painter and glazier, first working at the University of Virginia. Jefferson's friend Gen. John Hartwell Cocke had recommended him to the University's proctor as "the faithful Servant of our late lamented Rector." Afterward Colbert worked for many of Jefferson's friends and family members. In the 1830s, he painted at Isaac Coles's Enniscorthy and Carter H. Harrison's Valmont in southern Albemarle County. Colbert's stay at Valmont brought to Harrison's mind the "halcyon days" of his youth, when he had studied under Jefferson's direction at Monticello. In 1832 Colbert obtained his free register, which recorded his height as five feet ten inches, and in 1834 he married Elizabeth Battles, a free woman of color.[280]

In that same year of 1850, Burwell Colbert's enslaved daughter received a legacy. After his wife's death in 1819, Colbert's relatives had evidently taken his young children into their dwellings. His daughter Martha Ann was raised by his aunt Critta Hemings, the Monticello housemaid who became a free landowner after Jefferson's death. In 1827, Jefferson's grandson Francis Wayles Eppes purchased fifty-seven-year-old Critta Hemings, his nurse in his infancy, and immediately freed her so that she could join her husband, Zachariah Bowles, a free black farmer living north of Charlottesville. Critta Hemings Bowles inherited a life estate in her husband's ninety-six-acre farm, and when she died, in 1850, she made Martha Ann Colbert, "a female slave, raised by me," her sole heir.[281]

The question of providing for the old age of Burwell Colbert's and Wormley Hughes's mother provides another illustration of the Hemings family's vigorous support system. By the 1830s Betty Brown was in her seventies. The first member of her family to come to the mountaintop, at the age of twelve, she was one of the last to remain. This "old Woman no Value," as the appraisers of Jefferson's estate viewed her, stayed in her house at Monticello for several years after the dispersal of the community. Cornelia Randolph wrote her sister in 1830 about a visit to their former residence: "Finding our old servants about us when we went there it did seem something like home, but when they are gone (as all are now but Betsey's family and old Bet) it will be deserted indeed." A hard winter in 1831 prompted Cornelia's sister Virginia Randolph Trist to write that "this bad weather makes me think of poor Old Bett at Monticello."[282]

Seven months later, however, Cornelia Randolph reported to Virginia that "Old Bet is a greater virago than ever." This letter nevertheless reveals that family loyalties and memories of better times sustained the efforts by Betty Brown's children and, to some degree, her owner to arrange the best conditions for her last years. The four-way discussion involved Martha Randolph and at least three of Betty Brown's children. An enslaved son living in Lexington, Virginia, and a free daughter in Washington, D.C., both offered to give her a home. In the end, it was apparently her granddaughter Martha Ann Colbert who lived with and cared for Betty Brown until her death.[283]

The fate of the family of Betty Brown's son Wormley Hughes highlights the emotional complexity of the master-slave relationship and reveals some of the motivations of a "faithful servant." Wormley Hughes, who at Monticello had been nail maker, gardener, coachman, and hostler, displayed skill in yet another occupation after Jefferson's death. He was a domestic servant in various households of Jefferson's grandchildren and great-grandchildren. Thomas Jefferson Randolph's wife Jane wrote from Edgehill in 1829 of Hughes's attendance on her brother-in-law James, ill with fever: "We have Wormley to attend on him and I never saw such a servant as he is. He keeps his room like a picture. Harriet goes in to make his bed twice a day and Wormley does every thing else and there is never a spot on the paint or hearth."[284]

In mid-January 1827 Hughes's wife, Ursula, and their four youngest children had been sold to University of Virginia professor George Blaettermann; a Charlottesville merchant bought three of his older children. Within days, however, most of the family was reunited at Thomas Jefferson Randolph's Edgehill plantation. A disapproving witness illuminates the transactions. Randolph's mother-in-law, Margaret Smith Nicholas, wrote her daughter two weeks after the sale: "We both consider the exchange of Doll for Urcela a most excellent bargain, and sincerely congratulate you upon your good luck, in getting rid of Doll so happily." She was not so happy about the purchase of Ursula's son and brother, writing that she was "at a loss to understand why Jefferson [Thomas J. Randolph] should have given in these scarce times, above five hundred dollars a piece for two such worthless boys as Cornelius, and Archy." Her final comment reveals the genesis of some of these actions: "I must beg you my dear, not to count too largely upon Ursella's gratitude, as I consider gratitude in a slave as one of those prodigies of nature, that we rarely meet with."[285]

It is evident that Ursula Hughes was at the center of a combined family effort to minimize separation, which succeeded in bringing to Edgehill, where her husband lived, not just herself and five of her children but her parents, Bagwell and Minerva Granger, at least four of her siblings, and two nephews. In a second sale in 1829, Thomas Jefferson Randolph purchased the entire family of Ursula's sister, Virginia, an action that triggered further scolding from Peggy Nicholas. "I can assure you," she wrote her daughter, "that I was not a little horrified at hearing that you had saddled yourselves with such an additional number of them. Your feeling for those you purchased was very natural, but my dear, your love for your seven helpless little girls ought to have deterred you from indulging such feeling." Of thirty slaves that Thomas J. Randolph purchased from the estate of his grandfather, at least eighteen of them were close relatives of Wormley and Ursula Hughes.[286]

The bonds between Betty Brown's sons and Jefferson's children and grandchildren persisted well beyond Jefferson's time. After the Randolphs left Monticello in 1827, Burwell Colbert remained on the mountaintop and continued to carry the keys, although the house—with the family gone and the furniture sold—was empty. Jefferson's granddaughter Virginia wrote that "Burwell has given many proofs this winter of attachments to our family, as well as to Monticello. He has staid there ever since the sale and he appears to have taken pleasure in trying to keep the house clean, and even the yard he has attempted to keep in some sort of order." One day, when the granddaughters went back to check on the empty house, they found evidence of Colbert's preparations: "The doors and windows all open, the floors rubbed bright, the old remaining chairs and marble table . . . all set in order and the whole place seemed to welcome us. . . . He seems to take pleasure in keeping things as they used to be."[287]

In 1856 Ellen Randolph Coolidge wrote of Wormley Hughes's "loyal attachment" to her family, "having passed through four generations, for he is particularly devoted to Mrs. Ruffin's children, the great, great grand children of his old Master." Both brothers were remembered by the Randolphs after their deaths. Following the conflict that gave freedom to all Colberts and Hugheses, Thomas Jefferson Randolph recalled "Burwell Colbert Mr. Js confidential servant a gentleman in manners and character: located in a comfortable tenement on my farm off to himself. Expressed himself a happier man than President Polk because Mr. Polk was troubled with public business and he was not." Randolph's brother George Wythe Randolph, ruined by the war, contemplated his prospects in 1866: "As old Wormley used to say 'I am in no wise discouraged.' "[288]

But it is an image of a third son of Betty Brown that most hauntingly evokes the labyrinth of conflicting attachments and loyalties that an enslaved Virginian had to navigate. Colbert and Hughes's younger brother Robert, not known to

have occupied a position of trust in the Monticello household, was sold, for unknown reasons, in 1820. Sold twice again soon after, he twice tried to run away.
His first attempt ended in capture on the way to Pennsylvania, while his second
produced a rare description of a member of the Hemings family. Robert was
working on a bateau, or tobacco boat, on the James River when he ran away on
an August morning in 1824. Asbury Crenshaw described him as "a young negro
man; named BOB . . . of small stature, yellow complexion, straight, black hair,
somewhat of the appearance of an Indian's, speaks slowly, almost droning, has at
first view of him a simple appearance, but on examination will be found to be
shrewd and intelligent." Crenshaw named the locations where Bob had relations: Monticello, Poplar Forest, Richmond, Tuckahoe plantation in Goochland
County, and Wilton in Henrico County. Crenshaw thought it most probable
that "he is making his way either to Albemarle, or the plantation near Lynchburg" and offered fifty dollars if he was brought back from out of state, ten dollars if committed to jail in Virginia. It is not known if Betty Hemings's grandson
ever was able to rejoin family members; no further reference to him has been
found.[289]

1867

In the second year of peace, some of the fourteen thousand newly freed slaves
of Albemarle County decided the time was right to build a church and a school.
Several men approached the largest landholder in their neighborhood, a man
who had recently claimed many of them as his property. The deed Jefferson's
grandson Thomas Jefferson Randolph gave to these Baptist deacons reflected
the freedmen's recent struggles to live as full American citizens. In March, the
Reconstruction Act had been passed, and three weeks before the signing of this
deed, former slaves in Albemarle County had voted for the first time, sending a
southern Unionist and a black man to the state constitutional convention.
Throughout the year newly enfranchised black voters had joined the Union
League and other Republican clubs in droves, and the air was filled with talk of
Confederate disenfranchisement and land redistribution. Thomas J. Randolph,
who must have been aware that both the Bible and the Declaration of Independence were usually conspicuously displayed at these political meetings, was as
alarmed as other plantation owners about these developments. His deed for an
acre on the margins of the Edgehill plantation stated that while he wished "to
afford the congregation of the Union Branch, all the assistance in his power
for religious exercises or the purposes of education he does not desire the grant
to be abused by affording a place for political Gatherings." He retained the right
to dismiss an objectionable teacher as well as to take back the land "if at any
time a political assemblage is held upon the said parcel."[290]

Rev. Robert Hughes (1824–1895).
(Courtesy of Union Run Baptist
Church, Keswick, Virginia)

Among the members of the Union Branch Church were the children and grandchildren of David and Isabel Hern and the great-grandchildren of George and Ursula Granger and of Betty Hemings. Lewis Hern and George Hughes, son of Wormley and Ursula Hughes, were deacons. George Hughes's younger brother Robert was the minister, serving in that office until his death in 1895. Over almost thirty years, Rev. Robert Hughes officiated at the marriages of the Union Branch flock. In 1871 he presided at the wedding of Sanco Davis and Lily Hern, who exchanged their vows just a few miles from the mountain where they had both spent much of their lives. Davis, a nephew of the Hubbard brothers, had been a Monticello woodworker. David and Isabel Hern's daughter Lily, twice married while at Monticello, had been bought by a professor at the University of Virginia in 1827. Sanco Davis remained a slave at Edgehill until Emancipation, while Lily Hern's home after 1827 is not known. On March 2, 1871, after decades of family disruption and dispersal, they were boldly making this commitment at the respective ages of seventy-four and eighty. The Davises lived together, at Edgehill, well into their eighties. Other Herns and Hugheses also continued to live in the same neighborhood, their communal efforts to achieve the political and educational rights of American citizenship bound together in the Union Branch (now Union Run) Church that flourishes to this day.[291]

"My grandmother talked to me about the beauty of Monticello and the ugliness of slavery," a descendant of one of Monticello's African American families told us in 1995. Since 1993, the staff of Monticello's Getting Word oral history project have been interviewing the descendants of Jupiter and Suck, George and Ursula Granger, David and Isabel Hern, Betty Hemings, and other residents of Monticello in Jefferson's time. My colleague Dianne Swann-Wright and I, often with consultant Beverly Gray of Ohio, have searched through countless court records and newspaper files and listened to the family histories of over 130 people. We have learned that the skills practiced at Monticello were carried to all parts of the country and that the fight for education, freedom, and family integrity that characterized its African American residents continued after they left the mountaintop.[292]

In Alabama, Jupiter and Suck's descendants told us stories of the British occupation of Monticello in 1781 that perpetuate the memory of Jefferson's dependence on his resourceful enslaved labor force. In southern Ohio, we saw one building that was constructed by Madison Hemings and another that was the site of his brother Eston's musical performances. We heard of the ongoing struggle against slavery at stations on the Underground Railroad and read about Joseph and Edith Fossett's great-grandson William Monroe Trotter, who raised his voice on behalf of racial equality in his own Boston newspaper and "laid the first stone of the modern protest movement." Memories of ministers and teachers, as well as the founding of churches and schools, taught us the enduring importance of education and religion for the descendants of families like the Hemingses and Hugheses.[293]

Family has been the one theme common to all our interviews—the strength of its bonds as well as the harsh realities of American society that can break them. The severing of ties when runaways like James Hubbard left Monticello were echoed years later in the families split by the departure of members who chose to improve their lives by crossing the racial border. Not all the stories we heard have been positive ones, for the descendants of Monticello's African Americans have carried the burden of slavery through the generations. The economic and social discrimination that followed the legal injustice of bondage brought frustrated hopes and blasted dreams as doors to educational opportunities and suitable employment remained closed. We continue to seek information about the more than six hundred people held in bondage during Jefferson's lifetime. Because time has not erased the connection to Monticello felt by many descendants of its African American families, they have been getting word back to us about their lives and their memories of their ancestors.

Part III

———

FAMILIES
IN FREEDOM

Monticello to
Main Street

The Hemings Family
and Charlottesville

O N a bitterly cold day in January 1827, many of the citizens of Charlottesville made their way to the top of a small mountain two miles to the southeast. They were attending the auction of the estate of Thomas Jefferson, at which tables and chairs, sheep and mules, and men, women, and children were sold amid lively bidding. Thomas Jefferson Randolph, executor of his grandfather's estate, had advertised that 130 slaves would be included in the sale, the "most valuable for their number ever offered at one time in the State of Virginia." This winter scene at Monticello was like "a captured village in ancient times," Randolph recalled many years later. Surviving documents reveal the purchases, if not the impressions, of five of the Charlottesville residents. They successfully bid on furnishings and works of art, carrying home mirrors and mattresses, prints of former presidents, a Franklin stove, and a mule. They saved their highest bids for the most valuable part of Jefferson's property and became the owners of at least nine members of one extended family.[1]

The set of interlocking relationships that led to these purchases illustrates how members of a remarkable enslaved family formed a link between Monticello and Charlottesville and made a significant impact on the character and development of its main street. The descendants of Elizabeth (Betty) Hemings—in bondage and in freedom—lived on Charlottesville's Main Street, constructed some of its buildings, and provided much of its entertainment. Her family's fortunes ebbed and flowed over more than a century: some of her grandchildren were heirs, while others were inherited; in some years they were considered white, in others, black; and while one branch of the family lived all their lives on Main Street, their cousins were forced to leave it.[2]

This essay was originally published in *Magazine of Albemarle County History* 55 (1997): 94–126.

1827–1837

Betty Hemings's family has come to dominate most discussion of slavery at Monticello. When she and her ten children came to Monticello in the mid-1770s, they took the first step in a progression westward from slavery to freedom, from the Virginia Tidewater to the Old Northwest, even, ultimately, to California, where one of her great-great-grandsons became the first black state legislator.

As one former Monticello slave recalled, "folks said" that some of Hemings's sons and daughters were the children of John Wayles of Charles City County, whose death in 1773 precipitated her family's westward motion. Wayles, an Englishman of humble origins who prospered in Virginia as an attorney and merchant (he engaged in the commerce of enslaved Africans, among other enterprises), left an estate of over 20,000 acres and more than 300 slaves.[3] In 1774, on the division of Wayles's estate, his daughter Martha Wayles Jefferson and her husband inherited 11,000 acres of land and 135 slaves, including Betty Hemings and her children.

Betty Hemings's grandson also referred to her relationship with Wayles, specifically identifying their six children—Sally Hemings and her older siblings Robert, James, Thenia, Critta, and Peter. He did not include Betty Hemings's daughter Mary, who led the family migration to freedom and was the first member of the Hemings family to live on Charlottesville's Main Street.[4]

A dwelling on the corner of Main and East Second Streets (Lot 23) was occupied by the descendants of Betty Hemings for just over a century. The story began in 1784, when Thomas Bell, originally of the South River district of Augusta County, bought two half-acre lots on the north side of the road known first as the Three Notched (or Chopped) Road and finally as Main Street. On this square—the equivalent of a city block today—was a modest log house built in the 1760s, formerly used as a tavern. Bell added to the structure, opened a general store, and began to build a reputation as a respected merchant and citizen. His friend Thomas Jefferson called him a "man remarkable for his integrity."[5]

In 1787, while Thomas Jefferson was absent in France as American minister, Thomas Bell leased a slave from Monticello. Twenty-five-year-old Mary Hemings, the oldest child of Betty Hemings, was a domestic servant in Jefferson's household and had accompanied the family to Williamsburg and Richmond when he was governor. By 1784, she had four young children: Daniel (b. 1772), Molly (b. 1777), Joseph (b. 1780), and Elizabeth, or Betsy (b. 1783).[6]

Mary Hemings and her children lived in Bell's house on Main Street until 1792, when she took a significant step. She asked to be sold to Bell, who paid Jefferson £115 for Mary and her two youngest children, born since 1787. Jefferson, who had specified that he would sell Mary and "such of her younger children as she chose," retained Joseph and Betsy; he had already given Daniel and Molly to relatives.[7]

By becoming Bell's property, Mary Hemings also became the first of Betty Hemings's children to gain her freedom. By this time she and Bell had formed a relationship that was by every indication conjugal and openly acknowledged.[8] When Bell paid Jefferson £115 in 1792, he was purchasing his own son and daughter. In his 1797 will he bequeathed his property to his "natural" children, Robert Washington Bell and Sarah (Sally) Jefferson Bell, leaving Mary a life estate in "all my houses and Lotts" in Charlottesville.[9]

Betty Hemings's daughter and her children continued to live in the house on Main Street after Bell's death in 1800. Two years later the household expanded when Sally Bell married Jesse Scott, the son of an Indian woman and, as he believed, a white Virginian who became governor of Kentucky. Scott's mother was a favorite subject of family stories: "She could row a boat, shoot a bird on the wing, and perform wondrous feats of strength and skill." He had often seen her "shoot wild ducks with bow and arrow from the boat, and if they fell into the water she would spring into the stream and swim or dive in search of them."[10]

In a private collection there is a striking portrait of Jesse Scott holding a violin. A noted musician and composer of dance tunes, Scott and his sons were "famous throughout the south" for their musical talent, playing at private dances, University of Virginia balls, and the various Virginia springs.[11]

Jesse Scott was present in the crowd that gathered at Monticello on January 15, 1827, the family's emissary in an effort to mitigate a catastrophe. His

Jesse Scott (1781–1862), by unknown artist. (Courtesy of Olivia M. Dutcher)

mother-in-law, Mary Hemings Bell, had only one child remaining in slavery at Monticello.[12] Joseph, who had taken the surname Fossett, had begun his working life in the Monticello nailery, and some of the nails he made there in the 1790s were sold to the local community in Thomas Bell's store. He was also trained as a blacksmith, and in 1807 he took charge of Monticello's blacksmith shop. According to a Monticello overseer, Fossett was "a very fine workman; could do anything it was necessary to do with steel or iron." Jefferson's will gave Fossett his freedom, but Fossett's wife Edith and their seven children, ranging in age from two to twenty, were separated into six lots and placed on the auction block.[13]

Fossett could not purchase his entire family, nor could he have been a bidder at the sale, since he was not entitled to his freedom until the following July. Of the five children whose fate is known, four were bought by men from Charlottesville: fifteen-year-old Elizabeth-Ann (Betsy-Ann) was sold to merchant John Winn; Peter, age eleven, was bought by another local merchant, Col. John R. Jones; and the purchaser of Fossett's wife, Edy, and their two youngest children was Jesse Scott.[14]

The sum Scott bid was $505, well above the $325 appraised value of the three slaves. A purchase of this magnitude was unquestionably dependent on the inheritance from Thomas Bell. Although the settlement of Bell's estate was protracted, and in 1804, his executor had expressed the fear that its debts might exceed its credits, Mary Hemings and her Bell children had been left in possession of seven Charlottesville lots and the dwelling and store on Main Street.[15] Without this property, it is unlikely that Jesse Scott would have been extended the credit for such a purchase. Although it is now impossible to follow the trail of payment, one thing is clear: Jesse Scott's trip to Monticello mountain in 1827 entangled his family in transactions that contributed to a partial loss of their patrimony.

Mary Hemings Bell and her children may have staked their credit in several different quarters. Joseph Fossett had an agreement with John R. Jones to purchase his son Peter's freedom as soon as he had accumulated sufficient funds; Jones previously had assisted the family by acting as trustee when Robert W. Bell mortgaged his portion of his father's estate.[16] John Winn's purchase of Betsy-Ann Fossett was almost certainly made at the request of the family, since she was soon the property of her father and her inflated purchase price suggests a flurry of competitive bidding.[17] Winn and his partner Twyman Wayt were already financially involved in the fortunes of Mary Bell and the Scotts, as owners of a four-and-one-half-tenths interest in their house and all their Charlottesville lots. The family's inability to pay for the purchase of Betsy-Ann may have led to the suit brought by Wayt & Winn against Thomas Bell's heirs, forcing a sale in 1834 of their five lots on Water Street.[18] Whatever the particulars of these transactions, we will probably never know their nature. Jones's subsequent hostile behavior toward both the Fossetts and the West-Isaacs family raises questions about his motives for intervention, while Winn's agency may have been at least initially friendly.

At the time of the 1830 census, Joseph Fossett headed a household containing five slaves: his wife and their four youngest children (two born since the 1827 sale). He was compelled to keep his family in the safety of bondage because of an 1806 Virginia law requiring freed slaves to leave the state within a year. The location of their residence is not known but may have been in the second dwelling on the Bell lot—a one-story wooden house, once a granary, 24 by 14 feet, facing Church (East Second) Street. The larger house on Main Street was occupied by Mary Hemings Bell, Sally and Jesse Scott, and the Scotts' three sons, Robert, James, and Thomas. The appearance of this house is well documented by insurance declarations and photographs. Made entirely of wood, it was 30 by 24 feet, one-and-a-half-stories high, with a one-story wing of about 20 by 16 feet; a front porch was added by 1840. In 1823 it was insured for $1,500.[19]

Main Street in this period gave little hint of its future prosperity. A University of Virginia student remarked in 1835 on the "Irish filthiness" of the town's thoroughfares, and the courthouse square was still its commercial center. Newspaperman James Alexander remembered the Scott house as the only structure on the one-acre block for many years. He compared the Main Street of 1828 with a transformed scene almost fifty years later: "This street, when we first knew it, had few houses, and only two or three business places on it, now it has from one end to the other, fine houses and substantial business stores; then it was rough, and in winter season with mud enough to stall wagons passing over it; now it is macadamized and is well graded; then there were only patches of paved sidewalks, now there are wide sidewalks laid with brick or slate its entire length."[20]

Diagonally across from the home of the Scotts was a much larger wooden building, long the residence of a family closely connected with the Hemings descendants. Early in the 1790s another merchant was attracted to the small town of Charlottesville. David Isaacs moved his mercantile establishment from Richmond, eventually locating it in a combination residence and store on a half-acre lot (No. 36) that he purchased in 1802. Like his neighbor Thomas Bell, Isaacs also formed an enduring relationship with a free woman of color, Anne (Nancy) West, who was herself the daughter of a well-to-do white landholder and his slave. Prevented by both Virginia and Orthodox Jewish laws from marrying, from at least 1820 David Isaacs and Nancy West lived together in Isaacs's house with their seven children, born between 1796 and 1817. Two of those children married members of Monticello's Hemings family.[21]

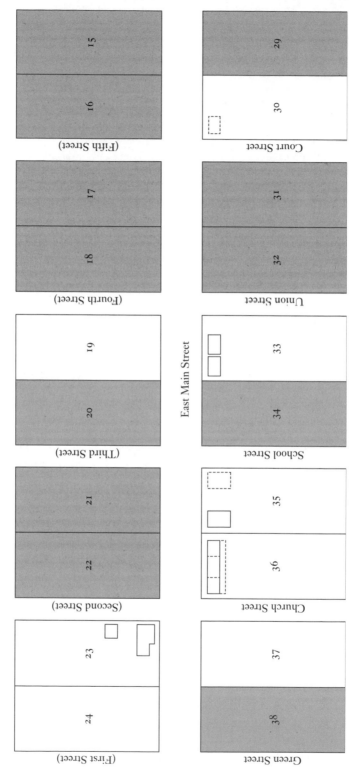

East Main Street, Charlottesville, showing lots owned by Hemings family members and their connections. (Lucia Stanton: Thomas Jefferson Foundation, Inc.)

Their son Tucker Isaacs and Joseph Fossett's daughter Betsy-Ann became husband and wife by 1831. Isaacs was a builder with special skills in painting and glazing. He and Betsy-Ann lived for a time with his parents in a structure that spanned almost the full width of Lot 36. It had a two-story central section, 32 by 18, with one-story wings at both ends, and was assessed at a value of $2,250. The family also had the use of the adjacent lot (No. 35) to the east, on which they paid taxes for its absentee owners. Any buildings they might have erected there before the 1840s had no taxable value.[22]

A block to the east were the dwellings of two of David Isaacs's and Nancy West's daughters. Lot 33, once owned by Nancy West's father, was, by 1823, her own property. One of her daughters married a son of Sally Hemings, for whom the crisis of January 1827 was less of a threat to family integrity than it had been for her nephew Joseph Fossett. Betty Hemings's daughter Sally knew that her sons Madison and Eston had been granted their freedom in Jefferson's will. Although she was not freed, she was almost certainly not among the slaves sold at the auction; Jefferson's daughter Martha J. Randolph presumably gave her "her time," that is, freed her unofficially so that she would not be subject to the 1806 removal law. Madison Hemings recalled that after Jefferson's death he and his brother took their mother to live in a rented house in Charlottesville.[23]

By 1832 both sons had married and set up separate households, Sally Hemings remaining with her son Madison, probably in his house on West Main Street. Eston Hemings married Julia Ann Isaacs in June 1832; Jane Isaacs married her cousin Nathaniel H. West in the same year. Nancy West gave both pairs of newlyweds portions of Lot 33, on which, about 1830, two contiguous two-story brick buildings had been erected. Measuring 30 by 20 feet, they were valued for tax purposes at $900 each. Julia and Eston Hemings lived in the house nearest the corner (present 320 East Main Street, approximately), while Jane West had her milliner's shop and residence in the westernmost structure.[24]

James Alexander's reference to a "small wood shop . . . used as a paint shop" on the corner of this lot (present Timberlake's Drug Store, 322 East Main Street) evokes the trades practiced by Eston Hemings and his brother-in-law Tucker Isaacs. Hemings had been trained in the Monticello joinery by his talented uncle John Hemings, and he pursued the woodworking trade after gaining his freedom. This corner of Main and Union (now East Fourth) Streets may have been the center of operations for the building enterprises of the Hemings-Isaacs family.[25]

Further to the east another member of the family had a blacksmith shop. Eston Hemings's cousin Joseph Fossett bought Lot 30 in 1831 and established his business in the corner shop, once owned by Opie Norris. Fossett's surviving accounts from 1827 to 1830—years when he may still have been working in the Monticello blacksmith shop—indicate that, in addition to shoeing horses, he spent most of his time mending and sharpening tools and agricultural implements. He also made a wide range of articles: clamps and staples, augers and hammers, wagon tires and plow parts, plates for skylights, and a newel post. Presumably, when he moved downtown, Fossett performed an even greater variety of tasks and may have provided the necessary ironwork for the new buildings of his Charlottesville relatives.[26]

Just outside the original eastern limits of the town was a quarter-acre Main Street lot owned from 1807 until his death in 1838 by a free black man named Daniel Farley. In what must have been a modest structure, as it had no taxable value, Farley lived and apparently operated a house of entertainment. According to Dr. Edgar Woods, Farley was a "frequent transgressor" of the gambling laws. He may have brewed his own malt beverages, since in 1812 he sold Thomas Jefferson a large amount of hops. Farley's residence was evidently a Sunday meeting place for slaves from the surrounding plantations, including Monticello. In March 1816 Jefferson's blacksmith Moses Hern broke his leg in a wrestling match and was noted as recuperating "at Farley's."[27]

Daniel Farley was a musician, his occupation listed as "Fiddler" in the 1833 special census (in 1829, to secure a $30 debt, he mortgaged his violin, as well as bedding, a bureau, and a set of china). It also appears that Daniel Farley was a Hemings. His age, close relationship with Joseph Fossett, and the shared given names of Farley's and Fossett's children all suggest that he was Mary Hemings's oldest child Daniel, born in 1772. Jefferson had given Daniel to his sister Anna Scott Jefferson in 1787, on her marriage to Hastings Marks of Louisa County.[28]

Daniel Farley was one of those present at the January 1827 sale at Monticello, and for one dollar he made a single purchase: "Peter. Old man." If Farley was indeed Joe Fossett's brother, he bought his uncle Peter Hemings, then aged fifty-seven, two years older than Farley himself. Hemings, who had been both cook and highly valued brewmaster at Monticello during Jefferson's lifetime (a "servant of great intelligence and diligence" in his master's eyes), supported himself in freedom as a tailor.[29]

At his death in 1838, Farley bequeathed his house and lot to his children John and Elizabeth-Ann and to Joseph Fossett, his executor. The next year they were purchased at public auction by yet another relative, James Scott, son of Jesse and Sally Bell Scott.[30]

1837–1850

The events of a single year, one of national economic crisis, reveal the vulnerability of this group of former slaves and their relations, highlighting the inherent instability of family for African Americans in the South, both enslaved and free. In the year of the financial panic of 1837, the death of David Isaacs in February came as the first blow—one, as the work of Joshua Rothman has revealed, for which preparations had been made. A strategic shifting of assets in the preceding years gave Nancy West a measure of control over her own destiny and resources to assist her connections.[31]

Charlottesville's free blacks lived in a kind of littoral zone, alternately submerged or exposed by the tides of law and public opinion. In the struggle to adapt to this unsettled environment, property was of primary importance. Because they were denied by law other means of achieving security and social standing (free blacks in Virginia could not legally vote, hold office, attend schools, or carry weapons, among other restrictions), the acquisition, preservation, and expansion of real estate constituted a critical aspect not only of success but of survival and the maintenance of family unity. A pattern of propertied free blacks working together to maximize security through all the legal means within their power is revealed in the public record, which shows the Isaacs, Hemings, Scott, and Fossett family members in frequent legal interaction with each other, as well as with other propertied free blacks. The web of connections was reinforced constantly by intermarriage, buying and selling property, serving as bondsmen, and witnessing legal documents.[32]

Tucker Isaacs, remembered by James Alexander as "a good citizen and much respected," was particularly visible in his efforts to increase the value of the family's property. Alexander noticed his role in the transformation of Charlottesville in the 1840s, when the commercial center began its shift from the Court Square vicinity to a Main Street lined with new brick buildings. Isaacs, he wrote, "built" two brick buildings on Lot 35 adjacent to his parents' house. Nancy West had purchased this lot at public auction in 1841 and, shortly afterward, erected a two-story brick dwelling on the corner valued at $1,200 (present Williams Corner Bookstore site). A few years later Isaacs added a two-story brick storehouse on the western edge of the lot. Both structures were presumably built to be leased out. By 1844, besides the brick house, 36 by 28 feet, and storehouse, the lot contained a wooden kitchen and meat house and a stable. Five years later it had as well a tailor's shop in a shed addition and—a kind of high watermark in the family's fortunes—a bowling alley.[33] Tucker Isaacs was also active in his trade of painter and glazier and probably worked on many of the buildings going up along Main Street in the 1830s and 1840s; there is a surviving contract, in 1848, for painting a new brick structure on the corner of Main and West Second Streets.[34]

Despite such enterprising schemes to solidify and expand their assets, Charlottesville's free blacks had to be continually vigilant merely to hold on to their pieces of ground. A recurring accompaniment to their efforts was the public sale. From 1827 to 1850 the members of the extended Hemings family witnessed over a dozen sales involving their possessions, real estate, or family members. On April 14, 1837, the sale that drew them together was that of the estate of David Isaacs. While Isaacs's will allowed Nancy West to retain some of their more valuable pieces of furniture, including a clock appraised at $50, those who attended had a chance to bid on most of the contents of the large wooden house on Lot 36. Tucker Isaacs, Eston Hemings, and Jesse Scott and his sons Robert and James each made modest purchases of books and crockery, spending little more than a dollar each. James Scott's successful bid of $2.25 for a four-volume edition of the writings of Thomas Jefferson was the most ambitious. All the rest of the books, barrels of whiskey, articles of kitchen and dinnerware, and pieces of furniture were dispersed to others.[35]

In 1837 there were also signs that the issue of leaving Virginia altogether was being vigorously discussed by family members. Joseph Fossett's September manumission of his wife, children, and grandchildren, who would by Virginia law be obliged to leave the state within a year, indicates an intent to emigrate. A month later Eston Hemings sold out his interest in his residence on Main Street and soon left for Ohio.[36] His brother Madison had preceded him the previous year, settling in a rural community of former Virginia slaves and free people of color located on the border of Pike and Ross Counties. Eston and Julia Ann Hemings chose to live in the town of Chillicothe, the Ross county seat. There Hemings pursued a dual career as a carpenter and musician. Described as a "master of the violin," his fiddling so lively that "there was only one thing to do, and that was—dance," he led a popular band, playing for the balls of the white population all over southern Ohio.[37]

Sally Hemings's son made a strong impression on his neighbors in Chillicothe. One man recalled many years later that Eston Hemings "was of a light bronze color, a little over six feet tall, well proportioned, very erect and dignified; his nearly straight hair showed a tint of auburn, and his face, indistinct suggestion of freckles. Quiet, unobtrusive, polite and decidedly intelligent, he was soon very well and favorably known to all classes of our citizens, for his personal appearance and gentlemanly manners attracted everybody's attention to him. And when it was rumored that Eston Hemings was a natural son of President Thomas Jefferson, a good many people accepted the story as truth, from the intrinsic evidence of his striking resemblance to Jefferson."[38]

The timing of the Fossett family's departure for Ohio is more difficult to determine. By at least 1843, they were settled in Cincinnati, where Joe Fossett pursued the blacksmithing trade with his sons and lived on a city lot he had purchased for $500. The next year he sold his Charlottesville lot to John Winn's son Benjamin for the same amount. It is apparent that between 1837 and 1843 the Fossetts were often on the road, shuttling between Virginia and Ohio in a continuing effort to reconstitute their family.[39]

When Joe and Edy Fossett left for the Northwest, only the four youngest of their ten children accompanied them. Still locked in bondage were James, Patsy, Isabella, and Peter, who recalled, sixty years later, that his master John R. Jones had "promised my father to let him have me when he could raise the money, but in 1833 he refused to let him have me on any conditions." In 1833 the governmental authorities had sent a powerful message to Virginia's free blacks. In the wake of the Nat Turner rebellion and the decision of the legislature to postpone measures for the eradication of slavery, the focus turned to ways to rid the state of a population of free people of color then numbering almost 50,000. The acts passed in 1833 appropriated funds for colonizing free blacks to West Africa and called for a special census in which they would be specifically asked about their willingness to emigrate. All 452 Albemarle County free blacks, including Sally, Eston, and Madison Hemings, Joseph Fossett, and Daniel Farley, declined the offer.[40]

As a trusted slave of John R. Jones, who owned stores on Main Street and Court Square and a residence on Jefferson Street, Peter Fossett probably was able to remain in regular contact with his family. His recollections suggest the mobility of slaves within the restricting confines of bondage and one of its consequences—the extensive communications network linking free and enslaved African Americans. While slaves from the surrounding farms are rarely mentioned in accounts of Charlottesville, there is every reason to believe that they were a regular presence, especially on Sundays. The gatherings at Daniel Farley's house have been mentioned. In Peter Fossett's case, the connection between town and plantation began when he was still a boy at Monticello. He recalled how a special suit of blue nankeen cloth, with red leather hat and shoes, given him by his free grandmother (Mary Hemings Bell), set him apart from "the plantation boys." In his years of bondage to Colonel Jones he attended summer revivals at the rural Baptist churches, one of which (Piney Grove) was the site of his own conversion experience.[41]

Peter Fossett's memories also included his secret movements, made at a time when education of both slaves and free blacks was severely restricted by law and custom. "I was teaching all the people around me to read and write, and even venturing to write free passes and sending slaves away from their masters," he recalled. Fossett had been taught to read and write by Jefferson's grandson Meriwether Lewis Randolph. His father had made an agreement with Colonel Jones's sons to continue Peter's education, but when Jones discovered his slave spelling on the hearth one night, he threw his book in the fire and promised him a whipping if he ever found him with a book again. Nevertheless, Jones's sons and daughter continued with their clandestine instruction.[42]

The situation for Peter Fossett's free Scott cousins, who were a generation older, had been quite different. Robert Scott remembered that "Mr. Jefferson had always been very kind to his father and had encouraged him to have his children educated" and that he and his brothers had attended white schools. The sons of David Isaacs and Nancy West, according to James Alexander, also "went to school with the white boys." And one of them used his knowledge in a continuing fight against slavery.[43]

The oral tradition of the descendants of Tucker and Betsy-Ann Isaacs—that their ancestor was an active forger in the cause of freedom—is confirmed in the county minute book for February 5, 1850. The clerk recorded that Tucker Isaacs was "led to the bar in custody of the Jailer" of the county court and charged with "falsly, wilfully and feloniously forging and counterfeiting a certain regis-ter of freedom" for a slave named Peter, the property of John R. Jones. Isaacs was released from jail the next day, after being found not guilty of the charge, while Peter's fate is revealed in a New York newspaper almost fifty years later. Interviewed in Cincinnati in 1898, Peter Fossett recalled his failed attempt to run away from Colonel Jones: "My parents were here in Ohio and I wanted to be with them and be free, so I resolved to get free or die in the attempt." Af-ter his second attempt, Fossett "was caught, handcuffed, and taken back and carried to Richmond and put in jail. For the second time I was put up on the auction block and sold like a horse." Accounts of his release from slavery vary, crediting his father, his brother-in-law Tucker Isaacs, and friends "from among my old master's friends" for making the purchase at auction. This diversity of support seems to indicate a banding together of various family members and friends to raise the money.[44]

It is possible that Peter Fossett forged his own free register, which used the pseudonym of a member of the prominent free black Battles family. It may have been the revelation of Fossett's secret literacy that swayed the court in Tucker Isaacs's favor.

Other events in 1850 besides his arrest were conspiring to push Tucker Isaacs and his family toward a final break with Charlottesville. The year of the Fugitive Slave Act brought another wave of antipathy to free blacks in Virginia, which led to a tightening enforcement of the 1806 removal act and a larger appropriation of funds for transporting blacks to Africa. The shifting tide of opinion affected another former Monticello slave at this time. Sally Cottrell's right to remain in Virginia was brought before the court in November, when, as one of her advisers wrote, "there has been a general examination into the subject of Free Negroes remaining in this State." The heightened insecurity of free blacks in the South in 1850 becomes strikingly apparent in the elaborate legal arrangements undertaken to assist her to remain.[45]

Most of the members of the Hemings family who were protected by special legislative permission to stay in Virginia had long since left for Ohio. In the last months of the year, those who remained who were not so protected—Nancy West, Tucker and Betsy-Ann Isaacs, Robert and James Scott, along with dozens of other free blacks—were brought before the court to answer the charge of "remaining in the Commonwealth without leave" and to make their cases for staying in Albemarle County. For the moment they escaped the harsh decree issued to some of those present with them in court: to leave the county within ten days or go to jail.[46]

In the case of Betsy-Ann Isaacs, the usually laconic clerk added this sentence to his entry: "No permission has been granted her to remain in the Commonwealth." These disturbing December incidents at the courthouse must have sealed her family's decision to sever its ties with Charlottesville forever. Betsy-Ann and her husband had been preparing their final exodus for years. After a few years in Ohio with her parents, Charlottesville was their primary residence until 1850, when they sold off their interest in the Charlottesville lots and moved permanently to Ross County, Ohio. They first lived in Chillicothe, where Isaacs built more brick buildings (James Alexander heard of him as a "man of large property") and pursued his trade as a "House, Sign, and Ornamental Painter, Glazier, and Paper-Hanger." In 1855 they purchased a farm of 158 acres located six miles outside the town. In the free state in the North the Isaacs household continued its fight against slavery and racial injustice. Stories are still told in Ross County about the light shining from their farmhouse as a beacon to fugitive slaves. Tucker Isaacs once brought suit against an Ohio hotel for refusing him accommodation. And their grandson carried on the tradition. William Monroe Trotter of Boston was one of the most militantly outspoken activists for civil rights and a key figure in the early days of the Niagara movement, precursor to the National Association for the Advancement of Colored People (NAACP).[47]

In the same period Betsy-Ann's cousin and sister-in-law also made a momentous decision. Early in 1849 Eston and Julia Ann Hemings had returned from Chillicothe to Charlottesville to sell all their remaining town property. Shortly after 1850 they left Ohio for Madison, Wisconsin, changing both their surname and their race in the process. As part of the white community there, the Jeffersons, as they were now known, gained some prominence. Both of their sons served in Wisconsin units during the Civil War, one afterward becoming a leading Madison hotel keeper, the other becoming one of the wealthier citizens of Memphis, Tennessee.[48]

End of a Century

In 1900 the members of Peter Fossett's church in Cincinnati helped raise the money to satisfy a long-held wish to return to his childhood home. In May, the eighty-five-year-old Baptist minister was driven up the mountain to Monticello by the son of one of the slaves he had taught to read and write years before. At the front door of Monticello he was welcomed "with most gracious hospitality" by its owner, Jefferson Monroe Levy, and his sister. After his freedom had been purchased in 1850, Fossett had joined the rest of his family in Cincinnati, married a former slave from Louisiana, and prospered, working as a whitewasher and waiter and eventually owning one of the most prominent catering firms in the city. In 1870 he was ordained a minister of the Baptist church and founded First Baptist Church, Cumminsville. He became widely known as one of the most respected Baptist ministers in Ohio.[49]

None of the relatives Peter Fossett had known fifty years before remained on Main Street to welcome him to Charlottesville in 1900.[50] The previous year, the passing of his first cousin Robert Scott warranted a headline in the town newspaper, as did the demolition of the Scott house in 1892. Both man and building were referred to as Charlottesville "landmarks," worthy of extended front-page commentary. The sale and removal of a structure described both as "one of the oldest" houses in Charlottesville and "at one time the only house" on Main Street was the occasion for a review of the history of that thoroughfare. The editor, consulting the memory of Robert Scott, recalled a time when wagons frequently stalled in the mud, chinquapin bushes flourished in the empty lots, and the only brick house (that of Joseph Bishop) lay outside the town limits. Now, in 1892, the Scott lot—to which Robert and James Scott had added two 20-by-60-feet brick storehouses—was "one of the most valuable pieces of property on Main street," drawing a final bid of $17,000 at auction.[51]

An anachronism on a street lined with tall brick storehouses, the small wooden dwelling in which Mary Hemings had established a beachhead a century before was virtually unchanged. A writer for the *Southern Workman and Hampton School Record* found Robert Scott in 1888 in an "old-fashioned weatherboarded house, with a long porch, sitting somewhat back from the street, in a shady little yard." Orra Langhorne observed the glass-and-china-filled sideboard in the hall, the cabinet organ and sewing machine in the parlor, and the Franklin stove from Monticello. She drank wine made from grapes from Scott's own vineyard and was particularly struck by her host, an imposing figure of over six feet, "whose aspect was truly venerable and interesting" and manner was "full of repose, grace, and dignity."[52]

Robert Scott (1803–1899) in front of his house on Main Street, ca. 1890. (Courtesy of Teresa Jackson Price)

She talked to Scott of Thomas Jefferson and undoubtedly heard one of his favorite memories, from the year of the Marquis de Lafayette's triumphal visit to the United States. Scott liked to recall the scene in November 1824, when Lafayette, Jefferson, Madison, and Monroe passed down Charlottesville's Main Street, crowded with cheering onlookers, in the landau carriage built by Scott's uncles Joe Fossett and John Hemings. Jefferson's liveried postilions rode two of the four bay horses. The Scott family provided music for the festivities—some apparently at Monticello—in honor of Charlottesville's celebrated visitor. Robert Scott also reported that "the taste for music shown by his family had early attracted Mr. Jefferson's notice, as he dearly loved music himself, and he had taken much kindly interest in the family," and would apparently stop at the Main Street house to hear them play. Memories of the Scotts' music making stirred aging Virginians in the same way that thoughts of Eston Hemings's fiddling affected newspapermen from Ohio: "Such music they made as the gods of Terpsichore will never hear again in this generation—such music as caused the old chateau to rock and reel to the cadence of the tripping feet and made old hearts young again!"[53]

The final assessment of Robert Scott's position in the Albemarle community followed the account of his sudden death, at age ninety-six, walking down Ridge Street: "While regarded as a colored man, Robert Scott was not a negro. He claimed a large degree of Indian blood in his veins, and his every lineament and his gigantic stature went far to prove his claim. He was a man of excellent principles, courteous as a king, gentle in manner, and even in the anti-bellum days, he and his brothers were regarded more as the comrades of the people they served than as menials doing their bidding."[54]

Betty Hemings's great-grandson's life spanned almost an entire century during which the inexorable forces of law worked hand in hand with the more ambiguous dynamics of society to fix assumptions about race. When Robert Scott talked, in 1888, of attending a white school in his boyhood, he noted that "the prejudice between the races was not so strong then as now, and he had never heard of any objection being made to the presence of the colored pupils in his school." According to Dr. W. C. N. Randolph, the Scotts were also allowed to vote, "the courts deciding they were nearer white than negro," and R. T. W. Duke recalled that Jefferson's grandson Thomas Jefferson Randolph had testified that the Scotts "were not Negroes."[55]

Until 1910 Virginia law declared that a free person with more than three-quarters white heritage was not black. Since three of their grandparents were white and the fourth, Mary Hemings, was of mixed heritage (her grandson described her as an "octoroon"), then Robert and James Scott were legally white. In 1888, Orra Langhorne said to her host: "You have scarcely any African blood in your veins." "None, I may almost say none," Robert Scott replied, "for my mother was almost white; we considered ourselves white people." She noted that the Scotts' appearance and manners had brought them special treatment; at the Springs, for instance, they were given private rooms and, after the paying guests had left, were waited on in the dining room.[56]

This middle ground was harder to maintain in the postbellum world, with fourteen thousand freedmen flooding the territory formerly claimed by the several hundred free blacks. By the 1890s Mary Hemings and the connection to slaves at Monticello was erased from the public versions of the Scott family history; in some accounts she has even become an Indian. In 1892 the death of James Scott provoked a lawsuit that hinged on this issue of racial identity and brought an end to the Hemings family's residence on Main Street. Because James Scott had never legally married (his wife was a slave), his daughter's right to his half of the Bell-Scott legacy was brought into question. Sarah Scott Raub's inheritance depended on the 1866 act legitimizing marriages of "colored persons" prior to the Civil War. Robert Scott opposed his niece by contending that her parents were white and lost both his case and his home.[57]

The division of the estate forced the 1892 sale of the lot Thomas Bell had purchased in 1784, and Peter Fossett thus saw the Rosser Building instead of his grandmother's house on his visit to Charlottesville in 1900.[58] By then his relatives were scattered all over the nation, carrying on the family traditions of concern for education and social justice. Two of Betty Hemings's Scott great-great-grandsons played a significant role as educators after the Civil War. Robert Scott, Jr., became one of the first black teachers in Albemarle County, while Jesse Scott Sammons was principal of what became the Albemarle Training School.

Descendants of those who had gone west included Madison Hemings's grandson, attending college in Colorado and destined to become the first black in the California legislature. Two of Eston Hemings's grandsons practiced law and medicine in Chicago. And, for Joseph Fossett's great-grandson William Monroe Trotter, a magna cum laude graduate of Harvard, the turn of the century marked his transformation from a member of Boston's black elite, growing wealthy from real estate, to an unremitting advocate of racial equality. At this time, he recalled later, "The conviction grew upon me that pursuit of business, money, civic or literary position was like building a house upon the sands, if race prejudice and persecution and public discrimination for mere color was to spread up from the South." Through reform societies, audiences with presidents, and his own newspaper, the *Boston Guardian*, Trotter, in the words of one historian, "laid the first stone of the modern protest movement."[59]

Bonds of Memory

Identity and the Hemings Family

LUCIA STANTON AND DIANNE SWANN-WRIGHT

FOUR years into our project to collect the oral histories of Monticello's African Americans, we made our first trip to New York City, arriving in Manhattan on a December morning on a bus from LaGuardia Airport. We were deposited, along with our bags of clothing, cameras, and recording equipment, on Harlem's 125th Street, to await the downtown bus. At this point in the project, we were used to sharing the same spaces but at different comfort levels, invariably determined by the fact that one of us is black and the other white.

DIANNE SWANN-WRIGHT (DSW): *The 125th Street bus stop provided a visual feast for my imagination. Small matter that over fifty years separated me from its Renaissance or that thirty years separated me from Malcolm X's physical presence on this very street. I stretched my neck looking for Claude McKay, Zora Neale Hurston, and Langston Hughes. I strained to hear the notes that just had to be coming from the uptown jazz clubs. Some of the brothers and sisters who had heard Malcolm speak must be somewhere close. They just had to be.*

In my mind's eye, I formed a bond with the folks who shared the actual present with me on this December morning. We were in Harlem, the home and center of black cultural expression. I was home.

LUCIA STANTON (LCS): *While I eyed the dark figures coming to life in the doorways and worried about the safety of our newly purchased video camera, I craned my neck to spot the bus that would take us away from Harlem and down to familiar streets with two-digit numbers.*

This essay, coauthored with Dianne Swann-Wright, was originally published in *Sally Hemings & Thomas Jefferson: History, Memory, and Civic Culture*, ed. Jan Ellen Lewis and Peter S. Onuf (Charlottesville, 1999), 161–183.

Conditions were reversed a few hours later, as we sat with a white family in a comfortable room, bright with Christmas presents piled on the sideboard and paintings decorating the walls. Three generations of descendants of Eston Hemings of Monticello, who 150 years earlier had moved from the black world into the white, were present to share their family history. When the collection of family photographs was brought out after the interview, we saw several arresting images on the first pages of an album dating from the turn of the century. Artfully staged and photographed in a professional studio, they showed Eston Hemings's grandson and a friend, costumed in blackface. The young men, dressed as pickaninnies, struck comical poses and, in one photograph, leered at their female companions, who wore little girls' dresses of virginal white.

DSW: *I was hopeful that the album might suggest links between the inhabitants of the house and an honored and respected black past. I stared at each image as someone else turned the pages. The image of Eston's grandson in blackface, mocking what he was slapped me in my own face. I needed the back of my chair to brace me from the insult, the disrespect.*

LCS: *With my mind wavering precariously between two equally strange possibilities—that Sally Hemings's great-grandson was ignorant of his race or that he knew it and was hiding or ridiculing it—I took refuge in sifting historical facts. At the time of the photograph, his family had been living as white for half a century. His grandfather Eston had died before his birth, but he had been raised by Eston's wife, his grandmother, who had been born a free woman of color in Virginia. Could he have been unaware of his racial heritage, acting like other white Americans who found the donning of blackface a titillating amusement? Or was he instead painfully conscious of his own masquerade, drawn to it unwillingly by the pleas of others or by his own need to fortify his whiteness by ridiculing blackness?*

The ambiguities and absurdities of racial definitions illustrated by this photograph seemed emblematic of our discoveries since the beginning of the project. It had been started in 1993, to give voice to Monticello's African American families, whose lives and contributions had gone largely unrecorded. In recognition of the importance of orality in the African American community, we named it Getting Word and hoped that present-day descendants would "get word" back to us about their ancestors' experiences at Monticello and their fates after Jefferson's death. Since 1993 we have conducted fifty-five interviews with more than one hundred descendants living in a dozen states, often with the help of our consultant, Beverly Gray, whose knowledge of the African American experience in Ohio has been indispensable. While our informants represent several enslaved Monticello families, two-thirds of them are descended from three daughters of Elizabeth (Betty) Hemings. It is particularly in our interviews with the descendants of two sons of Sally Hemings that we have learned about the legacies of miscegenation, the complexities of racial identity, and the power of memory. This chapter focuses on the different experiences of the families of Madison Hemings, who always remained a member of the black community, and Eston Hemings Jefferson, who at age forty-four crossed the color line, determined to live as a white man.[1]

Freed by the terms of Jefferson's will in 1827, Madison and Eston Hemings continued to live and work within a few miles of Monticello, as Jefferson's petition to the Virginia legislature exempted them from the 1806 law requiring freed slaves to leave the state within a year. Trained in woodworking by their highly skilled uncle, John Hemings, the Monticello joiner and cabinetmaker, they pursued this trade in Charlottesville and on plantations in Albemarle County. Eston Hemings also probably began to pursue a career as a professional musician. In 1830 the brothers bought a house and lot on the road between the town and the university and lived there with their mother.[2]

Within five years of their emancipation, both men had married, making choices that would perpetuate their mother's skin tone. Madison Hemings's wife, Mary Hughes McCoy, was the granddaughter of a white plantation owner and the slave he freed. Eston Hemings married Julia Ann Isaacs, member of a well-to-do mixed-race family in Charlottesville; her father was a Jewish merchant and her mother the daughter of a slave and a slaveholder. Both marriages ensured that, besides freedom, the children of these unions would have a passport to upper-class status within the black community and the probable option to enter the white race.[3]

After Sally Hemings's death in 1835, the brothers and their families moved to southern Ohio. Madison Hemings worked as a carpenter in Pike County, and Eston Hemings became well known in the area as a professional musician and leader of a dance band. Two Chillicothe residents, late in the nineteenth century, recalled the musician from Monticello. One described Eston Hemings as "a master of the violin, and an accomplished 'caller' of dances," who "always officiated at the 'swell' entertainments of Chillicothe." For the other, no ball in the 1880s could live up to those of the 1840s, when the Hemings band "struck up 'Money Musk' or 'Wesson's Slaughter House'" and capped the festivities with the Virginia reel. (The Scottish fiddle tune "Moneymusk" was evidently a favorite of Thomas Jefferson, too, as one of the rare musical manuscripts in his hand is a record of that tune.)[4]

Both newspaper accounts provide descriptions of Sally Hemings's youngest son, "a remarkably fine looking colored man." Tall, well proportioned, "very erect and dignified," he had nearly straight hair with "a tint of auburn" and a

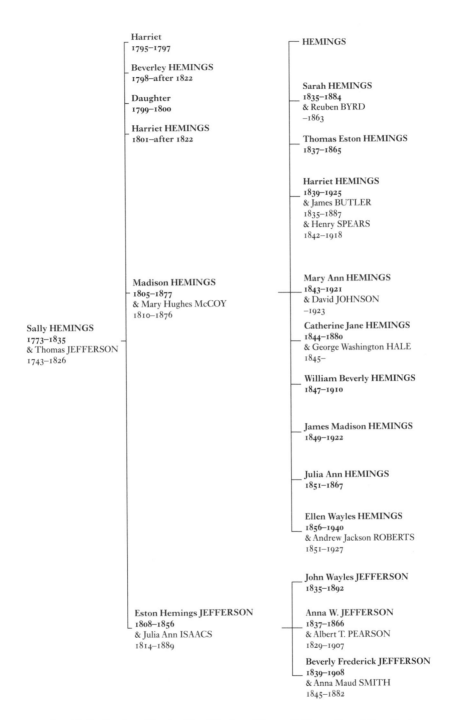

Family of Sally Hemings (Getting Word Project; Thomas Jefferson Foundation, Inc.)

"suggestion" of freckles: "Quiet, unobtrusive, polite and decidedly intelligent, he was soon very well and favorably known to all classes of our citizens, for his personal appearance and gentlemanly manners attracted everybody's attention to him." There was one drawback, however, on whatever ambitions Eston Hemings may have had: the color of his skin. He is described as "very slightly colored" and "a light bronze color." One writer stated that, "notwithstanding all his accomplishments and deserts," there would always be "a great gulf, an impassable gulf" between Hemings and whites, "even the lowest of them." The other concluded more crudely: "But a nigger was a nigger in those days and that settled it." Even the laws did not have the power to raise Eston Hemings in the eyes of his white neighbors. In both Virginia and Ohio, he and his brother were legally white, but social practice invariably invalidated the law for those who were known in a community or who had, as one of these newspapermen noted of Eston Hemings, a "visible admixture of negro blood in his veins," echoing a phrase that by then had statutory overtones. Efforts by light-skinned mulattoes to claim their rights to the vote or public education caused confusion in Ohio courts until general practice was codified in 1859, when "a distinct and visible admixture of African blood" became the legal litmus test for separating black from white.[5]

Seven years before this visible admixture law, Eston Hemings left Ohio, where he and his family were denied access to the courts, the polls, and the public schools. In 1845 a Cleveland newspaper, very possibly referring to Eston Hemings, expressed shock, "Notwithstanding all the services and sacrifices of Jefferson in the establishment of the freedom of this country, his own son, now living in Ohio, is not allowed a vote, or an oath in a court of justice!"[6] Since racial identities could be shifted only where one was unknown, Eston Hemings and his family had to move among strangers to claim their rights as citizens. In Madison, Wisconsin, he adopted a new name as well as a new racial identity, becoming Eston H. Jefferson. His northwestwardly course, from slavery to freedom and, finally, to whiteness and its associated privileges in Wisconsin provided his children with choices and considerations he had never had.

His brother Madison Hemings remained in Ohio, living for forty years with his family on the black side of the color line and becoming a pillar of his small rural community in Ross County, south of Chillicothe. He had at first supported his family in Ohio with his woodworking skills and, when interviewed in 1873, mentioned three buildings in Waverly for which he had crafted the woodwork, two of which are still standing. In 1865 he purchased a sixty-six acre farm, where he continued to pursue his trade while raising corn and hogs. According to Beverly Gray, descendants of white Ross County residents remember being told of Madison Hemings's reputation in the community. Known as the "junior president," his word, they recall, "was his bond." At his death in 1877, his estate was appraised at a value of almost $1,000.[7]

DSW: *Most historians can complete W. E. B. Du Bois's quotation, "The problem of the twentieth century is the problem of the ———." I wonder if Du Bois realized how true his declaration would prove to be. For me, the color line is more than a division, separating those with power and privilege from those without. For me, the color line is a hard, unhoeable row.*

Walls topped with broken glass surround buildings in Nairobi, Kenya. They protect serene courtyards and lush gardens from intruders who do not stay out of where they are not wanted. Anyone able to climb the wall can go over them, but few do unless they are willing to risk being cut to the core. I think that the color line in America is very much like the broken-glass-topped walls of Nairobi. They can be crossed but at a painful, bloody cost.

LCS: *Because my whiteness protected me from having to think about racial identity, my real consciousness of the color line came late. I was struck by the absurdity of racial categories in an Ohio living room in 1993, when three generations of people who looked white spoke of the indignities they had suffered because they chose to ally themselves with black family and community. A man who had lived in a white neighborhood growing up and whose friends were white played on the high school baseball team but could not join his teammates at the soda fountain afterward. His best friend's father, a barber, would not cut his hair.*

My response reminded me of the white travelers in the nineteenth century who realized the injustices of slavery only when they saw men and women as white as they were being taken down the Mississippi to the New Orleans slave market for sale. I still have difficulty visualizing the color line. It appears nebulous, shifting, at times a barricade guarded by gun-toting white men, at times a mist, a white mist into which people disappear.

The color line was both painful and permeable. In every generation of Sally Hemings's descendants, from her children in the first half of the nineteenth century to her great-grandchildren's great-grandchildren in the mid-twentieth century, some family members vanished into that mist. The experiences of descendants of both Madison and Eston Hemings illustrate the benefits and costs of passing for white. Madison's son William Beverly Hemings served in a white regiment—the 73rd Ohio—in the Civil War and died alone in a Kansas veterans hospital in 1910. His brother James Madison Hemings may be the source of stories among his sisters' descendants of a mysterious and silent visitor who looked like a white man, with white beard and blue, staring eyes. He slipped in and out of town to visit older family members but never formed ties with the younger generations. According to one family chronicler, neither of these sons married, perhaps because of concerns about revealing skin color. Several of Madison Hemings's grandsons also passed for white, divorcing themselves from their sisters who stayed on the other side.[8]

This pattern of brothers leaving sisters continued in the next generations. Descendants of Madison Hemings's oldest daughter Sarah Hemings Byrd have many stories of families fragmented by passing. Even though many of those who passed remained in southern Ohio, "we never heard from them," said one. Her cousin, conjuring up images of amputation, said: "They tended to cross over to the white community and not maintain any connection with the rest of the family. It was just sort of cut off." Important life passages like births, marriages, and deaths became painful reminders of family division, and only those remaining in the black community came to family reunions. One descendant related a bitter moment in his grandmother's life, when she was not notified of the death of her brother, who had passed for white and married a white woman years before. He had remained in touch, however, through cards and phone calls on certain meaningful occasions. His new family did not send word across the color line until months after he died, perhaps to ensure that no part of the black family appeared at the funeral.[9]

Passing was not always permanent. A great-grandson of Madison Hemings through Sarah Byrd became what his family calls an "ethnic person," adopting a variety of European accents along with his fictitious identities. At the end of his life, alone and in need of support, he returned to the care of a sister who had remained a person of color. According to one informant, when he came to live with her grandmother, "we didn't understand who [he] was because [he] had an Italian accent. . . . And then we found out actually he was our uncle. And that [he] had crossed over, he had been white. And he didn't have a whole lot to do with his family. . . . But at the point where he was an old man and he didn't have anywhere else to go, he ended up staying with Grandma and he stayed with her until he died." For others, intermittent passing became a strategy for securing anything from a job to a haircut. Their racial identities calibrated by the day or hour, they were white in the workplace and black at home, or borrowed a white surname to make a hairdressing appointment in a neighboring town.

There is no way to know exactly what governed the timing of Eston Hemings's decision to slip off his African American identity and move to Wisconsin, leaving his brother behind in Ohio. When Eston and Julia Hemings headed further northwest in 1852, their children were ages fourteen, sixteen, and seventeen. By crossing the color line in unison, before the children reached marriageable age, Eston Hemings's family avoided the fragmentation that had occurred in his own generation, with the departures of his siblings Harriet and Beverley. The disappearing brothers who haunted succeeding generations of Madison Hemings's descendants would not be a part of Eston Hemings's legacy, and his adoption of whiteness was successful in its probable intention—escape for his family from the economic and social subordination that prevailed under the "black laws" of Ohio. His daughter Anna married and lived as a white woman. Her brothers were both officers in white regiments in the Union army. Beverly F. Jefferson, who married a white woman, became a prosperous and respected hotel and transfer company owner, while John Wayles Jefferson moved to the South and became a wealthy cotton broker. His articles were published in Wisconsin and Tennessee newspapers, and he corresponded with President Benjamin Harrison about conditions in the postwar South. Eston H. Jefferson's grandsons even exceeded the success of his sons, becoming lawyers and physicians, as well as prosperous businessmen.[10]

By contrast, the children and grandchildren of Madison Hemings who remained in Ohio were bound by the restricted opportunities for blacks at the time. They were, for the most part, small farmers, storekeepers, laborers, domestic servants, or caterers. While their descendants speak above all of families of love and strength, there are stories of the breaking of the human spirit rather than its triumph, when racial prejudice blighted career expectations and dreams for children. Some lives, as we have also heard in other families descended from the Monticello enslaved community, were tinged with alcohol and anger.

A move to the other side of the color line brought its own set of costs, however. The persistent anxiety of hiding the past is shown in a newspaper account of the meeting of Eston's son John Wayles Jefferson, then a lieutenant colonel of the 8th Wisconsin, with a citizen of Chillicothe, Ohio, his former residence. "He begged me," recalled the writer, "not to tell the fact that he had colored blood in his veins, which he said was not suspected by any of his command."[11] Like Madison Hemings's sons, John W. Jefferson remained a bachelor, as did two of his nephews, one of whom was a suspected suicide; the other walked down the railroad tracks and "vanished off the face of the earth." The early deaths of an unusual number of Eston Hemings Jefferson's male descendants, if not attributable to genetic factors, may be symptomatic of the pressures of passing.

DSW: *It was December 1993, in Chillicothe, Ohio, the beginning of the Getting Word project, and we nervously awaited guests invited to a reception for descendants of Madison Hemings and his cousin Joseph Fossett. There were flakes of snow in the straight black hair of the first person to arrive. He rubbed long white fingers over his face and perfectly angled nose. I hated to send him back outside into the snowstorm, but I could not avoid telling him that the reception was only for descendants of the black people who lived at Monticello when Thomas Jefferson was alive.*

"Yes, I know. That's why I am here. I am one of them."

The next day, mindful that people are not as they appear, I approach everything with caution—even the old photographs strewn across the table.

Madison Hemings's granddaughter and her family were there, early in this century, standing and sitting in a farm's yard, facing the camera, their community, and me. There were no smiles; no one was touching. Two hunting dogs filled the space between the father and the son.

There was something else. I knew this family to be black. They looked white. The mother and daughters had clustered themselves at one side of the image. The brother stood alone at the opposite edge of the picture. Time and folding had creased the father. He appeared to be split into two parts.

Since that reception in 1993 we have learned that Sally Hemings's children and their descendants had been changing, reconstructing, or reinforcing their racial identities through all the generations from the time of slavery until the present. The light-skinned offspring of miscegenation in slavery had maintained their distinctiveness by marrying others who shared their physical appearance and its accompanying social status. In this way, subsequent generations of Sally Hemings's descendants continued to resemble their famous ancestor, who was

Madison Hemings's granddaughter Emma Byrd Young, her husband George Young, and their children, ca. 1915. (Courtesy of Ann Pettiford Medley)

described as "mighty near white."[12] Madison and Mary Hemings's descendants in Ohio were part of an endogamous community of very light skinned blacks that has continued for more than a century. Only recently has this self-perpetuating group living suspended between two worlds begun to blend into the rest of society, by expanding their marriage choices to include darker-skinned spouses.

Our interviews with Madison Hemings's descendants, all of whom identify themselves as people of color, reveal both the significance of light skin and a deeply felt allegiance to the black community. Similarities of appearance and social background were prerequisites for prospective mates and parents admonished their children of dating age to befriend only those who looked like themselves. One descendant said: "I think it is who you married. Those that were fair, perhaps, at the time married more white, because it was the way." Another descendant, recalling his first dating experiences as recently as the 1980s, told how his parents expressed their displeasure when he brought darker-skinned girls home; they let him know that his one experiment in dating a white girl was also unacceptable.

This pattern over two centuries—miscegenation in slavery, endogamy accompanied by some passing for white, and assimilation into black culture—was broken in one branch of Madison Hemings's family. His youngest daughter, Ellen Wayles Hemings, married a man described in the family as having "no white blood"; he was "pure African," "Nubian black." Some of Ellen's descendants tell an interesting story about the origin of this union: Madison Hemings, old and infirm, arranged this marriage for his last unmarried daughter, joining her, possibly against her will, with a much older man he recognized as able to support her. Ellen and Andrew J. Roberts's marriage record,[13] however, is dated a year after Madison Hemings's death and reveals Roberts to be only five years older than his wife. The story appears to be a family effort to explain the unusual choice of a dark-skinned husband.

A. J. Roberts, a schoolteacher at the time of his marriage, did indeed provide well for his wife and family. He took them to southern California where he started a very successful family mortuary business, "the pioneer establishment in the State." He and his son Frederick Madison Roberts, the first black member of the California legislature, are featured in a 1919 work, *The Negro Trail Blazers of California.*[14] But the variations of skin color within this family seem to have been a factor in shaping personal worth. Ellen Hemings Roberts, described in her family as looking like a white woman, seemed to prefer her grandchildren with Caucasian features. One brown-skinned granddaughter recalled the special favors given her brother, with his pale skin and golden curls, while she herself was called "little black gal." In another branch of Madison Hemings's family, a woman who married a dark-skinned man was remembered as having "stuck the wrong color into their family," and her brown-skinned daughters considered themselves the "black sheep" of the family.

Color prejudice was present in the black community outside the family as well. One of Sarah Hemings Byrd's descendants said that "the blacks don't like it because you're light skinned and the whites know you're black so you're just stuck there." Her mother, in her seventies, remembered the hostility of her black schoolmates: "They used to call us white niggers."

No matter their complexion, Madison Hemings's descendants were emphatic in their identification with blackness. Many elected to remain a part of the black community even when their appearance made passing possible. For one Sarah Byrd descendant, World War II provided two defining moments. When he enlisted in the navy, he was "really hurt" when he was recorded by the local recruiter as a negro of "dark" or "black" complexion. When he reached his assignment point, however, he adamantly refused to be placed in a white unit at the recommendation of the assigning officer, who was struck by his appearance. This forceful claim to African American identity was made in what seems to be a common scenario in which a white person is eager to offer a passport to white identity and the privilege it provides to blacks who appear white. One of Ellen Hemings Roberts's descendants, when asked if she had ever considered passing for white, responded: "Absolutely not! It was how we were brought up to take pride in who we were." She also was often told by white people that she could be "anything" she wanted, as if no sane person would wish to be black. This tendency of whites to want to make the rules about race is shown in a particularly revealing case, where a neighborhood street became a battleground over control of racial categories. Every summer evening in the 1970s a white boy pounced on Madison Hemings's great-great-great-grandson, knocked him to the ground, and pummeled his chest, shouting, "You're white. I know you're white." "No, I'm not. I'm black," was the response. After protesting his blackness over and over, he finally confessed to being what he knew he was not to bring the daily ritual to an end.

DSW: *A shadowbox containing a fifty-odd-year-old twist of tobacco and an ear of yellow corn, only a year or two younger, sits on a fireplace mantel in my office. My paternal grandfather grew them both in one of the Piedmont, Virginia, fields he sharecropped. Before the shadowbox came to this Monticello office, its contents had hung against the wall of my parents' kitchen for decades. My grandfather gave them to my parents' home when they married and moved north. Tobacco and corn were symbols for my ancestors—of how hard they worked and who they were. They are now markers for me.*

LCS: *I cherish and display—at risk to its existence—one piece of family memorabilia that has come down to me: a framed document inset with a small photograph of a young man in uniform. He is my paternal great-grandfather, appointed in the document as acting master in the Confederate navy, 1863. By framing these fading manuscripts, someone in the family had chosen to mark his decision to leave his inland home in the Union state of Kentucky for the seacoast and the Confederacy. And I had chosen to exhibit them, emblems of the slave-owning side of my family; my maternal ancestors were all Yankees. Other ancestors on my father's side had produced a Georgia plantation mistress who neglected to tell her slaves that the war was over and they were free, as well as a Pulitzer Prize–winning journalist who fought the Ku Klux Klan. Master Stanton stares out of the frame at the twentieth century, telling me that every American is implicated in the aftermath of slavery.*

We attach our memories to markers—people, places, events—that define and determine our identities.[15] Very much like icons on a computer screen, these familiar sites of memory can be opened to reveal a multitude of motifs and messages that influence our ideas and actions. These landmarks of the past usually undergo regular revision, changing their shapes and meanings as each new generation navigates its course toward identity. Thomas Jefferson remained a primary reference point for Eston Hemings's descendants, while in his brother Madison's family Sally Hemings survived as an additional marker of equal importance. For both families, however, the unacceptability of a significant part of their family tree has led to the suppression of the links and associations that might normally accompany sites of memory.

Whatever other parts of himself he left behind when he departed Chillicothe for Wisconsin, Eston Hemings took with him his connection to Thomas Jefferson. Although it was widely "rumored" in southern Ohio that he was Jefferson's son, he is not known to have made an unequivocal statement of his parentage, as did his brother Madison. When asked by another Chillicothe resident to comment on his "perfect and striking" resemblance to Jefferson, his response was more ambiguous: " 'Well,' answered Hemings quietly, 'my mother, whose name I bear, belonged to Mr. Jefferson,' and after a slight pause, added, 'and she never was married.' "[16] He made his most direct statement on the issue by suppressing his mother's name to a middle initial *H* and taking the surname of the man he so closely resembled. Unlike most who passed for white, who closed the door on their past and created new family histories, Eston Hemings risked exposure by adopting this well-known surname and sustaining the memory of his tie to Jefferson. This seems to indicate a strong identification with the man he knew as his father. They shared physical appearance and unusual stature, mastery of the violin, and the tunes to go with it. Eston Hemings may also have had Jeffersonian tastes, as he purchased a set of silver spoons at an estate sale in 1837, when about to leave Virginia.[17]

Passing usually required discarding the past and the creation of a new family story untainted by connection to blackness. Eston H. Jefferson's children, however, preserved their connection to Thomas Jefferson and Monticello. His son Beverly, who died in 1908, was described by a friend as Thomas Jefferson's grandson in a response to a notice of his death in a Chicago newspaper.[18] Within a few decades, however, a new history had been created by weaving fiction into core truths that were important to family identity. The Jefferson connection was preserved, but the pedigree was revised to prevent discovery by those who knew that Jefferson and his wife had no surviving sons. Growing up in the 1940s, Eston Hemings's great-great-granddaughter heard that she was related to Thomas Jefferson, not through direct descent but collaterally, through his uncle. Other small alterations were made to the past: Eston's name became Estis; Virginia remained the home state, but Albemarle County became Fairfax; and all references to the fifteen-year residence in Ohio, where the family had lived as blacks, were eliminated. Sally Hemings is conspicuously absent from this story.

Madison Hemings never took the Jefferson surname, and his recollections do not suggest that he identified with Jefferson in any way. He even pointed out their physical dissimilarity: "He [Jefferson] was a much smarter man physically, even at that age, than I am." But his several references to promises, and how they were broken by "white folks," indicate that, for him, Jefferson differed from other whites; he kept his promises. Referring to Jefferson's "solemn pledge" made in Paris to induce Sally Hemings to return with him to Virginia, he said: "We all became free agreeably to the treaty entered into by our parents before we were born." Because he remained a man of color, Madison Hemings did not have to twist Jefferson's relationship to him or to exclude his mother in his accounts of his history. Equal in importance, both parents appear in his 1873 recollections to a white journalist and in the stories told his children. They and succeeding generations were left to pass it on or to deny it according to their own racial and personal identities.[19]

Memory and personal identity are inextricably linked. One Madison Hemings descendant, the daughter of a California legislator, understands her father in terms of her ancestor's calling: "My father was a public servant, so it seemed kind of natural. My great-great-grandfather was a public servant. It came on down to my father." Another descendant said that, had he known of his connection to Thomas Jefferson while he was in architecture school, he never would have dropped out. Eston Hemings's descendants see their family's multiple talents and interest in the arts and music as links with their Jefferson heritage. Descendants now living on both sides of the color line described Thomas Jefferson in glowing terms. Young and old alike called him "a great man," and many described him as "brilliant," the brightest of our presidents. Younger descendants called him "interesting" and "contradictory," while their elders found ways to understand Jefferson's complicity in slavery. Two sisters living on different continents for the last thirty-five years shared the same view that Jefferson was not a "mean" master, but he was "caught" in his time and "was just torn about what to do." His family relationship mediated his role as a slaveholder: "Blood is thicker than water," as one sister said.

Even though no visual images of Sally Hemings exist, she is clearly present in the minds, memories, and identities of Madison Hemings's descendants. She is described by these, mostly female, descendants as "bright" and "intelligent," "very special" and "extraordinary." "I'd like to know more about her" and "I wish I could have met her" are common responses. They see the people and situations in their own lives through the lens of Sally Hemings. A human resources worker considers Sally Hemings in the context of her own workplace, with its concerns of sexual harassment and equal opportunity. Another descendant reviewed the parallels in the lives of Sally Hemings and her mother and grandmother, all single parents, and concluded: "My mother felt the same thing Sally did." One woman, a deputy sheriff in a large city, perceived her ancestor as "strong" and "independent."

A third marker for Madison Hemings's descendants was the relationship itself, the nature of the link between Jefferson and Sally Hemings. One descendant, confessing her imperfect recollection of her great-aunt's version of the family history, did remember that "it was more of a romantic story, it was about this captain of a ship." In two other branches there is a particularly strong oral tradition of a deep and abiding love between Jefferson and Hemings. As Ellen Hemings Roberts's granddaughter said, Sally Hemings was "dearly loved" by Jefferson. "This was passed down, down, down the oral history." In its most elaborated form, this version of the story removed the stain of illegitimacy by pointing to the laws that prevented Jefferson and Hemings from marrying, thereby allowing Sally Hemings to become a positive role model, in spite of her marital and social status.

In the 1940s Ellen Roberts's niece Nellie Johnson Jones wrote a two-page family history for a cousin in which she said her grandfather was "the son of Thomas Jefferson" (she was the daughter of Madison Hemings's daughter Mary Ann Hemings Johnson). While it is not known how widely she spoke of her actual descent from Jefferson outside of her family, she was not averse to making her connection to Monticello known. She had inherited from her mother several articles that had been Jefferson's—spectacles, a buckle, and an inkwell—and placed them for display in shop fronts in Illinois and houses in Los Angeles. In 1938 she wrote for advice to President Franklin D. Roosevelt and the postmaster general in her efforts to find the most appropriate location for these objects. Stating that they had descended to her from her great-grandmother Sally Hemings to Madison Hemings and then to her mother, and without directly mentioning Jefferson's paternity, she offered to sell the mementos to the Thomas Jefferson

Memorial Foundation at Monticello: "Knowing the esteem in which Thom. Jefferson is held; being a historical character who will live as long as America endures, I decided that some one might want these articles." She regretted her inability to donate them. The chairman of the board did not ask to view the objects and declined Mrs. Jones's offer; their current whereabouts are unknown.[20]

Nellie Jones's efforts to establish an almost public dimension for her connection to Jefferson were very much the exception. Her belief in a love story thwarted by unjust laws freed her to break the silence guarded so carefully by others of her generation. For the majority of Madison Hemings's descendants the paternity story remained a private matter, and its persistence in a hostile environment of disbelief is a striking demonstration of the strength of the oral tradition. One of the by-products of the public denial of the family's history was a potent and pervasive silence, both inside and outside the family circle. Descendants of three of Madison Hemings's daughters report that their elders talked little about the Jefferson-Hemings history. One heard the story from her father at the age of twelve: "But he said 'but we don't talk about it.' And I never mentioned it again to him and he never spoke about it. My grandmother didn't talk about it either." Personal encounters with skepticism reinforced the suppression of the story. As one man related: "It was never really, really talked about. You tell people and they would kind of laugh at you or didn't believe you or it would pass over their heads."

For members of an African American community where orality is honored and respected, silence became a family trait. The silence of the mysterious, staring son of Madison Hemings has been mentioned before. His sister is remembered as a loving presence, but her voice is forgotten. She was "very, very quiet." In describing their father and grandfather, three sisters used the word "quiet" over a dozen times, and a descendant in another branch stated: "You've been taught all your life to be quiet." The repressive climate of disbelief engendered a number of stories of documents or family Bibles that could have proved the Jefferson descent that had either disappeared or been burned in fires or car wrecks.

Society's repudiation was matched by denial within the family. Slavery itself was considered a shameful topic until recently, and the specter of illegitimacy further stifled discussion of the past. Said one descendant of her elders' injunctions to silence: "They seemed to feel because it was an illegitimate relationship that they didn't want it known." Many stories that might have flourished in a different climate vanished in the pervasive silence. Madison Hemings's woodworking talents were forgotten, his wife's freeborn status was lost, and no family accounts bearing on personality survive. Interestingly, the only information about Hemings's character comes from descendants of his white neighbors.[21]

Only the most important story, the one that was the hardest to believe, was held on to with remarkable tenacity. Because people pass on stories as part of the formation of identity, the account of descent from Thomas Jefferson and Sally Hemings became something very different from tales told around the dinner table or at bedtime to lull children to sleep. Madison Hemings's descendants chose the moments of transmittal carefully. They waited until children were old enough to understand, or until they reached an important transition point, or until their lives intersected with history. For Sarah Hemings Byrd's granddaughter, it was an occasion of both family pride and historical association that impelled her to pass on the story to her granddaughter. It was only when her granddaughter won a history prize in high school, sponsored by the Daughters of the American Revolution, that "she mentioned that we were related to the third president of the United States, Thomas Jefferson. She just took a lot of pride in the fact that we got that type of recognition. And she saw a connection there."

While Madison Hemings's descendants who remained black could openly identify with their slave ancestor, to erase their racial origins Eston H. Jefferson's descendants had to hide or deny her existence. It is apparently no accident that Dr. Eugene Foster, in pursuit of DNA samples, could find exclusively male-line descendants of Eston Hemings Jefferson but not of his brother Madison. In the Eston H. Jefferson branch, both the Y-chromosome and the memory of Thomas Jefferson were transmitted from generation to generation. The male markers of Madison Hemings's descendants seem to have disappeared as some men made the choice to pass for white and left no traces, while the women who remained behind never forgot Sally Hemings. The genetic markers in each line thus match the markers of memory.

DSW: *So much of what I've learned since the beginning of this project I've learned around kitchen tables. It was around Beverly Gray's kitchen table in Chillicothe, Ohio, that I first heard the phrase "bringing children out of Egypt." It was used in describing the deliberate behavior of enslaved women to gain freedom for their children. Bev Gray told me that "children could be brought out of Egypt or slavery" by having a father who could and would free them or by having skin light enough not to appear black.*

Bev's comment set my thinking of enslaved women on its head. In my mind, only Harriet Tubman and Sojourner Truth had such agency. Sally Hemings, Liberator. An interesting idea. If she and other enslaved women deliberately sought to "bring their children out," they were in some way doing what only God could do—freeing powerless people. A novel concept, to say the least—those without power exercising it, and those with power letting it seep away through sexual acts they were privileged to have simply because they were in power.

LCS: *I am sitting over breakfast, reading about the natural world in which I find so many metaphors for human behavior. Dianne and I have been talking, writing, and reading together for weeks in connection with preparing this essay, but at this moment I am, I believe, far away from Monticello and its messages. The monarchs are on the move in Mexico. Clouds of butterflies waft north to California and their summer feeding grounds. But many never complete their appointed journey. They alight and give birth and die, leaving their children to carry on the voyage and the family. Unbidden, Betty Hemings and her daughters Mary and Sally come to mind, making their long migration to freedom and fulfillment for their children.*

A number of Madison Hemings's female descendants are fascinated by the most evident moment of choice in Sally Hemings's life. Why did she leave freedom in Paris to return to slavery in Virginia? By her son's account, she refused to leave France until Jefferson promised her "extraordinary privileges" and "made a solemn pledge that her children should be freed at the age of twenty-one years. In consequence of his promise, on which she implicitly relied, she returned with him to Virginia."[22]

While we might find it hard to imagine making such a choice based on the fates of one's unborn children, Sally Hemings may have felt she was part of a continuum. Madison Hemings used the same term, *concubine*, for both his mother and his grandmother Elizabeth (Betty) Hemings. If through her connection to John Wayles, Betty Hemings had brought her children from the fields to the great house, could she, Sally, take her own one step further and bring them out of Egypt? Her sister Mary achieved this for some of her children when she formed a quasi-conjugal relationship with the white merchant who hired her in 1787. Thomas Bell, described by Thomas Jefferson as a "man remarkeable for his integrity," freed Mary Hemings, acknowledged his two children by her, and left them his substantial estate.[23]

Sally Hemings had partially accomplished her mission by 1822, when her oldest children Beverley and Harriet shed their slave identities and quietly left Monticello, evidently with Jefferson's blessing. Because they also discarded their African American identities, their emancipation required exile from their home. While proximity to family was sacrificed for the sake of freedom, it is apparent from their brother's recollections that Beverley and Harriet Hemings remained in touch with their mother and siblings. The close ties of this family are further indicated by the recurring names of siblings in the next generation, as well as actions after Jefferson's death in 1826. When Madison and Eston Hemings became free according to the terms of Jefferson's promise and his will, they and their mother took up residence together in Charlottesville, first in a rented house and then in one they purchased and, perhaps, built.[24]

Although no document granted Sally Hemings her freedom, she was evidently given "her time" by Jefferson's daughter Martha Randolph.[25] She lived to see a grandchild born in a house owned by her family. As property herself, she had little to give to her children, but she had negotiated to give them back what her enslaved condition had taken from them—their freedom. While the other men freed by Jefferson's will were in their forties and fifties, Madison and Eston Hemings began their adult lives as free men.

LCS: *From the time I read Dorothy Redford's* Somerset Homecoming *I could not help imagining a similar event at Monticello, bringing back descendants of all its former residents.*[26] *In the summer of 1997, Dianne and I took a first step in achieving such a goal, inviting the participants in the Getting Word project to come to Monticello for a weekend. We knew we wanted to have a naming ceremony, to acknowledge those who were unable to leave lasting records of their existence, whose talent and labor contributed to the creation and operation of Jefferson's house and plantation.*

As the date approached, I realized that projected attendance was nearing 130— the number of men, women, and children who lived in bondage at Monticello at Jefferson's death in 1826. I prepared 130 small cards, each imprinted with a name, and we placed them in a handmade white oak basket.

DSW: *What we called the Getting Word Gathering provided an opportunity to end the silence before it was too late. When this project began I did not know that one of our tasks would be to encourage the transmission of information through oral stories. The telling of stories—the speaking of things and events—was so much a part of African American experience, there should have been no need to promote it. There was. Decades of disbelief and unwelcoming reception had produced a righteous silence that threatened the magic and charm of black orality. The Gathering would give descendants a chance to speak their ancestors back into existence in the same way the Bible says that God spoke the world into being.*

A poem by a West African philosopher-poet, Birago Diop, came to mind.

> *Those who are dead are never gone;*
> *They are there in the thickening shadow.*
> *The dead are not under the earth;*
> *They are in the tree that rustles,*
> *They are in the wood that groans,*
> . . . .
> *They are in the hut,*
> *They are in the crowd,*
> *The dead are not dead.*

And so it was that a joint vision of a naming ceremony at the end of the Getting Word Gathering took form. On a warm clear evening in June, descendants and their families assembled on the mountaintop lawn, before the West Portico, with members of the Monticello staff. One of the fifty Betty Hemings descendants present spoke a prayer drawn from the Book of Timothy, encouraging each person to press on. Reminded of another verse in the same biblical chapter, a woman exclaimed that the Getting Word project had "come before winter," before all the memories were gone, before they were lost forever. Dianne read "The Dead Are Not Dead" and passed around the basket, from which everyone took a name card. One by one, descendants called out the names of those who had gone before, those 130 people who, on Independence Day 1826, were painfully aware that their fates hung in the balance. The economic realities of Jefferson's encumbered estate brought a train of events—appraisals, advertisements, and sales—that swiftly and harshly severed them from their homes and families. Sally Hemings and her sons were the only ones who were not separated from spouse, children, or parents. Her fifth great-granddaughter, a tow-headed ten-year-old, read out the name on the card in her hand—Sally Hemings— speaking her back into existence, breaking the silence.

"We Will Prove Ourselves Men"

Hemings Descendants in the Civil War

THERE are two major communal events in the story of the enslaved families of Monticello in the nineteenth century. One took place on five days in 1827, when over one hundred men, women, and children were sold from Jefferson's mountain and dispersed across central Virginia. The other unfolded over four years across the entire United States. From 1865 descendants of Monticello's African Americans have looked back at the Civil War through a split lens, seeing it in both positive and negative terms. Author and activist Pauli Murray expressed this double vision well when she described her grandparents as "viewing opposite sides of a coin." Her grandfather's memories of the war "evoked a youth fired with a great humanitarian ideal which had triumphed, Grandmother remembered slow starvation, invasion and disaster."[1] The wartime experiences of people connected to Monticello, whether they lived in Alabama, Virginia, Ohio, or Wisconsin, were similarly full of both rejoicing and suffering. In interviews conducted with over 150 descendants of Monticello's enslaved families, my colleague Dianne Swann-Wright and I were told no tales of the camp or battlefield. The few Civil War stories we heard came from the South, from those who were still locked in slavery. Yet at least ten men with a Monticello connection served in northern military units during the war. Eight were descendants of Elizabeth Hemings through her daughters Mary, Betty, and Sally, and two married her descendants.[2] Four of these ten soldiers served in white regiments.

———

Elizabeth Hemings's great-grandson Peter Fossett was the first to take the field, the only former Monticello slave known to have marched in a formal military unit. In September 1862, he served in the Cincinnati Black Brigade, months before the Union army officially enlisted black soldiers. Fossett, who became a well-known Baptist minister after the war, never mentioned his brief military role in numerous newspaper interviews. Almost the only information comes from the short history of the Black Brigade by Fossett's close friend Peter H. Clark, prominent educational and political leader. When the city was threatened by the Confederate army under Gen. Kirby Smith, martial law was declared. The mayor issued a proclamation calling for "every man, of every age, be he citizen or alien" to come to the city's defense. There was great excitement as thousands of instant soldiers from across Ohio, as well as Cincinnati, swelled the population. Local ladies provided meals on tables set up on the sidewalks, and Oberlin students sang antislavery songs.[3]

African American residents were understandably hesitant to come forward. At the beginning of the war, when they had organized a home guard, the Attucks Blues, to assist in the defense of the city, their participation had been scornfully rejected. They were harassed by the police and, according to Clark, were told, "We want you d—d niggers to keep out of this; this is a white man's war." After the rumors of invasion, however, the black men of Cincinnati were suddenly hauled forth to work on fortifications. Policemen charged into their homes: "Closets, cellars, and garrets were searched; bayonets were thrust into beds and bedding; old and young, sick and well, were dragged out, and, amidst shouts and jeers, marched like felons to the [mule] pen on Plum street."[4]

Fortunately, the white man assigned to command the African Americans was fair-minded and humane. Col. William M. Dickson, a Cincinnati judge, whose wife was a cousin of Mary Todd Lincoln, permitted the men to return home to reassure their worried families and then formed them into a separate Black Brigade of volunteers, described by Clark as "the first organization of the colored people of the North actually employed for military purposes." Over seven hundred men rallied to Dickson's more honorable call to serve, including forty-seven-year-old Peter Fossett, his brother-in-law Charles Williams, and his nephew Daniel Mundowney. Fossett was selected as one of a handful of African Americans among the seventeen company captains.[5]

Although they knew they could not bear arms or engage in combat, the men of the brigade marched across the pontoon bridge into Kentucky on September 8, "glowing with enthusiasm." "Receiving the treatment of men," wrote Clark, "they were ready for any thing." They carried into the land of slavery an American flag presented to them by Camp Commandant James Lupton, with the exhortation, "Rally around it! Assert your *manhood*." Quaker merchant and Underground Railroad leader Levi Coffin later recalled that the Black Brigade was "said to be the most orderly and faithful regiment that crossed."[6]

After three weeks of labor on fortifications far in advance of the Union lines, "with nothing but spades in their hands," the Black Brigade was disbanded when the Confederates turned their attention elsewhere. On September 20 the companies marched back through Cincinnati, with music playing and banners flying, and were dismissed by Colonel Dickson with these words:

> You have made miles of military roads, miles of rifle-pits, felled hundreds of acres of the largest and loftiest forest trees, built magazines and forts. The hills across yonder river will be a perpetual monument of your labors. . . .
>
> Go to your homes with the consciousness of having performed your duty—of deserving, if you do not receive, the protection of the law, and bearing with you the gratitude and respect of all honorable men.[7]

Black U.S. Army Regiments

55th Massachusetts Volunteer Infantry

Two days later Abraham Lincoln issued the preliminary Emancipation Proclamation, which went into full effect on January 1, 1863. At a grand jubilee in Cleveland to celebrate this long-awaited event, John Mercer Langston, born to a slave and a slaveholder thirty miles from Monticello and almost certainly well acquainted with its former residents in Ohio, advocated the right of blacks to fight with the Union. In his oration, Langston compared the Proclamation to the Declaration of Independence. The Proclamation, he said, was "a more perfect definition" of the Declaration, with its unfulfilled promise of freedom and equality.[8] Also in January, the War Department authorized the organization of all-black army regiments. African Americans soon were flocking to recruiting stations, eventually making up 10 percent of federal forces and becoming a significant factor in the Union victory. For the 180,000 black soldiers in the U.S. Army, the war provided their first chance to prove themselves in the eyes of a world beyond their immediate families and communities.

As a historian of the early republic, I never expected to read an entire Civil War regimental history. It became required reading because two men, who married granddaughters of Joseph and Edith Fossett of Monticello, enlisted in the 55th Massachusetts Volunteer Infantry. I followed the fortunes of the 55th in the words of its lieutenant colonel, Charles B. Fox, whose diary was the basis for the regiment's history. In more than two years of service, the soldiers traveled from Boston to South Carolina to Florida and back and experienced conflict with Union authorities as well as Confederate troops. William H. Dupree and James Monroe Trotter figure prominently in Fox's pages, as two of only three blacks in the regiment who gained commissions before the war's end. As I read the name of the third officer, I felt an excited twinge of recognition. Fox's biographical note on John Freeman Shorter, first sergeant and then second lieutenant, revealed that he had been born in Washington, D.C. Could he possibly be a descendant of Melinda Colbert Freeman, a granddaughter of Elizabeth Hemings who was born at Monticello and lived in the nation's capital with her free family from 1808 to her death? Further research provided the proof that Lt. John F. Shorter of the 55th Massachusetts was Melinda Freeman's grandson.[9] It was now clear that the only fully commissioned black officers in this renowned Civil War regiment were all connected to the Monticello enslaved community.

Governor John Andrew of Massachusetts, one of the strongest supporters of arming African Americans, led the way in organizing black infantry regiments. His chief recruiting agent in the West was John Mercer Langston, and one of Langston's deputies was William H. Dupree. In the late spring of 1863, Dupree, his best friend James M. Trotter, and John Freeman Shorter made the eight-hundred-mile journey from Ohio to Boston. Dupree, born free in Petersburg, Virginia, had attended school in Michigan and Ohio and in 1863 was working as a messenger for the livery stable and express business of Langston's brother-in-law in Chillicothe.[10] Trotter, son of a Mississippi enslaved woman and her master, had attended the Hiram Gilmore School in Cincinnati and the Albany Manual Labor Academy in Athens County. He was a schoolteacher in Pike County at the time of his enlistment. Shorter was raised in freedom in Washington and, in the words of Colonel Fox, "with few early advantages, acquired by hard study a good English education." He was working as a carpenter in Delaware County, Ohio, when he responded to the call to arms.[11]

When they reached Camp Meigs outside Boston in June, the better-known 54th regiment had already departed for South Carolina. All three therefore joined the 55th and, as men of some education, were quickly made first sergeants of their respective companies. In November, Trotter was promoted to sergeant major of the regiment.[12] Literate noncommissioned officers became the spokesmen for the thousands of African American men who served in Union regiments. In countless letters to the editors of northern newspapers, they drove home the point of Frederick Douglass's famous declaration: "Once let the black man get upon his person the brass letters, U.S., let him get an eagle on his button, and a musket on his shoulder and bullets in his pocket, there is no power on earth that can deny that he has earned the right to citizenship in the United States." Shorter wrote at least two such letters, and it is possible letters to editors from Trotter or Dupree survive hidden by a pseudonym. Trotter's surviving letters from the front were written to friends of the regiment in Boston.[13]

The experience of black soldiers in Union regiments has often been expressed as fighting a war on two fronts. They had not only to battle the Confederates but also to contend with the obstruction and prejudice of white men—in their units and in their government. For their white officers and members of Lincoln's administration, liberating slaves was one thing. The struggle for equality was quite another. The men in the Massachusetts 54th and 55th regiments soon learned of a significant "breach of faith" on the part of the government they were serving.[14] They had enlisted on the understanding that they would be paid, equipped, and treated on an equal footing with white soldiers. By the fall they knew that the War Department had decreed that their effective pay was to be half what white soldiers received. This issue, highlighted in the 1989 film *Glory*, produced many months of simmering unrest as well as letters and speeches of protest, with conspicuous participation by Shorter and Trotter. Both Massachusetts regiments refused to accept any pay until allowances were equalized.

In December 1863, the state of Massachusetts offered to make up the difference and sent its paymaster, Maj. James Sturgis, to the coastal islands near Charleston, where the 54th and 55th were in camp. After both regiments declined the funds, the soldiers were called together to explain themselves. A white captain wrote at the time, "The Sergeant-Major Trotter spoke in reply, stating the position in which the men stood and what their opinion was on the subject, and the result was that the Major entirely agreed with the men's ideas."

Lt. James Monroe Trotter (1842–1892). (Courtesy of the Division of Rare and Manuscript Collections, Cornell University Library)

Colonel Fox recorded in his diary that "several non-commissioned officers and privates expressed their views and those of their comrades, in a quiet and proper manner, the remarks of Sergt.-Major Trotter being especially good." The men then gave three cheers for Massachusetts, Governor Andrew, Major Sturgis, and their commanding officer, Col. Alfred S. Hartwell.[15]

Three months later James M. Trotter struck up a correspondence with Edward W. Kinsley, philanthropic friend of Governor Andrew and the 55th Massachusetts, who had accompanied Sturgis to the regiment's camp. In his 150-word opening sentence, Trotter expressed the gratitude of the soldiers for "how unceasingly you have advocated their cause in order that they might receive the same pay and treatment as other soldiers of their country, and by this means obtain, what is dearer to them than life without it, *the recognition of their manhood.*" He told Kinsley that although saddened by thoughts of their families facing destitution at home, the men were not discouraged. They drew inspiration for their patience from "the great Jehovah, who will not suffer this war to end until every trace of Slavery is gone."[16]

The summer of 1864 must have been particularly trying for the noncommissioned officers, who were crucial to containing the "mutinous spirit" of many of the men. As Colonel Fox stated, "To preserve a proper degree of order and discipline in a regiment thus situated was no light task." In May, John F. Shorter wrote his father that "the Regiment is in a perfect state of Demoralization. . . . I sometimes think to myself that I am more than Glad that I have no wife to undergo the Privations that the Long Delay of our pay would have exposed her to."[17] A few days later, Trotter poured out his thoughts to Edward Kinsley:

> We have been disheartened on account of the long delay, cruel and unnecessary of the *government at Washington*, some more so than others. You know how hard it must be for a husband and father to retain his evenness of mind and spirits when he knows that his loved ones suffer for his aid while he is so bound that he cannot give it. This circumstance has impelled many to grow disheartened, and others losing patience on account of government's refusing to accord to them the rights that they *knew* they had so dearly earned, and feeling that they were treated as slaves, have almost given over hoping. O, Mr. Kinsley, we have *all* been blue, very blue at times. Still there is at present a most cheerful state of feeling and your glorious letter has helped to cause it.
>
> God grant that soon, very soon, the dark clouds in sky may soon disappear, to give place to the bright sunshine of Equality and Manhood.

By this time soldiers had begun refusing duty, and on June 18, Private Wallace Baker was court-martialed and executed for having struck an officer, in other words, for mutiny. Everyone agreed that the crisis over unequal pay was at the root of such unfortunate incidents and the harsh response to them. According to Colonel Fox, "Had justice been done the enlisted men in regard to their position as soldiers, no such example would have been needed."[18]

In July, after thirteen months with no pay and no resolution to the issue, the men of John Shorter's Company D decided to write directly to President Lincoln: "To us money is no object. We came to fight for liberty, justice & equality. These are gifts we prize more highly than gold. For these we left our homes, our families, friends & relatives most dear to take as it were our lives in our hands to do battle for God & Liberty." They ended with a threat: "Be it further resolved that if immediate steps are not taken to relieve us, we will resort to more stringent measures." Shorter, whose signature, as first sergeant, appears at the top of the list of all the men in the company, probably played a part in composing the letter.[19] By the time the government relented, the soldiers of the 54th and 55th regiments had gone without compensation for eighteen months.

The first packets of equal pay finally arrived in October 1864, a milestone marked by the 55th with a day of celebration. John F. Shorter, at the center of festivities, provided African American newspapers with a long and lighthearted account. A procession led by the regimental band was followed by a prayer by Chaplain John R. Bowles, who had been William Dupree's schoolteacher and who would, after the war, officiate at the marriages of Dupree and Trotter as pastor of First Baptist Church, Chillicothe. Some of the sergeants made speeches, and Shorter read resolutions prepared for the occasion, including:

> Resolved, That we are determined to make it our first duty as soldiers—by promptitude, obedience, and soldierly bearing—to prove ourselves worthy of the responsible position assigned us by Providence in this, the grandest struggle of the world's history, between Freedom and Slavery; our first duty, as men, by every means possible, to contradict the slanders of our enemies, and prove to be true our fitness for liberty and citizenship, in the new order of things now arising in this, our native land.

The program was punctuated by music from the band and singing of patriotic songs. An "elegant supper" followed, with more speeches, toasts, songs, and cheers. Shorter concluded his letter, "Gentlemen sang that night who never were known to sing before. . . . The whole affair went off with *eclat.*"[20]

During the last six months of the pay crisis, there was an additional source of discontent in the regiment. The War Department's exclusion of black line officers was another example of the federal government's unequal treatment of its black soldiers. By 1864 most of the mixed-race officers of the Louisiana Native Guards had been purged; virtually the only blacks at officer grade were chaplains and surgeons, outside the chain of command. Governor Andrew and some of the officers of the Massachusetts regiments were determined to break this ban. The first sergeant to be promoted to second lieutenant was Stephen Swails of the 54th, on March 11. Two weeks later the 55th followed suit. The biographical sketch in Charles B. Fox's regimental history stated that, as first sergeant of Company D, John Freeman Shorter

> proved himself to be an excellent Orderly. Quiet, reserved, modest, he yet held his company in the firmest control. With every soldierly quality, from scrupulous neatness to unflinching bravery, he well merited the reputation of the best non-commissioned officer in the regiment. As such, he was selected for the first promotion from the ranks, and was commissioned as Second Lieutenant by Gov. Andrew, March 24, 1864.

A private in Shorter's company wrote his cousin back home in Indiana: "You must give three chers for the fortune that hapened in our regiment[.] our Seargeant John F. Shorter of Ohio is promoted second Luitenant[.] huraw huraw huraw."[21] James M. Trotter and William H. Dupree were promoted in April and May.

Initial joy in the regiment faded when the papers refusing these commissions began to arrive. One soldier wrote with bitter irony that "the U.S. government has refused so far to muster them because *God did not make them White*. No other objection is, or can be offered. *Three cheers for 'our country.'*" Sergeant Shorter took immediate action in the effort to break down the barrier to promotion by writing to his father in Washington, at the suggestion of his company captain. John Shorter, Sr., was a messenger in the Senate who might be able to shed light on the situation, "Being nearer the War Dept & perhaps acquainted with secretary Stanton Personally." The sergeant's father spoke, not to Edwin Stanton himself but to C. W. Foster, chief of the Bureau of Colored Troops. He learned that only the governor of Massachusetts had the authority to bring the subject before the War Department. Shorter, Sr., duly wrote Governor Andrew, who placed the matter in the hands of Massachusetts members of Congress, with an urgent request "to follow up the case fully and promptly." Andrew wrote Shorter that he wished he could personally travel to Washington to prosecute the case, "but I will never yield nor fail to pursue it. The law is plain; the right is clear. Your son's merits are eminent beyond doubt or cavil. He shall be mustered in under his commission, unless he dies or refuses it himself."[22]

Despite the strenuous support of Massachusetts officials and other proponents of black commissioned officers, the War Department did not budge on the issue for nearly a year. Meanwhile, Shorter, Trotter, and Dupree had to carry out the duties of a second lieutenant without its privileges. Trotter expressed his frustration in a letter to William Lloyd Garrison's sixteen-year-old son, Francis

J. Garrison, describing the uncomfortable middle zone he and his friends would have to navigate for the rest of the war:

> You have heard that 1st Sergts. Shorter and Dupree & Sergt. Maj. Trotter have been commissioned by Gov. Andrew as 2 Lieuts. So far, very good; but Gen'l Foster will not discharge them as enlisted men and muster them into service as officers claiming that "there is no law *allowing* it, they being colored men." Do you know any law that *prohibits* it? I am assigned to Co. K, and am performing the duties for which I was commissioned. So also is Shorter and Dupree. But this half and half arrangement is very unpleasant to us.

The prejudice *"in our very midst"* was especially dispiriting. Although the major and colonels remained staunch supporters, the lieutenants and captains (line officers) were less willing to accept black men as their equals:

> I am sorry to have to tell you also that most all the line officers give us the *cold shoulder.* Indeed, when our papers, returned the other day, disapproved those who have all along claimed to be our best friends, the line officers, seemed to feel the most lively satisfaction at the result. O how discouraging! How maddening, almost! . . . Several have resigned on account of it, and the disapproval of the muster papers alone prevent others from doing the same thing.[23]

It was only when the fighting had ended that the promotions of the three men were acknowledged and they could carry out their duties as officers with full official approval. In the meantime, they led their men into battle.

What was most important to the black soldier of every rank was the chance to prove himself on the battlefield. The men of the 55th had to wait over a year. Always before them was the example of the gallant but doomed charge of the 54th Massachusetts at Fort Wagner in July 1863. During the many months of the siege of Charleston they endured a wearisome round of picket and garrison duty and the exhausting labor of fatigue duty. Within range of Confederate batteries, they cut timber, built wharves, unloaded stores and ammunition, hauled heavy siege guns, and dug an endless array of trenches. As one soldier put it, they were "subjected to hard labor under a heavy cross fire of solid shot and shell."[24]

The first taste of combat finally came in July 1864 at Rivers Causeway on James Island. Although this was a minor and, in the end, unsuccessful action, it was of profound significance to the soldiers of the 55th. News of the Confederate slaughter of black soldiers at Fort Pillow in Tennessee had arrived six weeks earlier. The sense of outrage was fresh so that on the morning of July 2 the men were ready with a new rallying cry: "Remember Fort Pillow." In a long and color-ful account of the "expedition," James M. Trotter reported that, after two other regiments began retreating in panic, Colonel Hartwell cried, "Bring forward the 55th!":

> We were already advancing on the double-quick bayonets at a charge, and the men cheering, shouting, and the battle cry "Fort Pillow" came forth from many a throat. . . . [We were] within 200 yards of the battery, when we made a desperate rush, yelling unearthly. Here the Rebels broke, jumped on their waiting horses and by the time we had gained the parapet were far down the road leading to Secessionville. O how they did fly! They left behind two pieces of cannon. . . .
>
> Well, you may imagine how proud we felt when we found ourselves mas-ters of "Johnny's" fort and with what satisfaction we looked upon *our* pieces of cannon which now looked innocent enough but which a few minutes before had dealt death to so many [of] our brave fellows.

Nine men were killed, including three from Trotter's Company K, but the en-emy's relentless fire prevented their burial. Despite the ultimate failure of the action, letters from the soldiers, even those written forty years later, emphasize the thrill of reaching the parapet of the Confederate battery and capturing the two twelve-pound Napoleon guns, which were placed as trophies in front of the regi-ment's Folly Island headquarters.[25]

The Battle of Honey Hill on November 30 was the regiment's equivalent of the 54th's charge on Fort Wagner. It too was doomed from the start, part of an ill-conceived plan to cut the Charleston & Savannah railroad line in support of William Tecumseh Sherman's advance on Savannah. Union forces under Gen. John P. Hatch were carried by steamer up the Broad River past Hilton Head Island into a bewildering and fog-bound coastal landscape. Twenty years later Trotter's company captain Charles C. Soule recalled it as both a "disastrous episode" and a prime example of the "stubborn gallantry" of the troops: "To the Fifty-fifth Massachusetts this engagement gave the opportunity which the Fifty-fourth Massachusetts had at Fort Wagner, of proving that a black regi-ment, well disciplined and well officered, could behave as gallantly under fire as the best troops in the service." James M. Trotter, who lamented the "unavailing bloodshed" of the battle, wrote of the "desperate charge" of the 55th, which suf-fered thirty percent casualties and thirty men killed. Advancing toward the Confederate battery along a narrow road bordered by an impassable marsh, every shot from their guns "would mow down nearly a hundred of our brave fellows":

It was like rushing into the very mouth of death going up this road facing 7 pieces of death dealing cannon. Col. Hartwell and all of us knew this. But when commanded to charge 'twas not his to refuse, and so waving his hat while his eye looked upon his men, he smiled and cried, "Forward!" The order was promptly obeyed and in we rushed cheering and yelling. But ah! 'twas useless. The cannon on the hill opened. Shot, shell, grape and canister was hurled down the road as thick as hail and soon the Col. was wounded.

William Wells Brown devoted an entire chapter of *The Negro in the American Rebellion* (1867) to the Battle of Honey Hill, reserving special praise for the 55th, which occupied "the most perilous position" for most of the day, and mentioning Trotter and Shorter, who were wounded in the battle but fought on.[26] John Shorter's wound was severe, and he spent most of the rest of the war in the military hospital at Beaufort.

It was February 1865 before the rebel forces were finally dislodged from Charleston. The men of the two Massachusetts regiments had been burning to take this primary symbol of secession since they first arrived in South Carolina. Colonel Fox recalled the day his regiment marched into "the birthplace and hot-bed of rebellion" at the head of their brigade:

"The Fifty-Fifth Massachusetts Colored Regiment Singing John Brown's March in the Streets of Charleston." (*Harper's Weekly*, March 18, 1865)

Cheers, blessings, prayers, and songs were heard on every side. Men and women crowded to shake hands with men and officers. Many of them talked earnestly and understandingly of the past and present. The white population remained within their houses, but curiosity led even them to peep through the blinds at the "black Yankees."

The soldiers had been told that they must stay in formation but that "they might shout and sing as they chose." They sang "John Brown's Body," the "Battle Cry of Freedom," and "the national airs, long unheard there." As Fox recalled, "The glory and the triumph of this hour may be imagined, but can never be described. It was one of those occasions which happen but once in a lifetime, to be lived over in memory for ever."[27]

With the Confederate threat removed, the soldiers of the 55th were able to perform a sad task. Since the skirmish at Rivers Causeway the previous summer, rumors had spread suggesting that the Confederates had buried the white Union dead but not the blacks. Inspection of the battleground revealed that the bodies of their comrades had been left where they had fallen. They were brought back to the camp and buried with "appropriate ceremonies" and an address by Chaplain John R. Bowles. A lieutenant in the regiment told his mother that Reverend Bowles's words "did not tend to soften their feelings and I could see in the faces of the men a desire to revenge this insult." Rumors of atrocities committed against black people by bands of Confederate soldiers and guerrillas filtered back to the regiment throughout these chaotic weeks. The men became "greatly excited" and "effort was necessary to preserve discipline." But at midnight on Thomas Jefferson's birthday (April 13), they rushed out of their tents and cheered for hours when word of Lee's surrender came to their bivouac near Charleston. Jubilation turned to mourning a week later with news of the assassination of President Lincoln. In this period James M. Trotter and Company K were detailed to protect the freedpeople fleeing from their plantations in a mile-long train of every sort of wheeled vehicle, loaded with "feather-beds and tin-ware, looking-glasses and iron pots, earthenware, damask curtains, silk dresses, frying-pans, churns." In his vivid description of the scene, Colonel Fox noted as many as twenty-six children under five in one wagon, while the men, women, and older children "walked hour after hour beside the teams, toting heavy bundles on their heads." The intrepid Reverend Bowles had a risky encounter with an enraged ox, and when the camp was reached and the fires lit, "all the fatigue and hurry and vexation of the day seemed to be forgotten, and all were merry and happy together. Such an exodus is not often witnessed; once seen, it could never be forgotten."[28]

In May and June, the arrival of the commissions of Dupree, Trotter, and Shorter caused "quite a disturbance." Trotter wrote Edward Kinsley on May 27 that "some of our Officers have not yet got rid of their prejudices and consequently threaten to resign. . . . Our *best* officers do not manifest any 'Colorphobia.'" A month later, he did not know "how it will all turn out, but Dupree and I will try to do our duty as officers, let prejudice be as great as it may."[29] Reverend Bowles was back in Chillicothe when he heard the news. He immediately wrote to the *Weekly Anglo-African* that Shorter, Trotter, and Dupree, "after long waiting and faithful service, . . . have at last been permitted to wear straps on their shoulders and cords down the seam of their pants—three as worthy men as ever carried a gun. . . . The ball does move."[30]

Even with shoulder straps, a significant emblem of military authority, Trotter's "duty" was a challenge. From their base in Orangeburg, South Carolina, the officers of the 55th were responsible for maintaining peace between the freedmen and their former masters. Capt. Charles C. Soule, who headed the commission on labor contracts, described their task: "To avert disorder and starvation, officers detailed for the purpose were sent into the country to explain to white and black alike their condition under the new state of affairs, and to induce the laborers, if possible, to resume work upon the crops. . . . The officers engaged in this work have frequently ridden alone and unarmed twenty-five miles, or further, from the Post."[31]

One of those officers was Lt. James M. Trotter, who described his task as "quite arduous," but he was glad to do it because "I have ample opportunity to be of service to the freedmen." As he told Edward Kinsley:

> The former slaveholders wince under this new order of things. It seems to hurt them sorely—having to treat as intelligent free men and women, and draw up a written agreement to compensate for labor done those whom they have tyrannized over with impunity, treating them as so many cattle, but they have to do it. . . . I have several times been out on the plantations. I went 22 miles, without any guard save a good Colt revolver, which I had no occasion to call on. The Chivalry all treated me with respect and were very skillful in concealing whatever bitterness they may have felt when seeing a "nigger" with shoulder straps riding along the road to Columbia visiting their plantations in order to see that they were treating properly the colored people.[32]

At the end of August, the three second lieutenants were honorably discharged in Charleston and returned with the regiment to Boston. Trotter and Dupree settled there, returning to Ohio to marry the Isaacs sisters, Virginia and Maria Elizabeth. Their unique position as black army officers gave them a significant headstart in the city with the best reputation for race relations in the country. They were recognized as cultural and political leaders and were pioneers in the U.S. Postal Service (for many years Dupree was superintendent of a South End substation). Their former commanding officer, Col. A. S. Hartwell, whom Trotter called the "perfect soldier," was instrumental in Trotter's appointment as District of Columbia Recorder of Deeds in 1887, a lucrative position formerly held by Frederick Douglass. In the first decades of the twentieth century, James and Virginia Trotter's son, the famous firebrand William Monroe Trotter, continued his father's fight for the "great principle of equal rights" in picket lines, protests, and his Boston newspaper.[33]

James Monroe Trotter's family has preserved objects that are a perpetual reminder of the struggle for equality. His musket and sword now belong to his great-granddaughter Peggy Dammond Preacely. In the summer of 1864, Trotter had invoked the symbolic importance of these weapons, referring in one letter to "the wrong-avenging and freedom-securing musket" that Governor Andrew had boldly placed in the hands of African Americans. In another, to Francis J. Garrison, he recalled the moment when Andrew "said to us, 'boys take your muskets and wear your swords'":

> Franky, I wish you to give my high regards to your noble Father. I cannot of course ever forget *him*, he is too distinguished a friend of my race for that, but I remember particularly the happy speech he made to Co. "K" and the sword presentation. Do you recollect how you begged me not to call on "George" for a speech? Ah! we have seen some service since that time so have those swords.[34]

Peggy Preacely surmises that these tangible reminders of distinguished military service came to her mother, Ellen Craft Dammond, because she was the family historian. "As children we would take [the sword] out and we would look at it and it would be another source of conversation and historical remembrances." An illustration of the conjunction between family history and American history, the sword hangs in the main stairwell of her house, "so that the grandchildren can see black history and the families."[35] James M. Trotter's granddaughters knew their history better than the makers of *Glory*. When Ellen Dammond and her sister, Virginia Craft Rose, saw the film, they recognized their grandfather in the fictional figure played by Denzel Washington. James Monroe Trotter was one of the few spokesmen in the pay controversy—and perhaps the only one—to be cited by name at the time. His family preserved this leading role.[36]

Lt. John Freeman Shorter (1842–1865).
(Courtesy of the Division of Rare and
Manuscript Collections, Cornell
University Library)

John F. Shorter did not live to see the "new order of things" he had helped to bring about. He was exposed to smallpox on his journey back to Delaware, Ohio, to marry his fiancée. His constitution weakened by his wounds, he died just a few short weeks after reaching home. Charles B. Fox memorialized Elizabeth Hemings's great-great-grandson in his history of the regiment:

> The officers and men of the regiment will retain him in very pleasant and honorable remembrance. In person he was tall, of muscular build, with head carried a trifle forward, hair light, complexion almost white, and blue eyes, whose lively expression brightened a face otherwise somewhat grave. He was very reticent; but his few words were crisp, earnest, and to the point. A thorough soldier and a thorough man, he justified the friendship of the officers of the regiment and the State authorities of Massachusetts, who had urged upon the United-States Government the justice and the policy of the final recognition of the rights of his race, implied in opening to them promotion from the ranks.[37]

127th United States Colored Infantry

John Freeman Shorter's second cousin George Edmondson, a grandson of
Betty Brown, was still enslaved in Virginia when the men of the 55th Massachusetts were "comfortably encamped" in South Carolina in June 1864. On
June 11, Union troops under Gen. David Hunter made a memorable stop in the
Rockbridge County town where Edmondson lived. In its sweep up the Shenandoah Valley, Hunter's army destroyed mills, factories, and storehouses; carried
off horses and provisions; and liberated men, women, and children. As the Federal troops neared Lexington, its residents scurried to send off slaves, livestock,
and wagonloads of bacon and flour to safety in the Blue Ridge Mountains. Most
of the white men still in the town, including professors of Washington College
and the Virginia Military Institute, went with them. Thus it was mainly women,
children, and enslaved domestic servants who experienced the four-day occupation. Union forces shelled the town and set fire to the Military Institute and the
house of Virginia's recent governor John Letcher. They destroyed the mills and
ironworks near the Institute at Jordan's Point, where Edmondson's grandfather
Brown Colbert had worked as a blacksmith.[38]

The previous year, General Hunter, one of the earliest advocates of enlisting
blacks in the Union cause, had written a pugnacious letter to Jefferson Davis,
protesting the Confederates' outrageous treatment of captured black soldiers. He
reminded Davis of the words of Thomas Jefferson, misquoting a passage from
the *Notes on Virginia*: "The poor negro is fighting for liberty in its truest sense;
and Mr. Jefferson has beautifully said,—'in such a war, there is no attribute of
the Almighty, which will induce him to fight on the side of the oppressor.'"[39]
When Hunter's army arrived in Lexington in 1864, the actions of the enslaved
residents elicited contrasting responses from observers. For southerners it was
difficult to imagine that black people had minds and wills of their own. During
the Revolution, Jefferson had described his slaves as having been "carried off"
by Cornwallis rather than running away. Lexington's residents likewise saw the
invaders as the agents and the slaves as passive pawns of fate. When the wife of a
Virginia Military Institute professor wrote that "the servants are flocking away,"
she added that "the soldiers almost force them into the omnibuses." Hunter's
chief of staff, on the other hand, noted that "the Negroes take the first opportunity they find of running into our lines and giving information as to where their
masters are hidden and conduct our foragers to their retreats." He added that the
slaves "were continually running to us with information of all kinds and they are
the only persons upon whose correct truth we can rely." [40]

George Edmondson's enlistment in the 127th Pennsylvania regiment in
Wheeling, West Virginia, two months after Hunter's raid strongly suggests that

he took advantage of the turmoil and claimed his freedom by leaving with the Union soldiers. After June 18, when Confederate forces under Jubal Early defeated the Union army at Lynchburg, Hunter ordered its retreat, and wagon trains began streaming across the Allegheny Mountains into West Virginia. Since Edmondson's wife, Maria, gave birth to their second child in Lexington in September, his enlistment three hundred miles away on August 22 signals an irresistible desire to take part in a war of liberation.[41] Freedom—for themselves, their families, and their fellow slaves—was the first priority for most enslaved men who joined the Federal forces. By enlisting in a regiment of primarily northern freeborn men, Edmondson would have heard aspirations that went beyond the desire to stamp out slavery. Antislavery rhetoric had long equated manhood and equality. Once the Union army began to raise regiments of black soldiers, the Civil War provided the opportunity for demonstrating this equation. The motto of Edmondson's regiment—"We will prove ourselves men"— indicated their intent to display courage and patriotism, to prove themselves worthy of full rights as American citizens.

The 127th United States Colored Infantry, organized in Philadelphia in August 1864, became part of the all-black 25th Army Corps, which spent months in the grueling trench warfare of the siege of Richmond and Petersburg and was a factor in the final victory in Virginia. Yet, like so many black Union soldiers, Edmondson and his comrades spent far more of their time with pick and shovel, digging trenches and raising fortifications, than in combat. In October, men of the 127th were involved in a dispute over Confederate treatment of captured black Union soldiers who had been made to work on entrenchments in view of their own forces. Gen. Benjamin Butler responded by putting Confederate prisoners, especially members of the Virginia Reserves, to work in range of their own artillery fire, and he assigned soldiers of the 127th regiment to guard them. As a Philadelphia newspaper reported, "It was a curious sight to see the proud sons of the F.F.V.s, who had been accustomed to command negroes wherever they met them, humbly acknowledging the authority of the blackest of the race." [42]

In a minor engagement that fall, Private Edmondson was struck in the left arm by a shell, a wound that had disabling effects in later life. In December he was promoted to corporal. And in the early months of 1865, he participated in the final struggle of the Petersburg campaign. The 127th regiment was now part of Col. Ulysses Doubleday's brigade of black Pennsylvania units. On April 2, Doubleday was ordered to place his men "so that the enemy could see them, which was done, and they were consequently exposed for more than an hour to the fire of eleven pieces of artillery." The regiment's chaplain, Thomas S. Johnson, recalled that the Confederate batteries "were sending grape & canister & shells with great fury." The next day George Edmondson and his fellows in Double-

Carte de visite of *"We Will Prove Ourselves Men,"* painting by David Bustill Bowser for the regimental flag of 127th United States Colored Infantry. (Prints and Photographs Division, Library of Congress)

day's brigade were the first Union troops to enter Petersburg. Chaplain Johnson described the scene:

> The approach of the Union Soldiers was hailed with joy by all the colored population—which were the only people visible in the city—They came out and lined the streets—They filled the doors and windows with eager faces—Old men took off their hats and thanked "de Lord dat de good time had come"—Old matrons bowed their heads reverently as we passed—The young people were delighted that the day—the long expected day of their deliverance had come[—]The bands of music struck up and played the national airs and it was thrilling to hear the delightful notes of the Star "Spangled Banner" and "Yankee doodle" in the streets of the city which so lately was the home of the traitor and the hotbed of treason. The soldiers partook of the spirit of the occasion and marched finely through the city. Some recognized acquaintances who marched along and visited as they went—Others burst out in singing a song of which the chorus is—
> "Babylon is fallen Babylon is fallen"
> "And I'm a going to occupy the land." [43]

The brigade moved rapidly into Petersburg and out the other side in an epic six-day pursuit of Robert E. Lee's fleeing army—forty miles in one day. In his official report, Lt. Col. James Givin, commander of the 127th, said that his men, "though short of rations and almost worn out with fatigue, moved on without a murmur as long as there was an enemy to follow, and proved themselves to be a body of men upon whom the Government can safely rely in her hour of peril." Chaplain Johnson recalled the moment on April 9, when the surrender was announced to both armies gathered at Appomattox Court House: "A prolonged shout went up to Heaven from the Rebel Host when it was caught up by the Union Army that lay encamped all around and one & all joined in the shout till the air resounded with cheers of joy and gladness." [44]

After Lee's surrender, George Edmondson did not remain in Virginia as part of the Army of Occupation. The 25th Corps was transported to the remote Texas-Mexico border, a posting that felt to some like banishment after their participation in the arduous days of the final campaign. It was especially hard to watch the white Union soldiers mustered out of service, while the black soldiers, having enlisted later in the war, still had many months to serve. There was great suffering on the troop transport ships, and soldiers' letters were full of accounts of the harsh conditions along the Rio Grande. Of the barren island of Brazos Santiago, where Edmondson arrived in June, one wrote, "A more God-forsaken spot does not [exist] in the wide world; entirely without fresh water, and little or no facilities for making it; not a bush or a tuft of grass or a particle of vegetation within its entire area of twelve miles." The scarcity of water and fresh fruits and vegetables led to outbreaks of scurvy and other diseases. One overworked chaplain lamented that "no set of men in any country ever suffered more severely than we in Texas. . . . I have spent a great portion of my time at the hospitals and I never witnessed such fearful mortality in all my life." Death rates in the Union army from disease were appalling and dramatically higher for blacks than for whites: 33,000 of the 36,000 black soldiers who died in the war years succumbed to disease.

For most of his time in Texas, George Edmondson was confined to the post hospital at Brazos Santiago with dysentery and rheumatism. When he applied for his pension in the 1890s, he told the clerk that on his discharge at Brazos in September he "had to be assisted to the Boat" that carried him to New Orleans.[45] After the war he settled his family in Parkersburg, West Virginia, where he worked in a foundry and soon owned his own home. He was a trustee of the Methodist church, and although he could not write, he made sure his children acquired a good education (one son attended Wilberforce University). The "long and useful lives" of George and Maria Edmondson were noted in one newspaper, and another, in 1922, announced the death of one of Parkersburg's "leading citizens."[46]

Almost everything we know about the war service of George Edmondson comes from the written record. He seems to have been part of the long procession of silent veterans who have been returning from wars for centuries. We

George Edmondson (1836–1922).
(Courtesy of William Webb)

know that his grandchildren never heard him speak of his wartime experiences. We do not know if recollection of the march into Petersburg and the cheering at Appomattox—not to mention how he claimed his freedom with a musket in his hands—tempered memories of backbreaking labor, brutal combat, and dysentery in a sweltering Texas summer. Edmondson apparently chose to protect his family from the horrors of war. He expressed what was important about his year as a soldier quietly, by preserving papers that demonstrate that he served his country with honor and distinction. The documents for his honorable discharge and promotion to corporal were carefully passed down the generations between the pages of the family Bible. The silence of George Edmondson's war ended only when his great-grandson William Webb called up his military service and pension records from the National Archives in his quest to learn more about his ancestors.[47]

White U.S. Army Regiments

73rd and 175th Ohio Volunteer Infantry

If Sally Hemings's grandsons shared the sentiments of John F. Shorter and James Monroe Trotter, they could not have expressed them without risk.

Although they had lived all or a portion of their lives as members of the black community, they enlisted in white regiments. William Beverly Hemings was the first of Madison and Mary Hemings's sons to go to war. He was not yet seventeen when, in early 1864, he enlisted for three years with the 73rd Ohio Volunteer Infantry. Just a few weeks earlier, this regiment had marched through Chillicothe after two years in the thick of the action in Virginia, Pennsylvania, and Tennessee. It had fought at the Second Battle of Bull Run, held the line on Cemetery Hill at Gettysburg, and made a bold midnight charge near Chattanooga the previous October. William Hemings may have watched the veterans of the 73rd in their triumphal march through his county town and been fired, like many underage enlistees, with a wish to take part in a glorious adventure. He may also have been inspired by patriotism and political ideals we will never know about. Whatever his motivations, on February 10 a clerk recorded William Hemings's height (five feet six inches), black eyes and hair, and complexion ("dark" and "florid"), and he became a new recruit in the army of the Cumberland.[48]

The 73rd Ohio soon left for Georgia. William Hemings, however, missed the continuous combat of Sherman's Atlanta campaign, lying in a hospital bed for the whole four months. He apparently rejoined the regiment for the march to the sea at Savannah, thus passing through a stark landscape of slavery, with thousands of liberated slaves following the army in its train. His brigade then moved northward through the Carolinas and Virginia and, after the surrender of Gen. Joseph Johnston's forces at the end of April 1865, finally reached Washington. Hemings, therefore, was probably the only Monticello descendant to participate in the Grand Review of the Armies. On May 24, he marched down Pennsylvania Avenue in a stream of soldiers that lasted for six hours. Thousands of spectators crowded the sidewalks and watched from every door and window. Ulysses S. Grant described Sherman's army as a striking contrast to the more polished ranks of Meade's Army of the Potomac, which "had not had the experience of gathering their own food and supplies in an enemy's country."[49] If, like his kinsman George Edmondson, William Hemings had enlisted in a black rather than a white unit, he would have missed this day of triumph, since the three armies that marched in the Grand Review included none of the 160 black Union regiments.

The military career of Hemings's older brother, Thomas Eston Hemings, was short and tragic. In the summer of 1864, when he was twenty-six, he enlisted as a private in the 175th Ohio Infantry, recorded as five feet eight and one-quarter inches in height, with brown eyes and "dark" hair and complexion. Three months later he was captured near Columbia, Tennessee, in a skirmish with the forces of Gen. John Bell Hood. The records of the Ohio Adjutant General's office state that Hemings "died on or about Jan. 1, 1865, in Rebel Prison at Meridian, Miss."[50] While the lives of Madison Hemings's other sons are like shadows—they make only ghostly appearances in his descendants' recollections of childhood—Thomas E. Hemings's death became an indelible family memory. Eight years after the end of the war, Madison Hemings told a newspaperman that his son had died at the infamous Camp Sumter in Georgia: "Thomas Eston died in the Andersonville prison pen." Over seventy years later, in a brief history of her family, Hemings's granddaughter Nellie Jones wrote that her uncle "starved to death in Andersonville Prison (a rebel camp)."[51] This puzzling contradiction between the official records and family history may never be explained. If Madison Hemings paid twenty-five cents to purchase *A List of the Union Soldiers Buried at Andersonville* (1866), he would not have found his son's name among the 12,460 men in it. Thomas Hemings's body lies somewhere in an unmarked grave, either at Andersonville (one of more than four hundred marked "unknown") or at the site of the small stockade in Meridian or somewhere in between the two prisons. Because of the chaos of the final months of the war, with railroads in disarray and communication lines disrupted, just how, or if, Madison Hemings received reliable information about his oldest son is not known.[52]

Whether he died in Georgia or Mississippi, the agony of Thomas E. Hemings's last days is beyond question. Union soldiers captured in Tennessee were marched south, with no tents and little food, until they reached the nearest railhead for transfer east to the major prison camps at Cahaba and Andersonville. John Clark Ely, a sergeant in the 115th Ohio Volunteer Infantry regiment, was captured at the same time as Hemings. In his diary he recorded the march through December rains and the "usual mud," as they forded creeks in waist-deep water and went without rations for up to two days. Some men died of exposure and exhaustion along the way; others did not survive the few weeks spent at the Meridian stockade before moving east. When he eventually arrived at Camp Sumter on January 23, Ely did not try to put into words his first impression: "Of Andersonville the mind must draw its own picture." He at least had missed the horrific summer of 1864, when over thirty thousand men were crowded into the compound and over one hundred died every day. Nevertheless, the cold was severe, rations were short, and there were daily burials. Ely survived the notorious prison, as did a number of men from Thomas Hemings's regiment. If Hemings himself had lived, he might well have met a cruel fate. Paroled in March with thousands of others in Andersonville and Cahaba, an elated Sergeant Ely wrote, "Oh this is the brightest day of my life long to be remembered." On April 24, he boarded the steamboat *Sultana*, "a large but not very fine boat." Two days later, Ely and perhaps as many as 1,700 other returning Union prisoners of war were dead, after the explosion of a boiler on the overcrowded vessel—the worst maritime disaster in American history.[53]

The fear of discovery probably added to the misery of Thomas E. Hemings's experience. If his race were exposed, he would have had to endure both the open animosity of his captors and the latent prejudice of his fellow soldiers. At Andersonville black prisoners lived in their own enclave within the stockade. They were assigned to the burial detail and were sometimes whipped by the guards. When the federal government had begun to organize regiments of blacks, including former slaves, the Confederacy officially denied prisoner-of-war status to captured black soldiers who, in practice, encountered every response from ordinary imprisonment to hard labor on fortifications, reenslavement, and even murder. In the spring of 1863, the Lincoln administration suspended the exchange of prisoners until blacks and whites were treated equally. White Union soldiers languishing in southern prisons found a focus for their bitterness about the no-exchange policy. As one Andersonville prisoner confided to his diary, "It appears that the federal government thinks more of a few hundred niggers than of the thirty thousand whites here in bondage."[54]

William and Thomas Hemings left no testimony about their feelings about the color line and their reasons for crossing it to enlist. They would have known that had they joined one of the available Ohio black regiments, they would have been denied equal pay and equal access to advancement. As one man wrote in April 1864, we have "no chances for promotion, no money for our families, and we [are] little better than an armed band of laborers with rusty muskets and bright spades." The Hemings brothers had identified themselves as "colored" in their prewar lives. Thus every day spent with a thousand white soldiers must have been full of tension as well as the dread of discovery and its disagreeable consequences. The discomfort of passing for white was expressed by Private Charles R. Pratt of the 11th Ohio, who asked for transfer to the 55th Massachusetts in August 1864: "I am a colored man, and my position as private in a white Regiment is very unpleasant. My feelings are constantly outraged by the conduct of those who have no respect for my race." A month later, a white officer in the 1st Ohio Cavalry petitioned to transfer four men to a black regiment because of the "great dissatisfaction" their presence caused.[55]

William Hemings declared himself white to the military authorities, but it is hard to imagine that he was attempting to be fully accepted as a white man. The 73rd Ohio regiment was organized in Chillicothe, ten miles from his home, and the majority of his fellow soldiers were his neighbors in Pike and Ross Counties. Why was Hemings tolerated while, two years earlier, a Chillicothe mulatto, Albert Wall, was unceremoniously evicted from the same regiment (and same company) after his race was discovered? The beginnings of recruitment of blacks may have modified prejudice to an extent, but not enough to enable Hemings to be welcomed by many of his company cohorts. It does not appear to be an issue of social standing, since both the Wall and Hemings families were respected in the area.[56] The contrasting treatment of the two men suggests that Madison Hemings and his family were viewed, both because of their appearance and their standing in the community, as occupying some kind of intermediate racial zone, and thus eligible for some, if not all, of the privileges accorded to white people. After the war, William B. Hemings was a carpenter, farmhand, and farmer in Ohio, sometimes identified as black and sometimes as white. Plagued by poor health, probably derived from his year of war, he died a single white man in the National Military Home for Disabled Volunteer Soldiers in Leavenworth, Kansas, in 1910.[57]

1st and 8th Wisconsin Volunteer Infantry

William and Thomas Hemings's first cousins in Wisconsin unquestionably feared disclosure. When they joined the Union army in 1861, the sons of Eston and Julia Jefferson had been living as part of the white community in Madison for more than a decade. They were rising stars in the frontier city, members of local militia companies and a Masonic lodge. After his father's death in 1856, John Wayles Jefferson had begun to accumulate real estate and for several years ran a popular restaurant. In 1860, he was described as "one of the most energetic and obliging landlords" in the state. He was by then the owner and operator of Madison's oldest hotel, where his brother, Beverly, kept the sumptuous bar.[58] On May 17, twenty-two-year-old Beverly Jefferson enlisted as a private in the first volunteer regiment raised in the state, an early opportunity to serve his country that would have been impossible if he had remained in Ohio as a free person of color. The soldiers of the 1st Wisconsin Volunteer Infantry enlisted for only three months and were involved in one serious action, the Battle of Falling Waters (Hoke's Run), July 2, near Martinsburg in present West Virginia. It is now principally remembered as Thomas J. "Stonewall" Jackson's first engagement with Union forces. Beverly Jefferson returned to Madison in August and traded places with his older brother, who enlisted less than a week after Beverly was mustered out.[59]

Twenty-five-year-old John Wayles Jefferson started his war as one of three officers at the regimental level of the 8th Wisconsin Volunteer Infantry, a clear indication of his standing in the community. The *Wisconsin State Journal* assessed Major Jefferson at the beginning of his service:

He is favorably known in connection with the Governor's Guards of this place, and as an energetic and successful man of business. He has entered upon the discharge of his military duties with patriotic ardor, and so far with great success. He is highly popular with the soldiers, and with all who have the pleasure of his acquaintance. He promises to be a very able officer.

In September 1861, while Beverly Jefferson kept an eye on the family fortunes, taking over as landlord of the "best regulated hotel in Madison," Maj. John W. Jefferson joined the men of what became known as the Eagle Regiment. He provided an early account of the famous bird, dubbed "Old Abe," that gave the regiment its name and took part in many of its battles: "As the Chippewa Eagles [Company C] were coming into camp yesterday, with a live eagle perched upon their standard and their colors floating over it, the eagle caught the flag in its beak and spread its wings as if in the act of flying, and maintained the position for some time to the great delight of all who witnessed the scene."[60] For more than three years Major and ultimately Colonel Jefferson participated in arduous campaigns, protracted sieges, and hard-fought battles, principally in Mississippi and Louisiana. A steady stream of bulletins from soldiers of the regiment were published in Wisconsin newspapers, many of them commenting on their major.

John Wayles Jefferson also sent home observations on the regiment's progress as it passed through American scenes that were entirely new to him. He provided an account of Old Abe's first battle, a Union victory at Fredericktown in the slaveholding border state of Missouri. The weeks in Missouri, where he was in charge of 750 men guarding the Iron Mountain Railroad, were at first a rather lighthearted adventure, with hunting expeditions and trading with local farmers to vary both the diet and the dull round of army routine. As Federal forces moved toward the Arkansas border, his impression of the "southern" scenes he passed through was distinctly negative. He deplored the "miserable, old, dilapidated" dwellings, "built without the least regard to architectural taste," and found the inhabitants, with the exception of one family that unfurled a Union flag, "the very lowest, poorest and most ignorant kind, living in mud daubed cabins, tilling a few acres of land, and in many instances not any." The illiteracy of "these benighted people" surprised him. It was a man of color, the servant of his colonel, Robert C. Murphy, whose humor and cleverness lightened the monotony of camp life. On one occasion John wittily described his method of liberating some local sweet potatoes, and on another, he found a "shrewd way of getting even" with a "'secesh gent,' who, he claimed, had insulted him."[61]

By March 1862, the regiment, now part of Gen. John Pope's Army of the Mississippi, was living on corn bread, and Major Jefferson was yearning for "some of those good dinners" he used to "get up" at the American House. Yet, as another officer reported, "he has no desire to visit Wisconsin until he sees the old flag fl[y]ing from every town and village from Point Pleasant to the Balize."[62] The mood of exhilaration of the first months had faded in the face of the long marches and bruising combat of the Mississippi Valley campaign. One soldier summed up conditions for the 8th Wisconsin in 1862:

> Often on short rations, sometimes without rations at all; amid hunger and weariness; sultry days and chilly nights; shivering amid frost and snow in Missouri; parched beneath a burning summer sun in Mississippi and Alabama; sleeping without tents or blankets on the rain-soaked earth; splashing through mud and rain to-day, and choked and smothered with dust and heat to-morrow.

In May, in a major action at Farmington, Mississippi, Jefferson and Lt. Col. George W. Robbins "displayed great coolness and courage while leading the men on through the thickest of the fight, the shells were bursting all around them and the Major had a narrow escape from being killed, a cannon ball passed near his head." Soon afterward he fell seriously ill with dysentery and typhoid fever and had to be assisted from his tent to the ambulance when his commander and the surgeon insisted he leave for home. The Democratic editor of the Madison *Wisconsin Patriot* hailed the return of the "gallant Major Jefferson" and reported on his three months of recuperation.[63]

At the Battle of Corinth in October, he again displayed "great coolness and bravery under fire" and was "borne from the field" after being knocked off his horse by a spent bullet. Over the next two years, John Wayles Jefferson was twice wounded and twice had his horse shot from under him. In the spring of 1863, he evoked the grueling struggle to take Vicksburg in a letter to his brother:

> I have been continually on the March and fighting the rebels. I had not until to-day changed my clothes or had a decent meal for nineteen days. We marched around Vicksburg on the Louisiana side 90 miles, crossed the river at Grand Gulf, marched about 170 miles in a roundabout way to Jackson, Miss. Our brigade charged the rebel works at Jackson, and were the first troops in the town. . . . At Jackson Major General Sherman made me Provost Marshal of the town, had also charge of all the prisoners and was ordered to destroy five million dollars worth of rebel property. . . . We just lived on what we could pick up during the past three weeks, and I have been almost completely exhausted from hunger, loss of sleep and fatigue. Vicksburg will be ours in a day or two, but it has and will cost as many thousand lives.[64]

Six weeks later, on Independence Day, he sent an elated bulletin to Madison: "Vicksburg is ours. Glory! Glory! Glory! I have just returned from the city and actually saw the heads, hides and entrails of mules which the rebels have been subsisting on for days. We all feel so joyful today." He then linked this date to the one most associated with his grandfather: "Congress, at its next session, must be petitioned to add 24 hours to the 4th of July, making it 48 hours long, because hereafter we cannot possibly get done celebrating the day in 24 hours." Abraham Lincoln memorably marked this turning point of the war in the West in a famous letter, "The Father of Waters again goes unvexed to the sea."[65]

The next year of inconclusive actions and random movements, including the fruitless Red River campaign, must have been an anticlimax, not helped by the fact that Lieutenant Colonel Jefferson was suffering from bouts of the "ague" (malaria). Yet the wanderings of the Union army changed the course of his life. He got to know Memphis, the army's hub of operations in the West and a magnet for soldiers on leave, and was captivated by the cotton fields of the Deep South. During the siege of Vicksburg, Sgt. Maj. George W. Driggs had noted the impression made on the men of the 8th Wisconsin by the "large and magnificent plantations" along the banks of the Mississippi, which "presented a scene to the stranger's eye, so unusual to a Northerner, that we could not help gazing at them." When the regiment reached central Louisiana in the spring of 1864, Colonel Jefferson was reported as writing that "the country about Alexandria is the most beautiful he has ever seen, and that he had no conception of the wealth which exists there, or did exist there before the war."[66]

Over the course of the war, Jefferson rose from major to colonel, often commanded the regiment (and at least once an entire brigade), and several times served as Provost Marshal in the captured cities of the South. In their reports from the front, fellow soldiers sang his praises. Even allowing for exaggeration, from their wish to show the regiment in the best possible light, it is clear John Wayles Jefferson was a model army officer. The senior captain wrote, "None can avoid liking him." "Vox" stated that he was "idolized by his men." A second lieutenant believed there was no "worthier, more brave or gallant officer" in the army. Sergeant Major Driggs, who published his fifty-odd letters from the regiment, often mentioned him. In the fall of 1863, when Lieutenant Colonel Jefferson was acting commander of the Second Brigade, First Division, Driggs penned a long hymn of praise to the former hotel keeper. He said, in part:

> In this gallant and meritorious officer we have the utmost confidence. Ever attentive to the interest and welfare of his men and the service, he possesses the respect of all who come in contact with him. . . . Cool and determined in battle, he is also kind and courteous in camp. He has filled many high and honorable positions during the past two years of his service, with satisfaction to his superior officers, with honor to himself and credit to his command.[67]

Col. John Wayles Jefferson (1835–1892),
by Alexander Marquis, ca. 1864.
(Courtesy of the Museum of Wisconsin Art)

Throughout these years, when he was such a highly visible figure in the Union army, John Wayles Jefferson was in hiding. He was only a decade removed from life as a black teenager in Ohio and was painfully conscious of the risk of encountering someone who had known him in Chillicothe. His own commanding officer, Col. Robert C. Murphy, only seven years older than Jefferson, was raised in Chillicothe. It seems almost incredible that Murphy would not have recognized the officer he worked with every day as the son of Eston Hemings, who had been so well known as a musician in the town. The Jefferson surname also probably provoked frequent questions about the major's connection to the famous author of the Declaration of Independence. Some time in late 1863 or 1864, when Murphy had left the regiment and Jefferson had been promoted, he did meet someone who had known him in Chillicothe. The anonymous author of an article in 1902 recalled that the children of Eston Hemings "had scarcely a visible admixture of colored blood":

> I saw and talked with one of the sons, during the Civil War, who was then wearing the silver leaves of a lieutenant colonel, and in command of a fine regiment of white men from a north-western state. He begged me not to tell the fact that he had colored blood in his veins, which he said was not suspected by any of his command; and of course I did not.[68]

Coming of age in Madison's white community, the Jefferson brothers seem to have identified with their whiteness. Without it, John Wayles Jefferson could never have risen high in the military establishment and had his gallantry proclaimed in newspapers all across Wisconsin. He left the army as a colonel in October 1864 and, instead of returning to Wisconsin to live, settled in the heart of the South. The enterprising man of business as well as the weary soldier had ridden through those vast fields of cotton. He set up in business in Memphis while still in uniform and settled there after the war as a cotton broker, eventually acquiring plantations across the river in Arkansas and becoming "one of the largest cotton exporters" in the country. Wealthy, well traveled, and popular, the "jovial, genial" Jefferson never married and left no known descendants.[69] In his paean to his superior officer, George Driggs had predicted for him "an elevation which will prove the envy of his friends, and an honor to its possessor." Yet John Wayles Jefferson seems to have avoided the glare of the political arena.

Likewise, his brother, as well known in Madison as the colonel was in Memphis, steered clear of politics. Their geniality—a family trait that continued in subsequent generations—may have helped to mask a story that could not be told and lightened the burden of their father's decision to cross the color line in search of equality.[70] Beverly Jefferson left the hotel business in 1872, having built up a thriving omnibus and transfer line and, in the spirit of his famous grandfather, developed an "ingenious contrivance" to warm the interior of his coaches. He married the daughter of a prosperous farmer from Pennsylvania and sent three of his sons to the University of Wisconsin; two went on to law and medical school. At his death in 1908, he left an estate worth over $10,000, and his passing was lamented in long and lavish obituaries in Wisconsin newspapers. Chicago author and publisher A. J. Munson called him "one of God's noblemen—gentle, kindly, courteous, and charitable."[71]

For the Union soldiers connected to Monticello, the Civil War was an indelible memory that some of them perpetuated through ritual and reunion. Beverly Jefferson was a loyal "Three Months Man" who attended reunions of the 1st Wisconsin regiment. In 1875 his brother took part in Decoration Day ceremonies in Memphis, a mingling of the Blue and the Grey in a spirit of reconciliation noticed around the country. John Wayles Jefferson and about a hundred other "ex-federals" were said to have "never taken part in any public demonstration before."

In 1887, James Monroe Trotter initiated what he called "the first reunion of colored veterans of the Union" since the war. Veterans of the Massachusetts 54th and 55th Infantry and 5th Cavalry regiments came to Boston for a two-day event, which included a pilgrimage to the grave of Governor John Andrew. As chairman of the executive committee, William H. Dupree called the meeting to order. Among the speakers were the two Harvard-educated commanders of the 55th, Col. N. P. Hallowell and Col. A. S. Hartwell, and also Trotter, whose words were loudly cheered. He told the men he had no prepared remarks, preferring to await "the inspiration that comes to every true soldier when he meets a comrade who with him went through all the dangers, all the sufferings and went down nearly to death for the sake of liberty." He paid tribute to the memory of Governor Andrew and "that grand, highminded, generous noble boy," Col. Robert Gould Shaw, and recalled his comrade John Freeman Shorter and his long wait, suffering in a hospital bed, for his commission. Shorter's brother, Charles Henry Shorter, who had served in the 22nd United States Colored Infantry, was for many years an officer in a Washington post of the Grand Army of the Republic.[72] And in 2010, almost 150 years after it was minted, Bill Webb applied for and received the previously unclaimed Civil War medal of his great-grandfather George Edmondson. Bearing the legend "Honorably Discharged," it depicts a soldier being crowned with laurel by the figure of Liberty.

Fulfilling the
Declaration

*Descendants of Monticello's African
American Families*

I N 1993, to commemorate Thomas Jefferson's 250th birthday, Monticello inaugurated new public programs—particularly those dealing with slavery and
the African American community. Jefferson left an archive of over sixty thousand documents, one that dwarfs the dozen letters and handful of recollections
of his slaves. How could we at Monticello correct the imbalance of the testimony?
Perhaps by listening to the descendants of enslaved families, we could hear the
voices of their ancestors and learn their perspective on life on Jefferson's mountaintop. Could they *get word* back to us about who they were, where they went
after they left Monticello, what dreams they had for their children? That December my colleague Dianne Swann-Wright and I went to Ohio to meet our
consultant, Beverly Gray, and to conduct the first interviews for an oral history
project called Getting Word.[1]

My initial expectation that we would collect full-blown stories of life at Monticello turned out to be a pipe dream. Time—four to six generations of it—was
part of the problem. Also, the human urge to erect a mental barrier against a
negative past, in this case, the cruelties and indignities of centuries of slavery, has
erased great swaths of historical memory. What remains today is what was most
important to the tellers and listeners, what validated their identities and preserved their values. Chosen pieces of the past were transmitted carefully from
person to person, shaped and polished by generations of hands. Since 1993 we
have traveled thousands of miles to collect these shards of history, recording interviews with over 170 people and spending hours in church graveyards and
dusty courthouse cellars to fill in some of the blanks on the map of a forgotten
landscape.

We have encountered the almost universal themes of the importance of education, the centrality of the church, and the formidable strength of family bonds. In

the case of the Hemings family, we have heard the enduring story of descent from Jefferson and met the ambiguous issues of racial identity.[2] We have also been continuously reminded that people enslaved at Monticello and their descendants were untiring in their efforts to make Jeffersonian ideals a reality—to make this country live up to the promise of its founding document. They believed in the truth of the Declaration's preamble, cherished the hope that it would one day be more than an ideal, and joined with, and often led, countless other African Americans in the cause. This propensity to wage a continuous campaign to end slavery, oppression, and social injustice is especially conspicuous in the descendants of Elizabeth Hemings. Betty Hemings, the daughter of a slave and an English sea captain, came to Monticello with her children in the 1770s. She was a domestic servant who, according to her grandson, had six children by Jefferson's father in law, John Wayles. And one of those children, her daughter Sally, had six children by Jefferson himself.[3] From records research and in interviews with eighty of Betty Hemings's descendants, we have learned of a remarkable number of men and women who were crusaders, often on the front lines.

Descendants of Sally Hemings (1773–1835)

Descendants of Sally Hemings made their marks in two worlds, white and black. One of her grandsons, John Wayles Jefferson, commanded a white Wisconsin regiment in the Civil War, while a great-grandson, Frederick Madison Roberts, became the first black member of the California legislature. Roberts was the grandson of Madison Hemings, who moved with his family to southern Ohio in the late 1830s. Hemings initially worked as a carpenter and joiner in Waverly, one of the first so-called sundown towns, where no black people were permitted to live from its founding in 1829 until well into the twentieth century. He settled in a farming community of mostly light-skinned free blacks from Virginia (at least twenty of these families came from Albemarle County). Beverly Gray, Ohio historian and the generous and knowledgeable consultant for the Getting Word project, is descended from one of those mixed-race families. As a child she used to look after the cattle in her uncle's barn and always wondered why it had such a well-crafted staircase. Years later—after she began studying Afro-Virginians who settled in Ohio—she discovered that the barn had once been Madison and Mary Hemings's house. As she put it, she had been "standing in history" and did not know it.[4]

While Madison Hemings was able to fulfill the Jeffersonian dream of ownership of a small farm of sixty-six acres, he lived in a part of Ohio where there was

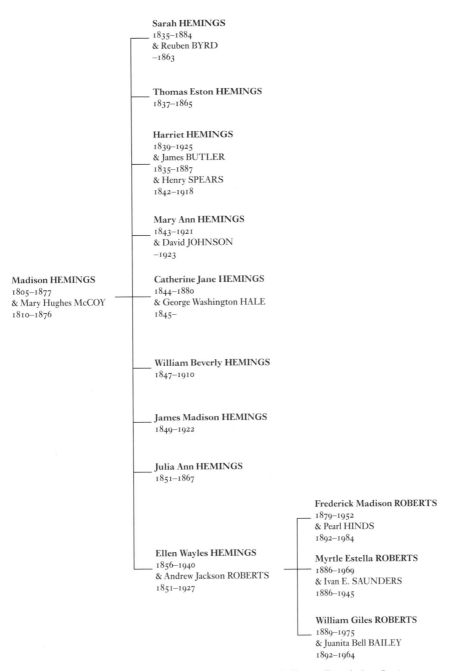

Sarah HEMINGS
1835–1884
& Reuben BYRD
–1863

Thomas Eston HEMINGS
1837–1865

Harriet HEMINGS
1839–1925
& James BUTLER
1835–1887
& Henry SPEARS
1842–1918

Mary Ann HEMINGS
1843–1921
& David JOHNSON
–1923

Madison HEMINGS
1805–1877
& Mary Hughes McCOY
1810–1876

Catherine Jane HEMINGS
1844–1880
& George Washington HALE
1845–

William Beverly HEMINGS
1847–1910

James Madison HEMINGS
1849–1922

Julia Ann HEMINGS
1851–1867

Frederick Madison ROBERTS
1879–1952
& Pearl HINDS
1892–1984

Myrtle Estella ROBERTS
1886–1969
& Ivan E. SAUNDERS
1886–1945

Ellen Wayles HEMINGS
1856–1940
& Andrew Jackson ROBERTS
1851–1927

William Giles ROBERTS
1889–1975
& Juanita Bell BAILEY
1892–1964

Hemings-Roberts Family (Getting Word Project; Thomas Jefferson Foundation, Inc.)

intense antiblack feeling. Some local whites were provoked by the prosperity of the Virginia mulatto community and "made almost constant war" on them, burning their hay and grain, harassing their livestock, and even making an armed raid on one home.[5] Several of the black families left the area forever. Madison and Mary Hemings remained, and by the time their youngest daughter, Ellen Wayles, was born in 1856, the violence had passed but not the hostility. In years when efforts to maintain schools were always under attack, the Hemingses made sure their children received a basic education. Ellen Wayles Hemings married a schoolteacher who studied at Wilberforce University and Oberlin. In 1884, when they had two young children, Ellen and Andrew Jackson Roberts became "pioneers." They left Ohio for southern California, arriving in Los Angeles in the midst of a boom. Roberts started out by hauling goods and people in a two-horse wagon. This modest beginning developed into the very successful Los Angeles Van, Truck and Storage Company. In his fifties, he opened the first black-owned mortuary in the city.

We have interviewed four of Ellen Hemings Roberts's grandchildren, only three generations distant from ancestors at Monticello. Like their cousins in Ohio, they have quietly and steadily passed on the story of descent from Jefferson as a genealogical fact. Patricia Roberts said, when we asked her connection to Monticello, "Thomas Jefferson is my great-great-grandfather. Period." What Roberts descendants chose to emphasize about their family was their California identity: in community service and leadership and as "one of the first founding families of Los Angeles."[6] Some are, however, perplexed by the marriage of Ellen Hemings to a man Patricia Roberts recalled as "Nubian black." A. J. Roberts, who described himself as "pure African," was a novelty in this family whose members were often indistinguishable from white people. Ellen Roberts herself, in the words of her granddaughter Lucille Balthazar, "looked like a Caucasian woman," with "very piercing blue eyes."[7]

When Dianne and I first went to Ohio, we mistook some of Madison Hemings's descendants for white people. Generation after generation, they have maintained their light complexions by choosing marriage partners who looked like themselves. While every generation had cases, principally men, who chose to cross the color line to live as white, those who remained identify themselves proudly as people of color. George (Jack) Pettiford, a descendant of Ellen Roberts's sister Sarah Hemings Byrd, had to strenuously resist being placed in a white unit when he enlisted in the navy in World War II. His widow remembered him saying, "I want to be what I am." Patricia Roberts was often asked, "What are you? (They couldn't quite get it.) Are you Tahitian?" When we asked her if she had ever considered passing for white, she responded, "Oh, oh, absolutely not! Under any circumstance! That was the way we were brought up, to take pride in who we were." When Ellen Hemings Roberts was asked by her grandchildren if she was black or white, "she would not answer."[8]

Ellen Hemings's marriage to a dark-skinned man was so unusual that her family seemed to need to find reasons for it other than mutual affection. And her way of playing favorites with her grandchildren did nothing to dispel this perception. Lucille Balthazar told us that her blond, blue-eyed brother was usually greeted with, "Billy, now what would you like Grandmother to cook for you?" But there were no special doughnuts and fried apple pies for brown-skinned Lucille, whom Ellen called "little black gal."[9] Some of Ellen Roberts's descendants believe that she resented her father for compelling her, at age sixteen, to marry an older, darker man who would be able to care for her after his death. The records show, however, that she and her husband were twenty-two and twenty-seven when they married and that the wedding took place a year after Madison Hemings died. The fact that Ellen Roberts named her firstborn son after her father also conflicts with this explanation.

No one heard of an arranged marriage from Ellen Roberts herself. In fact, she was never heard to speak of her father or her family back in Ohio. Everyone remembered her as well-spoken, with a caustic wit, but her actual words have been forgotten. When Gloria Roberts lived with her grandmother during her childhood, they never talked much; they just knitted, quilted, or washed dishes together. When the fish wagon came by, "Grandmama would pick out what fish

Andrew J. Roberts (1851–1927) and Ellen Wayles Roberts (1856–1940), Los Angeles. (Courtesy of the African American Museum and Library at Oakland)

she wanted and she'd always get a tiny little fish for me so that . . . while she's cleaning the fish, I had my little fish to try to clean." She was "my playmate, my best friend, my everything." Ellen Roberts showed her resourcefulness in 1927 when her husband died while they were vacationing in Baja, California. When the Mexican authorities refused to allow the return of his body to Los Angeles, she had him well dressed and placed beside her in the backseat of their car. They were then driven across the border. As Patricia Roberts said, "She was feisty right to the end."[10]

The son of the very dark A. J. Roberts and his nearly white wife stood out from the crowd from an early age. Frederick Madison Roberts was the first black to graduate from Los Angeles High School, attended the University of Southern California, and was a debater and football star at Colorado College. He remained for some years in Colorado Springs, where he was a county tax assessor and edited a weekly newspaper. He took time out in 1907 for a gold-prospecting adventure in western Nevada, during which he was lost in the desert near Death Valley for two days and nights. He studied mortuary science in Chicago and returned to Los Angeles to join the family firm. In the pages of the weekly *New Age*, which he purchased in 1912 and edited for decades, he championed a golden West of equality and opportunity, encouraged black business enterprise, and launched fierce attacks against all forms of discrimination. Fred Roberts was an active member of the local branch of the NAACP and the National Urban League, of which his father was a vice president. In 1915 he protested production of D. W. Griffith's film *The Clansman* (soon retitled *Birth of a Nation*) and joined in the unsuccessful effort to ban it in Los Angeles theaters, fearing the film would destroy "the best feeling" in the West: "Money rather than morality will rule the situation."[11]

Late in 1915 Roberts was called to lead the Normal and Industrial Institute in the all-black community of Mound Bayou, Mississippi, returning to Los Angeles after a year. In 1918, he boldly ran for the state assembly in an overwhelmingly white district. His Democratic adversary circulated campaign cards bearing the statement, "My opponent is a nigger," while Roberts ran on "his merit as an American citizen" and won that election and seven more. He introduced seventeen bills in his first session, one of them to strengthen the civil rights law. Yet in his sixteen years as a legislator, he focused on far more than race issues, promoting a broad range of public welfare initiatives. In the words of his widow, he was not just the first black California assemblyman but "the first black elected to a State office west of the Mississippi."[12]

In the 1920s, Frederick Roberts struggled to maintain his faith in an ideal of the egalitarian West, as white southerners flocked to Los Angeles and the Ku Klux Klan, its revival ignited by *Birth of a Nation*, gained a foothold in the city. When the film was brought back in 1921, shortly after the devastating race riot in

Frederick Madison Roberts (1879–1952).
(Courtesy of Patricia Roberts)

Tulsa, Oklahoma, he again spoke out. *Birth of a Nation*, he wrote, was "not an entertainment, it is un-American propaganda." The next year, in speaking of the threat to the western ideal posed by southern racial views, he said that "the very existence of the principles, upon which our nation was founded are at stake."

Roberts remained a loyal Republican and thus lost his ninth contest for a seat in the legislature in 1934, when blacks were realigning behind Franklin D. Roosevelt's Democratic Party. He twice ran for Congress and lost, the second time to Helen Gahagan Douglas, who in 1950 would originate the term "Tricky Dick." Although Roberts's political career wound down, his reputation in California and in the national Republican Party always remained high. As one author noted, "No Negro on the whole Pacific coast is more influential among his own people or among the population in general." In 1952, Roberts was apparently "slated to receive an ambassadorship" if Dwight D. Eisenhower was elected—he had always wanted to go to Africa—but his life was cut short by an automobile accident shortly after his return from the Chicago convention.[13]

Descendants of Betty Brown (1759–after 1831)

Elizabeth Hemings's daughter Betty Brown had seven surviving children. Wormley Hughes, the oldest, was head gardener and coachman at Monticello. His wife, Ursula, was a niece of Isaac (Granger) Jefferson, whose photograph in his blacksmith's apron has been an iconic image of a once-enslaved man since its first publication in the 1950s. Wormley and Ursula Hughes's children remained in slavery until the end of the Civil War, after which they made rapid strides in acquiring land, building schools, and founding churches in Albemarle County. Some of their present-day descendants trace their strong characters and family values to Monticello and their ancestors there. We have as yet found no descendants of Hughes's half brother Burwell Colbert, Monticello butler and Jefferson's last, and much valued, personal servant. Colbert's younger brother Brown, who worked in the Mulberry Row nail-making shop, formed a union with a slave belonging to John Jordan, a resident white brick mason. In 1805, when Jordan was about to leave Monticello, Brown Colbert asked to be purchased so he and his wife would not be separated. Colbert thus became a blacksmith in Jordan's flourishing mills and workshops on the Maury River in Lexington, in Virginia's Shenandoah Valley.

In 1832, Brown Colbert wanted to be free. But how could an enslaved blacksmith living in rural Virginia achieve freedom for not only himself but his wife and a number of children? His chances of being emancipated were almost nil, and running away with a large family was a virtual impossibility. It would have taken decades to save enough money from "overwork" in his free time to purchase so many enslaved people. Brown Colbert made the courageous decision to take the one available path to freedom: he removed with his family to the west coast of Africa and thus fulfilled a provision of a plan that Jefferson endorsed all his life but did little to implement—a plan of gradual emancipation that called for the removal of freed people from the United States. John Jordan evidently freed Colbert and his wife, and the freedom of their two youngest sons was purchased with funds from the American Colonization Society; all the emancipations were contingent on the Colberts' departure from American soil. In January 1833 Brown Colbert, described as "a pious man & first rate blacksmith," boarded the brig *Roanoke* in Norfolk with his wife Mary, sons Edwin and Burwell, a sister, and a niece. They had an easy crossing to the Liberian capital, Monrovia. Tragically, half the family fell immediate victim to the west African malarial fever that killed 25 percent of American emigrants in their first year. Of the six Colberts, only the son Burwell survived to appear in the first census ten years later. If Burwell Colbert lived another five years, he saw the colony become Africa's first independent republic. Its Declaration of Independence, modeled on

Jefferson's, included the words: "We recognize in all men certain inalienable rights; among these are life, liberty, and the right to acquire, possess, enjoy, and defend property."[14]

The pathos of the family's fateful journey was heightened by the fact that Brown and Mary Colbert had crossed the ocean without their older children, who remained in slavery in Virginia for another thirty years. Descendants of their two oldest sons, in keeping with the pattern of suppressing negative memories, had never heard of their ancestors' gamble on freedom in Africa. Then, in 2007, we were contacted by a descendant of the Colberts' daughter Melinda, who had escaped our notice, hidden in the post-Emancipation records by her husband's surname. As a boy, Bill Webb would often climb up to the attic, unwrap an old family Bible, and read the information in the family record pages. He was fascinated by an entry that said: "Brown Colbert . . . emigrated to Liberia in 1833 and died soon after landing." Years later, he and his wife Eva Kobus-Webb embarked on an extensive research project on Melinda Colbert Edmondson's line and have shared with us stacks of material on this previously unknown branch of the Colbert family, full of new and interesting personalities.

Melinda Colbert Edmondson's son George Edmondson served with the all-black 25th Army Corps in the last year of the Civil War and was among the first Union troops to enter Petersburg after the siege was broken. Her granddaughter Mary Franklin married John R. Clifford, eminent West Virginia attorney and newspaper publisher. Mary Clifford's sister was, as far as we know, the most publicly active female descendant of the Monticello enslaved community. One day, as Dianne and I sat at my dining room table trying to turn fifteen years of research into a book, we asked each other, "Who was the first descendant of Monticello's African Americans to go to college?" We guessed that it would be one of the grandsons of Eston Hemings, whose family lived as white from about 1850. Or perhaps a member of one of the families that became free well before the Emancipation Proclamation. To our surprise, the first college graduate was black, not white, achieved freedom only after the Civil War, and was a woman.

Brown Colbert's great-granddaughter Coralie Franklin Cook left no descendants to remember her, but she spoke and wrote her way into the historical record. She graduated from Storer College in 1880, a few years before Eston Hemings's grandsons graduated from the University of Wisconsin. Storer, in Harper's Ferry, West Virginia, was not yet a B.A.-granting college, but she completed its college-level program, one of the few in the Upper South open to blacks. She was described, while still at college, as "an elocutionist of grace, skill and power."[15] She pursued further studies up and down the eastern seaboard, taught English and elocution at Storer and then at Howard University, and was constantly called to the podium. She impressed her white audiences at meetings of the National

Council of Women, giving the "finest paper" at the Atlanta Exposition in 1895 and being hailed as "a revelation" in New York in 1899.[16]

In 1896 Coralie Franklin was one of the founders of the National Association of Colored Women, an organization of black women activists formed more than ten years before the NAACP and still active today. It campaigned for improved education and child welfare and against lynching and Jim Crow laws. When she was thirty-seven, Franklin married George William Cook, also born in slavery, who served Howard University for almost sixty years as professor, dean, secretary-treasurer, acting president, and trustee. In Washington, she served on many boards, was active in numerous civic organizations, and was a speaker at countless graduations and cultural and commemorative events in the city. She was the longest-lasting member of the District of Columbia Board of Education in a turbulent period, serving for twelve years, and she has made her way into just about every biographical dictionary of black women.

In 1902, Susan B. Anthony hosted a "brilliant" reception for Coralie Cook, who was in Rochester on a lecture tour. Cook considered Anthony a friend and greatly admired her, describing her as one of "the immortal few who have stood for the great principles of human rights" and predicting, after her death in 1906, that "thousands of torches lighted by her hand will yet blaze the way to freedom for women."[17] But Coralie Cook's experience in the Woman Suffrage Association was, in the end, disheartening. In 1921 she wrote that although "born a suffragist" and "once an ardent supporter and member," she was no longer active, as the organization "had turned its back on the woman of color." Cook and other African Americans who came of age after the Civil War and lived into the

Coralie Franklin Cook (1861–1942). (From November 1917 issue of the *Crisis Magazine*; courtesy of the Crisis Publishing Co., Inc.)

twentieth century had to face a demoralizing transformation. A time of great hope, when it seemed that the promise of equality might be fulfilled, gave way to decades of lynchings and Jim Crow laws. When they were in their fifties, Coralie and George Cook found comfort in the Baha'i Faith, based on the principle of the oneness of mankind and the equality of all races and of women and men. A letter she wrote to the son of the founder of the faith in 1914 illustrates how she held on to her ideals in the midst of bitter discouragement. Speaking of the efforts of "hot-headed demagogues" to annul the effects of the Fourteenth and Fifteenth Amendments to the Constitution, she welcomed the "uncompromising opposition from some few members of both houses of Congress who have not yet forgotten the Declaration of Independence nor that message handed down through the ages: 'He hath made of one blood all nations of men.'"[18]

Descendants of Mary Hemings Bell
(1753–after 1834)

Elizabeth Hemings's oldest child, Mary, was hired out to and then purchased and freed by white Charlottesville merchant Thomas Bell. Although the laws of Virginia prevented their legal marriage, they lived as husband and wife, and Bell bequeathed his considerable estate to their two children. Mary, described in one court document as Bell's "relict & widow," received a life interest in it. While Mary Hemings Bell lived in freedom, four of her older children remained in slavery. One of them, Joseph Fossett (1780–1858), head blacksmith at Monticello, was progenitor of a line of strong-willed activists.

All three branches of the Hemings family have stories of descent from Jefferson. Whereas this is the main—and often the only—story in Sally Hemings's line, it is secondary for Mary Hemings's descendants. Their stories highlight actions to end slavery and bring about racial equality, reflecting essential values in Fossett family memory. They recalled industrious, resourceful, and courageous ancestors who successfully helped people out of unjust situations. The core truth of these stories is borne out by the historical record. Jefferson, who described Joseph Fossett as "strong and resolute," gave him his freedom in his will. Six months later Fossett watched his wife, head cook Edith Hern Fossett, and their children sold from the auction block. The blacksmith struggled to reunify his family, working at his trade to buy them out of slavery and take them to the safety of the free state of Ohio. In the case of his son Peter Fossett, this took twenty-five years. Peter in the meantime secretly perfected his writing skills and taught his fellow slaves to read late at night, by the light of a pine knot. Some he liberated by forging free papers. Peter Fossett and most of his family were eventually re-united in freedom in Cincinnati, where they were prominent in a wide range of community activities. They were in the forefront of the struggle for educational opportunities, their homes were safe houses in the Underground Railroad, and they were pillars of the Baptist church. In 1870 Peter Fossett became a minister and founded his own church. His brother Jesse, ever going against the grain, was a particularly conspicuous example of the independent spirit in the Fossett family. Described as "a power among his own people," he instigated several civil rights test cases and was an early advocate of dividing the black vote, an unpop-ular position in the face of the vast majority of blacks still loyal to the party of Abraham Lincoln.[19]

Peter and Jesse Fossett's sister Ann-Elizabeth had married Tucker Isaacs, a "much respected" free man of color in Charlottesville, a successful contractor and painter who erected some of the first brick buildings on Main Street. In 1850 Isaacs was arrested for forging free papers for his enslaved brother-in-law Peter Fossett. Although charges were dropped, shortly afterward the Isaacses thought it best to sell their properties in Charlottesville and leave for Ohio, where they eventually settled on a 158-acre farm on a hill east of Chillicothe. In the summer of 1995, Beverly, Dianne, and I bounced up that hill in the back of a pickup truck to what is still called the "Isaacs place." We saw a well-maintained barn, packed with bales of hay, and an uninhabited log house drifting toward ruin. Ann-Elizabeth Fossett's cupboard, its glass panes painted sky blue, still perched on the broken floor boards in what had evidently been the kitchen. We talked to descendants of the Isaacses' white neighbors and heard how the black and white families shared hunting expeditions and farming tasks. The farm was "good wheat ground" and, after the grain was cut, Ann-Elizabeth Isaacs would lay on a splendid harvest supper for all. She put a bit of vinegar on the tomatoes to keep her guests "from getting the bellyache." We also were told of the light that shone from the Isaacs farmhouse as a nighttime beacon to fugitive slaves. Theirs was a safe house on one of the main routes of the Underground Railroad for runaways from Virginia.[20]

After the Civil War and the end of slavery, Tucker Isaacs did not abandon his fight for justice. He tested an Ohio civil rights law by seeking accommodation at a hotel and suing it when he was refused a room. This was a courageous act, since the hotel was the building that Madison Hemings had helped to construct in the intolerant "sundown" town of Waverly. Isaacs was an early defector from the Republican Party, warning of its "coming betrayal." Fifty years later family memory portrayed him as having to protect himself "from his hostile colored auditors with his big hickory cane."[21] Because they acted on a domestic stage,

Ann-Elizabeth Fossett Isaacs
(1812–1902). (*Ebony Magazine*,
November 1954)

Joseph and Edith Fossett's daughters and granddaughters reveal their characters only faintly in the historical record. That they, too, carried the family traits of independence, strength and determination, and a passion for equality can be inferred from their marriage choices. Tucker and Ann-Elizabeth Isaacs's daughter Virginia married a man in the mold of her father and grandfather. James Monroe Trotter, who often spoke of his admiration for "grit," displayed it in the political arena and on the field of battle.[22]

At least eight of Betty Hemings's great- or great-great-grandsons served in the Union army in the war, four of them in white regiments. Trotter, son of a white Mississippi plantation owner and a slave, and his close friend William H. Dupree, who married Virginia Isaacs's sister, responded to the call for recruits in 1863, when the first regular army regiment of African American soldiers was raised. They headed for Boston and, arriving too late to join the 54th Massachusetts Volunteer Infantry, they enlisted in its sister regiment, the 55th. As we began to explore the frighteningly vast resources on the conflict, we were astounded to realize that the only three black men in the 55th Massachusetts who were fully commissioned officers by the end of the war were all connected to

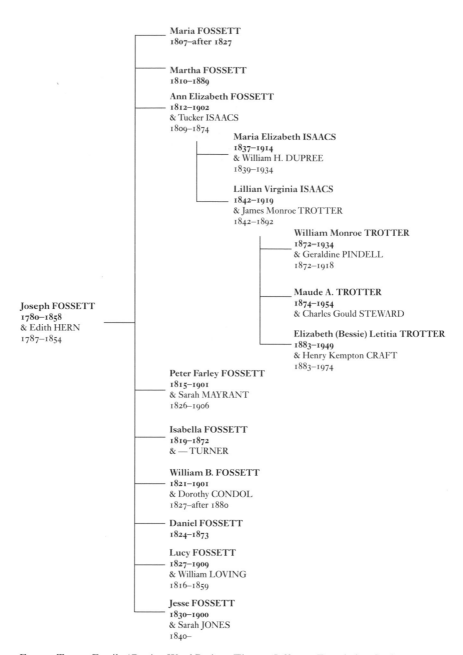

Maria FOSSETT
1807–after 1827

Martha FOSSETT
1810–1889

Ann Elizabeth FOSSETT
1812–1902
& Tucker ISAACS
1809–1874

Maria Elizabeth ISAACS
1837–1914
& William H. DUPREE
1839–1934

Lillian Virginia ISAACS
1842–1919
& James Monroe TROTTER
1842–1892

William Monroe TROTTER
1872–1934
& Geraldine PINDELL
1872–1918

Maude A. TROTTER
1874–1954
& Charles Gould STEWARD

Elizabeth (Bessie) Letitia TROTTER
1883–1949
& Henry Kempton CRAFT
1883–1974

Joseph FOSSETT
1780–1858
& Edith HERN
1787–1854

Peter Farley FOSSETT
1815–1901
& Sarah MAYRANT
1826–1906

Isabella FOSSETT
1819–1872
& — TURNER

William B. FOSSETT
1821–1901
& Dorothy CONDOL
1827–after 1880

Daniel FOSSETT
1824–1873

Lucy FOSSETT
1827–1909
& William LOVING
1816–1859

Jesse FOSSETT
1830–1900
& Sarah JONES
1840–

Fossett-Trotter Family (Getting Word Project; Thomas Jefferson Foundation, Inc.)

Monticello by marriage or descent: Trotter, Dupree, and John Freeman Shorter, a great-grandson of Mary Hemings's sister Betty Brown. The experience of the soldiers of the 55th Massachusetts paralleled that of the more famous 54th. They too went without pay for a year and a half, rather than accept less than what white soldiers received.

Virginia Craft Rose and Ellen Craft Dammond, Elizabeth Hemings's fourth great-granddaughters, never knew their grandfather James M. Trotter. They did know about his stand on the pay issue. Virginia Rose, then ninety-two, told us that her grandfather "instigated a protest" against unequal payment for black soldiers. She and her sister went to see the 1989 film *Glory*, and when Denzel Washington took the lead in the pay crisis scene, they looked at each other and said, "'Do you think that's Grandfather Trotter?' Because we had remembered that story. That was just one of the family stories." They wondered if Washington "had known about Grandfather Trotter and was emulating him or whether that was just a part that he was given." While they were right to see Trotter as a model for Denzel Washington's role, it is unlikely the actor knew of their grand-father. The film script created fictional characters for the black soldiers, while Robert Gould Shaw and some other white officers were historical figures. The actual men of the 54th and 55th were invisible in the film, despite plentiful information about them. Trotter was one of the most vocal spokesmen in this struggle for equal pay, and white officers at the time mentioned him as a leader in the controversy. On one occasion his remarks were described as being "especially good." As Trotter explained his position in a letter, the soldiers of the two Massachusetts regiments stood on "the great Principle . . . for the attainment of which we gladly peril our lives—Manhood & Equality."[23] Trotter's Civil War sword is proudly displayed in his great-granddaughter's front hall.

Trotter, Dupree, and Shorter were promoted to second lieutenant in the spring of 1864, but because the War Department did not allow black officers until the end of the war, they had to carry out their officer's duties without recognition or privileges. Their commissions finally arrived after General Lee's surrender—and after Shorter and Trotter had been wounded in November 1864, helping to lead their companies in the Battle of Honey Hill. Both Trotter and Shorter wrote of "the new order of things now arising" that Shorter did not live to see and in which Trotter and Dupree played significant parts.[24]

After mustering out, they settled in Boston, returning to Ohio to marry the Isaacs sisters. As the only fully commissioned black army officers in the city, they were conspicuous figures, with influential white friends and a broader choice of careers than most black men. They joined the U.S. Postal Service as clerks, pioneers in one of the few white-collar workplaces then open to African Americans. The Trotters moved to the suburban town of Hyde Park, a mostly white neighborhood of large houses, wide lawns, and tall elm trees. There they raised three children in an atmosphere that was far more free from segregation than Ohio. It was a kind of golden age in race relations in Boston, soon to fade. The Trotters and Duprees were prominent in the ranks of the Boston black elite, deeply committed to high culture. James Monroe Trotter published a book on African American classical musicians and composers, the first survey of American music of any kind, described as a "landmark in the field." He and Dupree managed the careers of several black musicians and elocutionists, including the soprano Madame Marie Selika, who toured Europe to rave reviews. All the Trotter children had piano lessons, and they went to Harvard, Wellesley, and in the case of the youngest, Bessie, the New England Conservatory of Music. After a visit to Boston, African American newspaper editor T. Thomas Fortune named Virginia Trotter and Maria Dupree among the ladies "who impressed me with their charming sociability and cultured manners."[25]

James Monroe Trotter resigned from the post office in 1883, again in protest against unequal treatment in connection with compensation. He left to "once more breathe the pure air of freedom" and to "win my bread in a manly way." Like his wife's father and uncle, he, too, renounced the "oldtime usual tame Negro obeisance to the Republican party," believing that blacks "could only get just and fair treatment by the wise and judicious use of the ballot." He worked with reform-minded white Republicans (soon to be called Mugwumps) and tried to persuade Massachusetts blacks to become "colored Independents."[26]

In 1884 he campaigned for Grover Cleveland and thereafter accepted the label Democrat. In a controversial move in 1887, since Trotter was a nonresident as well as a black man, President Cleveland appointed him Recorder of Deeds for the District of Columbia. The position, which had earlier been held by Frederick Douglass, was the highest government office then open to blacks and one of the most lucrative civil service posts in the nation. The appointment, which everyone expected would be rejected by the Republican Senate, was national news for several days—a period Trotter referred to as "this great race crisis."[27] The Senate confirmed him, however, for mainly political reasons, although Trotter's war record was a definite benefit. Republicans feared a mass defection of Massachusetts blacks if they blocked the appointment, and it was clear that the president was determined to fulfill, in this instance at least, his inaugural pledge to accord African Americans their full rights as citizens. Two weeks later, the new Recorder fell seriously ill with pneumonia at the boardinghouse of Harriet Jacobs, the famous former slave who had hidden for years in an attic room in Edenton, North Carolina. Summoned by telegraph from Boston, Virginia Trotter joined Jacobs in caring for her husband, who was unable to resume his duties for two months.[28]

William Monroe Trotter (1872–1934), ca.
1895. (Courtesy of Harvard University
Archives; call no. HVD 295.04, vol. 2)

Trotter held his profitable post until early 1890, when Republican president
Benjamin Harrison appointed his successor, ex-Senator Blanche K. Bruce. He
never fully regained his health, withdrew from politics, and died at only fifty
in 1892. The Trotters' son was then a freshman at Harvard. William Monroe
Trotter, who would become the most famous of known descendants of Monticello's enslaved families, was valedictorian of his class at Hyde Park High
School, his best friends were white boys, and he was always striving to live up to
the boundless expectations of both of his parents. He graduated magna cum
laude from Harvard, becoming the first African American in its chapter of Phi
Beta Kappa. For years he viewed Harvard as his cousin Frederick M. Roberts
viewed California, as "the exemplar of true Americanism, freedom, equality,
and real democracy." When his father died, Monroe Trotter had offered to leave
college to help his mother manage the family real estate investments. But, as
one family account put it, she "proved equal to the task to carry on."[29] She supported her son's enterprises financially after 1901 when he gave up his real estate
business and upper-class lifestyle to begin publishing a weekly newspaper, the
Boston Guardian, which was soon read all over the country.

   After breathing the democratic air of Hyde Park and Harvard, William Monroe Trotter's world was beginning to contract, as the Jim Crow line moved in-
exorably up from the South. Boston hotels, restaurants, and theaters that had

been open to all started to close their doors to blacks. The harder he fought, the worse the national situation seemed to get, and Trotter's intransigent independence was not always an effective strategy. He first trained his sights on the accommodationist principles of Booker T. Washington, whom he labeled the Benedict Arnold of the Negro race, among other epithets. In 1903, two thousand people gathered in Boston to hear Washington speak. The event ended in chaos, and it is now impossible to know what really happened. Did someone really throw cayenne pepper at the speaker's stand? Did Trotter's sister Maude jab a policeman with her hatpin? William Monroe Trotter definitely led some vigorous heckling in an effort to get Washington to answer questions such as, "Is the rope and the torch all the race is to get under your leadership?" During what was called the Boston Riot, Trotter was taken directly to jail. The *Boston Globe* reported that "Mrs. Trotter, mother of the editor, went bail" for him, and probably not for the last time. In his long, militant, and uncompromising fight for "full equality in all things governmental, political, civil and judicial," Trotter presented petitions, led picketing and demonstrations, and confronted presidents in the White House. His methods of protest have been called fifty years ahead of his time.[30]

In 1905 Trotter and W. E. B. Du Bois took the lead in founding the Niagara movement, the seed that developed into the NAACP, and together they drafted its Declaration of Principles: "We pray God that this nation . . . will return to the faith of the fathers, that all men were created free and equal, with certain unalienable rights." Trotter kept his distance from the biracial NAACP, casting his lot with the older and "racially autonomous" organization, the National Equal Rights League.[31] In 1914 he had a turbulent encounter with President Woodrow Wilson, whom he had supported in the 1912 election, over the issue of segregation of black federal employees. Thus it is not surprising that Wilson did not look kindly on Trotter's efforts to influence the Treaty of Versailles in 1919. The Wilson administration denied passports to Trotter and most other African Americans who wished to participate in the Paris peace talks. This generated one of the family's favorite stories about "Uncle Monroe." As Virginia Rose put it, her uncle "stowed away on a ship as a cook and sailed to Versailles." He evidently took a crash course in cooking and haunted the New York docks until he got a post as a galley hand on a freighter. After jumping ship in Le Havre, he spent three months in Paris, sending telegrams, publishing appeals in newspapers, meeting with foreign delegates—pointing out the military contributions of racial minorities and deploring their exclusion from the benefits of liberty and democracy.[32] While he failed to get antidiscrimination provisos into either the peace treaty or the covenant of the League of Nations (referred to by Trotter as Woodrow Wilson's "Magna Charta of a new order of things"), he was a hero to many on his return, getting back "in time for his feeble mother to see Boston's welcome." In "her last hours" he told her of his unrelenting efforts on behalf of amendments to the treaty in the Senate Foreign Relations Committee. Speaking for the National Equal Rights League at the August hearings, he proposed adding to the treaty a clause pledging the participating nations to "agree to vouchsafe to their own citizens the possession of full liberty, rights of democracy, and protection of life, without restriction or distinction based on color, race, creed, or previous condition." Joseph and Edith Fossett's granddaughter Virginia Isaacs Trotter died in October 1919. Her son penned a tribute to her, in the third person:

> She taught [him] to stand against any denial of right because of race as a principle of self-respect. It was not strange she encouraged him when he entered the lists against race discrimination as only a true mother can, daily offered him cheer and confidence, and backed him for organ and organization with her earthly means. . . . That her sacrifice may not have been in vain we fight on.[33]

The ongoing exertions of William Monroe Trotter, who died a possible suicide in 1934, were mostly unavailing, as race relations continued to deteriorate. He struggled to keep the *Guardian* alive and quarreled with leaders of his own race (one friendly commentator wrote that he "has never been able to play ball on any team"). In the sesquicentennial year of 1926, Trotter made another trip to the White House and his last national effort, described at the time as a movement for "the fulfillment of the preamble of the Declaration of Independence." He invoked Jefferson's words in asking President Calvin Coolidge to end segregation in government offices on the anniversary of the "Republic's first document which enunciated equality and freedom." On July 2 he delivered a pile of petitions with 25,000 signatures to the president, who did little to remedy the situation. The next year one African American newspaper said of Trotter, "He stands as a lone figure" whose voice "comes like a hollow cry from a wilderness." Yet "he stands undaunted, unbroken and defiant."[34]

William Monroe Trotter's younger sister Bessie often told her daughters what it was like to grow up in the Hyde Park household, a center of energetic protest, a place to hammer out strategies for carrying on the crusade. According to her daughter Ellen Dammond, "When the arguments got heated, when the pounding on the table became vociferous, . . . she would hide under the table and they would be beating the table above her head and she would be scared to death, but later she became a little more militant in her attitude, but she was always very sweet and gentle and quite a lady."[35] Their fighting forefathers and foremothers are models and inspirations for Trotter descendants today. Virginia Rose had

Bessie Trotter Craft (1883–1949).
(Courtesy of Peggy Dammond Preacely)

brought W. E. B. Du Bois's collected writings to her interview, and she read out what he said about her uncle for the videocamera and three generations of her family in the room. Du Bois summed up the colleague who had often tried his patience as "a man of heroic proportions, and probably one of the most selfless of Negro leaders during all our American history." Virginia Rose told us, "What I want the children to know is that, whatever you feel strongly about, fight for it because that's part of your heritage."[36]

Distant ancestors were replaced in family recollection by those closer in time who embodied the same spirit. Monticello, too, faded from memory as larger-than-life figures like William Monroe Trotter took the place of Joseph Fossett and Ann-Elizabeth Isaacs. Trotter's great-niece Peggy Dammond Preacely was active in the civil rights movement in the 1960s, sitting at hostile lunch counters and spending many days in jail. She felt her activism was "a continuation of some of my ancestors" and that she "had to do something in my lifetime to make a difference because Uncle Monroe did." She titled her essay in a recent book about the experience of women in the Student Nonviolent Coordinating Committee, "It Was Simply in My Blood."[37]

WE often speculate about whether these descendants of Sally, Betty, and Mary Hemings, who pursued the American dream in unison in different parts of the country, knew each other. William Monroe Trotter was often in Washington, D.C., Coralie Cook traveled to California, and Frederick Roberts went east for Republican conventions. Cook's brother-in-law worked with Trotter in the Niagara movement, and all three had some association with the NAACP. We may never know if they met each other or knew they had a common ancestor. Cook, Roberts, and Trotter can represent all the other Monticello descendants who did not make headlines but who also took stands in the continuous effort to fulfill the promise of the Declaration: families who literally built their churches and schools after Emancipation, parents who made sacrifices for educational opportunities for their children, fathers who cast votes in hostile southern towns, and mothers who helped desegregate playgrounds. In 1915, the year Booker T. Washington died, Elizabeth Hemings's descendants carried on their missions. In Los Angeles Frederick Madison Roberts unveiled a new masthead for his newspaper—a black Lady Liberty amid Californian mountains and orange groves—and protested the screening of *Birth of a Nation*. On the opposite coast William Monroe Trotter was again arrested and jailed for leading a demonstration against the film at a Boston theater. And in the nation's capital, Coralie Franklin Cook wrote a heartfelt plea for the enfranchisement of women, published in the NAACP's *The Crisis*: "Enlightened womanhood has so far broken its chains as to be able to know that to [serve humanity], woman should help both to make and to administer the laws under which she lives."[38]

Notes

Introduction

1. *MB.*
2. Kenneth M. Stampp, *The Peculiar Institution: Slavery in the Ante-Bellum South* (New York, 1956).
3. Peter S. Onuf, ed., *Jeffersonian Legacies* (Charlottesville, 1993).
4. This famous phrase was coined by novelist L. P. Hartley in *The Go-Between* (London, 1953).

"Those Who Labor for My Happiness"

The title of this essay in drawn from TJ's letter to Angelica Church, 27 Nov. 1793: "I have my house to build, my feilds to form, and to watch for the happiness of those who labor for mine" (*PTJ*, 27:449).

I would like to thank the Virginia Foundation for the Humanities and the Thomas Jefferson Memorial Foundation for their support of work on a related project. I could not have written this essay without those months spent considering the lives of Jefferson's slaves. I am also grateful to Peter Onuf, for suggestions about structure that were vital to the final product.

In my work on this subject I am following trails already blazed by others, notably James A. Bear, Jr., whose longtime interest in the Hemings family of Monticello has nourished my curiosity and informed far more of his work than the directly relevant "The Hemings Family of Monticello," *Virginia Cavalcade* 29, no. 2 (Autumn 1979): 78–87. Other useful accounts of the African American residents of Monticello include "To Possess Living Souls," chapter 4 in Jack McLaughlin, *Jefferson and Monticello: The Biography of a Builder* (New York, 1988), 94–145; and Elizabeth Langhorne, "The Other Hemings," *Albemarle Magazine*, Oct.–Nov. 1980, 59–66, and "A Black Family at Monticello," *Magazine of Albemarle County History* 43 (1985): 1–16. Note that in her discussion of the fate of Sally Hemings after Jefferson's death, in the latter article and in chapter 37 of *Monticello: A Family Story* (Chapel Hill, 1987), Langhorne mistakes her for Sally Cottrell, who was held by the Randolphs. Material on Jefferson and Monticello contributes to an excellent discussion of larger issues in Mary Beth Norton, Herbert G. Gutman, and Ira Berlin, "The Afro-American Family in the Age of Revolution," in *Slavery and Freedom in the Age of the American Revolution*, ed. Ira Berlin and Ronald Hoffman (Urbana, 1986), 175–191. Beware, however, of table 3, on page 184, which credits Jefferson with twice as many slaves as he actually had.

1. *Charlottesville Central Gazette*, 13 Jan. 1827. Only fragmentary documentation survives for the Jan. 1827 sale. Transactions are mentioned in occasional letters and in almost 30 sales slips, which note the purchase of only thirty-four slaves (Monticello Dispersal Sale receipts, ViU: 5291). Apparently all 130 slaves were not actually sold in 1827, as an account of a second sale of 33 slaves, 1 Jan. 1829, also survives (ViU: 8937).

2. Mary J. Randolph to Ellen Coolidge, 25 Jan. 1827, FLDA; Thomas Jefferson Randolph reminiscences, ViU: 1397. Randolph actually attended the sale; his sister Mary did not.

3. FB, 27.

4. TJ to Henry Rose, 23 Oct. 1801, *PTJ*, 35:495; TJ to Craven Peyton, 14 Nov. 1819, Betts, *Farm Book*, 145; TJ to James Madison, 26 July 1806, DLC; TJ to M. B. Jefferson, 2 Aug. 1815, Betts, *Farm Book*, 39.

5. Because of his surname, it has been suggested that Joseph Fossett may have been the son of William Fossett, a white carpenter working at Monticello from 1775 to 1779 (*MB* 391, 483, 486). Some of Joseph Fossett's descendants make the claim that Jefferson was his father (See Lerone Bennett, "Thomas Jefferson's Negro Grandchildren," *Ebony* 10 [Nov. 1954]: 78–80). Betty Hemings may actually have had 11 children at this time. Lee Marmon, researcher for Poplar Forest, makes the plausible suggestion that Doll (b. 1757), wife of Abraham, a carpenter, was her daughter ("Poplar Forest Research Report," pt. 3, Aug. 1991, 39).

6. Jefferson inaugurated his Farm Book with three lists of slaves at the time of the division of the Wayles estate: the first, a roll of his own 52 slaves in Albemarle County; the second, the 135 Wayles slaves and their locations; the third, a list of the combined total of 187, with new locations in three counties (FB, 5–18). In 1782 his Albemarle County total was 129, behind Edward Carter with 242 slaves and ahead of the estate of Robert Carter Nicholas, with 120 slaves (Lester J. Cappon, "Personal Property Tax List of Albemarle County, 1782," *Magazine of Albemarle County History* 5 [1944–1945]; 54, 69, 72). After the sale of his Goochland and Cumberland County lands in the 1790s, Jefferson's slave property was usually distributed in a ratio of three to two between his Albemarle and Bedford County estates—both about 5,000 acres. The combined totals for 1796, 1810, and 1815 were 167, 199, and 223 ("Jefferson's Slaves: Approximate Total Numbers," 8 Mar. 1990, Monticello Research Department). By the end of 1794, Jefferson had sold ninety slaves; he gave seventy-six to his sister and daughters on their marriages ("Negroes alienated from 1784 to 1794," Feinstone Collection, David Library of the American Revolution, on deposit at American Philosophical Society; this document is no doubt the missing page 25 of Jefferson's Farm Book).

7. TJ to John Wayles Eppes, 30 June 1820, ViU. On this particular occasion, he was grateful for Eppes's offer to buy slaves without moving them from Poplar Forest. This kept them "in the family." Isaac Jefferson's mother Ursula Granger was bought at the request of Martha Jefferson, because she was "a favorite house woman"; Jefferson purchased Nance Hemings the weaver on the resumption of textile production in 1795; and young men were needed for the digging of his canal in the 1790s (TJ to Archibald Thweatt, 29 May 1810, DLC; TJ to W. Callis, 8 May 1795, ViU; *MB* 957, 1153; TJ to John Jordan, 21 Dec. 1805, Betts, *Farm Book*, 21).

8. Jordan to TJ, 4 Dec. 1805, MHi; TJ to Jordan, 21 Dec. 1805 and 9 Feb. 1806, Betts, *Farm Book*, 21–22.

9. TJ to Randolph Lewis, 23 Apr. 1807, Betts, *Farm Book*, 26; TJ to Jeremiah Goodman, 6 Jan. 1815, *GB*, 540. This letter also suggests that Jefferson instructed his overseers to make some efforts to control behavior. Goodman, who interpreted the "home" rule too strictly, repeatedly "drove" Phill Hubbard from his wife Hanah's house and punished her for receiving him. Hubbard and his wife lived on different plantations, but both were part of the Poplar Forest estate. Jefferson intervened to facilitate their union.

10. TJ to Thomas Cooper, 10 Sept. 1814, *PTJ-R*, 7:651; Frederick Douglass, *Life and Times* (1881; repr. New York, 1983), 89.

11. TJ to Edward Coles, 25 Aug. 1814, *PTJ-R*, 7:605; Thomas Mann Randolph to TJ, 6 Mar. 1802, MHi; Martha J. Randolph to Nicholas P. Trist, 7 Mar. 1822, FLDA.

12. TJ to Joel Yancey, 17 Jan. 1819, MHi. Another statement expressing the value of slave women as producers of "capital" appears in TJ to John Wayles Eppes, 30 June 1820, ViU.

13. FB, 5, 52; TJ to Jeremiah Goodman, 5 Mar. 1813, *PTJ-R*, 5:663; "Negroes alienated from 1784 to 1794."

14. TJ to Randolph Jefferson, 25 Sept. 1792, *PTJ*, 24:416; TJ to Thomas Mann Randolph, 12 Oct. 1792, *PTJ*, 24:473; "Negroes alienated from 1784. to 1794."; TJ to W. Callis, 8 May 1795, *PTJ*, 28:346; FB, 24. Critta (ca. 1783–1819) eventually came to Monticello as the wife of the butler Burwell Colbert.

15. TJ to Nicholas Lewis, 12 Apr. 1792, *PTJ*, 23:408; "Negroes alienated from 1784. to 1794." Bell, whom Jefferson called "a man remarkeable for his integrity," acknowledged paternity of Bob and Sally and left his property in a life estate to Mary Hemings Wells [Wayles?] Bell in his will (TJ to William Short, 13 Apr. 1800, *PTJ*, 31:503; Albemarle County Will Book, No. 4, pp. 59–60.

16. Martha Randolph to TJ, 16 Jan. 1791, *PTJ*, 18:499.

17. FB, 41, 49.

18. Thomas Jefferson Randolph to [Pike County *Republican?*], 1874, ViU: 8937; Bear, 99–100; author's translation of F. A. F. La Rochefoucauld-Liancourt, *Voyage dans les Etats-Unis d'Amerique* (Paris, 1798–1799), 5:35. I use this in preference to the 1799 London edition, which, for

instance, translates *quarterons* as "mongrel negroes." The Comte de Volney also observed at Monticello, in the same summer, slave children "as white as I am" (Jean Gaulmier, *L'Idéologue Volney* [1951; repr. Paris, 1980], 371).

19. Madison Hemings's recollections (Fawn M. Brodie, *Thomas Jefferson: An Intimate Biography* [New York, 1974] 471–472); Bear, 4. Robert, James, Thenia, Critta, Peter, and Sally were allegedly the children of Jefferson's father-in-law John Wayles. In the words of Isaac Jefferson, "Folks said that these Hemingses was old Mr. Wayles's children" (Bear, 4). Madison Hemings stated the connection more emphatically in 1873. No reference to the Wayles-Hemings relationship has been found in the papers of Jefferson or his family. John Hemings was said to have been the son of Joseph Neilson, a white joiner resident at Monticello from 1775 to 1779 (Brodie, *Jefferson,* 475; *MB*, 390, 486).

20. The story that Jefferson was the father of slaves by Sally Hemings was first published by James Thomson Callender in the *Richmond Recorder* in the fall of 1802. It was carried through the nineteenth century in Federalist attacks, British critiques of American democracy, and abolitionist efforts to end slavery. Fawn Brodie's biography of 1974 revived the claim and suggested a romantic dimension—that the connection was not exploitative but a meaningful thirty-eight-year union. Oral traditions originating with the children of Sally Hemings strongly support the connection; Jefferson's daughter and grandchildren believed it a moral impossibility and suggested Jefferson's Carr nephews as more likely suspects. Both sides received their contemporary supporters, and Jefferson himself seems to have privately denied the charge in an 1805 letter to Robert Smith. Sources on the controversy include Douglass Adair, "The Jefferson Scandals," in *Fame and the Founding Fathers,* ed. Trevor Colbourn (New York, 1974), 160–191; Fawn Brodie's biography and her articles in *American Heritage* (23, no. 4 [June 1971]: 48–57, 97–100; 27, no. 6 [Oct. 1976]: 29–33, 94–99); Virginius Dabney, *The Jefferson Scandals: A Rebuttal* (New York, 1981); Dumas Malone, "Mr. Jefferson's Private Life," reprinted from *Proceedings of the American Antiquarian Society,* Apr. 1974; Minnie Shumate Woodson, *The Sable Curtain* (Washington, 1985), appendix. Michael Durey has recently somewhat refurbished Callender's image, demonstrating the likelihood that Callender took the story from what he considered reliable sources rather than making it up (Michael Durey, *"With the Hammer of Truth": James Thomson Callender and America's Early National Heroes* [Charlottesville, 1990], 157–163). Also, another birthdate has come to light. Sally Hemings's daughter, who did not survive infancy, was born about 7 Dec. 1799; Jefferson returned to Monticello from Philadelphia on 8 Mar. 1799 (TJ to John Wayles Eppes, 21 Dec. 1799, *PTJ*, 31:274; FB, 56).

21. Samuel Shepherd, *The Statutes at Large of Virginia* (Richmond, 1835), 1:123; TJ to Francis Calley Gray, 4 Mar. 1815, DLC.

22. Bear, 102, 122; FB, 130; Ellen Wayles Coolidge to Joseph Coolidge, 24 Oct. 1858, Coolidge Letterbook, 98–99, ViU. She cited the cases of "three young men and one girl" (Harriet Hemings). Besides Beverly Hemings, one of the three men was probably James Hemings (b. 1787), son of Sally's sister Critta. When he ran away from Monticello in 1804, only persuasion was exerted in an unsuccessful effort to bring him back. He briefly reappeared at Monticello in 1815, apparently as a free man (*MB*, 1315).

23. Gilbert Osofsky, ed., *Puttin' on Ole Massa* (New York, 1969), 64. Ellen Coolidge in 1858 blamed the "Irish workmen" building the Monticello house, "dissipated young men in the neighbourhood," and—in the case of the Hemingses—her own Carr uncles (Coolidge Letterbook, 100–102, ViU: 9090). Edmund Bacon reported that Thomas Jefferson Randolph's schoolmates were "intimate with the Negro women" (Bear, 88). Although no indictments of individual overseers have been found, the overseer class often took the blame, as the duc de La Rochefoucauld-Liancourt reported after his visit to Monticello in 1796 (*Voyage*, 5:35).

24. TJ to William Short, 18 Jan. 1826, Ford, 12:434. See also TJ to James Monroe, 24 Nov. 1801, *PTJ*, 35:719–720; TJ to Edward Coles, 25 Aug. 1814, *PTJ-R*, 7:604. The duc de La Rochefoucauld-Liancourt observed, in an unpublished paragraph of his travels, that fear of mixture lay at the root of Jefferson's reluctance to act on the emancipation issue: "The generous and

enlightened Mr. Jefferson cannot but demonstrate a desire to see these negroes emancipated. But he sees so many difficulties in their emancipation even postponed, he adds so many conditions to render it practicable, that it is thus reduced to the impossible. He keeps for example the opinion he advanced in his notes, that the negroes of Virginia can only be emancipated all at once, and by exporting to a distance the whole of the black race. He bases this opinion on the certain danger, if there were nothing else, of seeing blood mixed without means of preventing it" (author's translation, DLC microfilm of original manuscript in Bibliothèque Nationale).

25. Jefferson's first slave, Sawney, bequeathed him by his father, was described as "mulatto" (Peter Jefferson will, 13 July 1757, Albemarle County Will Book, No. 2, p. 33). So was Sandy, a carpenter who ran away from Shadwell in 1769 (advertisement, 7 Sept. 1769, *PTJ*, 1:33).

26. Harvest rolls 1795–1800, FB, 46, 58. At the time of Jefferson's death, Critta Hemings was married to free black Zachariah Bowles (Albemarle County Deed Book, No. 22, p. 412), and Mary was living in the property left her by merchant Thomas Bell. John Hemings's wife Priscilla was head nurse in the household of Martha and Thomas Mann Randolph. Peter Hemings's wife was also probably a Randolph slave, as she and her children lived at Monticello in 1810, after the Randolphs had moved there from Edgehill (Betts, *Farm Book*, 134).

27. "A slave . . . is born to live and labour for another," in *Notes on the State of Virginia*, ed. William Peden (Chapel Hill, 1954), 163.

28. TJ to J. B. Demeunier, 29 Apr. 1795, *PTJ*, 28:341.

29. FB, 111. Surviving nailery accounts are fragmentary. There are five pages of accounts, 1794 to 1796, bound with Jefferson's Ledger, 1767–1770, ViU, and a nailery account book, 1796–1800, in the William Andrews Clark Memorial Library, University of California, Los Angeles.

30. Nailery account book, Clark Memorial Library.

31. TJ to James Lyle, 10 July 1795, *PTJ*, 28:405; TJ to J. B. Deumeunier, 29 Apr. 1795, *PTJ*, 28:341.

32. TJ to James Maury, 16 June 1815, Betts, *Farm Book*, 490; TJ to Nicholas Lewis, 11 July 1788, *PTJ*, 13:343; TJ to Mary Jefferson Eppes, 11 Apr. 1801, *PTJ*, 33:570; TJ to Thomas Mann Randolph, 29 Jan. 1801, *PTJ*, 32:517.

33. TJ to Thomas Mann Randolph, 3 Feb. 1793, *PTJ*, 25:138; memorandum to Jeremiah Goodman, Dec. 1811, *PTJ-R*, 4:379–380.

34. TJ to Edmund Bacon, 6 Oct. 1806, MHi; Thomas Mann Randolph to TJ, 3 Jan. 1801, *PTJ*, 32:390–391; TJ to Randolph, 9 Jan. 1801, *PTJ*, 32:417–418; memorandum to Jeremiah Goodman, Dec. 1811, *PTJ-R*, 4:380.

35. Bear, 100; Ellen W. Randolph to Martha J. Randolph, 27–30 Sept. [1816?], FLDA.

36. FB, 77; TJ to George Jefferson, 3 Dec. 1801, *PTJ*, 36:10; Bear, 102; memorandum to Edmund Bacon, Oct. 1806, in Bear, 54.

37. TJ to Thomas Mann Randolph, 19 May 1793, *PTJ*, 26:65; TJ to Thomas Munroe, 4 Mar. 1815, Henry E. Huntington Library. Dinsmore's inventory of the Monticello joinery in 1809, listing over eighty molding planes among its tools, is further testament to the extraordinary work done on the mountaintop (inventory, 15 Apr. 1809, *PTJ-R* 1:135–136). Hemings usually spelled his name with two *m*'s.

38. TJ to Benjamin Austin, 9 Jan. 1816, LofA, 1371.

39. "Reminiscences of Madison Hemings," in Brodie, *Jefferson*, 474; Bear, 23. In 1799, thirteen-year-old nailer Phil Hubbard got a weekly ration of half a pound of beef and four salt herring, while Ned, a farm laborer the same age, had to share three-quarters of a pound of beef and six herring with five younger brothers and sisters (FB, 57; see also p. 135, for special meat rations for children working in both the nailery and the textile shop in 1810).

40. Nailery account book, Clark Memorial Library; *MB*, 1287. Davy, for instance, burned a kiln of 40 cords that yielded 1,276 bushels of charcoal, or 32 bushels to the cord; Jefferson therefore paid him a "premium" of 32 times $0.05, or $1.60 (*MB*, 1395).

41. *MB*, passim; see, for example, 1265, 1328, 1416.

42. Thomas Mann Randolph to TJ, 22 Apr. 1798, *PTJ*, 30:290; TJ to Randolph, 15 Feb. 1798, 29 Jan. 1801, *PTJ*, 30:114, 32:517; Randolph to TJ, 7 Feb. 1801, *PTJ*, 32:559; 3 Feb. 1798, *PTJ*, 30:79.

43. Bear, 97–99. Bacon names Jame Hubbard as the repentant thief. This is unlikely, however, as Bacon remembered that "he was always a good servant afterwards," whereas Hubbard was a chronic runaway throughout Bacon's tenure as overseer. His brother Phil is a more likely candidate for this incident.

44. TJ to James Dinsmore, 1 Dec. 1802, DLC; TJ to Thomas Mann Randolph, 23 Jan. 1801, *PTJ*, 32:499–500.

45. TJ to John Strode, 5 June 1805, DLC. The anonymous note in Jefferson's papers reporting the flogging of a slave woman, printed in McLaughlin, *Jefferson and Monticello*, 97, should be assessed with great caution. Jean Gaulmier, in *L'Idéalogue Volney*, gives the erroneous impression that Jefferson was the farmer Volney observed encouraging the pea planting of his slaves with an almost comic frenzy of whipping (370). This man was actually a French settler elsewhere in Virginia. I am grateful to C. M. Harris, editor of the William Thornton papers, for sharing his knowledge of Volney's manuscript journal, now in a private collection.

46. Bear, 97; TJ to Jeremiah Goodman, 26 July 1813, 6 Jan. 1815, *PTJ-R* 6:331, *GB*, 540. Nineteen-year-old Hercules's escapade was only the beginning of a life of resistance. He was involved in a poisoning case in 1819 and the assault of an overseer in 1822, after which he was sold (Joel Yancey to TJ, 1 July 1819, Betts, *Farm Book*, 44; TJ to Charles Clay, 9 Aug. 1819, typescript in ViU; McLaughlin, *Jefferson and Monticello*, 117–118).

47. TJ to Jeremiah Goodman, 26 July 1813, *PTJ-R*, 6:331; TJ to John Gorman, 18 Feb. 1822, Betts, *Farm Book*, 46. Most examples are from Poplar Forest, but some of the same behavior may be assumed for Monticello, where no letters had to be written to restore harmony.

48. I use the term "Monticello plantation" to encompass Jefferson's entire 5,000-acre operation in Albemarle County. It included the farms of Monticello and Tufton south of the Rivanna River and Shadwell and Lego on the north side.

49. Thomas Mann Randolph to TJ, 26 Feb. 1798, *PTJ*, 30:145; John Wayles Eppes to TJ, 10 Feb. 1803, ViU; TJ to James Madison, 16 Aug. 1810, *PTJ-R*, 3:35; *MB*, 1250–1251, 1271; James Oldham to TJ, 26 Nov. 1804, MHi; TJ to Thomas Mann Randolph, 5 June 1805, Betts, *Farm Book*, 153. Young James Hemings ran away because of Lilly's treatment (Oldham to TJ, 16 July 1805, MHi). For other harsh overseers, see TJ to Thomas Mann Randolph, 24 June 1793, *PTJ*, 26:356; TJ to Joel Yancey, 17 Jan. 1819, Betts, *Farm Book*, 43.

50. TJ to Reuben Perry, 16 Apr. 1812, *PTJ-R*, 4:620. Jefferson's grandson Thomas Jefferson Randolph continued this practice. One incident stuck fast in the memory of Randolph's six-year-old nephew, after a visit to Edgehill from his home in Boston. His uncle brought a slave guilty of a theft "before the house, in front of which all the slaves were assembled, and flogged him with a horsewhip" (*T. Jefferson Coolidge 1831–1920: An Autobiography* [Boston, 1923], 3).

51. Bear, 97.

52. TJ to Thomas Mann Randolph, 8 June 1803, Betts, *Farm Book*, 19. Jefferson's belief in the power of positive and negative example is apparent throughout his writings. He invoked example's "terror" at least twice more in this period. In 1803 he thought a convicted slave trader should serve his term "as a terror to others." In 1809 he fervently hoped that a slave who had plundered his baggage on its way up the James River should be hanged: "Some such example is much wanting to render property waterborne secure" (TJ to Christopher Ellery, 19 May 1803, Ford, 9:467; TJ to John Barnes, 3 Aug. 1809, *PTJ-R*, 1:408). I am indebted for these citations to Philip J. Schwarz, who generously shared his "Thomas Jefferson and Slavery: A Calendar of Manuscripts and Other Primary Sources."

53. TJ to John McDowell, 22 Oct. 1798, *PTJ*, 30:563; TJ to Reuben Perry, 10 May 1811, *PTJ-R*, 3:612–613.

54. Thomas Mann Randolph to TJ, 6 Mar. 1802, *PTJ*, 37:14; TJ to Randolph, 19 Apr. 1792, *PTJ*, 23:436, and 18 Feb. 1793, *PTJ*, 25:230.

55. TJ to Stevens Thomas Mason, 27 Oct. 1799, *PTJ*, 31:222; TJ to William Strickland, 23 Mar. 1798, *PTJ*, 30:212.

56. TJ to Joseph Dougherty, 31 July 1806, Betts, *Farm Book*, 22.

57. Bear, 104. John Freeman and Jack Shorter, footman and groom at the President's House, had accompanied Jefferson to Monticello (see *MB*, 1188).

58. Edy was at the President's House from at least the fall of 1802 until the spring of 1809. She bore three children in that period: an infant that did not survive in Jan. 1803; James, born Jan. 1805; and Maria, born Oct. 1807 (*MB*, 1091; FB, 128). Edy, who was only fifteen when she went to Washington, may have been considered too young by her parents for formal marriage. There seems to be no way of knowing whether Jefferson gave her the option of remaining at Monticello with Joe Fossett, and her family was ignorant of the depth of her connection, or knew it and chose to disregard it.

59. This section title is drawn from Isaac (Granger) Jefferson's reminiscences, in Bear, 19.

60. For stories told by descendants of Joe Fossett and his relatives, see Lucy C. Williams to Pearl Graham, 14 July 1947, ca. 22 Jan. 1948; Charles H. Bullock account of Peter Fossett, ca. Oct. 1949, DHU. The silver under the portico story was also told by the Jefferson-Randolph family; butler Martin Hemings fended off the British search while Caesar shared the dark space with the silver for eighteen hours (Henry S. Randall, *The Life of Thomas Jefferson* [Philadelphia, 1865], 1.338–339). Isaac Jefferson told another story of silver saved by his father, when Benedict Arnold's forces invaded Richmond earlier in the year (Bear, 8).

61. Bear, 13–14; Martha J. Randolph recollections, undated, *PTJ*, 16:168.

62. See, for instance, TJ to John McDowell, 22 Oct. 1798, *PTJ*, 30:563; TJ to John Hartwell Cocke, 3 May 1819, ViU; TJ to James Madison, 11 Apr. 1820, Betts, *Farm Book*, 420; TJ to John W. Eppes, 13 Oct. 1820, CSmH.

63. Brodie, *Jefferson*, 477; TJ to Thomas Mann Randolph, 4 Feb. 1800, *PTJ*, 31:360.

64. TJ to J. N. Demeunier, 26 June 1786, *PTJ*, 10:63; TJ to Thomas Cooper, 10 Sept. 1814, *PTJ-R*, 7:651; "Memorandums on a Tour from Paris to Amsterdam," 19 Apr. 1788, *PTJ*, 13:36, note 29; TJ to Thomas Mann Randolph, 28 July 1793, *PTJ*, 26:578; Richard Beale Davis, ed., *Jeffersonian America* (1954; repr. Westport, 1980), 149; Peden, *Notes*, 139, 143.

65. TJ to Nicholas Lewis, 29 July 1787, *PTJ*, 11:640; TJ to Samuel Biddle, 12 Dec. 1792, *PTJ*, 24:725; TJ to Edward Bancroft, 26 Jan. 1789, *PTJ*, 14:492; TJ to Thomas Mann Randolph, 19 Apr. 1792, *PTJ*, 23:436.

66. Margaret Bayard Smith, *The First Forty Years of Washington Society*, ed. Gaillard Hunt (New York, 1906), 68; Betts, *Farm Book*, 6; TJ to Edmund Bacon, 27 Feb. 1809, Betts, *Farm Book*, 28; memorandums to Jeremiah Goodman, 13 Dec. 1812 and 11 Nov. 1814, *PTJ-R*, 5:489, and Princeton University Library.

67. TJ to Jeremiah Goodman, 6 Jan. 1815, *GB*, 539; FB, 152, 165, 167.

68. *Charlottesville Daily Progress*, 25 May 1900; George Ticknor, *Life, Letters and Journals* (Boston, 1876), 1:36; Charles M. Wiltse and Harold D. Moser, eds., *The Papers of Daniel Webster* (Hanover, 1974), 1:371.

69. *MB*, 1245, 1392, 1399, 1402; FB, 116, 152; Edmund Bacon to TJ, 9 Sept. 1822, MHi.

70. Record of Cases Tried in Virginia Courts, 1768–1769, DLC; Mary Rawlings, ed., *Early Charlottesville: Recollections of James Alexander 1828–1874* (Charlottesville, 1963), 2. Jefferson's early legal notebook was later used for Monticello household accounts by his wife Martha (1772–1782) and granddaughter Anne Cary Randolph (1805–1808). In the three years of the latter's records, every adult slave (except Sally Hemings and the two cooks) sold chickens or eggs to the Jefferson household; more than half the adults sold garden produce.

71. *MB*, 928, 974, 1341, 1348; Nicholas Lewis accounts, 19 Sept., 28 Nov., 9 Dec. 1790, Ledger 1767–1770, ViU; Record of Cases, DLC; Lucia Goodwin, "Two Monticello Childhoods," in *Anniversary Dinner at Monticello* (Monticello, 1976), 2–3.

72. Peden, *Notes*, 139; TJ to Richard Richardson, 10 Feb. 1800, *PTJ*, 31:363; Bear, 22.

73. Eliza Trist to Nicholas P. Trist, 30 June 1819, DLC: Trist Papers; Virginia J. Randolph to "Mrs. and Miss Randolph," undated, FLDA; Bear, 4; Judith P. Justus, *Down from the Mountain: The Oral History of the Hemings Family* (Perrysburg, 1990), 89; Mary J. Randolph to Virginia Randolph, 27 Dec. 1821, FLDA.

74. Martha Jefferson to TJ, 3 May 1787, *PTJ*, 11:334; Martha Randolph to Benjamin F. Randolph, 27 Jan. [1836?], ViU. Eugène Vail published six songs and two stories in French in *De la Littérature et des hommes de lettres des Etats Unis d'Amérique* (Paris, 1841), 321–333. I am grateful to Mechal Sobel for providing copies of the relevant pages of this rare text. Elizabeth Langhorne provided commentary and translations back into English in "Black Music and Tales from Jefferson's Monticello," *Journal of the Virginia Folklore Society* 1 (1979): 60–67. See also Mechal Sobel, *The World They Made Together: Black and White Values in Eighteenth-Century Virginia* (Princeton, 1987), 141–142. I now (2011) think the Monticello informant was one of Martha's daughters.

75. Brodie, *Jefferson*, 474; *Charlottesville Daily Progress*, 25 May 1900; *New York World*, 30 Jan. 1898; Ellen Randolph to Virginia Randolph, 31 Aug. 1819, FLDA; Robert Pleasants to TJ, 1 June 1796, 8 Feb. 1797; TJ to Pleasants, [27 Aug. 1796], *PTJ*, 29:120, 177–178, 287–288; Peden, *Notes*, 137; TJ to Jared Sparks, 4 Feb. 1824, LofA, 1487.

76. TJ to Edward Bancroft, 26 Jan. 1789, *PTJ*, 14:492–493; Davis, *Jeffersonian America*, 149; instructions to Edmund Bacon, Oct. 1806, Bear, 54.

77. Israel Jefferson reminiscences, Brodie, *Jefferson*, 481; TJ–John Hemings correspondence, MHi; kitchen inventory, 20 Feb. 1796, *PTJ*, 28:610–611; Hannah to TJ, 15 Nov. 1818, MHi (there is a possibility this letter was written by an amanuensis); TJ to Thomas Mann Randolph, 25 Jan. and 8 Mar. 1798, *PTJ*, 30:56, 170; Albemarle County Deed Book, No. 29, p. 492, No. 36, p. 122.

78. There is one ambiguous payment in the 1806 Memorandum Book, to Benjamin Snead "for 2 1/2 mo[nth]s tuition of George's son" (*MB*, 1189). Isaac Jefferson's brother George Granger (1759–1799), a blacksmith, was always listed alone in Jefferson's Farm Book. His wife was probably either a free woman or a slave on a nearby plantation. Snead was a teacher at the neighborhood school attended by Jefferson's grandson, and if he was the same Benjamin Snead with whom Jefferson had dealings in the 1760s, he was also a weaver (Martha J. Randolph to TJ, 12 May 1798, *PTJ*, 30:346; *MB*, 150).

79. TJ to James Pemberton, 21 June 1808, DLC.

80. Mary J. Randolph to Ellen Coolidge, 11 Sept. 1825, FLDA; Cornelia Randolph to Ellen Coolidge, 30 May 1830, ViU. For "poisons" and "poisoners," see, for instance, Thomas Mann Randolph to TJ, ca. 19 Apr. 1800, *PTJ*, 31:523, and Joel Yancey to TJ, 1 July 1819, Betts, *Farm Book*, 44.

81. Auguste Levasseur, *Lafayette in America, in 1824 and 1825* (New York, 1829), 218. Fossett did pass on at least one overheard conversation to overseer Edmund Bacon (Bear, 117).

82. Mary J. Randolph to Ellen Coolidge, 25 Jan. 1827, FLDA; Monticello dispersal sale receipts, ViU: 5921.

83. TJ to Joseph Dougherty, 31 July 1806, Betts, *Farm Book*, 23; *Acts Passed at a General Assembly of the Commonwealth of Virginia* (Richmond, 1827), 127; Justus, *Down from the Mountain*, 121; Albemarle County Deed Book, No. 29, pp. 491–492. The shop on Lot 30 on Main Street was reserved in this deed but was probably purchased from its owner, Opie Norris, in a separate unrecorded transaction. Fossett bought the lot for $325 and sold it for $500 in 1844 (Deed Book, No. 42, pp. 9–10).

84. Albemarle County Deed Book, No. 4, pp. 59, 62–69, No. 35, pp. 219–220; William L. Norford, *Marriages of Albemarle County and Charlottesville, 1781–1929* (Charlottesville, 1956), 181. Since John Winn sued Jesse Scott and the Bells for a debt, they may have bought Betsy Ann from him (Deed Book, No. 29, p. 442, No. 36, pp. 121–122).

85. See Charlottesville Deed Book, No. 3, p. 270, for sale of the building out of the family 15 July 1892. Another probable link between Monticello and Charlottesville is Daniel Farley, whose house in the town may have been a Sunday gathering spot for Jefferson's slaves. In 1816 Moses

broke his leg "in a trial of strength in a wrestle with one of his fellows" and was "at Farley's" (Frank Carr to TJ, 18 Mar. 1816, Betts, *Farm Book*, 40). County records, which need further study, suggest that Farley is Mary Hemings's son, and Joe Fossett's brother, Daniel (b. 1772), given in the 1780s to Jefferson's sister Anna (FB, 24; "Negroes Alienated"; Albemarle County Will Book, No. 13, p. 44; Deed Book, No. 36, pp. 27–28).

86. Orra Langhorne, *Southern Sketches from Virginia 1881–1901*, ed. Charles E. Wynes (Charlottesville, 1964), 81–83. Sally and Jesse Scott's children did, in fact, attend the white school in Charlottesville. This work and a number of other sources on the Scotts were kindly brought to my attention by the staff of the Albemarle County Historical Society. Olivia Summers Dutcher deserves credit for sparking my interest in Jesse Scott and the resultant discovery of his connection with the Hemingses of Monticello. She is the owner of a delightful oil portrait of Scott with his violin, and she and her late husband assembled a great deal of information on the musician and his instrument.

87. *Charlottesville Daily Progress*, 25 May 1900; Justus, *Down from the Mountain*, 122–124; Charles H. Bullock account of Peter Fossett, ca. Oct. 1949, DHU.

88. Justus, *Down from the Mountain*, 122–124; Fossett obituary, Cincinnati newspaper, 1901, GWA.

Looking for Liberty

1. *Letters of Thomas Moore*, ed. Wilfrid S. Dowden (Oxford, 1964), 1:50–52; Howard Mumford Jones, *The Harp That Once—A Chronicle of the Life of Thomas Moore* (New York, 1937), 59. Moore and his contemporaries believed the odes he translated were the work of the sixth-century Greek poet Anacreon. The "Anacreontic" odes are now known to be productions of the Roman and Byzantine periods.

2. *Letters of Moore*, 1:66, 69; Jones, *The Harp That Once*, 68–69, 75–77.

3. Edmund Quincy, *Life of Josiah Quincy* (Boston, 1869), 92–93. The precipitating occasion had been a dinner at which Jefferson offered his arm and the place beside him at table to Dolley Madison, leaving Mrs. Merry to establish her own beachhead two seats further down. The president explained the pellmell policy as based on "the equality of individuals," which was the "principle of society as well as of government with us" (Merrill D. Peterson, *Thomas Jefferson and the New Nation* [New York, 1970], 731–734).

4. *Letters of Moore*, 1:67–68; preface to volume two of Moore's *Poetical Works* (1841), in *The Poetical Works of Thomas Moore* (New York, 1854), 22; Jones, *The Harp That Once*, 79, 253; Thomas Moore, *Epistles, Odes, and Other Poems* (London, 1806), 268.

5. Moore, *Epistles, Odes*, viii, 175–176, 178, 180, 214.

6. *Jeffersonian America: Notes on the United States of America Collected in the Years 1805–6–7 and 11–12 by Sir Augustus John Foster*, ed. Richard Beale Davis (1954; repr. Westport, 1980), 10–11; Sidney P. Moss and Carolyn Moss, "The Jefferson Miscegenation Legend in British Travel Books," *Journal of the Early Republic* 7 (Fall 1987): 257–258; Moore, *Epistles, Odes*, 209–211 (Moore slightly altered the wording of the quoted stanza in his 1841 edition). See Linda Kerber, *Federalists in Dissent* (Ithaca, 1970), 21–22, on Federalist use of "philosophical."

7. *Richmond Recorder*, 1 Sept. 1802; Kerber, *Federalists*, 51–52.

8. TJ to George Logan, 20 June 1816, Ford, 6:527; TJ to Martin Van Buren, 29 June 1824, Ford, 12:371–372; TJ to Thomas Allen, 12 Mar. 1805, DLC; TJ to William Short, 6 Sept. 1808, Albert Ellery Bergh, ed., *The Writings of Thomas Jefferson* (Washington, 1907), 12:159–160; TJ to Samuel Kercheval, 12 July 1816, Ford, 12:14; Margaret Bayard Smith, *The First Forty Years of Washington Society*, ed. Gaillard Hunt (New York, 1906), 396–397; William A. Burwell memoir, Burwell Papers, DLC.

9. Henry S. Randall, *The Life of Thomas Jefferson* (Philadelphia, 1857), 3:118–119; Davis, *Jeffersonian America*, 11.

10. Ellen Wayles Coolidge Letterbook, ViU, 76–79.

11. *Letters of Moore*, 1:397, 458–459; *The Journal of Thomas Moore*, ed. Wilfrid S. Dowden (Newark, 1983–1988), 1:39, 4:1380, 1385, 5:1903, 1908.

12. E. Millicent Sowerby, comp., *Catalogue of The Library of Thomas Jefferson* (Washington, 1955), vol. 4, nos. 4406, 4519; *Twopenny Post-Bag* in *The Poetical Works of Thomas Moore*, ed. A. D. Godley (London, 1929), 152; Ellen Randolph to Virginia Randolph, 28 Feb. [1816], FLDA; Ellen Coolidge Letterbook, ViU, 79; Ellen Coolidge to Martha J. Randolph, 11 Mar. [1831?], ViU: 9090. Moore's verses make repeated appearances in the Jefferson family scrapbook, M. E. R. Eppes souvenir album, and the Monticello music collection, all in ViU; in the album, Jefferson's granddaughter Cornelia inscribed Moore's "Song of Fionnuala," accompanying it with a water-color of Lir's daughter as a swan.

13. Ellen Coolidge Letterbook, ViU, 79; Randall, *The Life of Thomas Jefferson*, 3:118–119; Leon O'Broin, *The Unfortunate Mr. Robert Emmet* (Dublin, 1958), 164; *Irish Melodies* in Godley, *Poetical Works*, 181.

14. Jones, *The Harp That Once*, 59. Johnson's quotation appeared in *Taxation No Tyranny*; see *Political Writings*, ed. Donald J. Greene (New Haven, 1977), 454, in the *Yale Edition of the Works of Samuel Johnson*.

15. Sowerby, *Library*, vol. 1, no. 509; Frances Wright, *Course of Popular Lectures* (New York, 1829), 7; Wright, *Views of Society and Manners in America*, ed. Paul R. Baker (Cambridge, 1963), 175–176, 197, 267.

16. TJ to Frances Wright, 22 May 1820, *Thomas Jefferson Correspondence Printed from the Originals in the Collections of William K. Bixby*, ed. Worthington Chauncey Ford (Boston, 1916), 254–256; TJ to Lafayette, 4 Nov. 1823, Ford, 12:324. Jefferson referred to "our master Epicurus" in a letter to William Short, 31 Oct. 1819, Ford, 12:143.

17. Sarah N. Randolph, "Mrs. Thomas Mann Randolph," in *Worthy Women of Our First Century*, ed. Mrs. O. J. Wister and Miss Agnes Irwin (Philadelphia, 1877), 48; Frances Wright to Martha J. Randolph, 4 Dec. 1824, DLC; Wright to Julia and Harriet Garnett, 12–14 Nov. 1824, Houghton Library, Harvard University.

18. Jane Blair Cary Smith, "The Carysbrook Memoir," ca. 1864, ViU: 1378, pp. 72–73.

19. Lafayette to TJ, 1 June 1822, Gilbert Chinard, ed., *The Letters of Lafayette and Jefferson* (Baltimore, 1929), 409—see also 407, 437; Israel Jefferson's reminiscences, printed in Fawn Bro-die, *Thomas Jefferson: An Intimate History* (New York, 1974), 481; Drew R. McCoy, *The Last of the Fathers: James Madison and the Republican Legacy* (Cambridge, 1989), 309; Wright, *Views of Society*, 268; Wright to Julia and Harriet Garnett, 12–14 Nov. 1824, Houghton Library. "God grant that it be acted upon," wrote Wright of Jefferson's own emancipation plan, first drawn up in the 1770s. He evidently hoped that it would be introduced at a constitutional convention, the "step" toward abolition that he expected Virginia to take that winter; it did not meet until three years after his death.

20. Wright to TJ, 26 July 1825, Swem Library, College of William and Mary; Wright to Julia and Harriet Garnett, ca. Oct. 1820, Cecilia Helena Payne-Gaposchkin, "The Nashoba Plan for Removing the Evil of Slavery," *Harvard Library Bulletin* 23, no. 3 (July 1975): 225; TJ to Wright, 7 Aug. 1825, Ford, 12:410–411. Wright soon abandoned her concession to southern prejudice— separate colonization of freed slaves—and advocated the amalgamation of the two races as the proper solution to the problem.

21. Robert Owen to TJ, 25 Nov. 1825, DLC; G. D. H. Cole, *The Life of Robert Owen* (London, 1965), 238; Owen addresses, 24 Feb. and 7 Mar. 1825, in Oakley C. Johnson, *Robert Owen in the United States* (New York, 1970), 31, 52; TJ to Cornelius Blatchly, 21 Oct. 1822, Bergh, *Writings*, 15:399; *Life of Robert Owen by Himself* (New York, 1920), 274, 278; McCoy, *Last of the Fathers*, 205–213. The family of Nicholas and Virginia Trist kept up their attachment to the elder Owen. After hearing from him in 1847, Virginia wrote her husband that "our dear old friend" was the world's "best friend"; in the 1850s her daughter Martha sent Owen the gift of a scarf (Virginia

Trist to Nicholas Trist, 21 May 1847, DLC: Trist Papers; *Robert Owen's Rational Quarterly Review* 1 [1853]: 123).

22. TJ to Wright, 7 Aug. 1825, Ford, 12:410–411; Owen's Declaration, in Johnson, *Robert Owen*, 68, 70, 72–73.

23. George Flower to TJ, 6 Aug. 1816, MHi; TJ to Flower, 12 Sept. 1817, Bergh, *Writings*, 15:141; George Flower, *History of the English Settlement in Edwards County Illinois* (Chicago, 1882), 28, 43–45, 79.

24. Robert Dale Owen, *Threading My Way* (New York, 1874), 264; *Robert Dale Owen's Travel Journal 1827*, ed. Josephine M. Elliott (Indianapolis, 1977), 24; Frances Trollope, *Domestic Manners of the Americans*, ed. Donald Smalley (New York, 1949), 18, 69–70.

25. Trollope, *Domestic Manners*, 71–73, 244–245. Trollope also gave a significant middle name to the sadistic overseer in her antislavery novel of 1836, *Jonathan Jefferson Whitlow*.

26. Lafayette to TJ, 25 Feb. 1826, Chinard, *Letters*, 437; Ellen Coolidge to Virginia Trist, 21 July 1829, ViU: 9090; Virginia Trist to Nicholas Trist, 7 Oct. 1829, NcU: Trist Papers; Nicholas Trist to Robert Dale Owen and Frances Wright, 2 Nov. 1828, quoted in McCoy, *Last of the Fathers*, 213.

27. Ellen Coolidge to Martha J. Randolph, 6 June 1830, ViU: 9090.

28. Harriet Martineau, *Society in America* (1837; repr. New York, 1966), 2:312, 3:298; Martineau, *Retrospect of Western Travel* (1838; repr. London, 1942), 1:205.

29. Smith, *The First Forty Years*, 356, 363, 366, 368; Ellen Coolidge Letterbook, ViU, 29. A letter of Virginia Trist to her husband, 21 Jan. 1835, reveals that there was worried discussion of the ear trumpet even before the dinner (DLC: Trist Papers).

30. The quotations from Hamilton and Dickens are cited in Moss and Moss, "The Jefferson Miscegenation Legend," 263–266, 271.

31. Moore translated the lines from Anacreon as: "A scanty dust, to feed the wind,/Is all the trace 'twill leave behind." See Douglas L. Wilson, *Jefferson's Literary Commonplace Book* (Princeton, 1989), 130, 218, 224–235; Sarah N. Randolph, *The Domestic Life of Thomas Jefferson* (1871; repr. Charlottesville, 1978), 429; Smith, *The First Forty Years*, 315–316; Randall, *The Life of Thomas Jefferson*, 3:545. Photostats of Jefferson's "Adieu" and two family copies are in the office of the Papers of Thomas Jefferson, Princeton University Library (48628, 44203); the wording of the Monticello "It is Not the Tear" varies slightly from Moore's version. Henry Randall wrote that Jefferson had left Moore's "melody" as a souvenir for his daughter; no copy, however, has been found in his handwriting. TJ quoted Anna Laetitia Barbauld at length in a letter to John Adams 1 June 1822, *The Adams–Jefferson Letters*, ed. Lester J. Cappon (Chapel Hill, 1959), 2:578.

32. *Life of Robert Owen by Himself*, 274–275; *Rational Quarterly Review* 1 (1853): 122–125; Wright, *Course of Lectures*, 7–8; preface to volume two of Moore's *Poetical Works*, in *Poetical Works* (New York, 1854), 22.

"A Well-Ordered Household"

The quotation in the title is from: Margaret Bayard Smith, "The President's House Forty Years Ago" [1841], in *The First Forty Years of Washington Society*, ed. Gaillard Hunt (New York, 1906), 392.

Grateful thanks for research assistance are due to Charles T. Cullen, C. M. Harris, Amy Henderson, Jane Henley, Holly Shulman, Eleanor Sparagana, Andrew Trout, Gaye Wilson, Hobson Woodward, and staffs of the Papers of Thomas Jefferson, both in Princeton and Charlottesville.

1. William Plumer to Jeremiah Smith, 9 Dec. 1802, William Plumer Papers, DLC, quoted in Lynn W. Turner, *William Plumer of New Hampshire, 1759–1850* (Chapel Hill, 1962), 94.

2. Tailor Thomas Carpenter had just delivered the winter suits of livery. Thomas Carpenter, invoice, 14 Oct. 1802–26 Apr. 1803, Thomas Jefferson Papers, CSmH.

3. Mahlon Dickerson to Silas Dickerson, 21 Apr. 1802, *Letters of the Lewis and Clark Expedition, with Related Documents, 1783–1854*, ed. Donald Dean Jackson (Urbana, 1978), 2:677.

4. TJ to William Evans, 22 Feb. 1801; TJ to Philippe Létombe, 22 Feb. 1801; TJ to Meriwether Lewis, 23 Feb. 1801; TJ to Robert Morris, 26 Feb. 1801—all in *PTJ*, 33:38, 43, 51, 81–82.

5. TJ to Létombe, 22 Feb. 1801, *PTJ*, 33:43.

6. TJ to Joseph Rapin, 14 Aug. 1801, *PTJ*, 35:89–90.

7. Ellen Randolph Coolidge to Henry S. Randall, 13 Feb. 1856, in Coolidge Letterbook, 48, ViU: 9090; Létombe to TJ, 11 July 1801, *PTJ*, 34:544–545.

8. Thomas Jefferson Randolph, recollections, n.d., 6, ViU: 1397. Monticello overseer Edmund Bacon described Lemaire as "a very smart man, [he] was well educated, and as much of a gentleman in his appearance as any man" (Edmund Bacon, recollections, in Bear, 105). Rapin returned to Philadelphia for personal reasons, making a special trip there to find his own replacement. While Jefferson spent the summer at Monticello, Rapin and Lemaire overlapped at the President's House to ensure a smooth transition (TJ to Rapin, 14 Aug. 1801, *PTJ*, 35:89–90).

9. Smith, "President's House Forty Years Ago," 391.

10. Louisa Catherine Adams, "Adventures of a Nobody," 161, Adams Family Papers, MHi.

11. Smith, "President's House Forty Years Ago," 391–392.

12. TJ to Rapin, 14 Aug. 1801, *PTJ* 35:89–90.

13. Hemings had been *chef de cuisine* in Jefferson's households in Paris and Philadelphia, after several years of training in the French capital. Freed in 1796, he was working in a Baltimore tavern in 1801 and "died a suicide" later in the year. See Lucia Stanton, "Free Some Day: The African American Families of Monticello," this volume, 174–175, 184–187.

14. Létombe to TJ 26 Mar. 1801, *PTJ*, 33:449–450; *Washington National Intelligencer*, 31 Dec. 1830. An anonymous "cookwoman" worked in the kitchen for two months before Julien's arrival and during his first weeks (TJ, entry for 1 June 1801, *MB*, 1042).

15. Smith, "President's House Forty Years Ago," 391.

16. Samuel L. Mitchill to Catharine Mitchill, 10 Feb. 1802, Mitchill Collection, Museum of the City of New York, New York.

17. *Washington National Intelligencer*, 25 July 1832; William Seale, *The President's House: A History* (Washington, 1986), 101; TJ to Joseph B. Varnum, 19 Sept. 1811, *PTJ-R*, 4:164. See also TJ to Samuel H. Smith, 15 Aug. 1813, *PTJ-R*, 6:399.

18. *Washington Evening Post*, 20 Apr. 1802, in Henry Adams, *History of the United States of America During the Administrations of Thomas Jefferson* (New York, 1986), 133–134. The chariot was evidently used only during the two visits of Jefferson's daughters (TJ to Martha Jefferson Randolph, 18 June 1802, *PTJ*, 37:619; Smith, "President's House Forty Years Ago," 393).

19. TJ to Samuel H. Smith, 15 Aug. 1813, *PTJ-R*, 6:399.

20. Smith, "President's House Forty Years Ago," 392.

21. Thomas Carpenter, receipted invoices, 1 Jan.–30 Mar., 1 May–1 July 1801, *PTJ*, 33:503, 34:488–489. Jefferson's contracts with his footmen called for two livery suits a year (TJ, entries for 12 Mar. and 27 May 1801, *MB*, 1035, 1042). In Washington, livery seems to have been restricted to the households of the president, foreign diplomats, and wealthy residents like John Tayloe (Barbara G. Carson, *Ambitious Appetites: Dining, Behavior, and Patterns of Consumption in Federal Washington* [Washington 1990], 94–95.)

22. Linda Baumgarten, *What Clothes Reveal: The Language of Clothing in Colonial and Federal America—The Colonial Williamsburg Collection* (New Haven, 2002), 128–132. The livery of John Tayloe's servants was also blue and red (Carson, *Ambitious Appetites*, 94–95).

23. Edward Maher, John Christoph (known as Christopher) Süverman, and John Kramer/Jean Cremer, hired in the spring of 1801, all worked a year or less. The "fickle" Maher was addicted to changing places; Süverman could not carry out his duties because of increasing blindness; and Kramer apparently left because of marital difficulties. His replacement, William Fitzjames, remained for five years and disappeared from the record without remark (TJ to Lemaire, 14 May 1802; Lemaire to TJ, 10 May 1802, 19 Apr. 1804; Rapin to TJ, 17 May 1802, *PTJ*, 37:441, 463, 471; Jefferson Papers, MHi).

24. TJ to Lemaire, 14 May 1802, *PTJ*, 37:463.

25. TJ, entry for 1 June 1801, *MB*, 1043; Lemaire to TJ, 10 May 1802, *PTJ*, 37:441.

26. Rapin to TJ 3 Apr. 1801, *PTJ*, 33:531; Lemaire to TJ, 19 Apr. 1804, MHi; Donald Jackson, "On the Death of Meriwether Lewis's Servant," *William and Mary Quarterly*, 3rd ser., 21 (1964): 445–448. Golden was possibly a son or relative of Abraham Gaulding of Albemarle County (TJ, entry for 3 Aug. 1778, *MB*, 469; Lester J. Cappon, ed., "Personal Property Tax List of Albemarle County, 1782," *Papers of the Albemarle County Historical Society* 5 (1944–1945): 57; Edgar Woods, *Albemarle County in Virginia* [1901; repr. Bowie, 1991], 74). The family name was spelled variously Gaulding, Golden, and Golding.

27. TJ to John Wayles Eppes, 7 Aug. 1804, CSmH.

28. TJ, entry for 1 June 1801, *MB*, 1043. John Freeman's owner was Dr. William Baker of Prince Georges County.

29. William Brent, certificate, 22 Oct. 1827, Carter G. Woodson Papers, DLC.

30. Nicholas P. Trist, memorandum to Henry S. Randall, n.d., Randolph Family Manuscripts, DLC.

31. Maria Jefferson Eppes to TJ, 11 Jan. 1803, Betts and Bear, 240. A local barber came to the Executive Mansion to shave Jefferson and dress his hair (TJ, entries regarding Edward Frethey and William Conner, *MB*, index).

32. Maria Jefferson Eppes to TJ, 11 Jan. 1803, Betts and Bear, 240.

33. John Shorter was undoubtedly a member of the large extended free black Shorter family living in the District of Columbia. See Dorothy S. Provine, *District of Columbia Free Negro Registers, 1821–61* (Bowie, 1996), 76 and passim.

34. TJ, various entries, *MB*; Etienne Lemaire, accounts, Jan. 1806–Mar. 1809, CSmH. Some of the outside workers may have been slaves who hired their own time from their owners.

35. TJ, entries for 2 Nov. 1801, 13 July 1802, 7 Nov. 1803, 1 Oct. 1806, *MB*, 1057, 1077, 1111, 1189. Edy Fossett's arrival is indicated by an increase of $2 in the servants' wages. See also TJ to Martha Jefferson Randolph, 18 June, 10 July 1802, *PTJ*, 37:619, Betts and Bear, 233; Edmund Bacon, recollections, Bear, 55. Ursula, the daughter of farm laborers Bagwell and Minerva Granger and wife of Monticello head gardener Wormley Hughes, was inoculated against smallpox in May 1801, soon after her arrival (Edward Gantt, invoice, ca. 2 Mar. 1802, DLC). Edy Fossett, the daughter of carpenter David Hern and his wife Isabel, was the wife of Monticello blacksmith Joseph Fossett. Fanny Hern, the daughter of Edward and Jane Gillette, was the wife of wagoner David Hern. See Stanton, "Free Some Day," 138–139, 187–188. The records indicate that even during Jefferson's long summer vacations, the enslaved cooks remained at the President's House.

36. TJ, entries for 1801–1809, *MB*. The monthly wages, totaling an average of $140, were: Lemaire, $30; Julien, $25; Dougherty, $14; the footmen-porters, $12; Jack Shorter, $8; washerwomen, $7; other women, $8. For a brief period at the end of 1801 there were thirteen servants at wages totaling $175; from the fall of 1807, ten servants received $122 each month. In the two instances when Jefferson totaled the annual cost of "servants," his total was 10 percent or less of his salary, but he did not include the cost of their meals, which, according to his calculations, averaged $33 to $45 per week (TJ, entries for 8 Mar. 1802, 4 May 1803, *MB*, 1067, 1098).

37. TJ to Rapin, 3 June 1802, *PTJ*, 37:536.

38. Women servants usually received only $1 a month in drink money. John Freeman's gratuity was increased to $4 a month by the fall of 1804, when he was Jefferson's property (TJ entry for 2 Oct. 1804, *MB*, 1137). Jefferson also gave Freeman and Jack Shorter special gratuities of $5 during the two annual vacations at Monticello.

39. Jefferson's granddaughter Ellen Randolph Coolidge, who thought Lemaire "a civil and a useful man" who "merited reward," had some reservations about the steward, "of whose honesty his master had a higher opinion than the world at large, and who I fancy made a small fortune in his employ" (Ellen Randolph Coolidge to Henry S. Randall, 13 Feb. 1856, Coolidge Letterbook, 48, ViU: 9090).

40. See, for example, TJ, entries for 11 Oct. 1801, 8 Mar., 21 June 1802, 3 Jan. 1803, 9 Oct. 1806, 16 Jan. 1807, *MB*, 1055, 1067, 1075–1076, 1089, 1190, 1197, and passim 1801–1809. On 5 Nov. 1804, Jefferson began recording monthly, in chart form (1139). Lemaire's own accounts, 1806–1809, in phonetic French, survive in CSmH. A number of invoices of those who provided regular supplies of milk, meat, and bread also survive there. Jefferson's method for determining the average weekly cost of one person's dinner was to divide the total for "provisions" by the number of people who dined at the President's House each week. From 3 Jan. 1803, he refined the dinner cost analysis by deducting a set amount each week for the cost of feeding the servants (1089).

41. Smith, "President's House Forty Years Ago," 392.

42. Ibid., 384.

43. TJ to Létombe, 22 Feb. 1801, *PTJ*, 33:43; Lemaire to TJ, 6 Aug. 1803, 12 Aug. 1805, MHi; Joseph Dougherty to TJ, 26 July, 16 Aug. 1805, and others, MHi; Edward Gantt invoice, ca. 2 Mar. 1802, *PTJ*, 36:671. In the same way, Jefferson, like his fellow slave owners, referred to all the residents of his Monticello plantation as his "family." See, for example, FB, 27.

44. See Edward Gantt, invoices, ca. 2 Mar. 1802, *PTJ*, 36:671; ca. Nov. 1802, Jefferson Papers, DLC; Joseph Dougherty to TJ, 25 Apr. 1802, *PTJ*, 37:331; Lemaire to TJ, 6 Aug. 1803, 17 Sept. 1804, MHi.

45. TJ to Martha Jefferson Randolph, 20 Mar. 1807, Betts and Bear, 304.

46. Lemaire to TJ, 17 Aug. 1802; TJ to Edmund Bacon, 7 Nov. 1808, Jefferson Papers, MHi, Lemaire, accounts, 12, 19 Nov. 1808, Jefferson Papers, CSmH. Lemaire considered the death of the unidentified child a blessing, as "he would have been infirm all his life." The only women living in the President's House in the summer of 1802 were Julien's wife, Mary Dougherty, and the washerwoman (probably Sally Houseman), although it is also possible that Ursula Granger did not leave Washington in July, as records imply (TJ, entries for 5, 13 July 1802, 9 May 1803, *MB*, 1077, 1100). Margaret Bayard Smith remembered that "when the family of one of his domestics had the whooping cough," Jefferson wrote to a lady living at a distance (probably herself) for a remedy that had been successful in her family (Smith, "President's House Forty Years Ago," 392).

47. Ursula Granger's child was probably the first born in the President's House (22 Mar. 1802), Edith Fossett's children were born in Jan. 1803, Jan. 1805, and Oct. 1807, and Fanny Hern's child probably in 1808 (TJ, entries for 22 Mar. 1802, 28 Jan. 1803, *MB*, 1069, 1091; Edward Gantt invoice, ca. 2 Mar. 1802, *PTJ*, 36:671; FB, 128; Lemaire accounts, 7 Nov. 1807, CSmH).

48. Edmund Bacon, recollections, Bear, 104.

49. TJ to Joseph Dougherty, 31 July 1806; Dougherty to TJ, 3 Aug. 1806; Lemaire to TJ, 5 Aug. 1806, MHi. The news that precipitated Fossett's escapade is not known.

50. John Freeman to TJ, [18 Apr. 1804], DLC; copy of 3 July 1804 bill of sale of John Freeman, dated 22 Oct. 1827, Woodson Papers, DLC; John Wayles Eppes to TJ, 16 July 1804, ViU; TJ to Eppes, 7 Aug. 1804, CSmH. This is a radically abbreviated account of a complex set of negotiations, many aspects of which are not entirely clear.

51. Lemaire to TJ, 10 May 1802, *PTJ*, 37:441.

52. TJ, entry for 3 July 1807, *MB*, 1206; Lemaire to TJ, 11 Aug. 1807; Joseph Dougherty to TJ, 31 Aug., 17 Sept. 1807; TJ to Dougherty, 6 Sept. 1807, MHi.

53. Joseph Dougherty to TJ, [25 Apr. 1802], *PTJ*, 37:331.

54. TJ to James Oldham, 30 Nov. 1804, DLC.

55. Rapin to TJ, 3 Apr. 1801; TJ to Rapin, 17 Apr. 1801, *PTJ*, 33:531, 605. Jefferson's letter implies that he was familiar with John Freeman before he assumed office. Freeman may have worked at McMunn's boardinghouse, or he may have been a servant in the household of one of Jefferson's Washington acquaintances.

56. TJ to Lemaire, 14 May 1802, *PTJ*, 37:463.

57. TJ to Martha Jefferson Randolph, 6 May 1805, Betts and Bear, 270.

58. Jefferson's Weather Memorandum Book, 3 Apr. 1807, MHi; Isaac A. Coles, diary, 3 Apr. 1807, private collection (copy in Jefferson Library, Monticello). This section presents only a fraction

of the activities of a single day. Unannotated actions are educated guesses, based on a combination of primary sources and household routines of the period. I am very grateful to C. M. Harris for reminding me of the existence of Coles's diary.

59. Rapin to TJ, 3 Apr. 1801; TJ to Lemaire, 14 May 1802, *PTJ*, 33:531, 37:463; 26 July 1806, MHi.

60. Lemaire, accounts, 2 Apr. 1807, CSmH. Monticello overseer Edmund Bacon remembered of a visit to Washington that he often got up at 4:00 A.M. to accompany Lemaire and Dougherty on their marketing mission (Bacon, recollections, in Bear, 105).

61. Accounts with Jacob Miller; Lemaire, accounts, CSmH; Joseph Dougherty to TJ, [25 Apr. 1802], *PTJ*, 37:331.

62. TJ, entry for 7 Apr. 1809, *MB*, 1201; Rapin to TJ, 3 Apr. 1801, *PTJ*, 33:531; TJ to Roches frères and to Jones & Howell, 3 Apr. 1807, MHi. Rapin mentioned that Jefferson's cabinet "is found arranged by six in the morning when you descend."

63. Coles, diary, 3 Apr. 1807; TJ, memorandum of meeting of 3 Apr. 1807, "The Anas," in *The Writings of Thomas Jefferson*, ed. Paul Leicester Ford (New York, 1892), 1:324.

64. TJ, entry for 3 Apr. 1807, *MB*, 1200.

65. Smith, "President's House Forty Years Ago," 393, 410; *Jeffersonian America: Notes on the United States of America Collected in the Years 1805–6–7 and 11–12 by Sir Augustus John Foster, Bart.*, ed. Richard Beale Davis (San Marino, 1954), 9. According to Foster, only in uncivilized Washington could Jefferson have appeared "without attendants, when he took a ride, fastening his horse's bridle to the shop doors." For a particularly elaborate version of the citizen-president encounter, said to have been related by Jefferson himself, see John Bernard, *Retrospections of America 1797–1811* (New York, 1887), 240–242.

66. Washington Boyd, carriage tax receipt, 6 Nov. 1806, Missouri Historical Society, St. Louis. Jefferson's horses and the chariot had cost a staggering $3,100 (TJ, entries for 3 Feb. 1801, 20 Apr. 1801, 8 Mar. 1802, *MB*, 1034, 1038, 1067–1068).

67. Coles, diary, 3 Apr. 1807, for food; President's House inventory, 19 Feb. 1809, Jefferson Papers, DLC, for copperware.

68. Coles, diary, 3 Apr. 1807; Lemaire, accounts, 28 Mar. 1807, CSmH.

69. TJ to Létombe, 22 Feb. 1801, *PTJ*, 33:43. Among the recipes that survive in the Jefferson Papers, six are credited to Lemaire and only one to Julien.

70. Coles, diary, 3 Apr. 1807; Lemaire, accounts, 1–2 Apr. 1807, CSmH.

71. Smith, "President's House Forty Years Ago," 387–388; Seale, *President's House*, 104–105.

72. Thomas Jefferson Randolph, recollections, ViU; Benjamin Henry Latrobe to Mary Elizabeth Latrobe, 24 Nov. 1802, *The Correspondence and Miscellaneous Papers of Benjamin Henry Latrobe*, ed. John C. Van Horne et al. (New Haven, 1984), 1:232.

73. Coles, diary, 3 Apr. 1807.

74. Coles, diary, 1–3 Apr. 1807.

75. Samuel L. Mitchill to Catharine Mitchill, 10 Feb. 1802, Mitchill Collection.

76. Smith, "President's House Forty Years Ago," 392–393.

77. TJ, entry for 6 Apr. 1807, *MB*, 1200.

78. TJ to Lemaire, 16 Mar. 1809, *PTJ-R*, 1:56.

79. TJ, entries for 11–17 Mar. 1809, *MB*, 1243–1244; Bacon, recollections, in Bear, 106–107; TJ to Lemaire, 25 Apr. 1809; Lemaire to TJ, 6 May 1809, *PTJ-R*, 1:162, 188–189.

80. "Notes of Mr. Jefferson's Conversation 1824 at Monticello," in *The Papers of Daniel Webster: Correspondence*, ed. Charles M. Wiltse and Harold D. Moser (Hanover, 1974), 1:371.

81. Smith, "President's House Forty Years Ago," 392.

82. TJ to Lemaire, 16 Mar. 1809, *PTJ-R*, 1:55–56.

83. Julien to TJ, 7 Nov. 1817; TJ to Julien, 25 Dec. 1817, DLC.

84. TJ to William D. Meriwether, 21 Aug. 1810; John Christoph Süverman to TJ, 5 May, 8 Aug. 1810; TJ to Süverman, 23 Sept. 1810; Gilbert C. Russell to TJ, 31 Jan. 1810; John Pernier to TJ, 10 Feb. 1810, *PTJ-R*, 2:191–192, 208–209, 364, 672–673, 3:49, 110.

85. *Washington National Intelligencer,* 8 Jan., 1 June 1810; Julien to TJ, 1 Jan. 1810, 2 July 1812, 11 Sept. 1818, 14 Jan. 1825; TJ to Julien, 8 Jan. 1810, 6 Oct. 1818, 27 Jan. 1825; Joseph Dougherty to TJ, 18 Dec. 1823, *PTJ-R,* 2:115, 128, 5:204, and DLC. In his 27 Jan. 1825 letter, Jefferson wrote that the canvasbacks had "enabled me to regale my friends here with what they had never tasted before."

86. Nicholas P. Trist to Virginia J. Trist, 23 Nov. 1828, Nicholas Philip Trist Papers, Southern Historical Collection, NcU; *Washington National Intelligencer,* 31 Dec. 1830; Seale, *President's House,* 259.

87. Stanton, "Free Some Day," 140–141, 202, 204.

88. John Freeman to TJ, [2 Mar. 1809], DLC. Melinda Colbert was subject to the 1806 Virginia law making it illegal for a freed slave to remain in the state for more than a year after manumission.

89. Deed of John Freeman, 19 Apr. 1809, *PTJ-R,* 1:156; Paul Jennings, "A Colored Man's Reminiscences of James Madison," *White House History* 1, no. 1 (1983): 48, 50; James Madison to Dolley Madison, [28 Aug. 1814], James Madison Papers, DLC; Dolley Madison to Anna Cutts, 5 July 1816 and [1815 1816], *The Dolley Madison Digital Edition. Letters 1/88–June 1836,* ed. Holly C. Shulman (Charlottesville, 2004). Jennings's account described Freeman as "butler" in Madison's staff, perhaps indicating enlarged responsibilities but not suggesting that he ran the household; that role fell to Madison's French steward or maître d'hôtel.

90. Washington city directory, 1827 and 1830; Nicholas P. Trist to Virginia J. Trist, 27 Jan. 1829, NcU: Trist Papers; Letitia Woods Brown, *Free Negroes in the District of Columbia, 1790–1846* (New York, 1972), 118; John Freeman, will, 10 Aug. 1839, District of Columbia Archives, copy in GWA.

91. Joseph Dougherty to TJ, 10 Feb. 1819, DLC.

92. Joseph Dougherty to TJ, 15 May 1809, *PTJ-R,* 1:199.

93. Joseph Dougherty to Thomas Mann Randolph, 20 July 1819, DLC. Dougherty also directed the wagoning of Jefferson's almost 7,000-volume library from Monticello to Washington, after he sold it to Congress in 1815.

94. Mary Dougherty to TJ, 25 Oct, 7 Dec. 1823, DLC; TJ, entry for 30 Dec. 1824, *MB,* 1401.

95. Joseph Dougherty to Thomas Mann Randolph, 20 July 1819, DLC; Margaret Bayard Smith to Mrs. Kirkpatrick, 31 Mar. 1830, in Smith, *First Forty Years,* 313–314; *Washington National Intelligencer,* 25 July 1832.

Jefferson's People

This essay reexamines, after fifteen years, the themes of the first essay in the present volume in a chronological format that takes a broader view of Jefferson's management of the Monticello plantation as a whole.

1. Peter Jefferson will, 13 July 1757, Albemarle County Deed Book, No. 2, p. 33. In the first Albemarle County tax list, in 1782, Thomas Jefferson owned the second-largest number of slaves (Lester J. Cappon, ed., "Personal Property Tax List of Albemarle County, 1782," *Papers of the Albemarle County Historical Society* 5 [1944–1945]: 47–73).

2. TJ to Edward Coles, 25 Aug. 1814, *PTJ-R,* 7:604.

3. François Jean, Marquis de Chastellux, *Travels in North America in the Years 1780, 1781 and 1782 by the Marquis de Chastellux,* ed. and trans. Howard C. Rice, Jr. (Chapel Hill, 1963), 391–392.

4. TJ to Francis Willis, 15 July 1796, *PTJ,* 29:153; TJ to Thomas Leiper, 23 Feb. 1801, *PTJ,* 33:50.

5. FB, 5–18.

6. TJ to Edward Bancroft, 26 Jan. 1789, *PTJ,* 14:492.

7. FB, 27.

8. *MB*, 246–247; Lucia Stanton, "*Free Some Day: The African American Families of Monticello*," this volume, 21, 26.

9. *MB*, 371; Stanton, "Free Some Day," 104.

10. *MB*, 380; "Negroes Alienated from 1784–1794 Inclusive," in Lucia Stanton, *Slavery at Monticello* (Charlottesville, 1996), 16.

11. TJ to Nicholas Lewis, 29 July 1787, *PTJ*, 11:640.

12. TJ to Edward Bancroft, 26 Jan. 1789, *PTJ*, 14:492.

13. TJ to Nicholas Lewis, 29 July 1787, *PTJ*, 11:641.

14. TJ to Angelica Church, 27 Nov. 1793, *PTJ*, 27:449.

15. Merrill D. Peterson, ed., *Visitors to Monticello* (Charlottesville, 1989), 28; TJ to Philip Mazzei, 30 May 1795, *PTJ*, 20:270.

16. *MB*, 282; FB, 69.

17. FB, 46.

18. TJ to Samuel Biddle, 12 Dec. 1792, *PTJ*, 24:725.

19. TJ to Thomas Mann Randolph, 19 Apr. 1792, *PTJ*, 23:436; TJ to Thomas Mann Randolph, 18 Feb. 1793, *PTJ*, 25:230.

20. TJ to Thomas Mann Randolph 25 Jan. 1798, *PTJ*, 30:56; Randolph to TJ, 13 Jan., 3, 26 Feb. 1798, *PTJ*, 30:28, 79, 145.

21. One prospect was "a very good manager; but his severity puts him out of the question" (TJ to Thomas Mann Randolph, 26 Aug. 1811, *PTJ-R*, 4:101).

22. TJ to Stevens T. Mason, 27 Oct. 1799, *PTJ*, 31:222.

23. TJ to Thomas Mann Randolph, 18 Feb. 1793, *PTJ*, 25:230.

24. Thomas Jefferson, *Notes on the State of Virginia*, ed. Frank Shuffelton (New York, 1999), 170.

25. Peterson, *Visitors to Monticello*, 28.

26. TJ to Thomas Mann Randolph, 23 Jan. 1801, *PTJ*, 32:499–500.

27. *MB*, 1001; TJ to John Wayles Eppes, 21 Dec. 1797, *PTJ*, 29:586.

28. "Statement of Nailery Profits," *PTJ*, 29:540–541.

29. Thomas Mann Randolph to TJ, 3 Feb. 1798, *PTJ*, 30:79.

30. Thomas Mann Randolph to Nicholas P. Trist, 22 Nov. 1818, ViU: 10487.

31. TJ, statement of recommendation for Richard Richardson, 1 June 1801, *PTJ*, 34:232; TJ to Thomas Mann Randolph, 25 Nov. 1785, *PTJ*, 9:60.

32. TJ to Joel Yancey, 15 Nov. 1818, Betts, *Farm Book*, 41.

33. John Hemmings spelled his surname differently from other members of his family.

34. Peterson, *Visitors to Monticello*, 30.

35. *Richmond Recorder*, 1 Sep. 1802.

36. Henry S. Randall to James Parton, 1 June 1868, Harvard University Library.

37. Ellen Coolidge to Joseph Coolidge, 24 Oct. 1858, copy in Coolidge Letterbook, ViU: 9090, 98–99.

38. Martha J. Randolph to TJ, 15 Jan. 1795, *PTJ*, 28:247.

39. TJ to Thomas Mann Randolph, 8 June 1803, Betts, *Farm Book*, 19.

40. Edward Ross to David Parish, 23 Nov. 1813, St. Lawrence University Library.

41. TJ to Martha J. Randolph, 27 Feb. 1809, Betts and Bear 385.

42. Madison Hemings recollections, *Pike County* [Ohio] *Republican*, 13 Mar. 1873; reprinted in Annette Gordon-Reed, *Thomas Jefferson and Sally Hemings: An American Controversy* (Charlottesville, 1997), 245–248; FB, 116, 152.

43. *MB*, 1287, 1354, 1361, 1395; TJ to George Fleming, 29 Dec. 1815, Betts, *Farm Book*, 252–253.

44. TJ to Jeremiah Goodman, 6 Jan. 1815, *GB*, 540; Stanton, "Free Some Day," 148–149.

45. TJ to Randolph Lewis, 23 Apr. 1807, Betts, *Farm Book*, 26.

46. TJ to Joel Yancey, 17 Jan. 1819, Betts, *Farm Book*, 43; TJ to Jeremiah Goodman, 6 Jan. 1815, *GB*, 540.

47. TJ to James Pemberton, 21 June 1808, DLC.

48. TJ to Clement Caines, 16 Sept. 1811, *PTJ-R*, 4:157.

49. TJ to Jean Baptiste Say, 1 Feb. 1804, in LofA 1144.

50. TJ to Joel Yancey, 17 Jan. 1819, Betts, *Farm Book*, 43.

51. TJ to Henry Clark, 18 Oct. 1820, Betts, *Farm Book*, 46; TJ to John Wayles Eppes, 30 June and 29 July 1820, ViU.

52. TJ to Reuben Perry, 16 Apr. 1812, Betts, *Farm Book*, 35.

53. Auguste Levasseur, *Lafayette in America, in 1824 and 1825* (New York, 1829), 218.

54. Israel Gillette Jefferson recollections, *Pike County Republican*, 25 Dec. 1873, Gordon-Reed, *Thomas Jefferson and Sally Hemings*, 250.

55. TJ to Joseph Dougherty, 31 July 1806, Betts, *Farm Book*, 23.

56. Peter Fossett recollections, *New York World*, 30 Jan. 1898.

Perfecting Slavery

1. TJ to Angelica Church, 27 Nov. 1793, *PTJ*, 27:449. Until the publication of volume 27, "my feilds to farm" was the usual rendering of the phrase. Whether or not Jefferson intended it, he certainly wrote "to form."

2. TJ to John Adams, 28 Feb. 1796, *PTJ*, 28:618.

3. TJ to Thomas Leiper, 23 Feb. 1801, *PTJ*, 33:50.

4. TJ to Philip Mazzei, 30 May 1795, *PTJ*, 20:270; TJ to Elizabeth House Trist, 23 Sept. 1795, *PTJ*, 28:478.

5. TJ to George Washington, 14 May 1794, *PTJ*, 28:75.

6. TJ to John Adams, 12 Sept. 1821, in *The Adams-Jefferson Letters: The Complete Correspondence between Thomas Jefferson and Abigail and John Adams*, ed. Lester J. Cappon, 2 vols. (Chapel Hill, 1959), 2:575; TJ to William Ludlow, 6 Sept. 1824, L&B, 16:75.

7. TJ to Elizabeth House Trist, 23 Sept. 1795, *PTJ*, 28:478. For further references to "barbarous" agricultural practices, see TJ to John Taylor, 29 Dec. 1794, *PTJ*, 28:233; TJ to George Washington, 12 Sept. 1795, *PTJ*, 28:494; and TJ to Francis Willis, 15 July 1796, *PTJ*, 29:153.

8. TJ to Francis Willis, 15 July 1796, *PTJ*, 29:153.

9. François-Alexandre-Frédéric de La Rochefoucauld-Liancourt, *Travels through the United States of North America*, 4 vols. (London, 1799), 2:75.

10. FB, 46.

11. For instance, the plan called for 18 cradlers and 24 scythes, and in June 1796, "the 18. mowers had been fixed on & furnished with 27. scythes" (FB, 46, 54).

12. Francis Bacon, *The Advancement of Learning* (New York, 2001), 58.

13. FB, 46.

14. FB, 54.

15. TJ to John Holmes Freeman, 21 Dec. 1805, Betts, *Farm Book*, 417.

16. *Weevils in the Wheat: Interviews with Virginia Ex-Slaves*, ed. Charles L. Perdue Jr., Thomas E. Barden, and Robert K. Phillips (Charlottesville, 1976), 26 [indications of pronunciation removed].

17. FB, 58. Squire was the man with the grindstone in a cart in the 1799 harvest. No such role is listed in the harvest plan for 1800. For "ambulatory shop," see e.g., the letter from "Agricultor," in the *Farmer's Register* 1, no. 1 (June 1833), 48. In the two subsequent harvests for which calculations are possible (1799 and 1812), the average for each cutter was only one and a half acres per day (FB, 58; Betts, *Farm Book*, 143).

18. *The Correspondence of the Three William Byrds of Westover, Virginia, 1684–1776.* ed. Marion Tinling, 2 vols. (Charlottesville, 1977), 1:355.

19. TJ to David B. Warden, 12 Jan. 1811, *GB*, 451. Of more than thirty overseers employed at Monticello in Jefferson's lifetime, only one, George Granger, was an enslaved man.

20. Ellen Randolph Coolidge to Joseph Coolidge, 24 Oct. 1858, Coolidge Letterbook, 98, ViU: 9090. Thomas Jefferson Randolph recollections, ca. 1873, ViU: 1397; recollections of Edmund Bacon and Isaac (Granger) Jefferson, in Bear, 23, 97; and recollections of Peter Fossett, in *New York World,* 30 Jan. 1898.

21. TJ to John Strode, 5 June 1805, *GB,* 302–303; Thomas Mann Randolph to TJ, 27 Mar. 1792, *PTJ,* 23:347; TJ to Thomas Mann Randolph, 19 Apr. 1792, *PTJ,* 23:435–436; and TJ to Thomas Mann Randolph, 24 June 1793, *PTJ,* 26:356.

22. TJ to Jacob Hollingsworth, 22 Nov. 1792, *PTJ,* 24:656.

23. TJ to Thomas Mann Randolph, 18 Feb. 1793, *PTJ,* 25:230. This statement was made in connection with Jefferson's effort to find tenants as well as overseers in Cecil County; he was unsuccessful in luring any tenants from Maryland to Monticello.

24. TJ to James Madison, 15 Feb. 1794, *PTJ,* 28:22.

25. Biddle vanished from the local scene, while Alexander became a permanent Albemarle County resident, at one point leasing from Jefferson the lands he had previously managed (for the lease [dated 21 July 1805], see Betts, *Farm Book,* 171–172).

26. TJ to Sir John Sinclair, 23 Mar. 1798, *PTJ,* 30:206.

27. TJ to Jean Baptiste Say, 1 Feb. 1804, in LofA, 1144; Second Inaugural Address, 4 Mar. 1805, LofA, 518.

28. TJ to Joel Yancey, 17 Jan. 1819, Betts, *Farm Book,* 43.

29. TJ comparison of marriage settlements [1797], MHi. The four children were Judy Hix's sons Ben and Kit, Mary Hemings's daughter Betsy, and Betty Brown's daughter Melinda Colbert.

30. TJ to Thomas Mann Randolph, 19 May 1793, *PTJ,* 26:65.

31. TJ to William Short, 13 Apr. 1800, *PTJ,* 31:502. On Jefferson's nailery, see David Howard Shayt, "The Nailery of Thomas Jefferson; Ironworking in Arcadia," 8 May 1983, unpublished manuscript in the Jefferson Library at Monticello. Shayt provides excellent background information on nail making at the time; some of his conclusions about nail making at Monticello are incorrect.

32. TJ to Caleb Lownes, 18 Dec. 1793, *PTJ,* 27:586.

33. See François-Alexandre-Frédéric de La Rochefoucauld-Liancourt, *On the Prisons of Philadelphia* (Philadelphia, 1796), 22; La Rochefoucauld-Liancourt, *Travels through the United States of North America,* 2:345–346; Negley K. Teeters, *The Cradle of the Penitentiary: The Walnut Street Jail at Philadelphia, 1773–1835* (Philadelphia, 1955), 36–38.

34. Teeters, *Cradle of the Penitentiary,* 39.

35. Teeters, *Cradle of the Penitentiary,* 36–62; LeRoy B. DePuy, "The Walnut Street Prison: Pennsylvania's First Penitentiary," *Pennsylvania History* 18 (Apr. 1951): 130–144.

36. La Rochefoucauld-Liancourt, *On the Prisons of Philadelphia,* 22.

37. Caleb Lownes, *An Account of the Gaol and Penitentiary House of Philadelphia* (Philadelphia, 1793), cited in Teeters, *Cradle of the Penitentiary,* 42.

38. TJ to James Buchanan and William Hay, 13 Aug. 1785, *PTJ,* 8:368; TJ to James Buchanan and William Hay, 26 Jan. 1786, *PTJ,* 9:222; Howard C. Rice, Jr., "A French Source of Jefferson's Plan for the Prison at Richmond," *Journal of the Society of Architectural Historians* 12 (Dec. 1953): 28–30.

39. Robert Turnbull, *A Visit to the Philadelphia Prison* (Philadelphia, 1796), cited in Teeters, *Cradle of the Penitentiary,* 45.

40. La Rochefoucauld-Liancourt's account suggests that nail making was present in the first half of 1795. The first advertisement found for nails supplied from the prison, "on an extensive plan," is dated 30 July 1795 (*Pennsylvania Gazette,* 12 Sept. 1795). It is possible nails were made on a smaller scale before that.

41. As Jeremy Bentham stated on the title page to his *Panopticon; or, The Inspection House* (1787), the principles of the Panopticon were applicable "to any sort of establishment, in which

persons of any description are to be kept under inspection; and in particular to Penitentiary-Houses, Prisons, Poor Houses, Lazarettos, Houses of Industry, Manufactories, Hospitals, Work-Houses, Mad-Houses, and Schools."

42. Thomas Condie, "Plan, Construction and etc. of the Jail and Penitentiary House of Philadelphia," *Philadelphia Monthly Magazine*, Feb. 1798, printed in Teeters, *Cradle of the Penitentiary*, 129–132 (quotations, 129–130).

43. Benjamin Rush was one of the reformers who particularly mentioned the virtue-promoting properties of prisons. For a typical view of factories, see the letter to the editors of New Haven's *Connecticut Herald* for 9 Jan. 1811; written by officials of Humphreysville, Connecticut, it describes the Humphreysville Manufacturing Co. and expresses the view that manufacturing establishments, "instead of being productive of drunkenness, debauchery and vice, may become nurseries of sobriety, diligence and virtue" (*The Papers of James Madison: Presidential Series*, ed. J. C. A. Stagg et al. [Charlottesville, 1999], 4:148–149).

44. TJ to Jean Nicolas Démeunier, 29 Apr. 1795, *PTJ*, 28:341.

45. TJ to Thomas Mann Randolph, 23 Jan. 1801, *PTJ*, 32:500.

46. La Rochefoucauld-Liancourt, *Travels through the United States of North America*, 2:80.

47. Bear, 23. Called "Jefferson" by the Rev. Charles Campbell, who recorded his recollections, it is now known that Isaac's family name was Granger (see GWA). His statement about special rations is validated by Farm Book entries.

48. FB, 110–111; Thomas Jefferson, Nailery Account Book (1796–1800), at William A. Clark Memorial Library, University of California, Los Angeles. Jefferson, who had no success in decimalizing the nation's weights and measures, made sure that Monticello's scales were decimalized.

49. In the 1770s, the enslaved blacksmiths customarily received a "gratuity"; in later years, John Hemmings, joiner, and Burwell Colbert, butler, were given an "annual gratuity" (*MB*, 459, 1265, 1275, and passim).

50. *MB*, 925 (28 Jan. 1795). No explicit reference to training has been found; it is assumed that subsequent charcoal burners at Monticello—all enslaved—learned first from Silknitter and then from each other.

51. *MB*, 1001 (14 May 1799).

52. "Statement of Nailery Profits," 1794–1797, *PTJ*, 29:540–541; Memorandum to Richard Richardson, ca. 21 Dec. 1799, in *PTJ*, 31:271.

53. Jefferson, *Autobiography* (1821), in LofA, 44; Thomas Jefferson, *Notes on the State of Virginia*, ed. William Peden (Chapel Hill, 1958), 143.

54. TJ to John Wayles Eppes, 21 Dec. 1797, *PTJ*, 29:586. The blacksmith was Isaac Granger, apparently one of Jacob Silknitter's pupils in charcoal burning; Jefferson had given Granger to Eppes.

55. *MB*, 1354 (5 May 1819), 1361 (15 Feb. 1820).

56. TJ to Philip Tabb, 1 June 1809, *PTJ-R*, 1:252.

57. From its beginning in 1819, John S. Skinner's agricultural weekly, *The American Farmer*, evidences a rising tide of such references (see, as a sampling, 1:265, 329–330; 2:150, 165; 3:164; 4:90, 273–274).

58. *MB*, 1287 (17 Mar. 1813), 1329 (21 Dec. 1816), 1376 (26 June 1821).

59. "Statement of Nailery Profits," 1794–1797, *PTJ*, 29:540–541. In 1795, Granger's brother Isaac received a percentage as well.

60. TJ to John McDowell, 22 Oct. 1798, *PTJ*, 30:563; TJ to John McDowell, 21 Mar. 1799, *PTJ*, 31:83; TJ to Archibald Stuart, 14 May 1799, *PTJ*, 31:110.

61. "Statement of Nailery Profits," 1794–1797, *PTJ*, 29:540–541.

62. Jefferson purchased Ben and Cary from his brother Randolph Jefferson, and Philip Hubbard, John, and Davy were brought from Poplar Forest; all were born in 1785 or 1786 (see *MB*, 945 [3 Sept. 1796], 952 [9 Feb. 1797]; FB, 56; and Jefferson, Nailery Account Book).

63. See FB, 50–53.

64. Reports of the Commissioners for the University of Virginia, 4 Aug. 1818, LofA, 468.

65. Jefferson, *Autobiography* (1821), LofA, 41.

66. TJ to Thomas Mann Randolph, 23 Jan. 1801, *PTJ*, 32:500.

67. Thomas Mann Randolph to Nicholas P. Trist, 22 Nov. 1818, ViU: 10487. The suicide took place at Morven, the property of David Higginbotham.

68. La Rochefoucauld-Liancourt, *On the Prisons of Philadelphia*, 22. The judge was William Bradford.

69. Report to the Commissioners, in LofA 469.

70. TJ to Thomas Mann Randolph, 23 Jan. 1801, *PTJ*, 32:499–500.

71. Those seeking workers in this period invariably used some variation of the phrase "honesty, industry, and sobriety" in their advertisements (see, e.g., New York's *Columbian Gazetteer* for 24 Mar. 1794, and Charleston, South Carolina's *City Gazette* for 10 May 1794). For examples of Jefferson's appreciation of the same qualities in his employees, see TJ to John Harvie, 27 Sept. 1804, MHi; and TJ to Samuel H. Smith, 15 Aug. 1813, *PTJ-R*, 6:399.

72. Teeters, *Cradle of the Penitentiary*, 134.

73. Thomas Mann Randolph to TJ, 3 Feb. 1798, *PTJ*, 30:79.

74. TJ to Thomas Law, 13 June 1814, LofA, 1335–1338.

75. Fraser D. Neiman, "Changing Landscapes: Slave Housing at Monticello" (2003), available online at www.pbs.org/saf/1301/features/archeology.htm. I am indebted to Dr. Fraser D. Neiman, Monticello's director of archeology, for expanding my understanding of the late eighteenth-century transitional period at Monticello. For a full account of the effects of the transition, from tobacco to wheat, see his "The Lost World of Monticello: An Evolutionary Perspective," *Journal of Anthropological Research* 64 (Summer 2008): 161–193.

76. "Notes on Plan of a Prison," enclosure in TJ to James Wood, 31 Mar. 1797, *PTJ*, 29:337. Jefferson received a copy of Bentham's *Panopticon* from England in 1792 (Thomas Pinckney to TJ, 29 Aug. 1792, *PTJ*, 24:331; see also E. Millicent Sowerby, *Catalogue of the Library of Thomas Jefferson*, 5 vols. [Washington, 1952–1959], 3:28–29). For Jefferson's venetian blinds, see *MB*, (under index entry for "Furnishings and Furniture"); William L. Beiswanger, "Thomas Jefferson's Essay in Architecture," *Thomas Jefferson's Monticello* (Charlottesville, 2002), 20–22; and Jack McLaughlin, "The Blind Side of Jefferson," *Early American Life* 20 (Apr. 1989): 30–33.

77. Bentham, *Panopticon; or, the Inspection-House* (London, 1812), 1.

78. Interview with Peter Fossett, *New York World*, 30 Jan. 1898; Orra Langhorne, "Southern Sketches," *Southern Workman and Hampton School Record* 17 (Sept. 1888): 71.

79. TJ to Henry Remsen, 13 Nov. 1792, *PTJ*, 24:617.

80. Thomas Mann Randolph to TJ, 16 June 1805, ViU.

81. TJ to William Strickland, 23 Mar. 1798, *PTJ*, 30:212; TJ to Stevens Thomson Mason, 27 Oct. 1799, *PTJ*, 31:222.

82. TJ to James Dinsmore, 1 Dec. 1802, ViU.

83. Lucia Stanton, "Free Some Day: The African American Families of Monticello," this volume, 146–147, 151–152.

84. TJ to Thomas Mann Randolph, 8 June 1803, Betts, *Farm Book*, 19.

85. Lownes, *An Account of the Gaol and Penitentiary House of Philadelphia*, 19.

86. Bear, 98. The identity of the thief remains uncertain. Bacon named James Hubbard but described the man as a repentant who turned to religion and was "always a good servant afterwards," something that does not fit the rebellious Hubbard (Bear, 97–99).

87. TJ to John Wayles Eppes, 10 May 1810, *PTJ-R*, 2:378; see also *MB*, 1257 (11 May 1810).

88. For Jefferson, democracy was pure democracy—that is, a government in which every citizen participated directly in the business of governing (see TJ to Isaac H. Tiffany, 26 Aug. 1816, in L&B, 15:65–66; and TJ to Samuel Kercheval, 5 Sept. 1816, L&B, 15:71–72).

89. TJ to David Barrow, 1 May 1815, L&B, 14:296.

90. Ellen Wayles Coolidge to Mr. Maümur, 1845, Coolidge Letterbook, 24, ViU: 9090. Wormley Hughes was given "his time" by Jefferson's daughter Martha Randolph, a kind of unofficial freedom that allowed him to avoid the stipulations of the 1806 law that dictated that freed slaves had to leave Virginia within a year.

91. TJ, in conversation with Isaac Briggs, Nov. 1820, in *Visitors to Monticello*, ed. Merrill D. Peterson (Charlottesville, 1989), 90.

92. Frances Wright, *Views of Society and Manners in America* (London, 1821), 518; Harriet Martineau, *Society in America*, 2 vols. (New York, 1837), 2:120.

93. William H. Holcombe, *The Alternative: A Separate Nationality or the Africanization of the South* (New Orleans, 1860), 6. I thank Charles A. Miller for alerting me to this quotation.

94. For more on the Fossett family, see Stanton, "Free Some Day," 144–155, 188–190, and GWA.

95. *The Crisis*, May 1934, in *W. E. B. Du Bois: Writings* (New York, 1986), 1248–1249.

96. *Philadelphia Tribune*, 7 Apr. 1932, 9, 15.

The Other End of the Telescope

1. Ellen Coolidge to Henry S. Randall, 27 Jan. [1853?], 31 July 1856, Coolidge Letterbook, 9–18, 70–71, ViU: 9090; Thomas J. Randolph reminiscences, ViU: 1397.

2. Virginius Dabney, *The Jefferson Scandals: A Rebuttal* (New York, 1981), 46.

3. The substantial recollections of four men were recorded: Isaac (Granger) Jefferson (1775–ca. 1850), reprinted as "Memoirs of a Monticello Slave," in Bear, 3–24; Madison Hemings (1805–1877), in *Pike County [Ohio] Republican*, 3 Mar. 1873, reprinted as "The Memoirs of Madison Hemings," in Annette Gordon-Reed, *Thomas Jefferson and Sally Hemings: An American Controversy* (Charlottesville, 1997), 245–248; Israel Gillette Jefferson (1800–1873+), in *Pike County [Ohio] Republican*, 25 Dec. 1873, reprinted as "The Memoirs of Israel Jefferson," in Gordon-Reed, *Thomas Jefferson and Sally Hemings*, 249–253; and Peter Fossett (1815–1901), in *New York World*, 30 Jan. 1898, and in an unidentified Cincinnati newspaper, ca. July 1900, in clippings scrapbook, 97–98, Cincinnati Public Library (hereafter cited as Fossett 1898 and Fossett 1900).

Jefferson biographer Henry S. Randall included some of his conversations with former Monticello head gardener Wormley Hughes (1780–1858) in *The Life of Thomas Jefferson*, 3 vols. (New York, 1858), 1:69–70, 552–553; 3:332. One letter of the Poplar Forest slave Hannah and a dozen letters written by John Hemings (1776–1833), which are not discussed in this essay, survive in the Jefferson Papers, MHi.

Since 1993, more than 150 descendants of Monticello's African American community have been interviewed as part of the oral history project Getting Word. While this essay does not focus on these interviews, it does draw from material assembled as part of the project and related to interviews and conversations with descendants from the 1920s to the 1970s. This material is part of the GWA at Monticello.

4. Ross County, Ohio, Deed Book, No. 68, pp. 562–563; Madison Hemings estate, Ross County, Ohio, Probate Court records.

5. Dumas Malone and Steven H. Hochman, "A Note on Evidence: The Personal History of Madison Hemings," *Journal of Southern History* 41 (1975): 523–528.

6. "Memoirs of Madison Hemings," 245, 247.

7. Ibid., 247.

8. Ibid., 246–247.

9. Monticello's former overseer Edmund Bacon recalled that TJ "freed one girl [Harriet Hemings] some years before he died, and there was a great deal of talk about it. . . . People said he freed her because she was his own daughter" (Bacon recollections, in Bear, 102). Sally Hemings's brothers James and Robert both became free at about age thirty-one. Another James Hemings,

son of Sally Hemings's sister Critta, ran away to Richmond in his teens and, after negotiations for his return failed, was not pursued.

10. "Memoirs of Madison Hemings," 247; Ross County, Ohio, census, 1870; Malone and Hochman, "Note on Evidence," 526. The local oral tradition was communicated by Beverly Gray, Chillicothe, Ohio, consultant to Monticello's Getting Word project.

11. "Memoirs of Israel Jefferson," 252–253; Bear, 99–100.

12. "Memoirs of Israel Jefferson," 250–251; Eden Baptist Church records, in collection of Beverly Gray.

13. "Memoirs of Israel Jefferson," 249, 252.

14. "Memoirs of Madison Hemings," 247.

15. Pearl M. Graham, interviews with Anna Ezell, Lucy Williams, Minnie Arbuckle, and Charles Bullock, 28 July 1948 and [Dec.] 1949, typescript copy in ViU; Graham to Julian P. Boyd, 11 Jan. 1958, copy in GWA; Lerone Bennett, "Thomas Jefferson's Negro Grandchildren," *Ebony* 10 (Nov. 1954): 78–80. Recent interviews with Mary Hemings's descendants are in the GWA.

16. Fossett 1900; Fossett 1898.

17. Fossett 1900; *MB*, 1343, 1389; Albemarle County Will Book, No. 8, pp. 281–282, No. 9, pp. 20–21; Graham, interview with Charles and Lottie Bullock, [Dec.?] 1949, ViU.

18. "Memoirs of a Monticello Slave," 5, 12; "Memoirs of Israel Jefferson," 251; Graham, interview with Mary Cole Kenney, 28 July 1948; Fossett 1898.

19. Fossett 1898.

20. Ibid.; Orra Langhorne, "Southern Sketches," *Southern Workman and Hampton School Record* 17 (Sept. 1888): 71.

21. Fossett 1898; "Memoirs of a Monticello Slave," 7.

22. Randall, *The Life of Thomas Jefferson*, 1:338; Sarah N. Randolph, *The Domestic Life of Thomas Jefferson* (1871; Charlottesville, 1978), 56; Thomas J. Randolph reminiscences, ViU; Fossett 1898.

23. "Memoirs of a Monticello Slave," 8 and passim; Fossett 1898; Lucy Williams to Pearl Graham, ca. 22 Jan. 1948, and Charles Bullock to Graham, ca. Oct. 1949, Moorland-Spingarn Collection, DHU.

24. "Memoirs of a Monticello Slave," 9.

25. Ibid., 19–20; "Memoirs of Israel Jefferson," 249; Fossett 1900.

26. Thomas J. Randolph, undated letter to the *Pike County [Ohio] Republican*, ViU: 8937; Ellen Coolidge Letterbook, 5–6. In 1856, when Coolidge sent this paper to Henry Randall, she noted that it was in her handwriting but could not recall if she or her mother was its author.

27. TJ to John Wayles Eppes, 10 May 1810, *PTJ-R*, 2:378; Ellen Coolidge to Henry S. Randall, 13 Mar. 1856, Coolidge Letterbook, 57; Randall, *The Life of Thomas Jefferson*, 1:69–70.

28. Randall, *The Life of Thomas Jefferson*, 1:552–553; Martha J. Randolph, quoted in Randolph, *Domestic Life*, 152–153.

29. According to Randolph family versions of the story, Caesar was the man who spent hours in the cellar with the silver. Multiple versions from Alabama name either Caesar or Jupiter as the cellar's occupant. Because the Bankheads were so often intermediaries in the story's telling, it is now impossible to know Scott's version with certainty. My current view is that Scott was a granddaughter or great-granddaughter of Jupiter (1743–1800), who was probably Caesar's brother. The many varying accounts of the Bankhead and Scott descendants are compiled in Lucia Stanton, "Jefferson and Monticello Stories from Former Slaves and Their Descendants," GWA.

30. Anna Hotchkiss Gillespie, "A Faithful Servant," typescript copy, GWA; *Birmingham [Alabama] News*, 18 Feb. 1923; interview with Miss Cary Randolph Hotchkiss and Lessie Clay, Mar. 1971, copy, courtesy of Stewart Terry, in GWA; *Decatur [Georgia] Daily*, 9 Sept. 1977. When Isaac Jefferson referred to one of Jefferson's bouts of arthritis, he recalled that he and John Hemings "had to car him about on a han'barrow" ("Memoirs of a Monticello Slave," 19).

31. TJ to William A. Burwell, 28 Jan. 1805, in Ford, 10:126–127; Martha J. Randolph to a daughter, 17 Jan. 1827, in *Worthy Women of Our First Century*, ed. Sally Butler [Mrs. O. J.] Wister and Agnes Irwin (Philadelphia, 1877), 58; Ellen Coolidge Letterbook, 4–5; Thomas J. Randolph reminiscences, ViU.

32. Randall, *The Life of Thomas Jefferson*, 1:11, 3:544.

Free Some Day

I would like to thank the Thomas Jefferson Foundation, its trustees and staff, and particularly Daniel P. Jordan and Douglas L. Wilson, for continued support of my efforts to channel years of information retrieval into a publication that could make the story of the Monticello community accessible to a broad audience. I am also extremely grateful to Robert C. Vaughan and the Virginia Foundation for the Humanities and Public Policy for their support at critical moments over the last decade. My first uninterrupted thoughts about the lives of Monticello's African Americans took place within the walls of the Virginia Center for the Humanities, where I had a fellowship in 1992 and an office in 1997. Monticello's Getting Word oral history project, which has shed so much light into the darkness of slavery, was born with a grant from the Virginia Foundation.

I give special thanks to James A. Bear, Jr., my first guide to the pleasures, idiosyncracies, and complexities of Monticello's history. His curiosity about Monticello's human dimension and his pioneering work on its enslaved community have had a significant impact on my own perspective on Jefferson and his world.

Several colleagues have read all or portions of this work in its various stages, and my debt to them is considerable: James Horn, James O. Horton, Sarah S. Hughes, Peter S. Onuf, Philip J. Schwarz, Dianne Swann-Wright, Derry E. Voysey, and Douglas L. Wilson. The probing comments of Sarah Hughes, in particular, compelled me to grapple more strenuously with many of the issues I confronted. My six years of association with Dianne Swann-Wright and Beverly Gray in the Getting Word project have been of incalculable benefit to my understanding of slavery and African American history.

1. Exceptions to this origin as part of the estate of Peter Jefferson were the family of George and Ursula Granger, purchased in 1773, and Betty Brown, Martha Jefferson's personal servant.

2. In 1997 and 1998, Charles Irons, Melanie Kielb, and Joshua Rothman, Monticello graduate interns from the University of Virginia, compiled, from Jefferson's Farm Book, a database of over six hundred men, women, and children who at one time lived in slavery at Monticello or at Jefferson's other plantations in Bedford, Campbell, Cumberland, and Goochland Counties.

3. The name *Monticello* can be applied to a house, a farm, and a plantation. When used here without qualifiers, it applies to Jefferson's five-thousand-acre Albemarle County plantation, which consisted of several discrete farms (Monticello, Tufton, Shadwell, and Lego), as well as other contiguous properties that were not farmed.

4. *PTJ*, 15:654–655, 677. A reference in a letter to Jefferson's steward suggests that a significant number of the Wayles slaves had been purchased recently (TJ to Nicholas Lewis, 28 July 1787, *PTJ*, 11:640).

5. Unannotated information is presumed to come from Jefferson's Farm Book, reproduced in facsimile in Betts, *Farm Book*.

6. Since Jefferson's only brother was twelve years younger, his boyhood experience was probably similar to that of his grandson years later. "Having no companion of my own age," recalled Thomas Jefferson Randolph, "I associated entirely with the slaves and formed for them early and strong attachments" (Thomas Jefferson Randolph recollections, ViU: 1837). Jefferson refers to boyhood trapping in a letter to William Thornton, 24 Apr. 1812, *PTJ-R*, 4:667.

7. TJ to Daniel Hylton, 5 Feb. 1792, *PTJ*, 23:102; Bear, 5, 60; *MB*, passim (see Jupiter in index).

8. Jane Blair Cary Smith, "The Carys of Virginia," 18, ViU: 1397; Bear, 6, 10.

9. *PTJ*, 1:130; *MB*, 953; TJ to John McDowell, 22 Oct. 1798, *PTJ*, 30:563; Bear, 7–11. Isaac Jefferson was mistaken in including Jupiter among those taken from Richmond by the British (see *MB*, 504–505).

10. In Maplewood Cemetery (Edgar Woods, *Albemarle County in Virginia* [1901; repr. Berryville, 1984], 49).

11. Instructions to Manoah Clarkson, 23 Sept. 1792, *PTJ*, 24:413; *MB*, 411, 470; Rice account, Fee Book, CSmH; Nicholas Lewis accounts in Ledger 1767–1770, ViU; Thomas M. Randolph to TJ, 14 Aug. 1793, *PTJ*, 26:667.

12. Lucia Stanton, *Slavery at Monticello*, 16; TJ to Thomas M. Randolph, 11, 12, 18 Jan. 1796, *PTJ*, 20:580, 581, 592; *MB* index: Slaves: Health and Medicine.

13. Thomas Jefferson Randolph recollections, ViU: 1837. Jupiter may also have borne the surname Evans, but no confirming evidence has yet been found.

14. For references to "trusty" slaves, see TJ to Edmund Bacon, 11 Jan. 1808, MHi; TJ to John Wayles Eppes, 10 May 1810, *PTJ-R*, 2:378; TJ to Reuben Perry, 10 May 1811, *PTJ-R*, 3:612–613.

15. *MB*, 371.

16. *Truth Stranger than Fiction: Father Henson's Story of His Own Life* (1858; repr. Williamstown, 1973), 19, 51–53.

17. Thomas J, Randolph recollections, ViU: 1837; Anne Fontaine Maury, ed., *Intimate Virginiana: A Century of Maury Travels by Land and Sea* (Richmond, 1941), 18, 181, 201.

18. Henry S. Randall, *The Life of Thomas Jefferson* (Philadelphia, 1865), 1:68; Sarah N. Randolph, *The Domestic Life of Thomas Jefferson* (1871; repr. Charlottesville, 1978) 48–49; TJ to Thomas M. Randolph, 12 Feb. 1795, *PTJ*, 28:264; *MB*, 925.

19. Randall, *The Life of Thomas Jefferson*, 3:510.

20. Memorandum to Richard Richardson, ca. 21 Dec. 1799, *PTJ*, 31:270–271; TJ to Thomas M. Randolph, 4 Feb. 1800, *PTJ*, 31:360.

21. *MB*, 1011; Martha J. Randolph to TJ, 30 Jan. 1800, *PTJ*, 31:347.

22. TJ to Thomas M. Randolph, 4 Feb. 1800, *PTJ*, 31:360; TJ to Richard Richardson, 10 Feb. 1800, *PTJ*, 31:363; TJ to Maria J. Eppes, 12 Feb. 1800, *PTJ*, 31:368.

23. *MB*, 394; Ellen Coolidge to Sarah N. Randolph, 30 Feb. 1876, ViU: 1397.

24. Gerald W. Gawalt, "Jefferson's Slaves: Crop Accounts at Monticello, 1805–1808," *Journal of the Afro-American Historical and Genealogical Society* 13 (1994): 19–38.

25. Stanton, "'Those Who Labor,'" this volume, 20–21.

26. *MB* index: Slaves: Activities and Domestic Economy; TJ to Hugh Chisholm, 5 June 1807, MHi.

27. George W. Corner, ed., *The Autobiography of Benjamin Rush* (Princeton, 1948), 152; Joel Yancey to TJ, 14 Oct. 1819, Betts, *Farm Book*, 305.

28. Although references only to the Christmas holidays have been found in Jefferson's records, the Easter and Whitsun holidays were probably observed at Monticello, as elsewhere in Virginia.

29. Thomas J. Randolph recollections, ViU: 1397.

30. Philip D. Morgan, *Slave Counterpoint: Black Culture in the Eighteenth-Century Chesapeake and Lowcountry* (Chapel Hill, 1998), 524; Bear, 22; Eugène Vail, *De La Littérature et des Hommes de Lettres des Etats Unis d'Amérique* (Paris, 1841), 321–333; Elizabeth Langhorne, "Black Music and Tales from Jefferson's Monticello," *Folklore and Folklife in Virginia* 1 (1979): 60–67. Langhorne says that Vail's informant was Jefferson's daughter Martha Randolph, but it seems more likely to have been a granddaughter, possibly Ellen Randolph, who was most intimate with the Vail family (see correspondence in ViU: 9090).

31. Charles L. Perdue, Jr., Thomas E. Barden, and Robert K. Phillips, eds., *Weevils in the Wheat: Interviews with Ex-Slaves* (Charlottesville, 1976), 214. I have omitted indications of pronunciation from this and other quotations from interviews with former slaves.

32. TJ to Thomas M. Randolph, 30 Mar. 1800, Martha J. Randolph to TJ, 30 Jan. 1800; Thomas M. Randolph to TJ, 19 Apr. 1800, *PTJ*, 31:347–348, 473, 523.

33. *MB*, 334; TJ to Archibald Thweatt, 29 May 1810, *PTJ-R*, 2:425; Fee Book and Miscellaneous Accounts, 1764–1794, CSmH.

34. Isaac Jefferson's recollections appear in Bear, 3–24. See pp. 3, 8; Memorandum to Richard Richardson, ca. 21 Dec. 1799; TJ to Thomas M. Randolph, 4 Feb. 1800, *PTJ*, 31:270, 360; TJ to Randolph, 19 Oct. 1792, *PTJ*, 24:501.

35. *MB*, 377; Bear, 3–4, 20; blacksmithing accounts, 1792–1794, CSmH.

36. Nailery account book, 1796–1800, William A. Clark Memorial Library, University of California, Los Angeles; nailery accounts, 1794–1795, in Ledger and Miscellaneous Accounts, 1767–1797, ViU; *MB*, 987; Thomas M. Randolph to TJ, 22 Apr. 1798, *PTJ*, 30:290.

37. Bear, 15–16.

38. Bear, 7–11. Isaac recalled that his father, too, was at the Yorktown camp, but Jefferson's Memorandum Book indicates that George Granger was in Richmond shortly after the British left (*MB*, 505).

39. TJ to Nicholas Lewis, 11 July 1788, 29 July 1787, *PTJ*, 13:343, 11:641; TJ to Thomas M. Randolph, 3 Feb. 1793, *PTJ*, 25:138.

40. FB, 54; TJ to Thomas M. Randolph, 9 Jan. 1797; Randolph to TJ, 26 Feb. 1798, *PTJ*, 29:260, 30:145.

41. Thomas M. Randolph to TJ, 3 Feb. 1798, *PTJ*, 30:79; Thomas J. Randolph recollections, ViU: 1837; Randolph to TJ, 29 Apr. 1798; TJ to George Jefferson, 6 May 1798; George Jefferson to TJ, 14 May 1798, *PTJ*, 30:312, 337–338, 349.

42. Thomas M. Randolph to TJ, 3 and 26 Feb., 29 Apr., 3 June 1798, *PTJ*, 30:79, 145, 312, 385–386.

43. See Morgan, *Slave Counterpoint*, 218–225, 342–346; Eugene Genovese, *Roll, Jordan, Roll: The World the Slaves Made* (New York, 1976), 365–388; John W. Blassingame, *The Slave Community: Plantation Life in the Antebellum South* (New York, 1979), 258–261.

44. Stanton, " 'Those Who Labor,' " this volume, 14–15.

45. Thomas M. Randolph to TJ, 13 Jan. 1798; TJ to Randolph, 25 Jan. 1798, *PTJ*, 30:28, 55–56.

46. TJ to Henry Remsen, ca. 15 May 1799, *PTJ*, 31:106.

47. FB, 96; James Oldham to TJ, 26 Nov. 1804, MHi; Stanton " 'Those Who Labor,' " this volume, 23. References to written instructions left with George Granger suggest his literacy (Memorandum for Samuel Arnold, 12 Apr. 1798, *PTJ*, 30:271).

48. *MB*, 1010.

49. Bear, 3; *MB*, 4 May 1799, 1001; FB, 41.

50. TJ to Thomas M. Randolph, 7 Feb. 1796, *PTJ*, 28:608.

51. TJ to Thomas M. Randolph, 28 July 1793, *PTJ*, 26:578; FB, 47.

52. TJ to John Wayles Eppes, 30 June 1820, ViU; TJ to Joel Yancey, 17 Jan. 1819, Betts, *Farm Book*, 43; FB, 156.

53. Thomas J. Randolph recollections, ViU: 1837.

54. Maurice Duke, ed., *Don't Carry Me Back! Narratives by Former Virginia Slaves* (Richmond, 1995), 32–33; Jean Gaulmier, *L'Idéologue Volney* (1951; repr. Paris, 1980), 370; Thomas M. Randolph to TJ, 26 Feb. 1798, *PTJ*, 30:145; John W. Eppes to TJ, 10 Feb. 1803, ViU. Gaulmier's work gives the impression the pea-planting episode occurred at Monticello; Volney's manuscript journal, generously shared by C. M. Harris, makes it clear the scene was elsewhere.

55. FB, 67; TJ to Joel Yancey, 10 Nov. 1818, Betts, *Farm Book*, 41; Richard Beale Davis, ed., *Jeffersonian America: Notes on the United States of America . . . by Sir Augustus John Foster* (San Marino, 1954), 141–142.

56. Plat of Mulberry Row, Betts, *Farm Book*, 6; Stanton, " 'Those Who Labor,' " this volume, 20.

57. Nicholas Lewis account, pp. 584, 586, in Ledger and Miscellaneous Accounts, 1767–1797, ViU; *MB*, 928, 974, 1000, 1341, 1348, 1371; Gawalt, "Crop Accounts at Monticello," 22–36.

58. Nicholas Lewis account, p. 586; TJ to Thomas M. Randolph, 14 June 1798, *PTJ*, 30:410.

59. FB, 60; Betts, *Farm Book*, 168–170; Anne Cary Randolph to TJ, 18 Mar. 1808, *GB*, 367.

60. TJ to Edmund Bacon, 6 Oct. 1806, MHi.

61. FB, 160; Albemarle County Will Book, No. 9, p. 20; Monticello Dispersal Sale receipts, ViU; sales memorandum, 1 Jan. 1829, ViU: 8937.

62. Bear, 3–24.

63. Bear, 13–15; William T. Hutchinson and William M. E. Rachal, eds., *The Papers of James Madison* (Chicago, 1971), 7:304–305; *MB*, 808, 838, 896.

64. Bear, 13–16; William M. Kelso, *Archaeology at Monticello* (Charlottesville, 1997), 101.

65. TJ to John Adams, 27 May 1795, *PTJ*, 28:363; Nailery account book, 1796–1800, William A. Clark Memorial Library, University of California, Los Angeles; Stanton, "'Those Who Labor,'" this volume, 9–11.

66. Bear, 17; Nailery account book, University of California, Los Angeles.

67. "Negroes alienated . . . ," in Stanton, *Slavery of Monticello*, 16; Thomas M. Randolph to TJ, 13 Jan. 1798; TJ to Randolph, 25 Jan. 1798, *PTJ*, 30:28, 56; Bear, 16.

68. Bear, 3, 18–19, 21; *Travels in North America in the Years 1780, 1781, and 1782 by the Marquis de Chastellux*, ed. Howard C. Rice, Jr. (Chapel Hill, 1963), 2:394; TJ to Maria Cosway, 12 Oct. 1786, *PTJ*, 10:447; Merrill D. Peterson, ed., *Visitors to Monticello* (Charlottesville, 1989), 75, 112; *Notes on the State of Virginia*, ed. William Peden (Chapel Hill, 1955), 80–81.

69. Bear, 92, 23; Edmund Bacon account book, private collection, copy in Jefferson Library, Monticello.

70. *MB*, 992; Martha J. Randolph to TJ, 30 Jan. 1800; Thomas M. Randolph to TJ, ca. 20 Apr. 1800, *PTJ*, 31:347–348, 523.

71. Bear, 23–24. Randolph may have given Isaac Granger his "time," informally emancipating him so that he would not be subject to the 1806 Virginia law requiring freed slaves to leave the state within a year.

72. Morgan, *Slave Counterpoint*, 476.

73. TJ to William Gordon, 16 July 1788, *PTJ*, 13:363–364; FB, 29.

74. Sylvia R. Frey, *Water from the Rock: Black Resistance in a Revolutionary Age* (Princeton, 1991), 171; FB, 29; Randall, *The Life of Thomas Jefferson*, 1:342.

75. TJ to Nicholas Lewis, 19 Dec. 1786, *PTJ*, 10:615.

76. Jefferson family accounts of the events of June 4, 1781, appear in Randall, *The Life of Thomas Jefferson*, 1:337–339; Randolph, *Domestic Life*, 55–56; and Thomas J. Randolph recollections, ViU: 1837. Accounts by former slaves and descendants of Monticello slaves appear in *New York World*, 30 Jan. 1898; letters of Lucy Williams and Charles Bullock to Pearl Graham, 1947–1949, DHU; and in the files of the Getting Word project begun at Monticello in 1993 to locate and record the family stories and histories of descendants of Monticello's African American families. See also Lucia Stanton, "The Other End of the Telescope: Jefferson through the Eyes of His Slaves," this volume, 100–102.

77. Randall, *The Life of Thomas Jefferson*, 1:338–339; *New York World*, 30 Jan. 1898.

78. Randolph to TJ, 19 June 1793, *PTJ*, 26: 326; TJ to Manoah Clarkson, 23 Sept. 1792, *PTJ*, 24:413; Jocelyn Bailey, *The Village Wheelwright and Carpenter* (Aylesbury, England, 1975), 28–29. Hern's surname is known from the marriage license, 2 Mar. 1871, of his daughter Lily (Albemarle County Clerk's Office).

79. Memorandum to Richard Richardson, ca. 21 Dec. 1799, *PTJ*, 31:271; Eli Alexander to TJ, Apr. 1795, *PTJ*, 28:342; TJ to Manoah Clarkson, 23 Sept. 1792, *PTJ*, 24:413; Thomas M. Randolph to TJ, 9 Jan. 1793, *PTJ*, 25:43; FB, 67; Bacon to TJ, 11 Dec. 1807, ViU.

80. Memorandum to Richard Richardson, ca. 21 Dec. 1799; TJ to Edmund Bacon, 28 Dec. 1806, DLC; TJ to Randolph, 25 Jan. and 15 Feb. 1798, *PTJ*, 30:56, 114.

81. TJ to Francis Eppes, 30 Aug. 1785, *PTJ*, 15:622; Eppes to TJ, 31 Aug. 1786, *PTJ*, 15:631; Martha J. Carr to TJ, 2 Jan. 1787, *PTJ*, 15:633; Abigail Adams to TJ, 26 June 1787, *PTJ*, 11:502; Nicholas Lewis account, 19 May 1787, p. 570, in Ledger, 1767–1770, ViU; Gawalt, "Crop Accounts at Monticello," 23–36; *MB*, 1000; FB, 60.

82. Bear, 51.

83. TJ to Jeremiah Goodman, 6 Jan. 1815, *GB*, 540.

84. *MB*, 1162; Bear, 51.

85. Dr. Frank Carr to TJ, 18 Mar. 1816, Betts, *Farm Book*, 40; TJ to Edmund Bacon, 21 Nov. 1806, MHi; TJ to Randolph Lewis, 23 Apr. 1807, Betts, *Farm Book*, 26.

86. TJ to Jeremiah Goodman, 6 Jan. 1815, *GB*, 540.

87. Thomas J. Randolph recollections, ViU: 1837. On rituals of marriage in the nineteenth century, see Herbert G. Gutman, *The Black Family in Slavery and Freedom 1750–1925* (New York, 1976), 273–277; and Genovese, *Roll, Jordan, Roll*, 475–481.

88. Jefferson's instructions to Edmund Bacon, Bear, 55.

89. Although this designation for the President's House was not widely used until the 1820s, I use it for the sake of clarity.

90. Jefferson-Bacon correspondence, Oct. 1806–Dec. 1808, in DLC, MHi, and ViU.

91. *MB*, 1193 and passim; Bear, 104. There is a possibility that Bacon mistakenly remembered the troubled couple, who might have been Joseph and Edith Fossett, who were also parted by Jefferson's desire for French cuisine at Monticello. Whichever couple was involved, the case makes the same point about the difficulties of separation.

92. TJ to Bacon, 7 Nov. 1808, MHi; Lemaire accounts, 12 and 19 Nov. 1808, CSmH; Bacon to TJ, 17 Nov. 1808, ViU; TJ to Bacon, 22 Nov. 1808, MHi.

93. Bear, 106.

94. Betts, *Farm Book*, 120, 476–477; TJ to Barnes, 14 June 1817, DLC; Bear, 102–103. Bacon did not name Thruston Hern as the runaway, but the timing and circumstances fit his case.

95. Albemarle County Will Book, No. 8, pp. 281–282, No. 9, pp. 1–2, 20–21; Albemarle County Court Order Book, 1827, p. 144. No inventory and appraisal for Jefferson's Bedford County property survives. Records suggest he owned about two hundred slaves at the time of his death.

96. Monticello Dispersal Sale receipts, ViU.

97. Sales memorandum, 1 Jan. 1829, ViU: 8937; John Gorman to TJ, 30 Aug. 1823, MHi; Martha J. Randolph to Thomas J. Randolph, [June 1823?], ViU: Carr-Cary Papers; Brockenbrough to John H. Cocke, 6 Jan. 1829, 10 Mar. and 22 Oct. 1830, ViU: Cocke Papers. The original steps were replaced in marble in the 1930s.

98. Harriet Dunglison to N. P. Trist, 13 Jan. 1827, NcU; Robley Dunglison to Trist, 15 Jan. 1827, NcU: Trist Papers; sales memorandum, 1 Jan. 1829, ViU: 8937; Virginia J. Trist to Jane Hollins Randolph, 25 May 1840, ViU: 1397.

99. FB, 160; Joel Yancey to TJ, 20 and 26 Oct. 1819, 11 Feb. 1820, 22 and 31 May 1821, Betts, *Farm Book*, 44–46, and MHi; *MB*, 1359.

100. Inventory of Jefferson's Campbell County estate, 1 Jan. 1827, Albemarle County Will Book, No. 9, pp. 1–2; *Lynchburg Virginian*, 7 June 1832. Since Brooks did not provide the age of the fugitive, it is impossible to be certain that he was Moses Hern, but the references to his trade, his daughter, and the many relations in Albemarle County make him the most probable runaway.

101. Peterson, *Visitors to Monticello*, 28; FB, 46.

102. FB, 46.

103. Perdue, Barden, and Phillips, *Weevils in the Wheat*, 26 (indications of pronunciation removed); Richard Jefferies, "Walks in the Wheat-fields," in *Field and Hedgerow*, ed. Samuel J. Looker (London, 1948), 157–158.

104. Florence Whiting Lee, "Harvest Time in Old Virginia," *Southern Workman* 37 (Oct. 1908): 566–567; FB, 46.

105. TJ to John Wayles Eppes, 29 July 1820, ViU; FB, 123; TJ to George Jeffreys, 3 Mar. 1817, DLC; TJ to Craven Peyton, 27 Nov. 1815, Betts, *Farm Book*, 40.

106. FB, 54; TJ to James Monroe, 10 July 1796, *PTJ*, 29:147.

107. Daniel Bradley to TJ, 7 Sept. and 6 Oct. 1805; TJ to Bradley, 6 Oct. 1805, MHi; *MB*, 1170.

108. On the skills and independent character of slave watermen, see Morgan, *Slave Counterpoint*, 236–244, 337–342.

109. TJ to Bowling Clark, 21 Sept. 1792, *PTJ*, 24:409.

110. TJ to Demeunier, 29 Apr. 1795, *PTJ*, 28:341; Stanton, "'Those Who Labor,'" this volume, 9–11.

111. FB, 111; Nailery account book, University of California, Los Angeles; list of ten nailers and their output, undated, Missouri Historical Society; TJ to Thomas Mann Randolph, 9 Jan. 1801, *PTJ*, 32:417; *MB*, 925.

112. Bear, 62–63.

113. *MB*, 1081, 1150.

114. *MB*, 1001, 1004, 1081.

115. Randolph to TJ, 30 May 1803, ViU; TJ to Randolph, 8 June 1803, Betts, *Farm Book*, 19.

116. Daniel Bradley to TJ, 7 Sept. 1805, MHi.

117. S. Allen Chambers, Jr., *Poplar Forest and Thomas Jefferson* (N.p., 1993), 47, 49, 53–54, 62, 74; TJ to Edmund Bacon, 3 Jan. 1809, CSmH; TJ to Hugh Chisholm, 8 Sept. 1808, MHi; TJ to Jeremiah Goodman, 18 Oct. 1812, *PTJ-R*, 5:403.

118. TJ to Jeremiah Goodman, 6 Jan. 1815, *GB*, 540; Goodman to TJ, 30 Dec. 1814, ViU; Joel Yancey to TJ, 20 June 1819, MHi.

119. *Minutes of the Baptist Association . . . Caroline County, Virginia* (Fredericksburg, 1816), cited in Philip J. Schwarz, *Twice Condemned: Slaves and the Criminal Laws of Virginia, 1705–1865* (Baton Rouge, 1988), 118–120, 214; Peden, *Notes*, 142.

120. Bear, 97–99.

121. *MB*, 1043, 1162, and index, *sub* Freeman and Shorter.

122. Bear, 97; *Virginia Gazette* advertisement, 7 Sept. 1769, *PTJ*, 1:33; *MB*, 334, 1125; Martha J. Randolph to TJ, 14 Jan. 1804, Betts and Bear, 252; TJ to John Wayles Eppes, 30 June 1820, ViU.

123. TJ to Reuben Perry, 16 Apr. 1812, *PTJ-R*, 4:620; deed of sale to Perry, Feb. 1811, *PTJ-R*, 3:411–412; *MB*, 1275; account with Isham Chisholm, [ca. 1 May 1812], *PTJ-R*, 5:5.

124. John Hope Franklin and Loren Schweninger, *Runaway Slaves: Rebels on the Plantation* (New York, 1999), 209–233; *Richmond Enquirer*, 12 Apr. 1811 (a citation in Lee Marmon, "Poplar Forest Research Report," pt. 3, Aug. 1991, 111, led me to this advertisement).

125. Albemarle County Minute Book, 1807–1809, 3 Aug. 1807; also Order Book, 1806–1807, pp. 325–326, 330–332. Perhaps James's confession to Craven was a delaying tactic, made in the hope that he would be able to escape from his captor.

126. *MB*, 1180.

127. Philip J. Schwarz, *Slave Laws in Virginia* (Athens, 1996), 47–48, 68, 105. Among the ninety-eight slaves executed from 1800 to 1810 were thirty-six individuals convicted as part of Gabriel's conspiracy.

128. Condemned Slaves, Auditors Item 153, box 3, Library of Virginia. I am grateful for information about James's reprieve to Phil Schwarz, whose works are essential to understanding the issues in this chapter.

129. On 6 Oct. 1807 over a dozen Albemarle County men were paid for patrolling, some for as many as 120 hours (Albemarle County Court Order Book, 1806–1807, p. 461).

130. Albemarle County Minute Book, 1823–1825, 3 Mar. 1824; TJ to Jeremiah Goodman, 26 July 1813, *PTJ-R*, 6:331; Joel Yancey to TJ, 1 July 1819, Betts, *Farm Book*, 44; TJ to Charles Clay,

9 Aug. 1819, typescript, ViU; Elizabeth Trist to Nicholas P. Trist, 28 Nov. 1822, DLC: Trist Papers; William Radford to TJ, 26 Dec. 1822, MHi; Bedford County Court Order Book, No. 18, pp. 318–319.

131. TJ to Bernard Peyton, 5 Jan., 28 Aug. 1824, MHi; Wilson C. Nicholas to Thomas J. Randolph, 2 Mar. 1824, ViU: 1397.

132. Bear, 97; TJ to John Strode, 5 June 1805, DLC.

133. TJ to George Fleming, 29 Dec. 1815, Betts, *Farm Book*, 252; Joel Yancey to TJ, 14 Oct. 1819, Betts, *Farm Book*, 305.

134. See page 117.

135. Albemarle County Minute Book, No. 11 (1842–1844), p. 349; Israel Jefferson reminiscences, 25 Dec. 1873, in Annette Gordon-Reed, *Thomas Jefferson and Sally Hemings: An American Controversy* (Charlottesville, 1997), 251.

136. TJ memorandum, 6–29 Aug. 1822, ViU.

137. These are their names as told by Israel Gillette Jefferson (Gordon-Reed, *Thomas Jefferson and Sally Hemings*, 249). In Thomas Jefferson's records, many of Israel's siblings appear only with their diminutive names, Ned, Dick, Scilla, Aggy, and Sucky. Israel also mentioned a sister Jane, who does not appear in Jefferson's records.

138. TJ to Richard Richardson, 10 Feb. 1800, *PTJ*, 31:363; TJ to Edmund Bacon, 28 Dec. 1806, DLC; TJ to Eppes, 13 Oct. 1820, CSmH.

139. *MB*, 1324 and passim (see index); Gawalt, "Crop Accounts at Monticello," 23–36; Mary J. Randolph Memorandum Book, Sept. and Nov. 1827, Monticello Curatorial Collection.

140. FB, 111; Edmund Bacon to TJ, 19 Jan. 1809, ViU; TJ to Bacon, 6 Oct. 1806, MHi; *MB*, 1287, 1376; TJ to Joel Yancey, 13 Sept. 1816, MHi.

141. TJ to Edmund Bacon, 29 Nov. 1817, MHi; TJ to Joel Yancey, 11 Jan. and 18 Feb. 1818, MHi.

142. TJ to Joel Yancey, 25 June 1819, Betts, *Farm Book*, 44; Edmund Bacon to TJ, 26 July and 4 Aug. 1819, ViU and MHi; Elizabeth Trist to Nicholas P. Trist, 30 June 1819, DLC: Trist Papers; TJ to M. B. Jefferson, 2 Aug. 1815, Betts, *Farm Book*, 39.

143. Watkins invoice, 21 June 1820 to 21 Jan. 1821, MHi.

144. TJ instructions for Jeremiah Goodman, Dec. 1811, *PTJ-R*, 4:381; "Articles for contracts with overseers," 1773, *GB*, 40–41.

145. TJ to Dr. Henry Rose, 23 Oct. 1801, *PTJ*, 35:495; vaccination record, Mar. 1826, ViU. It was actually a local doctor who wielded the lancet.

146. FB, 152; TJ to Richard Fitzhugh, 27 May 1813, *PTJ-R*, 6:140.

147. Bear, 69; TJ to Jeremiah Goodman, 5 Mar. 1813, *PTJ-R*, 5:663; FB, 152.

148. Ellen Randolph Coolidge to Sarah N. Randolph, 30 Feb. 1876, ViU: 1397; TJ to James Maury, 16 June 1815, Betts, *Farm Book*, 490.

149. Gordon-Reed, *Thomas Jefferson and Sally Hemings*, 252; Thomas J. Randolph draft letter, post 25 Dec, 1873, ViU: 8937; Albemarle County Minute Book, No. 11 (1842–1844), p. 349.

150. FB, 114, 144; Ellen Coolidge to Henry S. Randall, 22 Feb. 1856, Coolidge Letterbook, p. 54, ViU; Thomas J. Randolph draft letter, ViU; Gordon-Reed, *Thomas Jefferson and Sally Hemings*, 252; TJ to Martha J. Randolph, 6 June 1814, *PTJ-R*, 7:400; Cornelia Randolph to Virginia Randolph, 22 Apr. 1821, NcU.

151. Ellen Randolph to Martha J. Randolph, 28 July 1819, ViU.

152. Gordon-Reed, *Thomas Jefferson and Sally Hemings*, 252.

153. Gordon-Reed, *Thomas Jefferson and Sally Hemings*, 249–250; Albemarle County Will Book, No. 8, p. 281; Monticello Dispersal Sale receipts, ViU; Marmon, "Poplar Forest Research Report," 71, 77.

154. Gordon-Reed, *Thomas Jefferson and Sally Hemings*, 250–251.

155. Gordon-Reed, *Thomas Jefferson and Sally Hemings*, 250–251. Beverly Gray, of Chillicothe, Ohio, is the generous source of information on Eden Baptist Church and its members, the Ohio Underground Railroad, and the lives of former Virginia slaves in southern Ohio.

156. Gordon-Reed, *Thomas Jefferson and Sally Hemings*, 251.

157. *New York World*, 30 Jan. 1898.

158. *Charlottesville Jeffersonian Republican*, 22 July 1892.

159. Gordon-Reed, *Thomas Jefferson and Sally Hemings*, 252.

160. *Acts Passed at a General Assembly of the Commonwealth of Virginia . . . 1830–1831* (Richmond, 1831), 107–108. I am grateful to Philip J. Schwarz for guiding me through the maze of Virginia laws relating to black education. A critical text on this topic is Janet Duitsman Cornelius, *"When I Can Read My Title Clear": Literacy, Slavery, and Religion in the Antebellum South* (Columbia, 1991).

161. Charles Bullock to Pearl Graham, 10 Oct. 1949, Moorland-Spingarn Collection, DHU; Orra Langhorne, "Southern Sketches," *Southern Workman and Hampton School Record* 17 (Sept. 1888): 92–93; *New York World*, 30 Jan. 1898; Madison Hemings recollections, Gordon-Reed, *Thomas Jefferson and Sally Hemings*, 247; Ellen Randolph to Virginia Randolph, 31 Aug. 1819, FLDA.

162. Stanton, "'Those Who Labor,'" this volume, 22–23; Fossett blacksmithing accounts, July 1827 to July 1830, ViU: 8937b.

163. Gordon-Reed, *Thomas Jefferson and Sally Hemings*, 251.

164. *New York World*, 30 Jan. 1898; Mrs. O. J. Wister and Miss Agnes Irwin, *Worthy Women of Our First Century* (Philadelphia, 1877), 47–48.

165. Eliza Trist to Nicholas P. Trist, 30 June 1819, DLC: Trist Papers; Virginia J. Randolph to "Mrs. and Miss Randolph," [ca. May–Sept 1819] FLDA; inventory of estate of John Neilson, 6 July 1827, Albemarle County Will Book, No. 9, p. 276; William Dinsmore will, 9 June 1836, Will Book, No. 12, pp. 191–193; TJ manuscript music, ViU: 5118; *Chillicothe* (Ohio) *Leader*, 26 Jan. 1887 (this last source, in typescript version, is in the collection of Beverly Gray, Chillicothe).

166. Cornelia Randolph to Virginia J. Trist, 22 Aug. 1831, NcU: Trist Papers. This chapter builds on the important work of James A. Bear, Jr. (see "The Hemings Family of Monticello," *Virginia Cavalcade* 29, no. 2 [Autumn 1979]: 78–87).

167. Bear, 99–100; Israel Jefferson recollections, Gordon-Reed, *Thomas Jefferson and Sally Hemings*, 252. No reference to this deathbed promise has yet been found in the papers of Jefferson or his Randolph and Eppes descendants. The bell descended to Mary Cole Kenney, whose connection to the Hemings family has not yet been determined. Her daughter Lucy K. Williams gave the bell to the Moorland-Spingarn Collection at Howard University; it is now on loan to Monticello (Susan R. Stein, *The Worlds of Thomas Jefferson at Monticello* [New York, 1993], 16).

168. Madison Hemings recollections, Gordon-Reed, *Thomas Jefferson and Sally Hemings*, 245; dower deed, 29 Apr. 1746, Henrico County Deed Book; John Wayles's will, 15 Apr. 1760, printed in *Tyler's Quarterly Magazine* 6 (1924–1925): 269. In Madison Hemings's account of Betty Hemings's life, Captain Hemings tried to purchase her, as an infant, from John Wayles, who refused to sell her. Since Wayles did not have ownership of Betty Hemings until 1746, it was some other man, most probably Francis Eppes, who "would not part with the child."

169. Gordon-Reed, *Thomas Jefferson and Sally Hemings*, 245; Bear, 4.

170. *MB*, 260, 263, 285, 290, 291, 297, 343; Bear, 4, 10; TJ to Thomas Mann Randolph, 19 May 1793, *PTJ*, 26:65; James Dinsmore to TJ, 23 Jan. 1802, *PTJ*, 36:422; TJ to Thomas Mann Randolph, 15 May 1791, *PTJ* 20:415; Gordon-Reed, *Thomas Jefferson and Sally Hemings*, 248.

171. *MB*, 342, 542, 546; Neil Jamieson to TJ, 14 July 1784, *PTJ*, 7:375–376.

172. Monroe to William Short, 23 Jan. 1786, *PTJ*, 9:191; TJ to Daniel Hylton, 1 July 1792, *PTJ*, 24:145. See also William Short to TJ, 14 May 1784, *PTJ*, 7:255; TJ to Martha J. Randolph, 8 Aug. 1790, *PTJ*, 17:326.

173. Bear, 100; Peterson, *Visitors to Monticello*, 34, 39, 53, 58, 64, 99, 101.

174. Thomas J. Randolph draft letter, post 25 Dec. 1873, ViU: 8937.

175. TJ to Martha J. Randolph, 4 Dec. 1791, 13 Dec. 1792, *PTJ*, 22:377, 24:740–741; FB, 41–42.

176. *New York World*, 30 Jan. 1898; Bear, "The Hemings Family of Monticello," 80–81; Lucia Stanton, "Monticello to Main Street: The Hemings Family and Charlottesville," this volume, 216–217; Stanton, "'Those Who Labor,'" this volume, 9. A possible exception to the Hemings marriage pattern is Doll (b. 1757), wife of Jefferson's slave Abraham and a farmworker, who, it has been plausibly suggested, was a daughter of Betty Hemings (Marmon, "Poplar Forest Research Report," 39).

177. *Richmond Recorder*, 1 Sept. 1802. For nineteenth-century attitudes, see Merrill D. Peterson, *The Jefferson Image in the American Mind* (New York, 1960), 181–187; and Sidney P. Moss and Carolyn Moss, "The Jefferson Miscegenation Legend in British Travel Books," *Journal of the Early American Republic* 7, no. 3 (Fall 1987): 253–274. Gordon-Reed's *Thomas Jefferson and Sally Heming* supersedes all previous accounts of the controversy and provides the most complete and balanced presentation of the known circumstances.

178. Gordon-Reed, *Thomas Jefferson and Sally Hemings*, 245; Bear, 4; Francis Eppes to TJ, 14 Apr. 1787, *PTJ*, 15:636.

179. TJ to Francis Eppes, 30 Aug. 1785, *PTJ*, 15:621–622; Eppes to TJ, 31 Aug. 1786, 14 Apr. 1787, *PTJ*, 15:631, 636; Martha J. Carr to TJ, 2 Jan. 1787, *PTJ*, 15:633.

180. Bear, 100; Abigail Adams to TJ, 26 and 27 June, 6 July 1787; Abigail Adams account with TJ, 10 July 1787, *PTJ*, 11:502–503, 551, 574.

181. Maria Jefferson to Kitty Church, 7 May 1789, *PTJ*, 16:xxxi; Marie de Botidoux to Martha Jefferson, Nov. 1789–10 Jan. 1790, ViU; *MB*, 731.

182. *MB*, 685, 930.

183. TJ to Anthony Giannini, 5 Feb. 1786, *PTJ*, 9:254; Perrault to TJ, 9 Jan. 1789, *PTJ*, 14:426; Madison Hemings recollections, Gordon-Reed, *Thomas Jefferson and Sally Hemings*, 246.

184. *MB*, 729, 734; correspondence of Martha Jefferson and Marie J. de Botidoux, 1789–1790, ViU; Wister and Irwin, *Worthy Women*, 20–22.

185. TJ to James Maurice, 16 Sept. 1789, *PTJ*, 15:433; Ellen Coolidge to Joseph Coolidge, 24 Oct. 1858, Gordon-Reed, *Thomas Jefferson and Sally Hemings*, 259; TJ to Count Diodati, 3 Aug. 1789, *PTJ*, 15:326; Madison Hemings recollections, Gordon-Reed, *Thomas Jefferson and Sally Hemings*, 246.

186. On the complex issue of the legal position of slaves in a "free" country, see Sue Peabody, *"There Are No Slaves in France": The Political Culture of Race and Slavery in the Ancien Régime* (New York, 1996).

187. Madison Hemings recollections, Gordon-Reed, *Thomas Jefferson and Sally Hemings*, 246, 248; TJ to Thomas Mann Randolph, 19 May 1793, *PTJ*, 26:65; Betts, *Farm Book*, 6.

188. Randall to James Parton, 1 June 1868, Gordon-Reed, *Thomas Jefferson and Sally Hemings*, 254; Bear, 46.

189. TJ to John Wayles Eppes, 21 Dec. 1799, *PTJ*, 31:274; Madison Hemings recollections, Gordon-Reed, *Thomas Jefferson and Sally Hemings*, 246–248.

190. Madison Hemings recollections, Gordon-Reed, *Thomas Jefferson and Sally Hemings*, 246, 248; Minnie Shumate Woodson, *The Sable Curtain* (Washington, 1985), appendix; Minnie Shumate Woodson, *The Woodson Source Book* (Washington, 1980), i–v, 20–55; Eugene A. Foster et al., "Jefferson Fathered Slave's Last Child," *Nature* 396 (5 Nov. 1998): 27–28.

191. Gordon-Reed, *Thomas Jefferson and Sally Hemings*, 141–147; Randall to Parton, and Ellen Coolidge to Joseph Coolidge, Gordon-Reed, *Thomas Jefferson and Sally Hemings*, 254–260; Bear, 4.

192. Unless the child born in 1790 did, in fact, survive.

193. Stanton, "'Those Who Labor,'" this volume, 7–8.

194. He used the spelling *Hemmings* (see note 237).

195. Gordon-Reed, *Thomas Jefferson and Sally Hemings*, 248. William Fossett was an apprentice carpenter at Monticello from 1775 through 1779 (*MB*, 390). The dates of his presence and

Joseph Fossett's choice of surname support the speculation that William and Joseph Fossett were father and son. The oral family history of Joseph Fossett's descendants, however, states that he was Thomas Jefferson's son (Lerone Bennett, "Thomas Jefferson's Negro Grandchildren," *Ebony* 10 [Nov. 1954]: 78).

196. F. A. F. La Rochefoucauld-Liancourt, *Voyage dans les Etats-Unis d'Amérique* (Paris, 1798–1799), 5:35; Gordon-Reed, *Thomas Jefferson and Sally Hemings*, 259; Bear, 88.

197. Oldham to TJ, 26 Nov. 1804, MHi.

198. Oldham to TJ, 16 and 23 July 1805, TJ to Oldham, 20 July 1805, MHi; Ellen Coolidge to Joseph Coolidge, 24 Oct. 1858, Gordon-Reed, *Thomas Jefferson and Sally Hemings*, 258; Bear, 102; Madison Hemings recollections, Gordon-Reed, *Thomas Jefferson and Sally Hemings*, 246. In 1815 at Monticello, Jefferson paid a "James Hemings" for finding the eyepiece of one of his telescopes. He probably was Critta's son, returning to visit family. As Ellen Coolidge recalled of the four runaways who were not pursued, "Their whereabouts was perfectly known but they were left to themselves—for they were white enough to pass for white" (*MB*, 1315).

199. Madison Hemings recollections, Gordon-Reed, *Thomas Jefferson and Sally Hemings*, 247; Fraser D. Neiman, "Coincidence or Causal Connection?: The Relationship between Thomas Jefferson's Visits to Monticello and Sally Hemings's Conceptions," *William and Mary Quarterly*, 3rd ser., 57, no. 1 (Jan. 2000): 198–210.

200. Madison Hemings recollections, Gordon-Reed, *Thomas Jefferson and Sally Hemings*, 246.

201. *MB*, 923; Bear, "The Hemings Family of Monticello," 80–81; Martha Randolph to TJ, 15 Jan. 1795, *PTJ*, 28:247. Mary Hemings was freed by her purchaser, Thomas Bell, sometime after 1792; Robert and James Hemings were manumitted by Jefferson in 1794 and 1796; the younger James Hemings was not pursued in 1805; Beverly and Harriet Hemings were allowed to leave Monticello in 1822; and John, Madison, and Eston Hemings, Joseph Fossett, and Burwell Colbert were freed in Jefferson's will.

202. Randall, *The Life of Thomas Jefferson*, 1:338–339; TJ to Daniel Hylton, 22 Nov. 1792, *PTJ*, 24:657. Randall's account gives the impression that an early death was the reason for Martin Hemings's vanishing from the records, but a letter of 1795 suggests that he may in fact have been sold (TJ to Martha J. Randolph, 22 Jan. 1795, *PTJ*, 28:249).

203. *MB*, 371; George Wythe to TJ, 31 Dec. 1781, *PTJ*, 6:144.

204. Bear, 99; Ellen Randolph to Martha J. Randolph, 27 Sept. 1816, ViU.

205. FB, 111; Thomas M. Randolph to TJ, 3 Jan. 1801, *PTJ*, 32:390; *MB*, 1150; TJ instructions to Bacon, ca. Oct. 1806, Bear, 54; Edmund Bacon to TJ, 26 Jan. 1809, MHi; *MB*, 1298; Ellen Randolph to Martha J. Randolph, 28 July 1819, ViU.

206. Thomas Mann Randolph postscript to Martha J. Randolph to TJ, 31 Jan. 1801, *PTJ*, 32:528; *MB*, 1265; Jefferson list of gratuity payments, 1816–1826, MHi; Bear, 99.

207. Bacon recollections, Bear, 94; Ellen Coolidge to Henry S. Randall, 13 Mar. 1856, Coolidge Letterbook, p. 61, ViU. Thomas J. Randolph, late in life, published a response to Bacon's memoir in which he noted that Bacon's "fertile imagination magnifies a row between two drunken men . . . in which neither skin was broken nor blood drawn . . . into a conflict almost as terrible as that of the Kilkenny cats" (Randolph, broadside, *The Last Days of Thomas Jefferson*, 1873, ViU).

208. Thomas J. Randolph draft letter, post-1873, ViU: 8937; TJ to Wilson C. Nicholas, 11 Aug. 1819, DLC; Ellen Randolph to Martha J. Randolph, 28 July 1819, FLDA.

209. Ellen Randolph to Martha J. Randolph, 28 July 1819, FLDA; to Virginia Randolph, 31 Aug. 1819, FLDA; Cornelia Randolph to Virginia Randolph, 28 July 1819, FLDA.

210. TJ to William O. Callis, 8 May 1795, *PTJ*, 28.346, *MB*, 957.

211. Ellen Randolph to Virginia Randolph, 31 Aug. 1819, FLDA. In his Farm Book, Jefferson noted Betty Brown as his "proper slave" in Jan. 1774, before the division of the Wayles estate that brought the rest of the Hemingses to Monticello (FB, 5).

212. Codicil of will, Bear, 121; Randolph reminiscences, Randall, *The Life of Thomas Jefferson*, 3:544; James A. Bear, Jr., "The Last Few Days in the Life of Thomas Jefferson," *Magazine of Albemarle County History* 32 (1974): 74–75.

213. *MB*, 555–557; TJ to William Short, 7 May 1784, *PTJ*, 7:229.

214. *MB*, 570, 673, 681.

215. Henry Adams, *History of the United States of America*, cited in Howard C. Rice, Jr., *Thomas Jefferson's Paris* (Princeton, 1976), 125; TJ to David Humphreys, 18 Mar. 1789, *PTJ*, 14:676.

216. Betts, *Farm Book*, 15–16.

217. Hemings inventory, 20 Feb. 1796, *PTJ*, 28:610–611; TJ to Mary Jefferson, 25 May 1797, *PTJ*, 29:399.

218. TJ to William Evans, 22 Feb., 31 Mar. 1801; Evans to TJ, 27 Feb. 1801; Francis Say to TJ, 23 Feb. 1801, *PTJ*, 33:38, 53, 91, 505.

219. *MB*, 1051; TJ to William Evans, 1 Nov. 1801; Evans to TJ, 5 Nov. 1801, *PTJ*, 35:542, 569–570; TJ to Thomas M. Randolph, 4 Dec. 1801, *PTJ*, 36:20.

220. Marie Kimball, *Thomas Jefferson's Cook Book*, 4th ed. (Charlottesville, 1987), 106–107; TJ to Martha J. Randolph, 2 Nov. 1802, Betts and Bear, 138–139.

221. TJ to William Short, 24 Nov. 1821, MHi; *MB*, 1043, 1053–1054, 1057, 1091, 1189.

222. Margaret Bayard Smith, *The First Forty Years of Washington Society* (New York, 1906), 391–392; John C. Van Horne and Lee W. Formwalt, eds., *The Correspondence and Miscellaneous Papers of Benjamin H. Latrobe* (New Haven, 1984), 1:232; Samuel Latham Mitchill letter, Jan. 1803, in *Harpers' New Monthly Magazine* 58 (1879): 744; Lucia S. Goodwin, "Barbarians and Savages in the President's House," *Monticello Anniversary Dinner Keepsake* (1983); TJ to John Barnes, 14 June 1817, DLC.

223. Bear, 105–107; *MB*, 1242, 1244; William Seale, *The President's House: A History* (Washington, 1986), 101; Lemaire to TJ, 6 May 1809, *PTJ-R*, 1:189.

224. Peter Fossett recollections, in unidentified Cincinnati newspaper, 1900, Clippings Scrapbook, p. 978, Cincinnati Public Library.

225. George Ticknor, *Life, Letters and Journals* (Boston, 1876), 1:36; Charles M. Wiltse and Harold D. Moser, eds., *The Papers of Daniel Webster* (Hanover, 1974), 1:371; Smith, *The First Forty Years*, 69.

226. TJ to Joseph Dougherty, 31 July 1806, Betts, *Farm Book*, 22–23. Giving credence to Joe and Edy's marriage is the surname taken by Edith's son, James, born in the White House in 1805: Fossett (several James Fossetts lived in Albemarle County after the Civil War, presumably descendants of Edith's son; see GWA). Another boy, born in 1803, died in infancy (*MB*, 1091).

227. Dougherty to TJ, 3 Aug. 1806, Betts, *Farm Book*, 23; *MB*, 1188; Stanton, "'Those Who Labor,'" this volume, 16–17; Etienne Lemaire to TJ, 5 Aug. 1806, MHi.

228. Bear, 8–11; TJ to Nicholas Lewis, 12 Apr. 1792, *PTJ*, 23:408. For a more extended account of Mary Hemings Bell and her family, see Stanton, "Monticello to Main Street."

229. TJ to J. B. Demeunier, 29 Apr. 1795, *PTJ*, 28:341; *FB*, 111; Stanton, "'Those Who Labor,'" this volume, 9–12.

230. Stanton, "Those Who Labor," this volume, 12, 20; Nicholas P. Trist to Virginia J. Trist, 8 May 1829, NcU: Trist Papers; Edmund Bacon to TJ, 11 Sept. 1822, MHi; *MB*, 1265, 1392, 1399, 1402; William Watson to TJ, 9 Mar. 1812, *PTJ-R*, 4:543; Bear, 102.

231. Bear, 6, 10; U.S. Census, 1850, Albemarle County.

232. Randall, *The Life of Thomas Jefferson*, 1:69; FB, 111; TJ to Thomas M. Randolph, 29 Jan. 1801, *PTJ*, 32:517, TJ to Edmund Bacon, 6 Oct. and 21 Nov. 1806, MHi.

233. TJ to Edmund Bacon, 24 Nov. 1807, 26 Dec. 1808, CSmH; TJ to Anne Cary Randolph, 16 Feb. and 22 Mar. 1808, Betts and Bear, 328, 337; Randall, *The Life of Thomas Jefferson*, 3:346.

234. Edmund Bacon to TJ, 19 Jan. 1809, ViU; TJ to Thomas M. Randolph, 9 Jan. 1801, *PTJ*, 32:417; FB, 70; TJ to Martha J. Randolph, 6 June 1814, Betts and Bear, 405.

235. Randall, *The Life of Thomas Jefferson*, 1:69–70; TJ to Thomas J. Randolph, 31 Mar. 1815, Betts and Bear, 409; *MB*, 1257; TJ to John W. Eppes, 10 May 1810, *PTJ-R*, 2:378.

236. *MB*, 1057, 1069, 1077; TJ to Edmund Bacon, 6 Oct. 1806, MHi.

237. To avoid confusion I use the spelling "Hemings" throughout. Madison and Eston Hemings, as well as Thomas Jefferson, used this spelling, while other members of the family (John Hemings and descendants of Joseph Fossett's sister Betsy) used the spelling "Hemmings."

238. Gordon-Reed, *Thomas Jefferson and Sally Hemings*, 248; memorandums for Manoah Clarkson, 23 Sept. 1792, *PTJ*, 24:413–414.

239. *MB*, 508, 517; Bear, 20, 54; "Memorandums with respect to Watson," ca. 22–25 Oct. 1793, *PTJ*, 27:267; *MB*, 985; TJ to Thomas Munroe, 4 Mar. 1815, CSmH.

240. Memorandum to Richard Richardson, ca. 21 Dec. 1799, *PTJ*, 31:271; Bear, 101–102; TJ to Joel Yancey, 17 Jan. 1819, Betts, *Farm Book*, 42; FB, 114; and TJ–Hemings correspondence, MHi (quotations from TJ to Hemings, 27 Nov. 1819, and Hemings to TJ, 29 Nov. 1821).

241. Martha J. Randolph to Thomas J. Randolph, 7 Feb. 1830, FLDA; FB, 114; TJ to Ellen Coolidge, 14 Nov. 1825, Betts and Bear, 461; Robert L. Self and Susan R. Stein, "The Collaboration of Thomas Jefferson and John Hemings: Furniture Attributed to the Monticello Joinery," *Winterthur Portfolio* 33, no. 4 (Winter 1998), 231–248; Fanny M. Burke to Stuart Gibboney, 8 Mar. 1928, Monticello Curatorial files.

242. Ellen Randolph Harrison, "Monticello Child Life," ViU; Ellen W. Randolph to Martha J. Randolph, [ca. 10 Nov. 1816], FLDA; John Hemings to Septimia Randolph, 28 Aug. 1825, ViU; Cornelia Randolph to Virginia Randolph, 25 Oct. [1816], FLDA.

243. Harrison, "Monticello Child Life"; Bear, 101 (Bacon recollects Priscilla's name incorrectly as Ursula); Ellen Randolph to Martha J. Randolph, 27 Sept. 1816, FLDA.

244. Cornelia J. Randolph to Ellen Coolidge, 30 May 1830, ViU.

245. John Hemings to TJ, 29 Nov. 1821, MHi; *MB*, 1265, 1275, 1352, 1373, 1385.

246. TJ will, Bear, 121–122. Jefferson bequeathed immediate freedom only to Burwell Colbert; Fossett and John Hemings were to be freed a year from the date of his death.

247. *Charlottesville Central Gazette*, 13 Jan. 1827.

248. Inventories, Albemarle County Will Book, No. 8, pp. 281–282; No. 9, pp. 20–22; John Forsyth to Thomas J. Randolph, 5 Dec. 1826, ViU: 8937-b.

249. Peggy Nicholas to Jane H. Randolph, 29 Jan. 1827, ViU; Thomas J. Randolph recollections, ViU: 1837; Mary J. Randolph to Ellen Coolidge, 25 Jan. 1827, FLDA.

250. Auguste Levasseur, *Lafayette in America, in 1824 and 1825* (New York, 1829), 218.

251. Israel G. Jefferson recollections, Gordon-Reed, *Thomas Jefferson and Sally Hemings*, 250; *New York World*, 30 Jan. 1898.

252. Israel G. Jefferson recollections, Gordon-Reed, *Thomas Jefferson and Sally Hemings*, 250; Thomas J. Randolph recollections, ViU: 1837; Jefferson will, Bear, 120–122; *Acts of Assembly* (Richmond, 1826), 127; Randall, *The Life of Thomas Jefferson*, 3:562; Martha Randolph will, 18 Apr. [1834], ViU: 1397; Ervin Jordan, Jr., "'A Just and True Account': Two 1833 Parish Censuses of Albemarle County Free Blacks," *Magazine of Albemarle County History* 53 (1995): 137; U.S. Census 1850, Albemarle County.

253. Monticello Dispersal Sale receipts, ViU: 5921; Mary J. Randolph to Ellen Coolidge, 25 Jan. 1827, FLDA.

254. Dispersal Sale receipts.

255. Dispersal Sale receipts; account of 1829 sale, ViU: 8937.

256. This word has so far defied interpretation.

257. Cornelia Randolph to Virginia Trist, 22 Aug. 1831, NcU: Trist Papers; Cornelia Randolph to Ellen Coolidge, 30 May 1830, ViU: 9090.

258. Cornelia Randolph to Virginia Trist, 22 Aug. 1831, NcU: Trist Papers.

259. "John Hemings: Documentary References," Monticello Research Library. Although Virginia law prohibited manumitting slaves over the age of forty-five unless provision was made

for their support, the skills of Hemings and Joseph Fossett (age forty-six when freed) protected them from enforcement of the letter of the law.

260. Jane Hollins Randolph to Sarah E. Nicholas, [Sept.?] 1831, ViU: 1397; Martha J. Randolph to Joseph Coolidge, 5 Sept. and 27 Oct. 1831, ViU; Albemarle County Minute Book, 1830–1831, p. 123.

261. Albemarle County Minute Book, 1830–1831, p. 123, and 1832–1843, p. 12; Albemarle County Deed Book, No. 29, pp. 276–277; Albemarle County marriage bonds, 1831 and 1832. Reference to Sally Hemings has been found in no records after 1833, and Madison Hemings's 1873 recollections give 1835 as the date of her death. A reference brought to my attention by C. Allan Brown, however, suggests that she may have been alive in 1837. An Italian count, passing through Charlottesville in the summer of 1837, was "shown a pretty [negress]—although she was no longer young—who had beautified the last days of Jefferson" (Count Francesco Arese, *A Trip to the Prairies and in the Interior of North America*, trans. Andrew Evans [New York, 1934], 29).

262. For more extensive accounts of Madison and Eston Hemings, see Lucia Stanton and Dianne Swann-Wright, "Bonds of Memory: Identity and the Hemings Family," this volume, 232–250, and Stanton, "Monticello to Main Street," 221, 224, 227.

263. Martha Randolph to Septimia Meikleham, 27 Mar. 1833, ViU: 4726.

264. Albemarle County Deed Book, No. 35, pp. 219–220.

265. Thomas J. Randolph recollections, ViU: 1837.

266. Bear, 122; *New York World*, 30 Jan. 1898; Stanton, "Monticello to Main Street," 216–218; Jefferson's optimism is indicated by the codicil to his will, which provided that the houses he wished built for John Hemings, Burwell Colbert, and Joseph Fossett be built "on some part of my lands convenient to them with respect to the residence of their wives."

267. Stanton, "Monticello to Main Street," 218–219; FB, 160.

268. Stanton, "Monticello to Main Street," 221–222, 224–225; *New York World*, 30 Jan. 1898.

269. Unidentified Cincinnati newspaper, ca. June 1900; *New York World*, 30 Jan. 1898.

270. *New York World*, 30 Jan. 1898; Cornelius, *"When I Can Read My Title Clear,"* 69–70.

271. *New York World*, 30 Jan. 1898; Charles H. Bullock recollections, ca. Oct. 1949, Moorland-Spingarn Collection, DHU.

272. *New York World*, 30 Jan. 1898; Stanton, "Monticello to Main Street," 225–226.

273. *New York World*, 30 Jan. 1898; unidentified Cincinnati newspapers, May and ca. June 1900, Jan. 1901, Clippings Scrapbook, Cincinnati Public Library; Cincinnati Directories, 1843–1856; U.S. Census, Hamilton County, Ohio, 1850; Stanton, "Monticello to Main Street," 221–222; 224–225; Wendell P. Dabney, *Cincinnati's Colored Citizens* (Cincinnati, 1926), 180, 349.

274. Dabney, *Cincinnati's Colored Citizens*, 109, 350–351; Cincinnati Directory, 1857; Charles Theodore Greve, *Centennial History of Cincinnati* (Chicago, 1903), 832–834; unidentified Cincinnati newspapers, May, ca. June 1900, Jan, 1901.

275. Unidentified Cincinnati newspaper, ca. June 1900; *New York World*, 30 Jan. 1898.

276. Dabney, *Cincinnati's Colored Citizens*, 180, 349, 375; unidentified Cincinnati newspapers, ca. June 1900, Jan. 1901; Stanton, "Monticello to Main Street," 226–227.

277. Dabney, *Cincinnati's Colored Citizens*, 180, 349; "First Baptist Church—Cumminsville 1870," church history, copy in GWA.

278. Unidentified Cincinnati newspaper, May and ca. June 1900, Jan. 1901; *Cincinnati Enquirer*, 8 Jan. 1901.

279. This census record provided the first knowledge of Wormley's surname, to which no reference has been found in Jefferson's papers.

280. Cocke to A. S. Brockenbrough, 17 July 1826, ViU; Elizabeth Langhorne, K. Edward Lay, and William D. Rieley, *A Virginia Family and Its Plantation Houses* (Charlottesville, 1987), 112; Harrison diary, Sept. 1834, ViU: 3226; Albemarle County Minute Book, 1832–1834, 6 Feb. 1832, p. 12; Albemarle County marriage bond, 5 Dec. 1834.

281. Maria Eppes to TJ, 6 Nov. 1801, 21 Apr. and 21 June 1802, *PTJ*, 35:579, 37:299, 647; deed of manumission, 20 Jan. 1827, Albemarle County Deed Book, No. 32, p. 412; Zachariah Bowles will, Albemarle County Will Book, No. 12, pp. 95–96; Critta Bowles will, Albemarle County Will Book, No. 20, p. 144. Whether Martha Colbert ever received the benefits of this legacy is not known. In a superseded will in 1834, Martha Jefferson Randolph indicated her intention to free the Colberts' daughters Emily and Martha Ann, but in 1836 she gave Martha Ann Colbert to her son Meriwether Lewis Randolph, who moved to the banks of the Terre Noir in Arkansas Territory. Although she was "certain that for [Martha Ann's] happiness she could not fall into better hands," Jefferson's daughter was aware of the impact of this gift. "The separation from her family will be but temporary I hope," she wrote to her son at this time, "as I live in hopes that you will finally settle where I can sometimes see you and yours." Both Martha and Lewis Randolph, however, died not long after these comments, and it is probable that Martha Ann Colbert remained in Arkansas with Randolph's widow (Martha J. Randolph wills, 18 Apr. 1834, 24 Jan. 1836, ViU: 1397, and Albemarle County Will Book, No. 12, p. 270; Martha J. Randolph to Meriwether Lewis Randolph, 6 Feb. 1836, Randolph Family Papers, ViU: 34869).

282. Manuscript inventory, ca. 1826–1827, ViU; Cornelia J. Randolph to Ellen Coolidge, 30 May 1830, ViU; Virginia J. Trist to Jane Hollins Randolph, 16 Jan. 1831, NcU: Trist Papers. The inventory is in the hand of Martha J. Randolph, except for the values, which are in an unknown hand.

283. Cornelia Randolph to Virginia J. Trist, 22 Aug. 1831, NcU: Trist Papers; Martha Randolph will, 18 Apr. 1834, ViU: 1397. Brown Colbert, whom Jefferson had reluctantly sold to brickmason John Jordan in 1806, wanted his mother to come live with him in Rockbridge County. Because of his enslaved condition he needed Martha Randolph's financial help to support her. Jefferson's daughter, living on a very restricted income, preferred an alternative arrangement. If Betty Brown went to live in Washington with her daughter Melinda, the financial burden on Martha Randolph would be lessened. Decades earlier Melinda Colbert had married John Freeman, Jefferson's dining room servant at the White House. Her husband, by now a free man, was able to earn a living for his family and would be able to contribute to his mother-in-law's expenses. In Cornelia Randolph's opinion, however, this was an unfortunate plan: "Poor Melinda, I really should be very sorry that the comfort and happiness of her family should be destroyed by this vixens tongue." Melinda and John Freeman did take in her invalid sister Mary, purchasing and freeing her in 1827 and 1828 (John Jordan to TJ, 4 Dec. 1805, 7 Jan. 1806, MHi; TJ to Jordan, 21 Dec. 1805, 9 Feb. 1806, MHi; John Jordan to Thomas J. Randolph, 29 Oct. 1827, ViU; Dorothy S. Provine, ed., *District of Columbia Free Negro Registers, 1821–1861* [Bowie, 1996], 140).

284. Jane Hollins Randolph to Margaret Smith Nicholas, 14 Mar. 1829, ViU: 1397.

285. Dispersal Sale receipts, ViU; Margaret Smith Nicholas to Jane Hollins Randolph, 29 Jan. 1827, ViU: 1397.

286. Account of 1829 sale, ViU; Margaret S. Nicholas to Jane Hollins Randolph, 17 Jan. 1829, ViU: 1397.

287. Virginia Trist to Ellen Coolidge, 1 May 1827; Cornelia Randolph to Ellen Coolidge, 18 May 1827, FLDA.

288. Ellen Coolidge to Henry S. Randall, 13 Mar. 1856, Coolidge Letterbook, p. 57, ViU: 9090; Thomas J. Randolph recollections, ViU: 1837; George W. Randolph to Mary B. Randolph, 3 Feb. 1866, ViU: 1397.

289. *MB*, 1363; *Lynchburg Virginian*, 20 Aug. 1824.

290. Deed, 11 Nov. 1867, Albemarle County Deed Book, No. 63, pp. 369–370; Eric Foner, *Reconstruction: America's Unfinished Revolution 1863–1877* (New York, 1988), 283–284.

291. Marriage license, 2 Mar 1871, Albemarle County Clerk's Office.

292. Quotation, Betty Ann Fitch. Results of the Getting Word project, which is sponsored by the Thomas Jefferson Foundation, Inc., and has been supported by the Coca-Cola Company, the

Ford Foundation, the River Branch Foundation, and the Virginia Foundation for the Humanities and Public Policy, can be seen in a Web site www.monticello.org/gettingword, a booklet published in 2001 available at GWA, and several essays in this volume: see Stanton, "Monticello to Main Street" and "The Other End of the Telescope"; also Stanton and Swann-Wright, "Bonds of Memory."

293. The quotation is by Lerone Bennett, Jr., cited in Stephen R. Fox, *The Guardian of Boston: William Monroe Trotter* (New York, 1970), 279.

Monticello to Main Street

Community history is a communal effort. Special thanks are due to Beverly Gray, Joshua Rothman, Gayle Schulman, Robert Vernon, and the staff and volunteers of the Albemarle County Historical Society, whose work has been of particular importance to this essay.

1. *Charlottesville Central Gazette*, 13 Jan. 1827; Thomas Jefferson Randolph's manuscript recollections, ca. 1870, Edgehill-Randolph Papers, ViU; Monticello Dispersal Sale receipts. ViU: 5291.

2. This essay represents only a preliminary exploration of this topic, leaving a wealth of documentation still to be mined for an understanding of the larger context within which the Hemings family members and their connections lived and worked. A closer examination of the parallel development of East Main Street by their white neighbors and the dynamics of black-white social and financial relationships is beyond the scope of this essay. Also, the settlement of West Main Street (involving Madison Hemings, the Scotts, Elizabeth Moore, and the Barnett sisters) has not yet been pursued. While following a chronological course of over a century, I have also leapt over defining events like the Civil War and Reconstruction and the arrival of the railroad without reference to their effects on the participants in this story. Investigating the free black presence in Charlottesville is, I have discovered, a window into a fascinating and much larger landscape of Albemarle County's early history.

3. Bear, 4. Wayles was described in a Green Springs manuscript as a "servant boy brought from England" (1839 copy of undated William Lee manuscript, courtesy of Sully Plantation).

4. Madison Hemings's recollections, *Pike County Republican*, 13 Mar. 1873, printed in Annette Gordon-Reed, *Thomas Jefferson and Sally Hemings: An American Controversy* (Charlottesville, 1997), 245–248.

5. Albemarle County Deed Book, Albemarle County Courthouse, No. 9, pp. 36–37; Joseph A. Waddell, *Annals of Augusta County* (1902; repr. Bridgewater, 1958), 288; James Alexander; *Early Charlottesville: Recollections of James Alexander 1828–1874*, ed. Mary Rawlings (Charlottesville, 1942), 89; TJ to William Short, 13 Apr. 1800, *PTJ* 31:503. Bell frequently appears in county records as a witness, trustee, or executor and was a county magistrate beginning in 1791 (Edgar Woods, *Albemarle County in Virginia* [1901; repr. Berryville, 1984], 90, 376). Robert Vernon's transcriptions of Albemarle County records on free blacks, shared with great generosity, have saved me countless hours of searching in unindexed record books.

6. Bear, 4, 6–8; FB, 15, 24. No indication of the identity of a husband appears in Jefferson's records.

7. TJ to Nicholas Lewis, 12 Apr. 1792, and TJ to Thomas Bell, 25 Sept. 1792, *PTJ*, 23:408, 24:416; "Negroes alienated from 1784 to 1794," Sol Feinstone Collection, David Library of the American Revolution, on deposit at the American Philosophical Society, Philadelphia. The last source, undoubtedly a detached page of Jefferson's Farm Book, is illustrated in Lucia Stanton, *Slavery at Monticello* (Charlottesville, 1996), 16. It is the document that firmly established that the Mary "Wells" of Thomas Bell's will and other public records was in fact Mary Hemings. She appears in the documentary record with three different surnames: Hemings, Wells (possibly a corruption of Wayles), and Bell.

Jefferson had given Mary's oldest child, Daniel, to his sister Anna Scott Marks on her marriage in 1787; he gave Molly to his daughter Martha on her marriage in 1790 ("Negroes alienated").

8. Although no manumission record has been found, Bell presumably freed Mary once she became his property. Marriage between the races had been prohibited by Virginia law since the beginning of the century (William W. Hening, *The Statutes at Large* [Philadelphia, 1823], 3:453–454). R. T. W. Duke, Jr., who was well acquainted with Bell and Hemings's grandsons, stated in his early twentieth-century recollections, "With the rather 'easy' morality of those early days no one paid any attention to a man's method of living and Col. Bell lived openly with the woman and had two children by her" (Recollections of My Life, ViU: 9521, 3:223). I am very grateful to Gayle Schulman for sharing her transcription of this memoir, which contains much new information about the Scotts.

9. Albemarle County Will Book, Albemarle County Courthouse, No. 4, pp. 59–60. Bell's nephew William Love was the third heir.

10. Marriage bond, 10 Oct. 1802, Albemarle County Clerk's Office; Orra Langhorne, "Southern Sketches," *Southern Workman and Hampton School Record* 17 (Sept. 1888): 92–93; Alexander, *Early Charlottesville*, 89. Ada Pyne Bankhead gave the name of Jesse Scott's mother as Annika Cumba (typescript copy of "Note inserted in Woods' History of Albemarle by Miss Ada Pyne Bankhead," on deposit at Monticello Research Department). One Scott who became governor of Kentucky was Gen. Charles Scott (ca. 1739–1813), originally of Powhatan County.

11. Langhorne, "Southern Sketches," 92–93; Alexander, *Early Charlottesville*, 89–90. Grateful thanks to Olivia Summers Dutcher, who brought to my attention her delightful portrait of Jesse Scott, thus setting in motion the research that led to a recognition of the connection between Monticello and the Bell-Scott family. A violin, sold in Charlottesville at the turn of the century, bore the story that it had been given to Jesse Scott by Thomas Jefferson. Its purchaser declared it a genuine seventeenth-century Amati, and it was played in public by several prominent violinists; it is now unlocated (Monticello Curatorial Files).

12. Betsy had been given to Jefferson's daughter Maria Eppes in 1797 ("Negroes alienated").

13. Nailery accounts, William Andrews Clark Memorial Library, University of California, Los Angeles; *MB*, 924, 926; Bear, 102; Stanton, "'Those Who Labor for My Happiness,'" this volume, 12. Historians have speculated that Joseph, since he took the surname Fossett, was the son of William Fossett, a free white carpenter who worked at Monticello from 1775 to 1779. Many of Fossett's descendants believe he was Thomas Jefferson's son. The Fossetts' oldest child, James, had been given by Jefferson to Thomas Jefferson Randolph in 1816 (FB, 160).

14. Patsy (b. 1810) was bought by University of Virginia professor Charles Bonnycastle for $325; the fates of Maria (b. 1807) and Isabella (b. 1819) are unknown. John Winn also purchased three other members of the Hemings family, the children of Betty Hemings's grandson Wormley Hughes (Monticello Dispersal Sale receipts; Peter Fossett recollections, *New York World*, 30 Jan. 1898; these recollections of life at Monticello were [re]discovered because of the work of the staff and volunteers of the Albemarle County Historical Society in computerizing county records). The two youngest Fossett children were William (b. 1821) and Daniel (b. 1824).

15. Robert Gamble report (Albemarle County Will Book, No. 4, pp. 164–168).

16. It is not possible to determine whether the agreement with Jones was made before or after the 1827 sale, and Jones later reneged on his promise (*New York World*, 30 Jan. 1798; Albemarle County Deed Book, No. 18, pp. 479–481).

17. Betsy-Ann sold for $450, $175 over her appraised value; her older sister Patsy brought only $395 (Monticello Dispersal Sale receipts; Albemarle County Will Book, No. 8, p. 281). Patsy Fossett ran away soon after the sale, so it is unlikely that Charles Bonnycastle's purchase was part of a family agreement (*Charlottesville Virginia Advocate*, 1 Sept. 1827). In Sept. 1837, Joseph Fossett freed his slaves, including his daughter Betsy-Ann (Albemarle County Deed Book, No. 35, pp. 219–220).

18. Wayt & Winn had bought Robert Bell's interest in the estate at public auction in 1818; Jesse Scott had purchased William Love's interest at auction in 1804 (Albemarle County Deed Book, No. 15, pp. 13–14; No. 18, pp. 479–481; No. 29, pp. 442, 444–445; No. 31, p. 436; No. 32, pp. 198–199; No. 36, pp. 121–122).

19. *The Revised Code of the Laws of Virginia* (Richmond, 1819), 436–437; Mutual Assurance Society declarations Nos. 953 (1809), 5244 (1823), 8228 (1833), 11,182 (1840) (microfilm in ViU).

20. Ronald B. Head, ed., "The Student Diary of Charles Ellis, Jr.," *Magazine of Albemarle County History*, 35–36 (1977–1978): 16; Alexander, *Early Charlottesville*, 67.

21. Since others have written extensively on David Isaacs and Nancy West, I discuss them only briefly here. See Carol Ely, Jeffrey Hantman, and Phyllis Leffler, *To Seek the Peace of the City: Jewish Life in Charlottesville* (Charlottesville, 1994), 3–5; Nancy E. Willner, "A Brief History of the Jewish Community in Charlottesville and Albemarle," *Magazine of Albemarle County History*, 40 (1982): 2–3; and Joshua D. Rothman, *Notorious in the Neighborhood: Sex and Families Across the Color Line in Virginia* (Chapel Hill, 2003), 57–90.

22. Tucker and Betsy-Ann Isaacs's first child, James, was born in June of 1832. As Betsy-Ann was a slave, they could not legally marry. Freed by her father in 1837, she did not become Isaacs's legal wife until 1848 (Albemarle County Deed Book, No. 35, pp. 219–220; Albemarle County Marriage Bonds, 1848; Isaacs family records, in private hands). Albemarle County Land Tax Book, 1823–1838; Mutual Assurance Society declarations Nos. 5249 (1823) and 8233 (1833). See also other insurance declarations, from 1802 to 1846 (Nos. 520, 619, 11,186, 14,489), all of which, except that of 1840, record that the structure was the residence of David Isaacs or, after his death, Nancy West. In 1840 it was occupied by George Norvell. Some time in the 1840s Tucker and Betsy-Ann Isaacs moved to a new house at the Water Street end of Lot 36 (Albemarle County Deed Book, No. 48, pp. 428–429).

23. Madison Hemings recollections, in Gordon-Reed, *Thomas Jefferson and Sally Hemings*, 248. In an 1834 will, superseded by an 1836 will after Sally Hemings's death, Martha Randolph gave "their time" to "Sally" and two other members of the Hemings family (Will, 18 Apr. [1834], ViU: 1397). The location of the rented house in Charlottesville is not known. Sally Hemings is listed as free in the 1833 special census (Ervin L. Jordan, Jr., "'A Just and True Account': Two 1833 Parish Censuses of Albemarle County Free Blacks," *Magazine of Albemarle County History* 53 (1995): 114–139). I am grateful to Mr. Jordan for giving me my first sight of these fascinating censuses.

24. The 1833 special census lists Madison Hemings and Sally Hemings as residents of St. Anne's Parish, probably in the house he owned on West Main Street; Eston Hemings is listed in Fredericksville Parish, of which East Main Street was a part (Jordan, "'A Just and True Account,'" 129, 136–137; Albemarle County Marriage Bonds, 1832). David Isaacs had sold Lot 33 to Nancy West in 1820, and later deeds refer to her gifts of portions of the lot to Eston Hemings and Jane West; Hemings's occupation of the most easterly house on Lot 33 is mentioned in both a deed and an insurance declaration (Albemarle County Deed Book, No. 22, p. 177; No. 35, pp. 264–266, 340; Mutual Assurance Society declaration No. 8597 [1837]; Albemarle County Land Tax Books, 1828–1838). According to James Alexander, Frederick Isaacs published the short-lived *Charlottesville Chronicle* in a building on Lot 33 (Alexander, *Early Charlottesville*, 77–79).

25. Alexander, *Early Charlottesville*, 78.

26. Albemarle County Deed Book, No. 29, p. 491; No. 41, pp. 519–520; Albemarle County Land Tax Books, 1832–1844; Fossett accounts with Thomas Jefferson Randolph and Thomas Jefferson's estate, July 1827 to July 1830, ViU: 8937-b. When Fossett purchased the lot, for $325, the Norris blacksmith shop was excepted from the deed; he probably purchased it soon after, as his deed of sale in 1844 mentions a shop. The structure on Fossett's lot was never valuable enough to be assessed for tax purposes.

27. Albemarle County Deed Book, No. 16, pp. 288–289; Albemarle County Land Tax Books, 1809–1840; Woods, *Albemarle County*, 110; *MB*, 1276; Dr. Frank Carr to TJ, 18 Mar. 1816, Betts, *Farm Book*, 40.

28. Jordan, "'A Just and True Account,'" 125; Albemarle County Deed Book, No. 27, p. 380; "Negroes alienated." Joseph Fossett was Farley's executor and a co-heir (Albemarle County Will Book, No. 13, p. 44; Albemarle County Deed Book, No. 36, pp. 27–28). Both had daughters

named Elizabeth- (Betsy-) Ann; Fossett had sons named Daniel and Peter Farley Fossett. No reference to Daniel Farley's manumission or freedom has been found in Louisa County records.

29. Monticello Dispersal Sale receipts; TJ to James Barbour, 11 May 1821, Betts, *Farm Book*, 421; William S. Bankhead guardian's accounts, 1833–1838, Albemarle County Will Book, No. 19, pp. 172–176. Peter Hemings had, despite his age, been appraised at $100 (Albemarle County Will Book, No. 8, p. 281). The token sale price suggests that the wish of his family members to purchase his freedom was recognized by those present at the sale.

30. Albemarle County Will Book, No. 13, p. 44; Albemarle County Deed Book, No. 37, pp. 235–236.

31. Rothman, *Notorious in the Neighborhood*, 57–87.

32. The family of free black Catherine Foster, living near the University of Virginia, was also often legally involved with the families of Main Street. To recapitulate some of the connections: Eston Hemings, Betsy-Ann Fossett, and Catherine Foster's son Jerman Evans all married children of Nancy West and David Isaacs; West and Isaacs and Eston Hemings and Tucker Isaacs sold land to each other; James Scott was bondsman for the marriage of Eston and Julia Ann Hemings, and Eston Hemings was bondsman for Jerman and Agnes Evans; Nathaniel H. West witnessed Daniel Farley's will, of which Joseph Fossett was executor; and Robert Scott and Eston Hemings witnessed statements by Catherine Foster and Nancy West (Albemarle County Marriage Bonds, 1832, 1836; Albemarle County Will Book, No. 13, p. 44). There were also property sales to other free blacks—Eston Hemings to Elizabeth Moore and Nancy West to William Spinner, for example; and Spinner was bondsman for Madison Hemings (Albemarle County Deed Book, No. 22, p. 467; No. 34, pp. 137–148; Albemarle County Marriage Bonds, 1831).

33. Alexander, *Early Charlottesville*, 84–86; Albemarle County Deed Book, No. 39, p. 232; No. 41, pp. 319–320; No. 43, pp. 282–283; No. 47, pp. 351–352; Albemarle County Land Tax Books, 1838–1850; Mutual Assurance Society declaration No. 376A (1857). It is at present unknown who lived in the large corner dwelling in the period of West-Isaacs ownership.

34. Albemarle County Deed Book, No. 46, pp. 226–227; Alexander, *Early Charlottesville*, 84. It is possible Isaacs learned his trade from his wife's cousin Burwell Colbert, a skilled painter and glazier and Monticello's butler for many years. Colbert, freed in Jefferson's will, also attended the 1827 Monticello sale, purchasing a mule and portrait prints of his former master and of Lafayette. He did some work at the University of Virginia.

35. Albemarle County Will Book, No. 12, pp. 396–398, 398–400. A few months earlier Eston Hemings had attended the sale of the estate of the eccentric merchant John Yeargain, making one purchase: six silver teaspoons for $4.60 (ibid., 384–386).

36. Albemarle County Deed Book, No. 35, pp. 219–220, 264–266. The deed of manumission, as well as Edith Fossett and family's registration as free persons of color two weeks later, gives ages and heights (Albemarle County Minute Book, 1836–1838, Albemarle County Courthouse, p. 259).

37. *Daily Scioto Gazette*, 1 Aug. 1902; *Chillicothe Leader*, 26 Jan. 1887, typescript. Both sources are in the collection of Beverly Gray, Chillicothe, Ohio, whose generous sharing of information and extensive knowledge of the African American settlement of southern Ohio have been invaluable.

38. *Daily Scioto Gazette*, 1 Aug. 1902. When he registered as a free person of color in Charlottesville in 1832, Eston Hemings was described as a "Bright Mulatto, six feet one inch tall" (Albemarle County Minute Book, 1832–1843, p. 12).

39. 1840 census (Albemarle County); Cincinnati Directory, 1843; Hamilton County (Ohio) Deed Book, No. 92, pp. 105–106; Albemarle County Deed Book, No. 41, pp. 519–520. The Albemarle County Land Tax Books record Fossett's residence as Charlottesville in 1840 and 1842 and "unknown" in 1841 and 1843.

40. *New York World*, 30 Jan. 1898; Jordan, "'A Just and True Account.'" The Scotts, Fosters, and West-Isaacs (other than Tucker) were not listed in the 1833 census, perhaps being considered white.

41. *New York World*, 30 Jan. 1898.

42. Ibid. Berkeley Bullock, a familiar figure in Charlottesville and at the University of Virginia after the Civil War, was one of the fellow slaves Peter Fossett taught to read (Charles H. Bullock recollections, ca. Oct. 1949, DHU).

43. Langhorne, "Southern Sketches," 92–93; Alexander, *Early Charlottesville*, 77, 84–85.

44. Albemarle County Minute Book, 1848–1850, pp. 308–310; *New York World*, 30 Jan. 1898; *Cincinnati Commercial Tribune*, May 1900; Wendell P. Dabney, *Cincinnati's Colored Citizens* (Cincinnati, 1926), 349; unidentified and undated Cincinnati newspaper, ca. July 1900, in scrapbook, Cincinnati Public Library.

45. *Acts of the General Assembly of Virginia* (Richmond, 1850), 7–8; Eugene Davis to Thomas H. Key, Nov. 1850, ViU: 2483-A. This very interesting letter was brought to my attention by the cataloging staff at the Alderman Library. Sally Cottrell, who had been a maid of Ellen Wayles Randolph, Thomas Jefferson's granddaughter, was sold to University of Virginia professor Thomas H. Key in 1826. When Key left for England in 1827 he made arrangements for her manumission, but it was not legally executed.

46. Albemarle County Minute Book, 1850–1854, pp. 5–13. Burwell Colbert was the only remaining one of the five slaves freed by Jefferson in his will and permitted, according to his petition to the legislature, to remain in the state (John Hemings had died in 1833).

47. Albemarle County Minute Book, 1850–1854, p. 13; Cincinnati Directory, 1843; Albemarle County Deed Book, No. 48, pp. 429–430; No. 49, pp. 200–202; *Scioto Gazette*, 15 May 1866; Ross County Deed Book, No. 54, p. 248; No. 57, p. 30; Alexander, *Early Charlottesville*, 84; personal communication of Beverly Gray, Chillicothe, Ohio; interviews in Chillicothe for Getting Word project (see GWA); Stephen R. Fox, *The Guardian of Boston: William Monroe Trotter* (New York, 1970).

48. Albemarle County Deed Book, No. 47, pp. 351–352; Ross County Deed Book, No. 50, pp. 574–575, No. 53, pp. 179–180; Fawn M. Brodie, "Thomas Jefferson's Unknown Grandchildren: A Study in Historical Silences," *American Heritage* 27 (Oct. 1976): 32–33.

49. *Charlottesville Daily Progress*, 13 June 1900; unidentified and undated Cincinnati newspaper, ca. July 1900, in scrapbook, Cincinnati Public Library; Charles H. Bullock recollections; Cincinnati Directories, 1857–1899; Dabney, *Cincinnati's Colored Citizens*, 180, 349–350.

50. Some of Robert Scott's children still lived in Charlottesville but no longer on Main Street. Fossett would have remembered well another family connection, if not relative. John West, adopted son and heir of Jane Isaacs West, left over fifty pieces of real estate at his death in 1927. In 1850, when he was nineteen, he had lived with the Scotts in their Main Street house, and he kept a barber shop on the Scott lot until its sale in 1892. After the division of the estate of James Scott, in 1892, West became owner of half of the outlot that had belonged to Daniel Farley (1850 census; Charlottesville Deed Book, Charlottesville City Courthouse, No. 3, p. 318; John West will, Albemarle County Will Book, No. 34, pp. 136–138).

51. *Charlottesville Jeffersonian Republican*, 22 June and 2 Nov. 1892; *Daily Progress*, 26 Sept. 1899; Mutual Assurance Society declarations Nos. 790A (1857), 21301 (1860); Charlottesville Deed Book, No. 3, 271; Alexander, *Early Charlottesville*, 90. In the 1880s the Adams Express Company occupied one of the storehouses and the barbershop of John West and James Ferguson was located in another structure on the lot.

52. Langhorne, "Southern Sketches," 92–93. Scott was six feet two and one-half inches tall (Albemarle County Minute Book, 1832–1834, p. 12).

53. *Jeffersonian Republican*, 22 June 1892; *Daily Progress*, 26 Sept. 1899; Virginia Writers' Project, *The Negro in Virginia* (New York, 1940), 39; Langhorne, "Southern Sketches," 92–93; statement of Elsie Curl Heiskell, 5 Jan. 1948, typescript, courtesy of Olivia S. Dutcher; Edward C. Mead, *Historic Homes of the South-West Mountains Virginia* (1898; repr. Bridgewater, 1962), 83. R. T. W. Duke, recalling the dances at which Robert Scott called the figures "in a stentorian

voice," wrote late in life that he had "never heard or danced to better music" (Duke, Recollections of My Life, 3:222).

54. *Charlottesville Daily Progress*, 26 and 29 Sept. 1899.

55. Langhorne, "Southern Sketches," 92–93; Ada Pyne Bankhead note; Duke, Recollections of My Life, 3:221.

56. *The Statutes at Large of Virginia* (Richmond, 1835), 1:123; *Virginia Acts of General Assembly, 1910* (Richmond, 1910), 581; Langhorne, "Southern Sketches," 92–93.

57. *Virginia Acts of General Assembly, 1865–66* (Richmond, 1866), 85–86; Duke, Recollections of My Life, 4:1–2; Virginia Writers' Project, *Negro in Virginia*, 39; George Hansbrough, *Reports of Cases Decided in the Supreme Court of Appeals of Virginia* (Richmond, 1892), 88:721–729. In the opinion of the presiding judge, while Sarah Raub's parents may have been legally white, they were "socially black."

58. The Rosser Building was followed soon after by Charlottesville's first "skyscraper," the eight-story National Bank Building.

59. Brodie, "Jefferson's Unknown Grandchildren," 94–95; final quotation is Lerone Bennett, Jr., in Fox, *Guardian of Boston*, 27, 279.

Bonds of Memory

Getting Word, Monticello's African American oral history project, was begun in the fall of 1993, with Lucia Stanton as project director, Dianne Swann-Wright as project historian, and Beverly Gray as consultant. Continuously supported by the Thomas Jefferson Memorial Foundation, it was initially funded by the Virginia Foundation for Humanities and Public Policy and received additional funding from Coca-Cola. The last two years of the project have been supported by a grant from the Ford Foundation. Beverly Gray, an educator and historian in Chillicothe, Ohio, has generously shared her papers, her knowledge, and her insights, all of which have contributed so much to the project and to this essay.

1. Our information is derived from interviews with twenty descendants of three daughters of Madison Hemings and four descendants of a son of Eston Hemings Jefferson, as well as documentary material relating to a branch of Madison Hemings's family through a fourth daughter. We would like to express our deep appreciation to the Hemings descendants who have so generously welcomed us into their homes and shared the thoughts, feelings, and memories that have made this essay possible. As of 2011, 100 interviews have been conducted with 170 people.

2. Albemarle County Deed Book, No. 29, pp. 276–277. A receipt in the University of Virginia Proctor's Papers notes payment to Eston Hemings for a violin case (receipt, June 1833, Box 10, Proctor's Papers). We are grateful to C. Allan Brown for pointing out this source.

3. Marriage licenses, 1831–1832, Albemarle County Clerk's Office; Lucia Stanton, "Monticello to Main Street: The Hemings Family and Charlottesville," this volume, 219–221.

4. *Daily Scioto Gazette*, 1 Aug. 1902; *Chillicothe Leader*, 26 Jan. 1887, typescript; Jefferson manuscript music, ViU: 5118. Both newspaper sources were brought to light by Beverly Gray, and the second one is in her collection.

5. Until 1910 Virginia law declared that a free person with more than three-quarters white heritage was not black; in Ohio the legal situation was more ambiguous, with some cases decided for mulattoes with more than one-half white heritage until the 1859 visible admixture law. Eston Hemings's cousin Robert Scott, grandson of his aunt Mary Hemings Bell, lost a lawsuit in 1892 because his family, although legally white, was deemed "socially black" (Stanton, "Monticello to Main Street," 230–231); Stephen Middleton, *The Black Laws in the Old Northwest: A Documentary History* (Westport, 1993). Madison and Eston Hemings were listed as white in the 1830 Virginia census and as mulattoes in a special Virginia 1833 census and in the Ohio censuses of 1840 and 1850.

346 Notes to Pages 236–252

6. *Cleveland American*, undated, cited in the *Liberator*, 19 Dec. 1845, a reference brought to our attention by Micah Fink.

7. Madison Hemings recollections, 13 Mar. 1873, in Annette Gordon-Reed, *Thomas Jefferson and Sally Hemings: An American Controversy* (Charlottesville, 1997), 248; Ross County Deed Book, Ross County Courthouse, Chillicothe, Ohio, No. 68, pp. 562–563; Madison Hemings estate, Ross County Probate Court records. His estate included, besides house, out-buildings, and land, a wagon and black mare, seven hogs, several plows, a large supply of lumber and wagon spokes, a workbench and tool chest, and assorted planes, augers, and chisels. Hemings's word as "his bond" was communicated by Beverly Gray, who interviewed a descendant of one of Hemings's white neighbors.

8. Fawn M. Brodie, "Thomas Jefferson's Unknown Grandchildren: A Study in Historical Silences," *American Heritage* 27 (Oct. 1976): 95; Nellie Johnson Jones manuscript family history, private collection.

9. Unless otherwise noted, all quotations are from interviews and notes of conversation in the GWA.

10. Brodie, "Jefferson's Unknown Grandchildren," 95.

11. *Daily Scioto Gazette*, 1 Aug. 1902.

12. Isaac Jefferson recollections, in Bear, 4.

13. In private collection.

14. Delilah L. Beasley, *The Negro Trail Blazers of California* (Los Angeles, 1919), 40–41, 137, 215–216, 255–256.

15. Our thoughts about memory have been enriched by the authors who made imaginative use of Pierre Nora's concept of *lieux de mémoire* in *History and Memory in African American Culture*, ed. Geneviève Fabre and Robert O'Meally (New York, 1994).

16. *Daily Scioto Gazette*, 1 Aug. 1902.

17. Stanton, "Monticello to Main Street," 343, note 35.

18. *Chicago Tribune*, 13 Nov. 1908.

19. Madison Hemings recollections, 245–248.

20. Nellie Jones to Stuart Gibboney, 29 July, 10 Aug. 1938; Gibboney to Jones, 1 Aug., 1 Nov. 1938, ViU.

21. Personal communication of Beverly Gray, Chillicothe, Ohio.

22. Madison Hemings recollections, 246.

23. Stanton, "Monticello to Main Street," 216.

24. Madison Hemings recollections, 246.

25. Stanton, "Monticello to Main Street," 221.

26. Dorothy Spruill Redford, *Somerset Homecoming: Recovering a Lost Heritage* (New York, 1988).

"We Will Prove Ourselves Men"

This essay is adapted from a chapter of a work-in-progress on the results of the Getting Word oral history project, begun in 1993 to record and preserve the stories and histories of Monticello's African American families and their descendants. I am grateful to Gary Gallagher for his valuable suggestions after reading an earlier draft of this piece.

1. Pauli Murray, *Proud Shoes* (New York, 1956), 156.

2. There were probably other men descended from Monticello families who served in the war, but none have yet come to light.

3. Levi Coffin, *Reminiscences of Levi Coffin* (London, 1876), 599–601.

4. Peter H. Clark, *The Black Brigade of Cincinnati* (1864; repr. New York, 1969), 5–7.

5. Clark, *Black Brigade*, 3, 26–27.

6. Clark *Black Brigade*, 9; Coffin, *Reminiscences*, 605.

7. Clark, *Black Brigade*, 10, 11, 13.

8. William Cheek and Aimee Lee Cheek, *John Mercer Langston and the Fight for Black Freedom 1829–65* (Urbana, 1989), 390.

9. [Charles B. Fox], *Record of the Service of the Fifty-Fifth Regiment of Massachusetts Volunteer Infantry* (1868; repr. Freeport, 1971), 28, 33, 75, 96–97. Dupree's and Trotter's comrade and friend Charles L. Mitchell received his commission as second lieutenant after his discharge.

10. Cheek and Cheek, *Langston*, 293, 395; William H. Ferris, *The African Abroad or His Evolution in Western Civilization* (New Haven, 1913), 2:781–782; William Wells Brown, *The Negro in the American Rebellion: His Heroism and His Fidelity* (Boston, 1867), 295–296; *New York Freeman*, 14 Mar. 1885.

11. Robert Stevenson, "America's First Black Music Historian," *Journal of the American Musicological Society* 26 (Autumn 1973), 388–391; *Record of the Fifty-Fifth*, 96, 125; 1860 census, Delaware County, Ohio.

12. William H. Dupree's military pension records, James M. Trotter's and John F. Shorter's Compiled Military Service Records NARA; *Record of the Fifty-Fifth*, 17–18. Dupree was in Company H, Trotter in Company K, and Shorter in Company D.

13. John W. Blassingame, ed., *The Frederick Douglass Papers: Series One: Speeches, Debates and Interviews* (New Haven, 1985), 3:596; Noah Andre Trudeau, ed., *Voices of the 55th: Letters from the 55th Massachusetts Volunteers* (Dayton, 1996); and Edwin S. Redkey, ed., *A Grand Army of Black Men: Letters from African-American Soldiers in the Union Army 1861–1865* (New York, 1992).

14. *Record of the Fifty-Fifth*, 17.

15. *Record of the Fifty-Fifth*, 17–18; Charles P. Bowditch to J. I. Bowditch, 15 Dec. 1863, "War Letters of Charles P. Bowditch," *Proceedings Massachusetts Historical Society* 57 (Oct. 1923–June 1924): 454.

16. James M. Trotter to Edward W. Kinsley, 13 Mar. 1864, in Trudeau, *Voices of the 55th*, 71–72.

17. *Record of the Fifty-Fifth*, 28; John F. Shorter to John Shorter, 29 May 1864, Shorter Case File, S-480, Letters Received, ser. 360, Colored Troops Division, Record Group 94, NARA. Shorter was apparently engaged to be married when he left Ohio. I am grateful to J. Calvin Jefferson for obtaining a copy of this letter.

18. James M. Trotter to Edward W. Kinsley, 2 June 1864, in Trudeau, *Voices of the 55th*, 108; *Record of the Fifty-Fifth*, 28–29, 33; Trudeau, *Voices of the 55th*, 113. Baker was in Company I.

19. Members of Company D to President of the United States, 16 July 1864, in Trudeau, *Voices of the 55th*, 117.

20. John F. Shorter to editors, *Philadelphia Christian Recorder* and *New York Weekly Anglo-African*, 14 Oct. 1864, in Trudeau, *Voices of the 55th*, 150–154.

21. *Record of the Fifty-Fifth*, 96; John Posey to Mathias Embry, 16 May 1864, in Trudeau, *Voices of the 55th*, 241.

22. "MON." to editor, *New York Weekly Anglo-African*, 24 July 1864, in Trudeau, *Voices of the 55th*, 127; John Freeman Shorter to John Shorter, 29 May 1864, John Shorter to John A. Andrew, 9 June 1864, and endorsement, 12 June 1864, by Governor Andrew, Shorter Case File, S-480, Letters Received, ser. 360, Colored Troops Division, Record Group 94, NARA.

23. James M. Trotter to Francis J. Garrison, 2 Aug. 1864, in Trudeau, *Voices of the 55th*, 141.

24. "A Soldier of the 55th" to editor, *New York Weekly Anglo-African*, 30 Jan. 1864, in Trudeau, *Voices of the 55th*, 56–57; *Record of the Fifty-Fifth*, 11–12.

25. James M. Trotter to Edward W. Kinsley, 18 July 1864, in Trudeau, *Voices of the 55th*, 121–122. On this engagement, see Trudeau, *Voices of the 55th*, 125–138; Redkey, *A Grand Army*, 99, 273; *Record of the Fifty-Fifth*, 30–32.

26. Charles C. Soule, "Battle of Honey Hill," *Philadelphia Weekly Times*, 10 May 1884; James M. Trotter to Edward W. Kinsley, 18 Dec. 1864, in Trudeau, *Voices of the 55th*, 193, 165–166;

Brown, *Negro in the American Rebellion*, 262–263; John F. Shorter Compiled Military Service Records, NARA. William H. Dupree missed the battle, left in command of his company on detached service on Folly Island. Colonel Hartwell's account of the battle, immediately afterward, is in U.S. War Department, *The War of the Rebellion: A Compilation of the Official Records of the Union and Confederate Armies* (Washington, 1894) (hereafter *Official Records*), ser. 1, 44:431–432.

27. *Record of the Fifty-Fifth*, 57–58.

28. *Record of the Fifty-Fifth*, 31, 67–68, 72–73; Charles F. Lee to Artemas Lee, 28 Mar. 1865, Charles F. Lee Papers, University of South Carolina.

29. *Record of the Fifty-Fifth*, 69, 74; Charles F. Lee to "my dear Mary," 16 July 1865, Charles F. Lee Papers, University of South Carolina; Compiled Military Service Records of Shorter, Trotter, and Dupree, NARA; Trotter to Edward W. Kinsley, 27 May 1865, 1 July 1865, in Trudeau, *Voices of the 55th*, 181, 184. Lieutenant Lee, of Company H, described his own response in this time of tension: "As one who believes in this thing I am determined to see it through: I should be ashamed to go home and have any one say (even were there no grounds for it and should I leave now there would be good grounds for so saying) that this was the reason of my resigning."

30. Rev. John R. Bowles to editor, *New York Weekly Anglo-African*, 16 Aug. 1865, in Trudeau, *Voices of the 55th*, 231.

31. Capt. Charles C. Soule to Maj. Gen. O. O. Howard, 12 June 1865, in Martin Abbott, "A New Englander in the South, 1865: A Letter," *New England Quarterly* 32, no. 3 (Sept. 1959): 390. Soule had been Trotter's company captain and was, in his opinion, "one of nature's noblemen" (Trotter to Francis J. Garrison, 2 Aug. 1864, in Trudeau, *Voices of the 55th*, 142).

32. James M. Trotter to Edward W. Kinsley, 1 July 1865, in Trudeau, *Voices of the 55th*, 182–183.

33. James M. Trotter to Edward W. Kinsley, 21 Nov. 1864, 29 Jan. 1865, in Trudeau, *Voices of the 55th*, 156, 179.

34. James M. Trotter to Edward W. Kinsley, 2 June, 21 Nov. 1864; to Francis J. Garrison, 2 Aug. 1864, in Trudeau, *Voices of the 55th*, 107, 143, 157. "George" was George Thompson Garrison, Franky's brother, a lieutenant in the 55th.

35. Interview with Peggy Preaceley, 16 July 2006, GWA. William Dupree, who had no surviving children, gave his own sword to a favorite nephew, Frederick Douglass Isaacs, a greatgrandson of Joseph and Edith Fossett. Isaacs's grandson Brian Isaacs was fascinated by it as a boy (interview with Brian Isaacs, 21 Oct. 1995, GWA).

36. Interview with Virginia Craft Rose, 15 July 2006, GWA; *Record of the Fifty-Fifth*, 18. For the film's treatment of black and white soldiers, see Martin H. Blatt, "*Glory*: Hollywood History, Popular Culture, and the Fifty-Fourth Massachusetts Regiment," in *Hope and Glory: Essays on the Legacy of the Fifty-Fourth Massachusetts Regiment*, ed. Martin H. Blatt, Thomas J. Brown, and Donald Yacovone (Amherst, 2002), 215–235.

37. *Record of the Fifty-Fifth*, 96–97.

38. *Record of the Fifty-Fifth*, 28; Elizabeth Preston Allan, ed., *Life and Letters of Margaret Junkin Preston* (Boston, 1903), 182–197; Fanny M. Lyle Wilson to her father, 17 June 1864, in undated newspaper article, Virginia Military Institute Archives.

39. Maj. Gen. David Hunter to Jefferson Davis, 23 Apr. 1863, in Ira Berlin, Joseph P. Reidy, and Leslie S. Rowland, eds., *Freedom: The Black Military Experience in the Civil War* (Cambridge, 1982), 573–574. Jefferson wrote, "The Almighty has no attribute which can take side with us in such a contest" (William Peden, ed., *Notes on the State of Virginia* [Chapel Hill, 1954], 163).

40. Allan, *Life and Letters*, 193–194; Cecil D. Eby, Jr., ed., *A Virginia Yankee in the Civil War: The Diaries of David Hunter Strother* (Chapel Hill, 1961), 254.

41. George Edmondson Compiled Service Records and Pension Records, NARA; Rockbridge County birth records, No. 1, 301. Information from the NARA records was collected and generously shared by William Webb.

42. Gen. Benjamin F. Butler, General Orders No. 126, 13 Oct. 1864, in Berlin, Reidy, and Rowland, *Black Military Experience*, 590; Noah Andre Trudeau, *Like Men of War: Black Troops in the Civil War 1862–1865* (Boston, 1998), 311–312.

43. Edmondson pension records, NARA; Gen. Ulysses Doubleday report, 26 Apr. 1865, *Official Records*, ser. 1, 46:1236; Thomas S. Johnson to Gen. Lorenzo Thomas, 30 Apr. 1865, Thomas S. Johnson Papers, Wisconsin State Historical Society, Oshkosh, manuscript Z32. Johnson's letters are published, with alterations of wording and placement, in "Letters from a Civil War Chaplain," *Journal of Presbyterian History* 46, no. 3 (Sept. 1968); 219–235.

44. Lt. Col. James Givin report, 22 Apr. 1865, *Official Records*, ser. 1, 46:1240–1241; Thomas S. Johnson to Gen. Lorenzo Thomas, 30 Apr. 1865, manuscript Z32.

45. "Rufus" to editor, *New York Weekly Anglo-African*, 12 Aug. 1865; Garland H. White to editor, *Philadelphia Christian Recorder*, 19 Sept. 1865, in Redkey, *A Grand Army*, 198, 200; Joseph T. Glatthaar, *Forged in Battle: The Civil War Alliance of Black Soldiers and White Officers* (New York, 1990), 218–221; Berlin, Reidy, and Rowland, *Black Military Experience*, 633; Edmondson pension records, NARA.

46. Wood County, West Virginia, censuses 1870–1920; undated, untitled newspaper clipping and *Parkersburg News*, 1 Dec. 1922, copies in GWA generously shared by William Webb.

47. With grateful thanks to William Webb and Eva Kobus-Webb for bringing George Edmondson to our attention and sharing the fruits of their outstanding research.

48. William B. Hemings Compiled Military Service Records, NARA.

49. *Personal Memoirs of U. S. Grant* (New York, 1886), 2:534.

50. Thomas E. Hemings Compiled Military Service Records, NARA; *Official Roster of the Soldiers of the State of Ohio in the War of the Rebellion* (Cincinnati, 1889), 9:517, 773. Hemings enlisted on 16 Aug. 1864 in New Lexington, Ohio, and was mustered as a private into Company E of the 178th Ohio regiment, which was absorbed into the 175th regiment, organized at Camp Dennison, outside Cincinnati, on 11 Oct. 1864. His records have contradictory notations about the date and place of his capture: "Absent with leave supposed to be taken prisoner at Block house No. Nov./64," "Prisoner of war Captured near Columbia Tenn Nov 24/64," and "Dec 1864 absent missing on retreat from Columbia or in action at Franklin Tenn Nov 30/64." A "Memorandum from Prisoner of War Records" of 1889 states: "No record subs. to Nov 24/64."

51. *Pike County Republican* (Waverly, Ohio), 13 Mar. 1873; Nellie E. Jones manuscript, post-1942, Shay Banks-Young collection, copy in GWA.

52. I am grateful to many people who contributed to an effort to understand this mystery, particularly to Daniel H. Reigle and other members of the Ohio Civil War Genealogical Society. Their conclusions are in *Ohio Civil War Genealogical Journal* 12, no. 4 (2008): 184–188. Thanks are also due to Ward Calhoun, Kevin Frye, Jack Lundquist, and Mary June Platten. This issue is treated at greater length in the chapter from which this essay was adapted.

53. Diary of John C. Ely, first sergeant in Company C, 115th OVI (private collection), copy in GWA, acquired with the generous assistance of Jack Lundquist, Jerry O. Potter, Dan Reigle, and Gene Salecker.

54. William Farrand Keys diary, 4 Sept. 1864, in William Marvel, *Andersonville: The Last Depot* (Chapel Hill, 1994), 148.

55. "Bay State" to editor, *New York Weekly Anglo-African*, 10 Apr. 1864, in Trudeau, *Voices of the 55th*, 88; Ira Berlin, Joseph P. Reidy, and Leslie S. Rowland, eds., *Freedom's Soldiers: The Black Military Experience in the Civil War* (Cambridge, 1998), 25.

56. Beverly Gray, "The Civil War in Southern Ohio," www.angelfire.com/oh/chillicothe. Albert Wall, the son of a North Carolina planter and his slave, was John Mercer Langston's brother-in-law. He studied at Oberlin after leaving the 73rd Ohio and then enlisted in the 54th Massachusetts. His half brother O. S. B. Wall became the first regularly commissioned black captain in the U.S. Army (Cheek and Cheek, *Langston*, 250–251, 409–410).

57. Fayette County, Ohio, censuses 1880, 1900; Leavenworth County, Kansas, census 1910; William B. Hemings pension records, NARA.

58. *History of Dane County, Wisconsin* (Chicago, 1880), 798–799, 1004; (Madison) *Wisconsin State Journal*, 13 Mar. and 7 July 1858, 8 Jan. 1860; 1860 Dane County, Wisconsin, census.

59. Beverly Jefferson and John Wayles Jefferson Compiled Military Service Records, NARA.

60. *Wisconsin State Journal*, 10 Oct. 1861; *Wisconsin Patriot*, 9 May 1863, (Madison) *Weekly Argus and Democrat*, 17 Sept. 1861.

61. [George W. Driggs], *Opening of the Mississippi; or Two Years' Campaigning in the Southwest* (Madison, 1864), 54; John W. Jefferson to editor, *Weekly Argus*, 21 Nov. 1861, John W. Jefferson scrapbook, Jefferson Family Papers (coll. 1218), Charles E. Young Research Library, University of California, Los Angeles. See also Fawn M. Brodie, "Thomas Jefferson's Unknown Grandchildren: A Study in Historical Silences," *American Heritage*, 27 (Oct. 1976): 94.

62. Capt. William B. Britton to editor of unnamed newspaper, [Mar. 1862], clipping in Quiner Scrapbooks: Correspondence of the Wisconsin Volunteers, 1861–1865, 4:61, Wisconsin Historical Society (hereafter Quiner Scrapbooks). I am extremely grateful for the expert assistance of Wisconsin Historical Society archivist Dee Grimsrud, who brought the invaluable Quiner Scrapbook collection to my attention.

63. "M" to editor of unnamed newspaper, [Oct. 1862], Quiner Scrapbooks, 4:127; Driggs, *Opening of the Mississippi*, 93; Lt. John Woodworth to editors, *Milwaukee Daily Sentinel*, 21 Aug. 1862; *Weekly Wisconsin Patriot*, 7 June and 19 July 1862.

64. Clippings in Quiner Scrapbooks, [Oct. 1862], 4:60, 123; John W. Jefferson to Beverly Jefferson, 21 May 1863, in *Weekly Wisconsin Patriot*, 13 June 1863. Jefferson's official account of the battle is in *Official Records*, ser. 1, 17 (pt. 1): 202–203.

65. John W. Jefferson to editor, 4 July 1863, in *Wisconsin State Journal*, 14 July 1863; Abraham Lincoln to James C. Conkling, 26 Aug. 1863, in *The Collected Works of Abraham Lincoln*, ed. Roy P. Basler et al. (New Brunswick, 1953), 6:409.

66. Driggs, *Opening of the Mississippi*, 128; excerpt from *Madison Journal* in *Milwaukee Daily Sentinel*, 14 Apr. 1864.

67. *Milwaukee Daily Sentinel*, 16 June 1864; Capt. W. B. Britton to editors, unnamed newspaper, ca. 26 Mar. 1862, Quiner Scrapbooks, 4:61; "Vox" to editor, *Cairo Daily Gazette*, ca. 16 Feb. 1862, Quiner Scrapbooks, 4:47, 61; Driggs, *Opening of the Mississippi*, 142–143.

68. *Daily Scioto Gazette*, 1 Aug. 1902, collection of Beverly Gray. Officers passing for white were more rare than passing enlisted men like the sons of Madison Hemings. Historian Joseph T. Wilson mentioned several examples, especially in Pennsylvania, New York, and Massachusetts regiments. "One of the prominent Ohioans of to-day [1890]," he wrote, had served on the staff of a major general (Joseph T. Wilson, *The Black Phalanx: A History of the Negro Soldiers of the United States* [Hartford, 1890], 179–180). One notable example, and one of the few passing officers who was later exposed, was Edwin Belcher, who was a captain in a white Pennsylvania regiment and a political leader in Georgia after the war (Berlin, Reidy, and Rowland, *Black Military Experience*, 310; Glatthaar, *Forged in Battle*, 249; Belcher obituary, *New York Globe*, 20 Jan. 1883).

69. John Wayles Jefferson Compiled Military Service Records, NARA; *Milwaukee Sentinel*, 14 June 1892; *History of Dane County*, ed. Elisha W. Keyes (Madison, 1906), 455–456; *Wisconsin State Journal*, 29 Sept. 1888; and documentary reference compilations in GWA. Jefferson's life in Memphis is still to be fully explored.

70. Driggs, *Opening of the Mississippi*, 142–143; Julia J. Westerinen interview, 19 July 2000, GWA. See Lucia Stanton and Dianne Swann-Wright, "Bonds of Memory: Identity and the Hemings Family," this volume.

71. *History of Dane County, Wisconsin*, 1004; *Wisconsin State Journal*, 22 Dec. 1870, 11 Nov. 1908; Keyes, *History of Dane County*, 454–456; *Chicago Tribune*, 13 Nov. 1908; and documentary reference compilations in GWA.

72. *Milwaukee Journal*, 2 and 3 July 1891; *Little Rock Daily Arkansas Gazette*, 25 May 1875; *Wheeling Register*, 25 May 1875; *Boston Journal*, 1 Aug. 1887; *Boston Daily Advertiser*, 2 Aug. 1887; and many other newspapers, which include Trotter's remarks.

Fulfilling the Declaration

This essay is adapted from a talk given to the Contemporary Club in Charlottesville, Virginia, in 2009, an effort to bring women in the Hemings family out of the shadows while telling the stories of descendants who led public lives.

1. The Getting Word project, sustained for almost twenty years by the Thomas Jefferson Foundation, Inc., has received additional support from the Coca-Cola Company, the Ford Foundation, the River Branch Foundation, and the Virginia Foundation for Humanities and Public Policy. The staff of the Getting Word project are myself, director; Dianne Swann-Wright, historian; and Beverly Gray, consultant. For sources except those for actual quotations, see the hundreds of compiled documentary references in GWA.

2. See Lucia Stanton and Dianne Swann-Wright, "Bonds of Memory: Identity and the Hemings Family," this volume.

3. I am in agreement with the conclusions of the report of Monticello's Research Committee on Thomas Jefferson and Sally Hemings, Jan. 2000: the combination of historical, statistical, and scientific evidence indicates the "high probability that Thomas Jefferson fathered Eston Hemings, and that he most likely was the father of all six of Sally Hemings's children appearing in Jefferson's records" (www.monticello.org/hemings-jefferson-report).

4. Interview with Beverly Gray, 1 Feb. 2003, GWA.

5. *Life and Reminiscences of Hon. James Emmitt as Revised by Himself*, ed. M. J. Carrigan (Chillicothe, 1888), 289.

6. Interview with Ellen Hodnett, Paula Sanford Henderson, Robin Roberts Martin, 4 Dec. 1998, GWA; Fawn M. Brodie, "Thomas Jefferson's Unknown Grandchildren: A Study in Historical Silences," *American Heritage* 27 (Oct. 1976): 28–33, 94–99.

7. Interviews with Patricia Roberts, 5 Dec. 1998, and with Lucille Balthazar, 23 Oct. 1995, GWA.

8. Interviews with Jacqueline Pettiford, 11 Sept. 2004, and Patricia Roberts, 5 Dec. 1998, GWA; Ellen Roberts's great-grandson Andrew Giles Roberts, in Brodie, "Thomas Jefferson's Unknown Grandchildren," 95.

9. Interview with Lucille Balthazar and accompanying notes, 23 Oct. 1995, GWA.

10. Interviews with Gloria Roberts, 12 Jan. 1999, and Patricia Roberts, 5 Dec. 1998, GWA. The Mexican border story was told to Beverly Gray by Lucille Balthazar.

11. Douglas Flamming, *Bound for Freedom: Black Los Angeles in Jim Crow America* (Berkeley, 2005), 55–58, 85–89 (quotations: 88–89), 168–174; this is the best account of Roberts, particularly his public career. For Roberts the gold prospector, see A. V. Buel, "Solon Misses Death Fred Roberts Lost on Desert," *Sacramento Bee*, n.d., Roberts collection, box 1, folder 4, AAMLO.

12. Delilah L. Beasley, *The Negro Trail Blazers of California* (Los Angeles, 1919), 255; *California Eagle*, 13 July 1918, in Flamming, *Bound for Freedom*, 172; Pearl Hinds Roberts recollections, AAMLO.

13. Flamming, *Bound for Freedom*, 198–200 (quotation: 198); Herbert B. Alexander, "Interesting Negroes," *San Jose Evening News*, 2 Sept. 1922; Pearl Hinds Roberts recollections, AAMLO.

14. Henry Ruffner to Rev. Ralph R. Gurley, 9 Oct. 1832, American Colonization Society Papers, DLC (I am grateful to Ellen Eslinger for first bringing this letter to our attention and to Karen Hughes White for providing a copy of it); Charles Henry Huberich, *The Political and Legislative History of Liberia* (New York, 1947), 1:145.

15. John Cromwell recalling a visit in 1877, *Journal of Negro History* 8, no. 3 (July 1923): 338.

16. *Harper's Bazaar* 28, no. 44 (Nov. 1895): 890; *New York Herald-Tribune*, 18 Feb. 1899.

17. Coralie Cook birthday tribute to Anthony, 1900, and Cook to Mary Stafford Anthony, 1906, in Ida Husted Harper, *The Life and Works of Susan B. Anthony* (Indianapolis, 1908), 3:1183, 1452.

18. Gwendolyn Etter-Lewis and Richard Thomas, eds., *Lights of the Spirit: Historical Portraits of Black Baha' is in North America* (Wilmette, 2006), 88, 239.

19. TJ to Joseph Dougherty, 31 July 1806, Betts, *Farm Book*, 23; *Cincinnati Enquirer*, 19 Apr. 1885, 22 July 1900; *Detroit Plaindealer*, 19 Aug. 1892.

20. James Alexander, *Early Charlottesville: Recollections of James Alexander 1828–1874*, ed. Mary Rawlings (Charlottesville, 1942), 84; interview with Forrest Cutright, 17 July 1995, GWA.

21. *Baltimore Afro-American*, 4 June 1932.

22. *New York Globe*, 3 Mar. and 28 Apr. 1883.

23. Interview with Virginia Craft Rose, 15 July 2006, GWA; [Charles B. Fox], *Record of the Service of the Fifty-Fifth Regiment of Massachusetts Volunteer Infantry* (1868; repr. Freeport, 1971), 18; James M. Trotter to Edward Kinsley, 2 June 1864, in Noah Andre Trudeau, ed., *Voices of the 55th: Letters from the 55th Massachusetts Volunteers* (Dayton, 1996), 108. On the film script, see Martin H. Blatt, "*Glory*: Hollywood History, Popular Culture, and the Fifty-Fourth Massachusetts Regiment," in *Hope and Glory: Essays on the Legacy of the Fifty-Fourth Massachusetts Regiment*, ed. Martin II. Blatt, Thomas J. Brown, and Donald Yacovone (Amherst, 2002), 215–235.

24. John F. Shorter to editors, *Philadelphia Christian Recorder* and *New York Weekly Anglo-African*, 14 Oct. 1864, and James M. Trotter to Edward W. Kinsley, 1 July 1865, in Trudeau, *Voices of the 55th*, 150–154, 182–183.

25. Eileen Southern, *The Music of Black Americans: A History*, 3rd (New York, 1997), 261; *New York Globe*, 6 Jan. 1883.

26. James M. Trotter to ——, 18 Sept. 1883, in *New York Globe*, 29 Sept. 1883; *New York Freeman*, 25 Sept. 1886; Trotter to T. Thomas Fortune, *New York Globe*, 17 Nov. 1883.

27. James M. Trotter to ——, 9 Feb. 1884, in *New York Globe*, 24 Feb. 1883; James M. Trotter to Charles L. Mitchell, 3 Mar. 1887, in *New York Freeman*, 12 Mar. 1887.

28. *New York Freeman*, 26 Mar. 1887; *Cincinnati Commercial Tribune*, 9 Apr. 1887; *Trenton Evening Times*, 9 Apr. 1887, among many other newspapers. Headlines in the two latter sources referred to Trotter's "Famous Nurse," the "Romance of Slavery Days," and the "Woman with a History" who attended him. Virginia Trotter's sister Maria Elizabeth Dupree moved out to Hyde Park to care for the Trotter children.

29. *New York Times*, 13 Jan. 1923, Stephen R. Fox, *The Guardian of Boston: William Monroe Trotter* (New York, 1970), 19; Almira Park, "A Little Boy Named Monroe," *Boston Guardian*, 18 Aug. 1952.

30. Fox, *Guardian of Boston*, 39; *Boston Globe*, 31 July 1903, in *The Booker T. Washington Papers*, ed. Louis R. Harlan (Urbana, 1977), 7:232–233, 238; *Thirtieth Anniversary Report*, Harvard Class of 1895 (Cambridge, 1925), 303.

31. Fox, *Guardian of Boston*, 89–92, 239.

32. Interview with Virginia Craft Rose, 15 July 2006, GWA; Fox, *Guardian of Boston*, 224–230.

33. *Baltimore Afro-American*, 4 June 1932; *New York Times*, 28 Aug. 1919; *Philadelphia Tribune*, 7 Apr. 1932; Fox, *Guardian of Boston*, 230–235.

34. Kelly Miller in *Philadelphia Tribune*, 19 Mar. 1932; *Philadelphia Tribune*, 7 Apr. 1932; William M. Trotter to Calvin Coolidge, 10 June 1926, and quotation from *Chicago Whip*, 6 Aug. 1927, in Fox, *Guardian of Boston*, 257–259.

35. Family recording of Virginia Craft Rose and Ellen Craft Dammond, 1996, recorded in interview with Peggy Dammond Preacely, 16 July 2006, GWA.

36. Interview with Virginia Craft Rose, 15 July 2006, GWA.

37. Faith S. Holsaert et al., eds., *Hands on the Freedom Plow: Personal Accounts by Women in SNCC* (Urbana, 2010), 163–172.

38. Flamming, *Bound for Freedom*, 107; Fox, *Guardian of Boston*, 191–197; Coralie F. Cook, "Votes for Mothers," *The Crisis Magazine* 10 (Aug. 1915): 184–185. Cook also wrote, "Disfranchisement because of sex is curiously like disfranchisement because of color. It cripples the individual, it handicaps progress, it sets a limitation upon mental and spiritual development."

Index

TJ refers to Thomas Jefferson; page numbers in italics refer to illustrations.